DEVELOPMENT OF URBAN SYSTEMS IN AFRICA

DEVELOPMENT OF URBAN SYSTEMS IN AFRICA

Edited by

R.A.Obudho
Salah El-Shakhs

PRAEGER

PRAEGER SPECIAL STUDIES • PRAEGER SCIENTIFIC

Library of Congress Cataloging in Publication Data

Main entry under title:

Development of urban systems in Africa.

    Bibliography: p.
    Includes index.
    1. City planning--Africa--Addresses, essays,
lectures. 2. Urbanization--Africa--Addresses,
essays, lectures. I. Obudho, Robert A.
II. El-Shakhs, Salah.
HT169.A3D48   301.36'096   78-19766
ISBN 0-03-047066-8

Published in 1979 by Praeger Publishers
A Division of Holt, Rinehart and Winston/CBS, Inc.
383 Madison Avenue, New York, New York 10017 U.S.A.

9 038 987654321

Printed in the United States of America

To the People of Africa

PREFACE

Issues of development planning in the African nations have gained added importance over the last few years in view of the recent political events on the continent (in Angola, Rhodesia, South Africa, Ethiopia, and so on) which have indeed occupied a center stage within the world community. Surprisingly, however, there has been little published on the problems, experiences, and approaches of spatial and urban development in Africa from a comparative and comprehensive view since our edited volume on <u>Urbanization, National Development, and Regional Planning in Africa</u> (Praeger) was published in 1974. The present volume is intended to help bridge that gap by bringing together a number of original contributions on spatial development and planning in Africa, covering a wide geographical and interdisciplinary perspective.

The essential focus is on comparative historical analysis of the urbanization process in Africa, the resulting limitations and problems of urban development, and consequent challenges and responses of development planning. Given the wide range of the countries involved, the disparities among their developmental contexts, and the lack of basic comparable data, this approach necessarily poses several problems. We have attempted to overcome them, however, by selecting case studies that analyze and evaluate systematically representative experiences against a background of common problems and colonial heritage.

The first part of the book attempts to provide a framework for understanding the nature of African urbanism, the limitations on that urbanism imposed by traditional nations, and analytical approaches to it. The failure of most recent attempts to implement spatial and regional planning in Africa may have been due to the lack of understanding of the nature and process of urbanization over time. This book, therefore, offers the basic facts, trends, and options that have emerged in various African countries. This reader's primary aim is to present a comparative perspective on the processes of urbanization and planning in the form of case studies centered on selected countries representing different regions and developmental contexts on the African continent. We hope that those for whom the book is intended—students, professionals, planners, and policy makers of African urbanization and development planning—will find it not only informative but also challenging in their continued search and interest in African urban development.

ACKNOWLEDGMENTS

This volume could not have been produced without the enthusiastic support and unrelenting patience of the contributors, who have not only responded to our initial queries but have also produced and revised manuscripts with a dispatch remarkable in academia. To them we must express special thanks since without them this book would have been impossible. Their efforts have been tireless and have produced, without financial reward, some outstanding pieces of scholarship. We hope that what we have assembled here will aid them in their continuing study of urbanization and development planning in Africa.

Organization, research, and editorial assistance have been provided by a number of people, both in Africa and overseas, and our thanks go to all concerned. The editors would like to express special thanks to the following individuals for their invaluable help: for organization, Margie Bahash, Beverly Braxton, Normarie Lindsey, Rhonda Valentine-Mitchell, and Francine Spradley; for typing, preparation of indexes, and editorial assistance, Jackie Leonard, Carol Saddington, Connie Nobile, and Ellen Rabinowitz.

All the above individuals are, however, absolved of guilt by association for any inaccuracies that remain herein.

CONTENTS

LIST OF TABLES

LIST OF FIGURES

INTRODUCTION

As a formal field of inquiry, the serious study of urbanization and development planning in Africa is a little more than three decades old. Early studies during this period have dealt mainly with social surveys of major urban centers, particularly the traditional or colonial capitals or primate cities. The focus was on the effects of urbanization on indigenous behavioral patterns among Africans and the relationship between urbanization and development.

The population of the continent as a whole, and of tropical Africa in particular, is still overwhelmingly rural (see Table I.1). The fact that Africa is the least urbanized continent in the world has given rise to a variety of views on the significance of urbanization in Africa and a variety of conceptual approaches to its study. While some (Trewartha and Zelinsky 1954) have concluded that the low level of urbanization, particularly in tropical Africa, makes African urbanization an uninteresting or insignificant area for detailed study, others (Miner, Lerner, and Spengler 1967) have seen this low level as a blessing enabling a more rational course of future development. [1]

The urban population in Africa is expected to more than triple by the turn of the century, and its major urban centers have recently displayed some of the world's fastest rates of population increase. Thus, while no one doubts the crucial importance and impact of urbanization in Africa on its future development, whether or not Africa will succeed in taking best advantage of this process is indeed a wide open question. [2] Any optimism on its prospects may be more theoretical than real. While African countries do have the opportunity to "determine the basic pattern of urban growth likely to emerge in the next decade,"[3] the adoption of unrealistic policies or the lack of sufficient political will and machinery to translate policies into executive action,[4] may prove such optimism unfounded. If this materializes, and, given the rates of population and urban growth and the low level of national economic resources, African cities would "be unable to absorb future rural-urban migration likely to result when limits to increasing rural income are approached."[5]

The study of African urbanization, therefore, has recently come to focus on a better understanding of the nature of this process, its historical and political context, the limitations on comparative applications of Western concepts and experiences, and the urgency of developing the appropriate tools, policies, and institutional machinery for development planning. Urbanization in Africa originated largely

xix

TABLE I. 1

Gross National Product and Urban Population in Africa

	GNP		Urban Population	
Country or Area	1973 Per Capita (U. S. dollars)	Average Annual Growth Rate 1965–73	As Percent of Total Population in 1973	Average Annual Growth Rate 1965–73
North Africa				
Algeria	570	4. 3	50. 4	7. 3
Egypt	250	0. 8	43. 2	3. 2
Libya	—[a]	—	52. 0[b]	—
Morocco	320	2. 5	36. 8	4. 7
Sudan	—	—	20. 0[b]	—
Tunisia	460	4. 9	44. 5	4. 7
West Africa				
Dahomey	—	—	11. 0[c]	—
Gambia	—	—	7. 0[c]	—
Ghana	300	0. 8	30. 8	5. 1
Guinea Bissau	110	0. 1	18. 0	7. 2
Ivory Coast	380	3. 0	18. 9	7. 0
Liberia	310	4. 7	13. 5	6. 0
Mali	70	0. 5	12. 9	4. 5
Mauretania	200	1. 2	10. 4	5. 6
Niger	—	—	5. 0[c]	—
Nigeria	210	8. 3	17. 4	4. 9
Senegal	280	2. 8	26. 2	4. 1
Sierra Leone	160	1. 5	14. 5	4. 0
Togo	180	2. 5	15. 2	7. 4
Central Africa				
Burundi	80	1. 4	3. 5	7. 1
Cameroun	250	4. 9	22. 4	6. 0
Central African Empire	160	1. 0	33. 4	6. 5
Chad	—	—	8. 0[c]	—
Congo	340	1. 9	31. 2	4. 9
Equatorial Guinea	—	—	10. 0[c]	—
Gabon	—	—	12. 0[c]	—
Zaire	140	2. 9	25. 1	5. 6

(continued)

Table I.1, continued

Country or Area	GNP		Urban Population	
	1973 Per Capita (U.S. dollars)	Average Annual Growth Rate 1965-73	As Percent of Total Population in 1973	Average Annual Growth Rate 1965-73
East Africa				
Ethiopia	90	1.6	11.0	6.9
Djibouti	—	—	70.0[b]	—
Kenya	170	3.3	10.7	6.4
Madagascar	150	0.9	16.8	5.5
Malawi	110	3.7	6.5	4.7
Rwanda	—	—	4.0[b]	—
Somalia	80	1.6	27.1	5.5
Tanzania	130	2.6	7.3	7.1
Uganda	150	1.2	7.7	7.0
Zambia	430	0.2	34.3	8.0
Southern Africa				
Angola	490	3.2	20.2	7.3
Botswana	—	—	12.0[b]	—
Lesotho	100	2.6	2.9	8.2
Mozambique	380	4.1	5.9	6.4
Namibia	—	—	32.0[b]	—
Rhodesia	430	3.5	19.1	5.8
South Africa	—	—	48.0[b]	—

[a]Dash indicates data not available.

[b]1978 estimates compiled by the editors from various sources.

[c]1970 figures from Colin Rosser, "Urbanization in Tropical Africa: A Demographic Introduction," Report of the International Urbanization Survey, Ford Foundation, New York, 1972.

Sources: United Nations, Global Review of Human Settlements (New York: Habitat, U.N. Conference on Human Settlements, A/Conf. 70/A/1, March 1976).

under conditions of dominant colonial economic and political policies.
It is currently proceeding faster and with more imbalances and constraints than did European urbanization. Urbanization within a culture
of capitalist dependency like Africa's not only resulted in the bifurcation of urban systems and structures but also in urban growth unac-
companied by expansion in the capacity of urban systems, in hierarchical and sectorial imbalances, inefficient institutional structures,
and distorted measurements, norms, goals, and planning approaches.

At this stage, the study of African urbanism requires a better
understanding of the emergence of African urban cultures and the contexts that gave birth to them. The interpenetration of traditional and
modern norms have created not a mixture but a new social order.
Attempts to understand today's urban African "as a mixture of primitive and modern," as Miner puts it, "run the risk of overlooking him
as a new kind of person dealing with new kinds of problems requiring
new kinds of solutions."[6]

The study of African urbanism and urban development, thus,
would have to take a fresh look at its approaches and tools of analysis.
As the first part in this book will suggest, the African normative system should provide a baseline for our investigations into the processes of social change. The interpenetration of modern patterns and
traditional norms is a two-way process of interaction and adaptation.
The emerging modes of socioeconomic organization are profoundly
affected by the outcome of such interaction and the conditions in which
it occurs. There is no simple explanation for the processes of African
urbanization as social and economic processes. Thus, a wide perspective on their historical development as well as recent and current
experiments and planning efforts is necessary for guiding future development approaches.

The countries studied have been organized by region: North
Africa, West Africa, East Africa, and Southern Africa (see Tables
I. 2 and I. 3). Despite diversities in sizes, levels of development,
colonial experiences, and current political ideologies among the individual countries in each region, they share broad historical backgrounds, cultural influences, and intraregional interactions which
provide predominant regional perspectives sufficient as frameworks
for comparative analysis.

The North African countries, discussed in Part Two, are generally more urbanized, have longer urban traditions, are predominantly Muslim, and have been exposed to pre-modern Mediterranean
influences. They generally have well-established national urban networks upon which their planning can be based and relatively more developed administrative structures within which planning can occur.
This region has a higher proportion of its population in cities of
100,000 or more inhabitants than does the rest of Africa.

TABLE I. 2

Population, Annual Rate of Natural Increase, and Percentage
of Urban Population in Africa, by Region, 1978

Region	Population (millions)	Annual Rate of Natural Increase (percentage)	Urban Population (percentage)
Northern	103	2.9	40.0
Western	128	2.7	19.0
Eastern	124	2.7	12.0
Central	50	2.4	27.0
Southern	31	2.5	44.0
Total	436	2.7	25.0

Source: Population Reference Bureau, 1978 World Population
Data, p. 1.

Part Three deals with the processes of political and economic
transformation in the West African nations. Next to North Africa
this region has a relatively long tradition of indigenous African urbanization. The most remarkable example of this is the so-called black
metropolis, which developed a complex pattern of rural-urban interdependence.[7] This region has had a long history of interaction with
North Africa across the Sahara, and cities such as Kano, Sokata,
Ibadan, and Kumasi have prospered for a long time. West Africa is
more urbanized than East Africa.

The East African countries covered in Part Four have had a
long orientation and exposure to the Arabian peninsula and the Indian
subcontinent. Most of their urban centers originated along the coast
in the precolonial era and were influenced by international trade and
migration. In general, their urban networks were superimposed colonial creations inaccessible to African populations until recently.
This may in part explain the low level of urbanization in this region's
interior.

Perhaps approximately, the last part of this book deals with
last remaining countries in Africa still seeking the liberation of their
economic and political systems. It focuses on the overwhelmingly
similar development issues in the Southern African nations. Although

that region is relatively more urbanized than the rest of Africa, this urbanization occurred without the meaningful participation of its African populations. Through apartheid, mobility restrictions, and conscious planning, these populations have largely been kept marginal, not only to the urbanization process but to economic, social, and political development as well. Clearly, any basic change in this structure requires a political reorientation that is already in the making for at least some countries in the region. The economic and spatial adjustments that would follow, however, will present development planners with major challenges and many constraints.

The first chapter in this volume considers the problems and prospects of planning in the African context. Planning involves not only technical capacities and solutions but also institutional implements and political choices. Such requirements present many obvious problems within the context of African development. These problems are further compounded by the discrepancies inherent in the environment of planning as a process of social change. These include the gap between the rate of urban growth and the pace of institutional change and spatial response, the gap between heightening expectations and national capacities, and the discrepancies between the national interest and special interests of elites and labor and professional aristocracies which, in many cases, developed in unison with colonial interests and continued dependencies. [8]

TABLE I.3

Estimated Percentage of Urban Populations, by Settlement Size, in Major African Regions, 1960 and 1967

Region	1960		1967		
	20,000+	100,000+	5,000+	20,000+	100,000+
North Africa	23.8	19.0	32.2	24.9	19.7
West Africa	10.7	7.3	16.6	11.7	8.8
Middle Africa	8.4	4.7	15.6	11.4	7.5
East Africa	5.6	3.1	9.5	7.6	4.9
Southern Africa	34.5	23.6	41.3	40.7	29.6
Total	13.7	9.7	19.8	15.8	11.5

Source: William A. Hance, Population Migration and Urbanization in Africa (New York: Columbia University Press, 1970), p. 222.

The dangers of applying unrealistic approaches or models have already been pointed out repeatedly in an earlier volume of ours on urbanization and regional planning in Africa. [9] There we maintained that Africa's leaders and planners are "learning from their own successes and failures as they go, on precious time," and that "the flexibility, adjustment, and experience to be gained from continuous monitoring and evaluation are of crucial importance"[10] in that process. The evaluations of different planning experiences included in this volume are presented as another step in that learning process.

NOTES

1. Colin Rosser, Urbanization in Tropical Africa: A Demographic Introduction. Report of the International Urbanization Survey, Ford Foundation, New York, 1972, pp. 1-3.

2. Salah El-Shakhs, "Development Planning in Africa," in Urbanization, National Development, and Regional Planning in Africa, ed. S. El-Shakhs and R. Obudho, (New York: Praeger, 1974), pp. 3-12.

3. Michael Cohen et al., The Task Ahead for the Cities of the Developing Countries, World Bank Staff Working Paper No. 209 (Washington, D.C., IRBD, 1975), p. 10.

4. Rosser, op. cit., p. 4.

5. Cohen, op. cit., p. 10.

6. Horace Miner, "The City and Modernization: An Introduction," in The City in Africa, ed. H. Miner, (London: Pall Mall Press, 1967), p. 1.

7. Akin L. Mabogunje, Urbanization in Nigeria (London: University of London Press, 1968), and P. C. Lloyd, A. L. Mahogunje, and B. Awe, eds., The City of Ibadan (London: Cambridge University Press, 1967).

8. El-Shakhs, "The Urban Crisis in International Perspective," American Behavioral Scientist 15, no. 4 (March/April 1971).

9. El-Shakhs and Obudho, op. cit., pp. 3-12.

10. Ibid., pp. 4, 11.

1

PROBLEMS AND PROSPECTS OF PLANNING IN AN AFRICAN CONTEXT

Michael L. McNulty
Frank E. Horton

INTRODUCTION

The past two decades have witnessed a dramatic increase in the volume of planning literature. The tone of much of that literature has been introspective, questioning existing planning practice and calling into question the very nature of planning.

Since the mid-1960's, nearly all of the assumptions under-lying economic planning in developing countries have been questioned, including the desirability of growth and the need for planning itself. Although recent policies reflect some agreement that the pace, direction, and benefits of growth in developing countries must be drastically altered, little consensus has emerged on what to do about planning. [1]

\ Despite the continuing debate over the proper role of planning and planners, there is a growing acceptance of planning as a necessary and desirable instrument for effecting orderly change in a variety of activities in the social and economic environment. Proponents of planning argue that it can contribute to more rational decision making,

An earlier version of this paper was presented at the 16th Annual Meeting of the African Studies Association, Syracuse, New York, in November 1973. We are indebted to S. A. Agunbiade and J. P. Lea for useful comments on that earlier version.

an accelerated pace of development, and more equitable distribution in the benefits of development.

Planning has become particularly attractive to people in those developing countries where limited resources require careful consideration of the nature, sequence, and location of resource allocation. While planning offers great prospects for aiding the development effort, at the same time it faces serious problems. Planning itself is a complex and demanding organizational task requiring coordinated effort not only of the professional planning staff but of political leaders and the general public as well.

This chapter addresses some of the problems and prospects of applying planning methodologies in an African context. Recognizing that it would be impossible to address adequately all aspects of this broad topic in a single chapter, we have chosen to select only a few specific conditions illustrating important aspects of planning activities in Africa.

PREREQUISITES TO EFFECTIVE PLANNING

Regardless of the specific characteristics of the country that undertakes planning activities to initiate, maintain, and direct development, there are two antecedents which enhance the likelihood of effective planning. Without public acceptance of planning as a legitimate function of government and a general framework to guide its activities, there can be little hope of successful planning.

The Acceptance of Planning as a
Necessary Function of Government

The relationship between individual action and government control has been a constant theme throughout the history of planning. In many nations the need to serve the broader "public good" has been used to justify the expansion of government planning activities into numerous areas of social and economic life. However, planning practice often has been criticized as serving only the narrow economic and political interests of the power elite. In many developing countries, planning was introduced initially as a method of achieving the dual objectives of colonial domination: efficient economic exploitation and effective administrative control. Whether planning will be viewed as a legitimate and useful function of government in the now independent countries of Africa depends on whose interests will be served by planning.

The Need for a Planning Paradigm

Even under the best of circumstances, the will to plan may not be sufficient to insure successful planning. Professor Dudley Seers argues that even though each of the principal forces of planning—the politician, the planner, and the administrator—"may play his role quite reasonably, by his own lights, the outcome is often nonetheless quite irrational, because of differences in the ways they approach their joint task, due to differences in the education and experience which have moulded them."[2]

Planning functions are performed at a number of different levels and by a variety of actors in numerous government or quasi-governmental bodies. As a result, decisions taken at one level or by one agency may prove to be inconsistent with, or even contrary to, decisions made by other planning agencies. This has been the case in a number of countries where national planning objectives have been frustrated by the decisions of regional or local planning officials and vice versa. The lack of coordination among the various agencies involved in planning may result in a waste of scarce resources and cause unnecessary delays in program implementation.

Integration of the planning effort must be undertaken both horizontally and vertically. Horizontal and vertical integration of planning is made more difficult by the lack of an acceptable planning paradigm, that is, a generalized framework within which planning activities may be organized and pursued. No such single paradigm for planning has been developed, and some would argue that its development is unlikely, owing to the diverse areas covered under planning.[3] Even without the benefit of an acceptable paradigm for planning, though, it is possible to suggest some desirable characteristics.

It is our contention that planning for development must be inte-grated.[4] There is a need to view the elements of the socioeconomic environment as an integrated system with explicit recognition being given to the interrelated nature of system elements.[5] As much attention must be given to the interrelations among system elements as has traditionally been given to the system elements themselves. It must be understood clearly that land-use planning, for example, cannot be divorced from transportation planning, nor can the planning for urban housing needs be undertaken effectively unless coordinated to some extent with rural development planning.

A second feature of the planning framework is that it must be explicitly spatial. National development planning is a spatial activity. To plan successfully for the "how" of development one must deal explicitly with the "where" of development. While some national development plans have been drawn up without concern for their spatial implications, successful planning for the future requires explicit treatment of the plan's spatial dimensions. [6]

An additional useful characteristic of planning is that it be based upon a clear conception of the nature of development as a process. Such a conception of development must not only take account of how various sectors of the economy and society are related but also how development is initiated and spatially diffused. The concepts or theories of development that have been advanced have too often focused on sectoral relationships. Considerably less attention has been given to the need for a spatial theory of growth. However, the elements of such a theory are contained in the writings of Perroux, Myrdal, Hirschman, Friedmann, and others, in which growth is viewed as a cumulative and circular process with strong tendencies to concentrate spatially. [7] This view of development gained considerable attention in both developed and developing nations and gave rise to an interest in what has been termed "growth pole theory." This concept and its possible use in development planning was the central focus of several international organizations interested in development throughout the world. [8] Recently, this growth pole strategy has been subject to increasing criticism on the basis of both ideological and efficiency considerations. [9]

Mabogunje reviewed the growth pole methodology in terms of its applicability to Nigeria. He referred to the rather "simplistic attitude [that] has characterized the use of the concepts in planning regional development especially in developing countries."[10] According to Mabogunje, part of the problem in the application of this methodology resulted from a misunderstanding of the concept as originally developed and subsequently modified. Because of the manner in which Perroux[11] initially stated certain propositions of the growth pole concept, there has been a tendency to erroneously equate the notion of growth pole with that of industrial center. Mabogunje suggests that the applicability of the concepts involved deserve much more attention than they have hitherto been afforded. The crucial question of the planner according to Mabogunje is "how to initiate a self-sustaining process of development in a lagging region."[12] The solution lies in the identification of existing or potential centers of growth together with sufficient infrastructural linkages to surrounding regions to allow for stimulation and rapid diffusion of development throughout the urban system and its tributary areas. Thus, according to Mabogunje,

> the critical issue is . . . the selection of the appropriate set of core units that will induce in the region maximum development responses in terms of both new functional linkages (forward and backward) and social structural changes whilst at the same time facilitating the endogenous

generation (and inflow of innovations from outside and their rapid internal diffusion.[13]

In order to undertake such a difficult assignment, the planner must operate within a theoretical framework and choose a set of particular techniques capable of answering the questions inherent in the charge to the planner. The need is for a theory and methodology capable of performing certain integrated functions including (1) a descriptive function capable of specifying those variables necessary to identify and characterize core units within the spatial system; (2) identification and explication of significant relationships between relevant variables and the generation of researchable hypotheses regarding the spatial structure of urban systems and the diffusion of development impulses; (3) normative capabilities for the specification of criteria for optimization and techniques to evaluate alternative planning strategies; and (4) identifying activities and system elements capable of being controlled through government action so as to achieve objectives specified within the plan.[14]

As Mabogunje notes, "In its present stage of development, the growth pole theory is far from satisfying these conditions."[15] At present one of the primary drawbacks to the use of this strategy is that the deliberate development of a regional growth center may in fact engender a sequence of growth leading to the decline of surrounding regions as the growth center attracts resources to itself. In this manner the growth center becomes "parasitic" with respect to the region it is supposed to aid in developing. That is, the "backwash" effects may be stronger than the "spread" effects, to use Myrdal's terms.[16] Without proper concern for what Mabogunje refers to as "functional complementarities" between a growth center and its region, the effects may be counterproductive. Such complementarities must "exhibit both a functional and a geographical dimension."[17] Unless such linkages are explicitly planned as part of the development strategy, it is possible that little growth will occur outside the core.

IMPLICATIONS OF PLANNING IN AN AFRICAN CONTEXT

To date, the methodology and most analytic techniques available to the urban and regional planner have been constructed and used primarily in the "developed" countries.[18] It is not surprising, therefore, that quite aside from the general and inherent problems associated with their use, the relevancy of these methodologies and techniques for use in an African context is subject to question.

Problems Associated with Application
of Planning Methodologies

Since the existing methodologies have been constructed in the
social, economic, and political milieu of a "developed" nation, many
of the assumptions of the methods, either explicit or implicit, may
be inappropriate to developing nations. In fact, several authors have
argued that because of the violation of these assumptions, many of
the methods are irrelevant to the planning needs of the developing
nations. They suggest that such methods need to be modified, or even
completely redesigned, in order to accommodate the different conditions of Third World countries. There have been appeals for the development of "indigenous economics," "indigenous urban theory,"
and so on. [19] It is therefore incumbent upon those most familiar with
conditions in developing nations to undertake such efforts to improve
upon the tenuous theoretical and methodological foundation of planning.

A second problem relates to the data required for the use of
even the most elementary methods of interest to the planner. Data
insufficiency, particularly time series information, is an endemic
problem in developing regions. Most of the models currently available
have a voracious appetite for data of an increasingly specific nature.
But in many of the African nations the conditions for obtaining such
information are also poorer than in the more developed nations. There
is a general suspicion and mistrust among the general public surrounding the process of data gathering. While the public in many developed
nations has become increasingly vocal about "invasion of privacy,"
they nonetheless have been more willing to submit to the task of providing data when required by policy makers and government planners.
Also, because of the number of institutional contexts, such as social
security forms, income tax returns, and applications for driver's
licenses, in which the public routinely interfaces with government
agencies, there are a greater number of data acquisition opportunities.
In African nations such points of interface are fewer, and the general
public is less willing to supply needed information. The experiences
of census teams in many African nations attest to the reluctance of
individuals to submit to inquiry into what they consider their private
lives. For example, in preparation for the 1973 census, Nigeria
mounted an intensive educational effort to alert and inform the general public of the importance of and need for accurate population data.
The experiences of the previous census, with the explosive political
implications of the results, obviously made the task more difficult.

A third area of concern within Africa is the general scarcity of
properly trained managerial and planning personnel. In discussing the
urban problems of Africa, Mabogunje has suggested that this is a
major problem in formulating and implementing effective urban de-

velopment.[20] While a goodly number of individuals are employed in Town and Country Planning Units in Nigeria, their training is often not the most desirable for the type of planning currently required. This is in part due to what Mabogunje refers to as an "erroneous belief that the training of architects is what is required for planning the growth and development of cities."[21] The manpower needs include the employment of individuals conversant with pertinent theories and methodologies of regional development. In short, the training of planners for developing nations must reflect a much more functional approach to planning in contrast to the strong traditional reliance upon physical planning and design.[22] Several authors have addressed the types of training required of modern planners and have stressed the role of analytical skills.[23]

A secondary consideration in this regard has been that most African nations, lacking such expertise in sufficient numbers, have had to rely upon foreign planners and analysts in formulating and implementing certain projects. This may be inadvisable for a number of reasons. Quite aside from the fact that many foreign "experts" are unfamiliar with the local political and social conditions of the host country, there are problems associated with depending too fully upon such individuals or consulting agencies. In approaching African development problems, foreign "experts," perhaps unwittingly, operate within their own basic frames of reference. For example, even in relatively straightforward engineering problems they may attempt to impose upon the developing nation standards which are consistent with practice in the United States or Great Britain but which may be totally irrelevant to the needs of the local population. Such problems call into question the role of the foreign advisory in developing planning, as well they should. This is not to argue that foreign research workers or planners should be ignored as a potentially useful resource for developing nations; rather their role should be clearly defined so as to insure that their contributions are useful and their influence on decision making kept in perspective.

A fourth problem derives from the fact that most African nations are only recently independent countries in which many segments of the society still hold strong allegiances to traditional local leaders or other persons of authority of a religious or a secular nature. Such traditional authorities are often ignored in the planning process and thus are either indifferent or actively opposed to the efforts of government planners. This has created a degree of animosity which has made it difficult to define the role of traditional leaders and make them effective participants in the search for solutions to problems. The difficulty of redefining the role of traditional elites has resulted in a "vacuum of enlightened leadership in virtually all African cities."[24] This condition derives in part from the colonial experience and the "emasculation of local leadership talent" implied by systems of direct or indirect colonial control. This condition will obviously be corrected in time, but in the shortrun there is a clear need to be able to work with and gain the cooperation of such traditional leaders and their supporters to insure the success of planning efforts.

A fifth problem of a related nature stems from the continued strong allegiance of present urban dwellers to their towns and regions of origin. Johnson and Whitelaw present data on urban-rural income transfers in Kenya and suggest that

> to the extent that rural and urban residence is a useful distinction in a country like Kenya, the magnitude of urban-rural income transfers implies a very significant increase in rural welfare from what is implied by comparisons of relative incomes alone. If, as is roughly the case in Kenya, the urban and rural wage bills are equal, then aggregate rural income is increased by 20 percent by the institution of remittances. This interpretation, however, can be somewhat misleading. Most urban residents still consider their home to be the village in which they grew up; their stay in Nairobi is principally for the purpose of making a good income. . . . Given that individual families are spread out in both urban and rural locations, it is not useful to consider the welfare of urban residents and rural residents as independent of each other. [25]

This linkage in itself is a strong and potentially beneficial force for the development of rural areas in many African countries, but in its more extreme versions it leads to a "high degree of social indifference to progress of the city where they make their fortune. "[26] Thus the populations of many of the larger cities in developing nations are unwilling to contribute substantially to the pool of fiscal and other resources necessary to facilitate development.

A sixth problem may be seen in what might best be characterized as the lack of a responsive bureaucratic infrastructure. Again, partly owing to the nature of the colonial administrations established in African nations, there was little chance for public input in defining planning objectives. Unfortunately, there are still few well-developed channels whereby public complaints, demands, and grievances may be forwarded to those in control of the planning functions. This has resulted in a situation wherein the general public has had little recourse short of riot or demonstration to call to planners' attention their dissatisfaction with certain decisions and policies.

A seventh and, some would argue, most important problem associated with the implementation of planning methodologies is related to the lack of fiscal resources. Planning itself is an increasingly expensive undertaking. The adequacy of planning efforts and the extent to which they are implemented are clearly related to the fiscal resources available. Few African countries, with Nigeria perhaps being the most notable exception, have had the resources necessary to make adequate plans, let alone implement them. Nigeria, in this regard, can clearly establish a position of leadership in the planning area. [27]

An eighth problem is related to the often strong dependence of developing nations on external governments as sources of capital. The nature of the colonial and neocolonial relationships in many developing areas means that the indigenous planner and politician often lack effective control over basic elements of the economy. Such dependence makes planning on the basis of national objectives difficult and perhaps impossible since it requires the implicit or explicit approval of plans by foreign governments, international lending agencies, and corporations. This condition has prompted efforts at indigenization of business and industry in several African countries.

Ninth, owing to the colonial past, many African nations have been organized to operate efficiently as export-oriented, primary producers. As this was consistent with the colonial objectives, the pattern of infrastructural development in most developing nations took place so as to serve most efficiently these objectives. [28] However, it is quite possible, and indeed probable, that the inherited pattern of infrastructure may be totally inappropriate, and even inimical, to the interests of independent African nations. Moreover, there continue to be strong forces within the economy and society that will attempt to thwart any attempt to alter this pattern. Undoubtedly this will make the planning process more difficult.

As a final observation, recognition must be given to the impact of political instability on the implementation of planning strategies. The political instability that has characterized many African nations since independence has obviously affected the atmosphere for planning and made it impossible to formulate and carry out long-range planning schemes. Frequent changes of government and shifting ideological bases of planning may result in a waste of effort and resources. The experience in Ghana with the development of the Accra-Tema motorway illustrates the effects of radical differences in the approach to planning of the Nkrumah government and that of the subsequent military and civilian regimes. The motorway, originally conceived as one link in an integrated urban-industrial transport network in and around the Accra-Tema complex now stands as an ill-used but magnificent monument to changes in objectives brought about by political instability. Even so, one would be reluctant to argue that political stability should be bought at any price. In this regard, some of the participants in a recent Society for International Development conference in Europe were moved to remark,

> Clash and conflict can no longer be regarded as a "failure" of a given system. Whenever conflict is likely to resolve rather than set back class contradictions, it should actually be promoted. The alternatives to conflict have simply shown themselves to be too slow. [29]

Prospects for Planning

The literature on developing nations is replete with studies purporting to identify and describe what are considered to be the major obstacles or problems associated with development efforts. In fact, the list of such factors has grown as the number of articles being written has swelled. It is therefore somewhat heartening to read the few studies that take a more positive perspective on the development opportunities of the new nations. This is not to play down the important issues in those many scholarly works focused upon the problems of development. It is, rather, to attempt to bring them into perspective and to insure against an overly pessimistic view. In this regard, Hirschman's article, with the intriguing title "Obstacles to Development: A Classification and a Quasi-vanishing Act,"[30] strikes a note which we wish to echo here. By adopting Hirschman's perspective, certain of the alleged obstacles to development may take on a different character.

Hirschman addresses the question of obstacles to development by positing the following question. Consider that some given country at a specific time has encountered a particular obstacle that has adversely affected the development of that country. Does this suggest that this same obstacle will constitute a similar problem in other countries and at a different time? Upon closer investigation, it is possible that the alleged obstacle may in fact be seen either not to constitute an absolute barrier, not to be an obstacle to development at all, or actually to be a positive advantage.

Hirschman illustrates these points with a number of interesting examples, including that of the role of the extended family. While many authors, particularly those from Western societies, have frequently cited the extended family as a possible hindrance to individual achievement, entrepreneurship, and so on, Hirschman presents an argument which suggests the extended family may turn out to be not an obstacle but a positive incentive to increased individual effort. Similarly, political instability and civil strife are often regarded as major obstacles to African development, yet in the U.S. experience

conflict associated with the settlement of the West necessitated a
methodical, well-planned, and gradual advance involving very close
logistical and cultural contact with established communities in the
East. Hirschman contrasts this with the experience in Brazil, where
the frontier was settled rapidly and without major conflict, conditions
which gave rise to isolated communities without close logistical ties
to other areas and which resulted in their rapid economic regression.

Let us now consider some other attributes of African countries
which may prove beneficial in carrying out planning tasks. First is
the general acceptance of planning as a legitimate function of government, at least among elites in Africa. Regardless of the approach,
many African nations have a development plan. The fact that these
nations have felt the need to put such plans into a published document
represents a commitment to planning that might well be envied in
some more developed nations. A second and related feature is the
accepted central role the government plays in the establishment and
execution of plans. Concomitantly, there is greater participation in
and control over investments in the private as well as the public sectors, particularly as countries attempt to decolonize their economies.
It would appear that this process is likely to continue in the future.
Even in those areas where private investment is being actively sought
and encouraged, efforts are being made to insure that such investment is consistent with the long-range planning objectives and guarantees participation by government or nationals.

As the newly independent countries of Africa attempt to cope
with the numerous and pressing developmental problems facing them,
one might hope that they will be in a position to study and learn from
the development planning experiences of other countries. In particular,
the developing countries have access, at least potentially, to a great
wealth of experience and a "technological backlog" accumulated through
other nations' development efforts. Perhaps through an understanding
of past development efforts, the developing nations may avoid some
of the setbacks and mistakes that marked early planning efforts of
other countries. However, in order to benefit from such a backlog of
technical information and experience, African countries must have
well-trained and highly qualified individuals who are conversant with
the nature of this backlog and who will participate in the selection of
the planning methods and technology, most appropriate to the needs
of their particular countries. In facing this task, many African nations would prefer not to have to rely on foreign advisers. As a consequence, they are encouraging students to seek advanced training
abroad and, increasingly, are attempting to provide local training
facilities and institutions of higher education.

Although the colonial experience had a definite impact upon
African space economies, the generally low level of infrastructure

development may allow African planners to redirect regional development to a greater extent than if faced with large amounts of "sunk capital." In this regard, developing nations may have a freer hand to initiate plans of an innovative and imaginative character. Moreover, since even minor additions or extensions to existing infrastructure may have dramatic impact, African nations may be in a position to effect significant changes in their spatial patterns of development. [31] While the need to break the colonial pattern of development remains a thorny issue, the development of certain areas in the country may be planned de novo. In this regard, students of planning and development will follow with interest the current efforts of the Nigerians to design and build a new federal capital at Abuja.

CONCLUDING REMARKS

While it is rather common to discuss the numerous problems associated with planning African development, we feel that these may arise in part from attempts to apply inappropriate planning methods in African contexts. Rather than bemoaning the fact that African conditions don't meet the stringent requirements of existing planning methods and models, perhaps we need to develop planning methods and techniques that are more appropriate to the specific contexts of African countries.

We have attempted to bring into focus several issues bearing on the application of planning methodologies in an African context. The absence of a well-established and tested planning paradigm within which development efforts may be evaluated and their impacts identified is perhaps the most critical concern at the moment. A great deal of additional thought and effort will be required before the elements of such a paradigm may be articulated fully, but it is almost certain that the major impetus and direction for such a new paradigm will be found in the efforts of Third World planners working on immediate problems in their respective countries. This experience has already called into question nearly every aspect of the "conventional wisdom" of Western planners and theorists. [32]

Superimposed on this already weak theoretical foundation is a set of techniques and methodologies which require refinement and deliberate modification before they may be applied satisfactorily in the context of African countries. Efforts to articulate more appropriate planning methods stress the need for more "action-oriented" approaches, [33] emphasizing planning as a process rather than preparation of plans, [34] greater local participation and decentralization, [35] more concern for people than projects, and planners motivated by a concern for greater social justice rather than narrow conceptions of economic efficiency. [36]

Finally, we might note that we have assessed certain problems and prospects of planning African development in the general context of individual national efforts. We would like to argue, however, that care should be taken to insure that in conceiving individual national plans, cognizance be given to the larger problems of regional or even continental concern, so that the parochial interests of one nation do not frustrate efforts toward intra-African cooperation. Every effort should be made at present to pursue policies strengthening ties between African nations through the efforts of the Organization of African Unity and the establishment of regional groupings, such as Economic Community for West African States (ECOWAS), for purposes of social, economic, and perhaps eventual political integration.

If one lesson of development is clear from the U. S. and Soviet experiences, it is that interregional integration of diverse elements of the economy and society is the basis of strength. The Balkanization of Africa resulting from the forces of colonialism and neocolonialism is perhaps one of the greatest barriers to effective planning in the continent. In order to insure effective developmental planning for the Africa of the future, the words of the late Dr. Nkrumah are still appropriate: "Africa must unite."

NOTES

1. Dennis Rondinelli, "Rethinking National Development," Journal of American Institute of Planners 44, no. 1 (January 1978): 84.

2. Dudley Seers, "The Prevalence of Pseudo-planning," in The Crisis in Planning, ed. Mike Faber and Dudley Seers, vol. 1 (London: Chatto and Windus, 1972).

3. J. S. McCallum, "Planning Theory in Planning Education," The Planner (Journal of the Royal Town Planning Institute) 60, no. 6 (1974): 738-41.

4. F. E. Horton and M. L. McNulty, "A Strategy for Coordinating Human and Technical Resources in Planning: The Lagos-Ibadan Corridor," in Urbanization, National Development and Regional Planning in Africa, ed. S. S. El-Shakhs and R. A. Obudho (New York: Praeger, 1974).

5. G. A. Chadwick, A Systems View of Planning: Towards a Theory of the Urban and Regional Planning Process (Oxford: Pergamon Press, 1971).

6. Alan Gilbert, ed., Development Planning and Spatial Structure (New York: John Wiley & Sons, 1976).

7. François Perroux, "Note sur la notion de pôle de crois-sance," Economie Appliqué, (1955); François Perroux, "Economic Space: Theory and Applications," Quarterly Journal of Economics (February 1950); Gunnar Myrdal, Rich Lands and Poor (New York: Harper & Brothers, 1957); Albert O. Hirschman, The Strategy of Economic Development (New Haven: Yale University Press, 1958); and John Friedman, Urbanization, Planning, and National Develop-ment, (Beverly Hills, Calif.: Sage, 1973).

8. Resources for the Future: Harvey S. Perloff et al., Design for a Worldwide Study of Regional Development: A Report to the United Nations on a Proposed Research-Training Program (Washington, D.C.: Resources for the Future, 1966); Antoni Kuklinski, ed., Growth Poles and Growth Centers in Regional Planning (Paris: Mouton, 1972); and several others in this series. A recent IDEP seminar on region-alization of development planning and regional planning was held in Ibadan, Nigeria, April 16-May 12, 1973. Papers presented there in-cluded John Friedmann et al., "Urbanization and National Develop-ment: A Comparative Analysis"; M. O. Filani, "The Creation of Urban Environments and General Urban Problems in Africa"; R. K. Udo, "Planning Growth Centers: New Towns vs. Expanded Towns"; among others. Akin Mabogunje, "Growth Poles and Growth Centres in the Regional Development of Nigeria," United Nations Research Institute for Survey Development (UNRISD) Report, no. 71.3 (Geneva, 1971).

9. Michael E. Conroy, "Rejection of Growth Center Strategy in Latin American Regional Development Planning," Land Economies 49, no. 4 (November 1973): 371-80.

10. Akin Mabogunje, "Growth Pole Methodology in Regional Planning" (Paper presented at IDEP Seminar, Ibadan, Nigeria, April 16-May 12, 1973).

11. Perroux, "Note sur la notion de pôle de croissance."

12. Mabogunje, op. cit.

13. Ibid.

14. Ibid.

15. Ibid.

16. Myrdal, op. cit.

17. Mabogunje, op. cit.

18. F. E. Horton and M. L. McNulty, Problems in the Applica-tion of Planning Methodologies in Developing Countries, Development Series Report, no. 2, Institute of Urban and Regional Research (Iowa City: University of Iowa, 1973).

19. Polly Hill, "A Plea for Indigenous Economics: The West African Example," Economic Development and Cultural Change (October 1966); and Harold Brookfield, Interdependent Development (Pittsburgh: University of Pittsburgh Press, 1975).

20. Akin Mabogunje, "Urbanization Problems in Africa," in Urbanization, National Development and Regional Planning in Africa, ed. El-Shakhs and Obudho, (New York: Praeger, 1974).

21. Ibid.

22. Ibid.

23. Harvey Perloff, "Education for Regional Planning in Less Developed Countries," and Antoni R. Kuklinski, "Education for Regional Planning," in Issues in Regional Planning, ed. David Dunham and Jos Hilhorst (The Hague: Mouton, 1971); and Anthony King, "Exporting 'Planning': The Colonial Experience," Urbanism Past and Present, no. 5 (Winter 1977-78); 12-22.

24. Mabogunje, op. cit.

25. G. E. Johnson and W. E. Whitelaw, "Urban-Rural Income Transfers in Kenya: An Estimated-Remittances Function," Economic Development and Cultural Change 22, no. 3 (April 1974); 477-78.

26. Mabogunje, op. cit.

27. K. M. Barbour, ed., Planning for Nigeria (Ibadan: University Press, 1972).

28. M. L. McNulty, "West African Urbanization," in Urbanization and Counter-Urbanization, ed. B. J. L. Berry, Urban Affairs Annual, 11 (1976).

29. Report of the Ad Hoc Working Group to the Plenary Session, Society for International Development European Regional Conference, September 1973.

30. Albert O. Hirschman, "Obstacles to Development: A Classification and a Quasi-vanishing Act," in The Political Economy of Development, ed. Uphoff and Ilchman (Berkeley: University of California Press, 1972).

31. S. El-Shakhs, "Planning for Systems of Settlements in Emerging Nations," Town Planning Review 47 (April 1976).

32. David Slater, "Geography and Underdevelopment—Part II," ANTIPODE pp. 1-31; and Milton Santos, "Planning Underdevelopment," ANTIPODE 9, no. 3, Clark University (December 1977): 86-97.

33. Avrom Bendavid-Val and Peter Waller, eds., Action-Oriented Approaches to Regional Development Planning (New York: Praeger, 1975).

34. Mal Rivkin, Land Use and the Intermediate-Sized City in Developing Countries (New York: Praeger, 1976).

35. Ann Siedman, Planning for Development in Sub-Saharan Africa (New York: Praeger, 1974).

36. Milton Santos, op. cit.

Part One

THE NATURE OF
AFRICAN URBANISM

2

MISCONCEPTIONS OF
AFRICAN URBANISM:
SOME EURO-AMERICAN NOTIONS

Azuka A. Dike

INTRODUCTION

This chapter attempts to point out some of the misconceptions
about African urbanism, briefly enunciating the principles that should
guide students of social change on that continent. A few works, which
tend to represent the approach of the majority of Africanists, have
been selected to illustrate the impact of Euro-American notions of
urbanism on the study of indigenous African towns.

The majority of Euro-American Africanists tends to see sociocultural change as a linear progression, the end result of which is
Western urbanism. Many Africans have also been educationally so-
cialized to accept this sociocultural process. This approach has influenced research on African urbanism toward studying African adjustment or adaptation to Western norms, as evidenced in the works
of A. L. Epstein, J. Clyde Mitchell, Leonard Plotnicov, and Immanuel Wallerstein. Thus, this approach has come to ignore or gloss over
the African normative system as if it were a passing phase incapable
of withstanding the concomitants of industrialism.

This approach tends to be unaware of the binary nature of African societies and cultures. When the duality of African sociocultures
is recognized, those aspects generated by colonialism are to measure
the inability of the Africans to respond positively to the newly imported
culture and to assert that traditional norms will inevitably be superseded by Western values. The duality in African societies and cultures
can be broadly identified as combining, first, the newly introduced
state-level organizations with their administrative and technological
networks and their normative concomitants, and, second, the local
indigenous level, which has constituted the primary base of encultura-

19

tion. The great majority of Africans have their sociocultural base at the local indigenous level. For them, Western norms do not constitute the core values. Even where the dual cultures clash, they are often synthesized by the new African elites, who are products of both African and Euro-American world views.

An alternative approach is to study the adaptation of Western norms to indigenous norms. This requires that the student first understand thoroughly the traditional cultures; that is, the traditional meaning of material artifacts, when and how the newly acquired artifacts become substitutes, and when the old is partially or completely discarded. This approach allows for the study of sociocultural formations in terms of national cultures. The overall standard of measurement implicit in this approach is the indigenous norm. It is my contention that the comprehension of the process of social change is incomplete and misleading without such an analysis allowing the student of culture change to separate—and reconcile—the local indigenous norms with imposed norms. In effect, it allows for the possibility that imposed norms can be indigenized, as has been recognized by Shelton in his study of Igbo-Igala Borderland. [1]

This approach may have unique philosophical implications as well as operational problems. The mere recognition of the significance of indigenous norms is in itself educational. It reorients scholars and laymen to an understanding of the indigenous normative structure and has serious implications for policy planning. The problems of operationalization, on the other hand, may result primarily from our preoccupation with Western indexes. If we realize, however, that it is hypotheses that often generate our operational definitions, the problems of operationalization can be minimized. More importantly, there are several research methods that do not require operationalization.

Methodologically, there are three broad models of urbanization: behavioral, structural, and demographic. They are conceptually different, and while models are not inherently wrong or incorrect, they can be misleading or incomplete. Briefly stated, the behaviorists, such as Louis Wirth and his school of thought, focus on the conduct of individuals or groups and patterns of behavior or thought irrespective of social environment or locale. [2] Behavior is classified as either urban or rural. In this approach, social change tends to be regarded as evolutionary and is seen conceptually as unilinear or one-dimensional, the ultimate stage being Euro-American industrial culture. On the other hand, the structural model, exemplified by the works of Eshref Shevky and Wendell Bell, focuses on patterned activities of whole populations. [3] Its primary interest is in the differential ordering of occupations, industries, location of recent and earlier migrants into the city, and other varieties of structured activities. Urban economists and geographers find this closer to their disciplinary approach. While most structuralists are not averse to the typical behavioral unilinear approach, their synchronic analysis may allow for differential evaluation of urbanism in time and space. Finally, the demographic approach, typified by the works of Hope Tisdale and even the ecologists Robert Parks and Ernest Burgess, focuses primarily on the interaction of population and space and the movement of people out of agricultural communities.[4] Our focus in this chapter is primarily on the first group, the behaviorists, particularly those whose analysis has been constrained by the impact of their intellectual, social, and cultural backgrounds.

ADAPTATION STUDIES OF AFRICAN URBANIZATION

Several Western scholars of sociocultural change in Africa have adopted Western cultural artifacts as their principal indexes. By basing their measures of change on Africans' response and adjustment to the material culture of urban and metropolitan centers, they run the risk of equating increasing acquisition of Western cultural materials with increasing Westernization. Powdermaker's Copper Town is a good example of an early work on urbanization in Africa that demonstrates such pitfalls.[5] It lacks good comprehension of the traditional normative structure and uses the adoption of Western cultural artifacts as the principal variable demonstrating cultural linearity. Its basic assumption is that the mere presence of Western objects in and of itself is a normative change. Other African sociocultural studies, by A. L. Epstein, J. Clyde Mitchell, and Leonard Plotnicov to mention a few, are concerned more with the extent of adjustment or maladjustment to imported cultural traits.[6] Epstein's approach is to "illustrate vividly the random or haphazard character of much of urban social life in Africa."[7] Plotnicov's purpose was "to describe and analyze the adjustments individuals make to modern conditions."[8] The primary concern here is to show the awkwardness of the African in what the authors perceive as Western urban conditions. There is no doubt of some maladjustment to any newly imposed norms, but where such norms are peripheral they should not be treated as if they constitute the standard.

Many Africanists' choice of indexes, or indicators, and hypotheses seem geared to validate and substantiate an a priori definition. Powdermaker, for example, states in Copper Town,

> The original problem was concerned with the communication of modern Western culture through the mass media—radio, movies and newspapers—and was part of a larger

study of leisure activities as an index of social change in
this mine community. [9]

While the author acknowledges the existence of traditional leisure
activities, she uses her limited knowledge of it only to gauge how
much the individual or the society "relates" to the modern world or
"returns to the past." She describes those who did not want to listen
to the radio or take advantage of new leisure activities as "intransigents" lacking the "ego strength" to move into the modern world and
instead "regress to exaggerated traditional values." [10]

The author clearly implies that those who have "accepted the
new moral order and internalized some of its values" [11] have resisted
the drunkenness and promiscuity that, in her view, characterize those
who want to cling to the old. While Powdermaker concedes that the
"polarities of African versus European appear to have been merged in"
the young African leaders, the thrust of her study was to demonstrate,
first the local native Africans' maladjustment to the new urban situation, second their normalization by adopting European ways, and,
third, the dichotomization of the urban dweller in opposition to the
rural inhabitant. [12] It may be argued that these conclusions are entirely due to the strict scientific approach which constrains the range
of technical control over natural processes. Nevertheless, it seems
that the hypotheses on which such studies are based are derivations
of a state of mind.

Willie Abraham, a noted African scholar, also tended to equate
increasing acquisition of Western cultural materials with increasing
westernization. He argued that there is no simple transplantation of
a borrowed item from its original native setting, where it would have
been surrounded by ideals, attitudes, and relationships, into a foreign
setting, particularly if the borrowed item is corrosive in nature. [13]
This, however, assumes that one item serves the same function for
all cultures, an assumption seriously questioned by Robert Merton
in his critique of functionalism. [14] While some cultures have the capa-
bility of adapting borrowed traits to other functions, others, as Shelton
has pointed out, put them to the same use but modify them to blend
into local values. [15] In some cases the foreign setting may already
possess items surrounded by similar ideals. If so, resilience and
traditionalization are two important factors to be considered in any
discussion of social change in Africa.

To borrow from David Apter, some traditional systems accept
innovation more readily than others. [16] Those with "instrumental"
values tend to traditionalize the newly acquired norms and are capable
of making use of newly introduced means to further their own ends,
while those with "consumatory" values tend to "fracture along well-
established lines" because their values are "strongly ritualized and

meaningful in and of themselves. "[17] In effect, the direction of change varies from culture to culture and is not necessarily a linear progression.

Southall and Gutkind saw the need to understand the new by looking at the old; they saw the culture as being transformed from tribal to Western norms. [18] They portrayed urban squalor, community atomization, and individualization. Their seeming inability to see beyond the squalor and perceive the integrative influence of traditional norms within the African urban milieu can only be explained by a linear perception of urbanization. [19] Their Townsmen in the Making, one of the first studies of African urban life, seemed to be based on a model designed for a society experiencing indigenously generated change. [20] The response of Londoners to their cultural innovation, which we must emphasize is merely a slightly modified extension of the original patterns, is different from the response of a divergent society with its own long-established norms and modes of behavior before the introduction of the alien foreign innovation.

While there may be similar physical conditions in New York, London, Lagos, Niarobi, and Tokyo, the different cultural backgrounds provide and generate different social norms and cultural organizations. The memorial service which some groups in Nigeria hold a year after the death of a loved one is a substitute for the indigenous second burial ceremony. The elaborate speechmaking, rituals, and the high table for special guests, mostly of high status, connected with Nigerian church weddings is a modification of indigenous norms. With the exception of some Mediterranean groups, these rituals, speechmaking, and even elaborate merrymaking are not typically Euro-American. It would appear, therefore, that norms induced or introduced by a foreign cultural agent would tend to conform to the indigenous norm when the indigenous group does not experience any forced transplantation or uprootment.

THE RURAL BASE OF AFRICAN URBANISM

Because of their linear progression approach, most Africanists failed to perceive that urban Africa is predominantly inhabited by men and women with rural upbringing and that there is a continuous and strong symbiosis between rural and urban life. Most urban Africans consider their rural abode their home. The works of Kenneth Little, Emmanuel Wallerstein, and A. J. Epstein, to mention a few, do not seem to recognize the strength of the continuous interchange of ideas between rural and urban Africa. Epstein sees traditional and urban values as contradictory when he states, "Africans in the town, are now beginning to group themselves from their fellows (in rural areas) in terms of . . . their general social values. Gradually, new associations come into being to express these different interests, and clashed with existing traditional bodies. "[21] Like Powdermaker, Epstein sees any remnant of traditional forms in the urban setting as an "internal inconsistency. " What they fail to recognize is that African urban voluntary associations are in some measure an outgrowth or a transformation of similar rural activities. As Meillassoux showed, the traditional voluntary associations of the Bamana and others in Mali were transferred to urban conditions. [22]

The concept of Isusu Union, a rotating credit association of men in urban areas of Nigeria, which primarily serves to put a large sum of money at the disposal of one of its members at regular intervals, is a concept derived from age-group farming associations. Here all members of the group would work for a member at stipulated intervals by rotation until each member of the group had received his share.

Lloyd acknowledges that some of the norms and forms of associations in industrialized urban areas owed their origins to traditional structures. [23] His primary concern, however, is "the adaptation of traditional West African society to modern conditions. "[24] This approach glosses over the normative foundation of a modern African community. With the main exception of Uchendu and Diamond, all contributors to The Passing of Tribal Man in Africa, edited by Gutkind, reiterated the views expressed above. The very title of the book confirms the argument that Western scholars generally see that African traditional norms are being wiped out by the presence of European technology.

Uchendu supports the thesis of continuous exchange of ideas between the rural and urban communities. He says,

Although the tribal and national groupings in West Africa are increasingly acquiring a wider frame of reference (politically), the old and the new still co-exist, and often interpenetrate. The Ghanaian national dress known to the outside world, is as much part of modern Ghana as the skirt of leaf of the Kusasi woman. An Ashanti medical doctor is as much an ashanti as he is a doctor and Ghanaian. The Igbo college professor who takes his village "title" is no less modern than he is Igbo. [25]

Uchendu conceptualizes the problem very clearly. He acknowledges the interpenetration of the old and the new and their coexistence without the suggestion of marginality or mental disorder found in the writings of some other Western scholars.

The norms of greetings vary from one region to another but not necessarily from urban to rural area. In urban or rural Nigeria one is still expected to greet one's elders or those of high social status. In the streets and offices of Lagos and Kano it is not uncommon to see children, men, and women genuflect or even prostrate themselves before their social superiors in the act of exchanging greetings. In Enugu, Onitsha, and Aba, where body bending is not a normative expression of courtesy or greeting, the norm of good manners requires that one greet his seniors or ask after the well-being of a person or group in the morning, afternoon, and evening or before soliciting any information.

The norm of kola nut presentation to a guest, or the apology for lack of it, as a demonstration of hospitality on the part of the host is an Igbo custom well entrenched in urban areas. The often extensive ritual of kola nut breaking, used to show respect to the oldest person or culturally revered group, is part of the accepted norm of both the Igbo university professor and the village farmer. The act of vacating chairs in home or in nonofficial places by the younger for older persons is a folkway found in both towns and villages among the Igbos and other ethnic groups.

Visitation to the bereaved person is a sine qua non for the urban or rural Igbo. An adult person remiss in this social obligation can be forsaken in times of distress. In fact, one of the bases for paying condolence visit to a person is the knowledge that he pays such visits to others.

In the analysis of urban cultures, many fail to recognize that the urban and rural people in each nation have a common cultural denominator and that an urban culture shares more with the rural culture of the same nation than with the urban culture of another country. The normative universals within each nation are more numerous than among nations. Within a national group (not state) the customary tenets prevalent in the rural area tend to predominate in the urban area. There are of course regional idiosyncrasies, but these are the extremes of our normal curve and do not represent the area between one or two standard deviations.

URBAN ETHNIC CONSCIOUSNESS

William and Judith Hanna assert that antagonistic relationships in urban Africa are a result of minimal ethnic interactions and the urban dweller's conception of "his traditional family home" as his true home. [26] The Hannas correctly observe that ethnic groups are "encapsulated within their own ethnic network in the urban centers." But in their view this "serves as a partial barrier between them and the wider urban social system." The implications of their work are, first, that Euro-American social conditions will inevitably be replicated in the African milieu, and, second, that the "melting pot" principle is the best social condition. As has been pointed out by Herbert Gans, Willmott and Young, and Whyte, [27] contrary to the prediction and postulation of Louis Wirth and other members of the Chicago school, the "melting pot" principle has not even materialized in the United States. The clustering of people of the same ethnic background is still a common feature of U. S. society. This is contrary to Wirth's assumption that size, density, and heterogeneity have their own dynamics without regard to ethnicity. He had postulated that as people come to the city they tend to live and interact mostly with their own kind, but as a result of physical proximity the different ethnic groups eventually melt into one group, completely disregarding any reference to ethnicity. This theory is negated by the African practice, and its negation contradicts the linear progression theory.

Uchendu seems to capture the true situation in the African context. He "views tribe and tribal society as a central feature of pluralism" and makes the assertion, with which I fully agree, that "tribalism as ideology and behavior is everywhere on the increase."[28] By tribalism I mean ethnic consciousness, the consciousness of belonging to a particular ethnic group, the sharing of ethnic custom, belief, language, and values, which guide individual behavior.

In a multinational state like Nigeria there is the evergrowing fear by some ethnic groups of their emasculation by the dominant groups. This threat or feeling, caused by visible and imaginary others, sustains ethnic consciousness through intensified intra-ethnic interaction. The resulting intensive intra-ethnic interaction in urban areas sustains ethnic cultures within metropolitan areas. Abner Cohen observed that the introduction of the Tijaniyya Order, a Muslim sect, into Sabo, Hausa Quarters in Ibadan, checked the disintegration of the foundation of Sabo's exclusive identity. [29] Hitherto the Hausas in Sabo worshipped and even intermarried with the Yorubas. But with the coming of the new order the Hausas of Sabo became socially exclusive, upholding only Hausa customs, values, and beliefs in the big metropolis of Ibadan.

It seems, then, that, contrary to the linear progression theory, ethnic consciousness and culture not only remain part of the urban sociocultural order, but quite often strengthen under such conditions.

METHODOLOGICAL IMPLICATIONS AND SUGGESTIONS

The proper study of urbanism in Africa should be based on a recognition of the theory of cultural relativity and diversity. Behavioral patterns in urban Africa may be shaped more by intra- and inter-ethnic composition than by the presence of Western norms. As Magubane indicates in his chapter on the city in Africa in this volume, urbanization and the city cannot be analyzed apart from their historical and social contexts. Failing to do so betrays the misconception that urbanization is an independent process in history.

The proper analysis of African sociocultural change needs to be seen through African eyes. It may be argued that objective analysis requires a disinterested party, but the question is whether research and conceptual analysis can be value-free. Even Talcott Parsons once maintained that the extended family is not conducive to the functional and efficient operation of an industrial system because of its inherent nepotistic tendencies. However, the Japanese experience indicates, according to Abegglen, that "the factory recruits involve and maintain their membership on a basis similar to that of the domestic and social groups of the society," and that industrial development took place with many fewer changes in social organization than would be expected in a Western model. [30] This contradicts Parson's theory and shows that even Parson's thought process was circumscribed by the social milieu in which he was enculturated. It further weakens the linear progression thesis by showing that the social organization of industry in Japan varies from its Western counterpart.

The use of Western indexes by Euro-American Africanists and some Africans may be mainly responsible for their adjustment and maladjustment studies. For students of African urbanism to understand the processes by which Western norms are adapted to indigenous norms, they have first to understand thoroughly the traditional culture. As indicated earlier, this implies a comprehension of the traditional meaning of the material artifacts, when and how newly acquired artifacts become substitutes or are used for other purposes for which they were not intended in their original culture. They have to understand the context in which the old is partially or completely discarded. This approach renders the study of sociocultural formations of national (ethnic) culture and their processes of assimilation and acculturation more meaningful. The point here is that the proper indexes for measuring sociocultural changes in a given culture should be based on and derived from its indigenous norms, not from the newly acquired norms peripheral to the original culture. Otherwise, indexes can only measure the extent of adjustment or maladjustment to the newly acquired elements, not the depth of cultural change. The study and comprehension of the process of social change would be incomplete, and even misleading, without an approach allowing the separation of the local indigenous norms from those imposed and aiding in synthesizing both. The possibility that imposed norms can be indigenized could thus be clarified if the indigenous normative structures is taken as the basis for the study.

For meaningful and accurate delineation and analysis of social change in Africa the combination of diachronic as well as synchronic method is most useful. While the analysis would attempt to capture the stages of development or sequences of changes it would also take a more limited time approach. The analyst would attempt to examine some value systems held by people at different times before and after European contact. In such a case, only a few operational variables should be used to allow for an in-depth study of the kind of changes that have taken place. Some good examples of such variables are work habits, marriage norms, sexual codes, funeral rites and ceremonies, food habits, and leisure norms. The following four sociocultural categories can be most useful as guidelines for such a study:

Traditional—pre-European contact norms;
Proto-modern—early contact acculturation with discrete practice of
    some Western and some traditional customs;
Modern—Western-oriented culture; and
Modern-traditional—a fusion of Western values and traditional norms.

Any or all of these can coexist almost contiguously at different geographical areas and times.

In closing, this chapter has attempted to show that the linear progression theory can be misleading in understanding the process of urbanism in Africa. The basic normative superstructure of urban Ibadan or Kano is Yoruba or Hausa, respectively, irrespective of metropolitan status and atmosphere. Africa or, to be accurate, specific areas of Africa, should be studied from the perspective of their unique historical and cultural circumstances. In so doing resilience and traditionalization are two important factors to consider in delineating and analyzing their social change.

NOTES

1. Austin Shelton, Igbo-Igala Borderland: Religion and Social Control in Indigenous African Colonialism (Albany: State University of New York Press, 1971).

2. Louis Wirth, "Urbanism as a Way of Life," American Journal of Sociology 44 (July 1938): 3-24.

3. Eshref Shevky and Wendell Bell, Social Area Analysis: Theory, Illustrative Application and Computational Procedures (Stanford: Stanford University Press, 1955).

4. Hope Tisdale, "The Process of Urbanization," Social Forces 20 (1942): 311-16.

5. Hortense Powdermaker, Copper Town: Changing Africa; the Human Situation of the Rhodesian Copperbelt (New York: Harper and Row, 1962).

6. A. L. Epstein, "The Network and Urban Social Organization," in Social Networks in Urban Situations: Analyses of Personal Relationships in Central African Towns, ed. J. Clyde Mitchell (Manchester: Manchester University Press, 1969), pp. 77–116; J. Clyde Mitchell, Tribalism and the Plural Society: An Inaugural Lecture (London: Oxford University Press, 1960); and Leonard Plotnicov, Strangers to the City (Pittsburgh: University of Pittsburgh Press, 1967).

7. Epstein, op. cit. , p. 80.

8. Plotnicov, op. cit. , p. 3.

9. Powdermaker, op. cit. , p. xiv.

10. Ibid. , p. 296.

11. Ibid. , p. 292.

12. Ibid. , p. 315.

13. Willie Abraham, The Mind of Africa (Chicago: University of Chicago Press, 1962).

14. Robert Merton, Social Theory and Social Structure (Glencoe, Ill. : The Free Press of Glencoe, 1964), p. 36.

15. Shelton, op. cit. , pp. 237–39.

16. David E. Apter, The Politics of Modernization (Chicago: University of Chicago Press, 1965), p. 85.

17. David E. Apter, The Political Kingdom of Uganda: A Study in Bureaucratic Nationalism; (Princeton: Princeton University Press, 1961), p. 87.

18. A. W. Southall and Peter C. W. Gutkind, Townsmen in the Making: Kampala and Its Suburbs (Kampala; East African Institute of Social Research, 1957).

19. Peter C. Gutkind, ed. The Passing of Tribal Man in Africa (Leiden: E. J. Brill, 1970).

20. See Sir H. Llewellyn Smith, London Life and Labour (London: n. p. 1830), pp. 930–35.

21. A. L. Epstein, Politics in an Urban African Community (Manchester: Manchester University Press, 1958), p. xv.

22. Meillassoux, Urbanization of African Community: Voluntary Associations in Bamako (Seattle: University of Washington Press, 1968), pp. 143–47.

23. Immanuel Wallerstein, Social Change: The Colonial Situation, (New York: Wiley, 1966).

24. Peter C. Lloyd, Africa in Social Change: Changing Traditional Societies in the Modern World (Baltimore: Penguin Books, 1969), p. 12.

25. Victor Uchendu, "The Passing of Tribal Man: A West African Experience" in The Passing of Tribal Man in Africa, ed. Peter C. Gutkind (Leiden: E. J. Brill, 1970), p. 64.

26. William Hanna and Judith Hanna, Urban Dynamics in Africa an Interdisciplinary Approach (Chicago: Aldine, Atherton, 1971).

27. Herbert J. Gans, The Urban Villagers Group and Class in Life of Italian Americans (New York: The Free Press of Glencoe, 1962); and William Foote Whyte, Street Corner Society: The Social Structure of an Italian Slum (Chicago: The University of Chicago Press, 1959).

28. Uchendu, op. cit., p. 5.

29. Abner Cohen, Custom and Politics in Urban Africa: A Study of Hausa Migrants in Yoruba Towns (Berkeley: University of California Press, 1969), pp. 183-87.

30. James C. Abegglen, "The Japanese Factory: Aspects of its Social Organization," in Urbanism in World Perspective: A Reader, ed. Sylvia F. Fara (New York: Thomas Y. Crowell, 1968), pp. 289-96.

3

THE CITY IN AFRICA: SOME THEORETICAL ISSUES

Bernard Magubane

This is a critical time for the social sciences, not a time for courtesies.

Lynd

INTRODUCTION

This chapter questions the conventional wisdom of studying African urbanization in terms of acculturation models. It attempts to analyze African urbanization in the light of the evolution of urbanism in the metropolitan countries, making a clear distinction between urbanism and industrialism. To do this requires a theoretical comprehension of the manifestations of urbanism in different parts of the world and an assessment of its meaning and social implications. A true comparative analysis should attempt to ascertain the underlying principles and major impacts of contemporary urban development.

Appreciation is expressed to the University of Connecticut Research Foundation for providing facilities for typing the first draft and the revised edition. A different version of this paper was written with Amelia Mariotti for the IXth International Congress of Anthropology held in Chicago, August 28–September 8, 1973. Though Ms. Mariotti did not rewrite this version with me, it still owes a lot to her brilliant insights. She is, however, not responsible for my errors.

There are many approaches to the comparative study of urbanism. An obvious one is to compare cities in different societies, that
is, crosscultural comparisons. A second approach is to compare
cities within a given society. A third approach is to compare cities
of one period with those of another historical epoch. The comparative
method is a purposeful and rigorous study of similarities and differences among a wide variety of cities that are assumed to share at
least some fundamental characteristics. The aim is to explain the
causal relationships and interrelationships underlying such alleged
regularities. It is thus important that the units being compared be
clearly defined in terms of their critical characteristics. Comparative studies are usually most useful if they are well grounded in a
theory of society. Theoretical clarity becomes even more essential
in view of the rapid growth of cities all over the world, the changing
forces behind this growth, and the opportunities created by such
change. But to seize upon these opportunities, as Harvey put it,

> We have to confront the forces that create cities as alien
> environments, that push urbanization in directions alien
> to our individual or collective purpose. To confront these
> forces we have first to understand them. The old structure
> of industrial capitalism once such a force for revolutionary
> change in society, now appears as a stumbling block. The
> growing concentration of fixed capital investment, the crea-
> tion of new needs and effective demands, and a pattern of
> circulation of surplus value are changing but they have not
> altered the fact that cities . . . are founded upon the ex-
> ploitation of the many by the few. An urbanism founded
> upon exploitation is a legacy of history. A genuinely hu-
> manizing urbanism has yet to be brought into being. It
> remains for a revolutionary theory to chart the path from
> an urbanism based in exploitation to an urbanism appropri-
> ate for the human species. And it remains for revolution-
> ary practice to accomplish such a transformation. [1] (em-
> phasis added)

URBANIZATION AND THE MODERN ERA

Max Weber and Arnold Toynbee defined the city as a settlement
in which the inhabitants engage primarily in nonagricultural productive activities. [2] Such a definition is of some value in that it identifies
certain general features that may be found wherever cities exist.
Placed in an historical context, however, these features assume a
complexity which cannot be explained by means of a rational abstrac-

tion. For a city is not an entity that can be analyzed apart from its historical and social context but rather an historical configuration reflecting the particular political economy and prevailing class relations in an historical epoch. The welter of competing definitions and special theories that fill the literature on cities reflects the attempt to treat the city as a static, superhistorical entity—to elevate various concrete, historical features to abstract universal principles. There is a failure to recognize that "between the cities of ancient and medieval times and the modern metropolis or conurbation there is a connection of name and in part of function, but nothing like identity."[3]

In contrast, Karl Marx views the city as a set of social relations in which the social processes of the division of labor through exchange become focused between spheres of production. For Marx, the whole economic history of society is summed up in the antithesis between town and country. That is, the division and opposition of city and country, industry and agricultural, in their modern forms, are the critical culmination of the division and specialization of labor which, though it did not begin with capitalism, was developed under it to an extraordinary and transforming degree.

> Here first become manifest the division of the population into two great classes, which is directly based on the division of labour and on the instruments of production. The town already is in actual fact the concentration of the population, of the instruments of production, of capital, of pleasures, of needs, while the country demonstrates just the opposite fact, isolation and separation. The antagonism between town and country can only exist within the framework of private property. It is the most crass expression of the subjection of the individual under the division of labour, under a definite activity forced upon him—a subjection which makes one man into a restricted town-animal, the other into a restricted country-animal, and daily creates anew the conflict between their interests. Labour is here again the chief thing, power over individuals, and as long as the latter exists, private property must exist.[4]

The city is, therefore, not merely a demographic agglomoration of population and growth. It is above all a social and economic process which profoundly affects traditional modes of socioeconomic organization; it provides the context within which new forms of the division of labor appear. In the Communist Manifesto, Marx and Engels argued that "the bourgeoisie has subjected the country to the rule of the times . . . has created enormous cities . . . has made barbarian and semi-barbarian countries dependent on the civilized ones." It is the familiar history of capitalism and imperialism. Engels further postulated that "socialism would abolish the contrast between town and country, which had been brought to its extreme point by present-day capitalist society." Thus, the Marxist tradition contains interesting clues to the opposition not only between town and country but between developed and underdeveloped areas. [5]

Urbanization processes in different historical epochs under various modes of production superficially may seem identical. It is this superficial identity that has occupied social scientists who have attempted to formulate abstract definitions of the city. However, the identities obtain only on the level of description. Any attempt at explanation must specify the dominant mode of production and the nature of the town-country dichotomy. It must also specify that classes dominated the mode of production. Perry Anderson's summary of urban-rural relations in Greco-Roman antiquity provides a point of departure that needs to be grasped. What he says is so important that he deserves to be quoted at some length:

> Graeco-Roman Antiquity had always constituted a universe centered on cities. The splendour and confidence of the early Hellenic polis and the later Roman Republic, which dazzled so many subsequent epochs, represented a meridian of urban polity and culture that was never to be equalled for another millenium. . . . Yet at the same time this frieze of city civilization always had something of the effect of a trompe l'oeil facade, on its posterity. For behind this urban culture and polity lay no urban economy in any way commensurate with it; on the contrary, the material wealth which sustained its intellectual and civic vitality was drawn overwhelmingly from the countryside. The classical world was massively, unalterably rural in its basic quantitative proportions. Agriculture represented throughout its history the absolutely dominant domain of production, invariably furnishing the main fortunes of the cities themselves. The Graeco-Roman towns were never predominantly communities of manufacturers, traders or craftsmen: they were, in origin and principle, urban congeries of landowners. Every municipal order from democratic Athens to oligarchic Sparta or senatorial Rome, was essentially dominated by agrarian proprietors. Their income derived from corn, oil and wine—the three great staples of the Ancient World, produced on estates and farms outside the perimeter of the physical city itself. Within it, manufactures remained few and rudimentary: the range of normal urban commodities never extended

much beyond textiles, pottery, furniture and glassware. Technique was simple, demand was limited and transport was exorbitantly expensive. The result was that manufactures in Antiquity characteristically developed not by increasing concentration, as in later epochs, but by decontraction and dispersal, since distance dictated relative costs of production rather than the division of labour. A graphic idea of the comparative weight of the rural and urban economies in the classical world is provided by the respective fiscal revenues yielded by each in the Roman Empire of the 4th century A. D. , when city trade was finally subjected to an imperial levy for the first time by Constantine's collatio lustralis: income from this duty in the towns never amounted to more than 5 percent of the land-tax. [6]

The country and the city are thus changing historical realities, and it is clear from the above passage that an idea derived from the past cannot explain the nominal continuity between ancient cities and the process of urban growth in the twentieth century. Marx saw this difference very clearly;

Ancient classical history is the history of cities, but cities based on landownership and agriculture: Asian history is a kind of undifferentiated unity of town and country (the large city, properly speaking, must be regarded merely as a princely camp, superimposed on the real economic structure); the Middle Ages (germanic period) starts with the countryside as the locus of history, whose further development then proceeds through the opposition of town and country; modern history is the urbanization of the countryside, not, as among the ancients, the ruralization of the city. [7]

The subsequent decline of the Greco-Roman city and the rise of the feudal city were bound up with changes in the modes of production of ancient society and the rise of feudal society which also implied shifts in social power. "With the gradual 'fall' of the Roman Empire in the West and the dissolution of its armies and state institutions, the cities as administrative centers almost ceased to exist. " When the trade routes in the Mediterranean vanished, with the Islamic invasions of the ninth century, and "Europe declined into Feudal Provincialism, " according to Ernest Harsch, the ruling class abandoned the cities as economic centers and moved back onto their country estates or demesnes, leaving behind empty hulks that now served only as religious centers or as the fortresses of the various princes who used them only in time of war."[8]

The emergence of capitalism as the dominant mode of production, however, brought about an extraordinary transformation of the urban-rural dimension that embraced the whole world. Thus, the model of city and country in economic and political relationships has gone beyond the boundaries of the nation-state and is seen and challenged as a model of the world. Looking back on English history and its "culmination in imperialism," for example, Raymond Williams asserts,

> I can see in this process of the altering relations of country and city the driving force of a mode of production which has indeed transformed the world. I am then very willing to see the city as capitalism, as so many now do, if I can say also that this mode of production began, specifically, in the English rural economy, and produced, there, many of the characteristic effects—increase of production, physical reordering of a totally available world, displacement of customary settlements, a human remnant and force which became a proletariat—which have since been seen, in many extending forms, in cities and colonies and in an international system as a whole. [9]

Cities today play an indisputably dominant role in modern life. As the focus of capital accumulation and productive life the city attracts large numbers of people from the hinterlands. Laborers are drawn or pressed into these centers by job opportunities created by expanding manufacturing and commercial activities. The configuration of urban space is determined by those classes which control the forces of production. "The exploitation of man and nature, which takes place in the country, is realized and concentrated in the city."[10] The dominant classes used laws to protect their own interests as early as the thirteenth century, as Thompson indicates. "Everywhere the wealthy classes controlled the local town government and local trade and industry, and passed statutes in support of their interests, like privileges and monopolies, or expressive of their contempt for the masses. "This led to riots and strikes, in the heavily settled industrial regions of Europe and to attempts on the part of the working classes to form unions in their own midst and even to knit together such combinations in adjacent towns. But all such efforts were abortive in the Middle Ages, except in Florence, and then only successful for a short season."[11]

The rise of the capitalist city was accompanied by the destructive invasion of the countryside. In England the enclosure laws displaced thousands of families from the country, who were forced to settle in the emerging industrial towns. At the same time this massive depopulation of the country condemned the rural population to what Frederick Engels described as thousands of years of degradation. [12] The antagonism between town and country destroyed the basis of the intellectual development of those who settled in the urban slums and the physical development of the rural population.

CAPITALISM AND COLONIAL DEPENDENCY

The destructiveness of capitalism reached appalling proportions in the colonies. Nearly all the cumulative benefits of the growth of urban culture that eventually accrued to the metropolis were lacking in the colonial towns. In the slums and shanty towns that grew on the periphery of colonial towns, a moral blight with its rampant debasement of family life, human solidarity, and dignity became the way of life because the capital invested in the colonies only served limited objectives of developing those primary industries that complemented the metropolitan economy. The festering slums that characterized the colonial and postcolonial towns reflected the conscious irresponsibility of the colonial bourgeoisie toward the living conditions of the colonial proletariat. [13]

Even when viewed against this background, a qualitative difference exists between the development of cities in the metropolis and in the colonies. In societies in which an indigenous capitalist class developed, cities were formed through the geographic concentration of accumulated social surplus product which the process of transforming the rural economy with a capitalist form had generated and concentrated into the hands of commercially active landowners. The surplus derived from earlier accumulation and exploitation was invested in urban ventures to produce further growth. Herein lies the crucial relationship between urbanism and the mode of economic integration under capitalism. Industrialization proceeds continuously and urbanization can be contained, more or less, by the widening economic framework. But in societies in which the capitalist mode of production was introduced and controlled by an alien bourgeoisie and developed without connection with the requirements of these societies, this process was distorted. Walter Rodney writes,

Colonialism provided Africa with no real growth points. For instance, a colonial town in Africa was essentially a centre of administration rather than industry. Towns did attract large numbers of Africans, but only to offer them a very unstable life based on unskilled and irregular employment. European towns had slums, but the squalor of towns in underdeveloped countries is a special phenomenon. It was a consequence of the inability of those towns to play the role of expanding the productive base. Fortunately, Africa was never as badly off in this respect as Asia and Latin America.

Instead of speeding up growth, colonial activities such as mining and cash-crop farming speeded up the decay of "traditional" African life. In many parts of the continent, vital aspects of culture were adversely affected, nothing better was substituted, and only a lifeless shell was left. The capitalist forces behind colonialism were interested in little more than the exploitation of labour. Even areas that were not directly involved in the money economy exported labour. [14]

The concept of dependent urbanization facilitates an examination of the internal situation of African cities as the result not of factors characteristic of traditional African societies but of the exigencies of colonial capitalism. To account for the social structures that developed in the African city requires that the consequences of capitalism in its imperialist development be understood. During the colonial era in Africa, imperialism built cities (some of them impressive) that reflected the well-being of the white settler classes, which tried to make them islands of privilege. After independence, economic stagnation and the agricultural crisis worsened the imbalance between city development and rural underdevelopment that had been inherent in the colonial system. Today the enjoyment of urban privileges are still limited to an infinitesmal part of the urban population. The masses, as always, are excluded. There is, however, a difference today because the contradictions of the system now continue directly under the noses of the masses who easily grasped their political meaning.

Fanon recognized that the colonial city is highly segregated residentially and that it exhibited colonial inequality in its most brutal and stark reality.

The settlers' town is a strongly-built town, all made of stone and steel. It is a brightly-lit town; the streets are covered with asphalt, and the garbage-cans swallow all the leavings, unseen, unknown and hardly thought about. The settler's feet are never visible, except perhaps in the sea; but there you're never close enough to see them. His feet are protected by strong shoes although the streets of his town are clean and even, with no holes or stones. The settler's town is a town of white people, of foreigners.

The town that belongs to the colonised people, or at least the native town, the negro village, the medina, the reservation, is a place of ill fame, peopled by men of evil repute. They are born there, it matters little where or how; they die there, it matters not where, nor how. It is a world without spaciousness; men live there on top of each other, and their huts are built one on top of the other. The native town is a hungry town, starved of bread, of meat, of shoes, of coal, of light. The native town is a crouching village, a town on its knees, a town wallowing in the mire. It is a town of niggers and dirty arabs. [15]

The spatial system and land-use patterns, according to Fanon, closely confirm social and economic inequalities. "The originality of the colonial context is that economic reality, inequality and immense difference of ways of life never come to mask the human reality." A close examination of the colonial context shows that "what parcels out the world is to begin with the fact of belonging or not belonging to a given race, a given species." The spatially defined inequality in Africa's urban areas was thus expressive of the colonial class structure. "In the colonies the economic substructure is also a superstructure. The cause is the consequence; you are rich because you are white, you are white because you are rich." [16]

The economic antagonism between town and country were, in colonial Africa, replaced by "the antagonism which exists between the Native who is excluded from the advantages of colonialism and his counterpart who manages to turn colonial exploitation to his account." [17] The leading towns of Africa—Dakar, Lagos, Nairobi, Dar es Salaam, Luanda, Lourenço Marques, and so on—displayed splendid mansions on streets lined with lawns and trees in which the rich white folks lived. In dirty, smoky houses, squalid and rickety shacks on joyless streets, lived the African workers, the source of the tremendous colonial wealth.

The picture of the town structure in Portuguese Africa drawn in the following passage by Kamm was typical of pre- and postcolonial Africa:

Luanda in Angola, Lourenço Marques and Beira in Mozambique are white man's cities—with downtowns of pleasant, Portuguese-style colonial houses of commerce of the last century, surrounded by the pompous public buildings of the authoritarian Government of Salazar Portugal and enveloped by the massive, shapeless concrete blocks of today's men of business. At the edges are housing developments for the "poor whites" and villas on tree-lined

streets for those less poor. One wonders how cities so
seemingly small can have population figures as large as
the 475,000 given for Luanda, 355,000 for Lourenço
Marques and 114,000 for Beira. The answer lies beyond,
in endless, warrenlike shantytowns of surpassing wretch-
edness. There the African population lives, and there it
becomes quite obvious that the population figures are, if
anything, understated and, more likely, guesswork.

Shack next to shack, of the most disparate bits of
wood, tin or anything else that will offer shade and shelter
but uniform in their shabby inadequacy, are crowded into
the plains of beaten dirt. It must have been savanna country, before, with grass, bushes and some trees, but only
at the edges do flashes of green relieve the dun barrenness
now. The houses are arranged, if the work is not too
strong for such unplanned mazes, to resemble the homesteads of families in the bush, with the shacks of the different members facing onto small patches of ground on
which children play without toys and often without clothes
and women cook over scraps of wood or charcoal. [18]

To account for this urban dichotomy in terms of cultural differences is to conceal the fact that this state of affairs is a fundamental
social condition or, more precisely, an inherent condition of bourgeois
urban social life. The picture drawn of Africa's urban areas is very
much similar to the picture drawn by Engels of living conditions of
the 290,000 workingpeople in Manchester who, as he observed,

live, almost all of them, in wretched, damp, filthy cot-
tages, that the streets which surround them are usually
in the most miserable and filthy condition, laid out without the slightest reference to ventilation, with reference
solely to the profit secured by the controller. In a word,
one must confess that in the working-men's dwellings of
Manchester, no cleanliness, no convenience, and consequently no comfortable family life is possible; that in such
dwellings only a physically degenerate race, robbed of all
humanity, degraded, reduced morally and physically to
bestiality, could feel comfortable at home. [19]

THE NATURE OF CAPITALIST URBANIZATION

The approach adopted by Engels in 1844 was, and still is, far
more consistent with the hard economic and social realities of capital-

ist urbanization than is the essentially cultural approach of urban anthropologists such as Voldo Pons (1969), Epstein (1967), Clyde Mitchell (1956, 1967), and Philip Mayer (1961). In fact, if one deleted Manchester and made other obvious modifications, Engel's description could easily be made to fit the conditions of Africans in colonial and current cities. For Engels, the despicable conditions and the "moral" depravity of urban workers were an inevitable result of an evil and avaricious capitalist system.

> Thus are the workers cast out and ignored by the class in power, morally as well as physically and mentally. The only provisions made for them is the law, which fastens upon them when they become obnoxious to the bourgeoisie. Like the dullest of the brutes, they are treated to but one form of education, the whip, in the shape of force, not convincing but intimidating. There is, therefore, no cause for surprise if the workers, treated as brutes, actually become such; or if they can maintain their consciousness of manhood only be cherishing the most glowing hatred, the most unbroken inward rebellion against the bourgeoisie in power. [20]

The industrial city, both in the metropolis and in the colonies, is a social form, a way of life predicated on a certain division of labor and a certain hierarchical ordering of the urban space which is consistent with the class structure of the dominant mode of production. The city functions to stabilize the class structure. Hence the city, both in colonial Africa and the metropolis, became the focus for the accumulated contradictions of industrial capitalism and its class conflict. The urban shanties in Africa present a stark resemblance to what the slums were in Europe.

> Every great city has one or more slums, where the working-class is crowded together. True, poverty often dwells in hidden alleys close to the palaces of the rich; but, in general, a separate territory has been assigned to it. Where, removed from the sight of the happier classes, it may struggle along as it can. . . . The streets are generally unpaved, rough, dirty, filled with vegetable and animal refuse, without sewers or gutters, but supplied with foul, stagnant pools instead. [21]

The picture of the slums drawn by Fanon and Kamm for Africa and that by Engels for Britain reveals the essence of the capitalist economy: in order to grow it must, besides providing employment, create a large industrial reserve army of labor. It is this reserve army that brings into a sharper focus a series of imbalances between supply and demand in the area of housing and urban services that constitute itself into urban slums, shantytowns, and <u>favelas.</u> The capitalist development has been an ambiguous process; it forced larger and larger populations to abandon the rural economy for the industrial areas and disclaimed any responsibility for the social consequences thus produced. The slums, shantytowns, and favelas are thus the obverse side of the extraordinary process of capital accumulation.

The phenomenon of urban slum or shanty is an abiding problem of capitalist cities and is very important in explaining the urban decay. It was no part of a capitalist economy to provide urban quarters for the working class except in terms that would furnish a handsome profit, that is, by overcrowding, skimping, niggardly provisions, even for light and air, a general worsening of the whole urban environment. [22]

The contradictory growth of capitalism as a process of development is displayed most starkly in the built-up environment of the city. For a vivid insight into this ambiguity let us look at Lagos, the capital of Nigeria, which has grown within living memory from what Rasheed Gbadamosi has called "a rather serene small town" of 100,000 people to a teaming shambles of over 1.5 million, a "rambling, ill-defined piece of urban landscape in which you can expect to spend hours of a working day for a journey that would take you no more than ten minutes on a Sunday, and which might take no more than 35 minutes if you were walking down the streets, as you were able to do twenty-five years ago, unmolested by traffic."[23]

What caused this change? According to Gbadamosi,

> "The colonial administration cared far more about commerce than the people, and closed their eyes to the human drama and turbulence of the growing city." It is the consequences of that neglect which are now being felt. The narrow roads, "built for convenience, to move the police when the natives were creating trouble," now carry huge oil trucks. The sewer project of the 1920's devised at a projected cost of $20 million, and rejected as too expensive, would now, it is estimated, run to $3.3 billion for the first phase alone. The postcolonial government has built no underground drainage, sewerage or storm drains, so that the stench has to be smelled to be believed. [24]

Capitalism is preeminently an exploitative economic system, and the growth of urban slums was the byproduct of economic exploitation. Almost accidentally does industry respond to the material requirements of those forced to work in factories. While the development of colonial capitalism led to the penetration of commodity-monetary relationships into every aspect of African life, the relatively small size of the modern industrial sector proved quite incapable of providing work for the whole considerable mass of workers seeking it. Unemployment and underemployment often reach high levels. In many African urban slums there is an excessive swelling of the semiproletarian strata and those groups of the working class connected with the primary sector of capitalist production, for example, miners recruited for a specific period.

To see this contradiction and its human consequences is to penetrate the mode of economic growth that produced the process of urbanization characteristic of Africa today. David Harvey quotes Castells who, for example, differentiated between the metropolitan forms of urbanism in North America and Western Europe and the dependent urban forms of much of the rest of the world. According to Castells, dependent urbanism arises in situations where the urban form exists as a channel for the extraction of quantities of surplus from a rural and resource hinterland for purposes of shipment to the major metropolitan centers. [25] The widespread (both in time and place) occurrence of the urban phenomenon should not be allowed to obscure its particular manifestations in the so-called Third World. An examination of urbanization must be related to the study of the mode of production on which urban forms grow.

Insofar as the essence and the dynamics of the bourgeois urban form are not identical to those of the cities of antiquity or medieval times, it is because the factory transforms the bourgeois city into a commercial and industrial unit. The modern city develops according to the laws of the capitalist market. That is, "Production for the sake of production, translated into urban terms, means the growth of the city for its own sake—without any intrinsic urban or human criteria to arrest that growth."[26] The study of the colonial city and the absence there of modern industry must be understood in terms of the dynamics of the political economy of capitalism in its imperialistic phase.

The bourgeois historical experience of industrialization is not to be separated from that of urbanization. Engels in his book, The Condition of the Working Class in England 1844 drew the conclusion of a broader import and described the main tendencies of capitalist urban growth. He examined the capitalist mode of production and showed how the world trade enhanced and benefited the English towns. For Engels, Manchester was a representative instance; it developed as an essential part of a global economy and more particularly as the center of that vast formal or informal "empire" on which its fortunes so largely rested from the seventeenth century.

Eric Williams, in his seminal work <u>Capitalism and Slavery</u>, reached the same conclusion:

> No growth of Manchester was intimately associated with the growth of Liverpool, its outlet to the sea and world market. The capital accumulated by Liverpool from the slum trade poured into the hinterland to fertilize the energies of Manchester; Manchester goods for Africa were taken to the coast in the Liverpool Steam vessels.[27]

Besides Liverpool and Manchester, Lancashire was converted from an obscure, ill-cultivated swamp into a very lively region, multiplying its population tenfold in 80 years. Giant cities, such as Bolton, Oldham, and Preston, also sprang up as if by magic.[28] They became elements in a complex system of national and overseas economy and society which was not in any simple way physically apparent. From that time on,

> what was happening in the "city," the "metropolitan" economy, determined and was determined by what was made to happen in the "country," first the local hinterland and then the vast regions beyond it, in other people's lands. What happened in England has since been happening ever more widely, in new dependent relationships between all the industrialized nations and all other "underdeveloped" but economically important lands. Thus one of the last models of "city and country" is the system we now know as imperialism.[29]

THE CITY IN MODERN AFRICA

The colonial city in Africa is therefore a reflection of the world economy and its priorities. Yet most social scientists only studied the ideological aspect of urbanism rather than the material aspects. Following the lead of the Chicago school, especially Park's formulation in the article "The City: Suggestions for the Investigation of Human Behavior in the Urban Environment," urbanism and urbanization became the focus of interest as an independent variable. Thus the development of new forms of social relations among peasants recently settled in the new towns became of tremendous interest to the social scientists (e.g., Hauser 1965, Reissmen 1964, Fava 1969). They looked to urbanization in the developing countries for a recapitulation of the European experience. For instance, Leonard Reissman says that urbanization in Africa provides a "rare opportunity to study . . .

cases of historical reiteration. "[30] And Phillip Hauser expresses the
hope that studies of Africa and Asia may "shed light on the antecedents
and consequences of urbanization in the West. "[31] When differences
in the urbanization of nineteenth-century Europe and that of colonial
Africa are observed, there is little attempt to explain them. Rather,
the African experience is characterized as a deviation from the Western model. [32]

Other theorists concern themselves with problems of definition
and categorization. The literature abounds with typologies of cities
based on origin, location, and function, among others. [33] Various indexes have been developed to study optimum location, size, density,
and composition of population; attributes of the city as a physical "con-
tainer"; the quality of social life and characteristic mentality of urban
dwellers. For the most part these criteria are only descriptive of the
empirical reality, yielding little in the way of explanation.

An elaboration of indexes is a common approach in urban studies;
it is a method which takes the city as a given entity and tries to isolate
those properties that seem to be common or unique to urban situations
or to various urban populations. If well conceived, the search for what
is distinctively urban may yield useful insights into the ways in which
city life differs from rural life or the ways in which the class structure of the city affects different populations. It cannot, however, explain why urban life is the way it is. This approach can provide at
best a familiarity with the superficial aspects of urban phenomena.
At worst, its resulting configurations are tautological and distorted,
as when it is argued that with urbanization has come "increased freedom of women, changes in reproductive behavior, and late marriages. "
These indexes are then taken as "a few of the factors which have
brought about direct changes within the indigenous family structure. "[34]

It is held by some that urbanization is equivalent to modernization, and to a certain extent this is true. But it has also been a source
not only of error but of ideologically prejudiced formulations. Cultural
change in urban areas was studied as a process of acculturation, and
terms such as "detribalization," "stabilization," and "westernization"
have been used to refer to the process of urbanization in Africa. Living
in towns is described as "civilized" in contrast to living in rural areas
which is "uncivilized. "[35] Another source of error is the attempt to
explain urbanization only in terms of the behavior of Africans in cities.
This leads to considerable discussion concerning objective criteria
for describing an "urbanized African. " These include number of years
of permanent residence in a city, permanent residence of wife in an
urban area, and absence of land rights in the countryside. [36]

Until recently, students of urbanization in Africa paid particular
attention to Africans who lived and worked in cities but retained land
rights in rural areas. Descriptions of African town dwellers who sup-

plemented their wages with agricultural production were a basis for
superficial analysis of a "dual" or "plural" society in urban and development literature. Attempts to explain the retention of rural land-
holdings or extended kin ties, the instability of urban residence, or
other features of urbanization in Africa pass over the objective structure of colonial urbanization to focus on the "backward" attitudes of
Africans or the tenacity of the traditional way of life. Low wages,
confiscation of unworked land, the tenuousness of urban work and
residence under labor contracts, work compounds, and racial preju-
dice are less significant in these analyses than conjectured reasons
for the rural-urban shuttling or people's perception and evaluation of
that aspect of the colonial system that they directly experience.

There is a general failure to recognize that the behavior and
attitudes of Africans are not the cause of the kind of urbanization that
Africa has experienced but rather the observable effect of the social
forces that initiated and shaped the process of urbanization itself.
These social forces were not generated by traditional African social
attitudes but by the development and expansion of the colonial capitalist mode of production. In reality, the city in Africa was a clear expression of the nature of underdevelopment: namely, the exploitation
of African raw materials by unskilled labor and the cumulative effects
which this process brought about.

The nature of urbanization in Africa requires that the relation
between Africa and certain European countries and of white settlers
be sought out and examined. In doing so, it becomes apparent that
much of what has been taken to be uniquely African is a consequence
of this relationship. Laws and policies were promulgated and administered in such a way that only those Africans whose labor power was
needed in the towns were admitted. Others were uprooted to create a
floating work force that could be used to undermine and depress the
wages of those employed in colonial industries. The Stallard Commission of South Africa spelled out unreservedly the status of Africans
in the city and was used as a model by various colonial governments
in one way or another. Among other things it stated, "The Native
should only be allowed to enter urban areas, which are essentially
the White man's creation, when he is willing to enter and minister to
the needs of the White man and should depart from there when he
ceases so to minister."[37]

In 1935, the Colonial Government of North Rhodesia produced
a booklet entitled Lusaka. This booklet was for private circulation
only and contained the plans of the new capital city that was being
planned. The writers of this booklet proposed,

> The miscellaneous African population of the Capital has,
> for purposes of accomodation, been divided into two classes,

personal servants and others, and these classes have been provided with separate compounds. It has been considered wise to discontinue the practice of providing each house with its own Native Compound. Quarters are only provided for one unmarried boy on each plot. The other servants with their families live at a distance in the Personal Servant's Compound. Thus, the residential areas are freed from picaninns and other manifestations of domestic untidiness. [38]

In East Africa, the British colonial administrators considered town life unsuitable for Africans whose natural habitat, it was argued, was the rural area. According to the East African Royal Commission,

> The theory of indirect rule as well as the personal inclinations of many administrators led to a concentration on the development of rural tribal societies rather than the training of an educated urban elite, and also to the view that the town was not a suitable habitat for a permanent African society: there has, indeed, been a tendency to look on the westernized African with suspicion. The towns have, therefore, been regarded rather as bases for administrative and commercial activities than as centres of civilizing influence, still less of permanent African population. [39]

The urban form that developed as a consequence of these policies is described by V. S. Naipaul;

> It was like another Sunday in the capital, which . . . in spite of deportations, remained an English . . . creation in the African wilderness. Not far from the capital were bush villages, half-day excursions for tourists. But in the capital Africa showed only in the semi-tropical suburban gardens, in the tourist shop displays of carvings and leather goods and souvenir drums and spears, and in the awkward liveried boys in the new tourist hotels, where the white or Israeli supervisors were never far away. Africa here was a decor. Glamour for the white visitor and expatriate; glamour too for the African, the man flushed out from the bush to whom, in the city . . . civilization appeared to have been granted complete. It was still a colonial city, with a colonial glamour. Everyone in it was far from home. [40]

The urban theorists who formulated principles of African urbanization in terms of African cultural attitudes about the city or in terms of the so-called tribal obligations were potently wrong. Phillip Mayer described a pattern of African urbanization in which some Africans accepted willingly to incorporate with urban life while others refused. The latter group was said to be subject to kinship patterns that pulled them back to the rural areas. For example,

> The triumph of incapsulation is that through its institutions the home agents of morality have been enabled to extend their grasp over distance and over time from rural homestead into the heart of the East London slums. The long arms of the parents, the long arms of the ancestors are constantly pulling the Red migrants back out of reach of the "perils" of urbanization. [41]

In this formulation "tribalism" is said to be responsible for the migrant labor system and acts as a pull back to the reserves of all those Africans who might stray and accept the values and culture of the cities. This is an ideological formulation of the process of urban development justifying the evil system of migrant labor.

The colonial city of the twentieth century in Africa and elsewhere was the creation of imperialism. It was the result of foreign capital. But when capitalism expanded overseas, it did not merely discover but created "new worlds" through the exploitation of raw materials needed for the developing capitalist industries. The "modern" city in Africa was created by the colonizer as commercial, administrative, or mining center. The African migrant and a handful of "proletarians" were engaged mostly in either the production of primary goods or in building railways and roads for the shipment across the ocean of these raw materials. This dynamic set Africa on a course of urban development as an aspect of the further capitalist development of Western Europe and later the United States. As David Harvey puts it,

> "Contemporary metropolitanism" is embedded in a global economy of great complexity. That economy is hierarchically ordered with local centres dominating local hinterlands, more important metropolitan centres dominating lesser centres, and all centres outside of the communist nations by being ultimately subordinate to the central metropolitan areas in North America and Western Europe. This economic structure, elaborated theoretically and empirically most perceptively in the works of Losch (1954) has been interpreted in terms of surplus appropriation and extraction. [42]

Harvey's position is supported by Portes who writes "The cities, especially the major ones [in the colonies] were not centres for advancement but, by and large, centres for exploitation of a subordinate periphery."[43]

One effect of imperialist dominance in Africa was the initiation, within the dominated societies, of processes which then followed internally the lines of alien development. Because the city in Africa confronts the African peasant with the global capitalist economy, the internal history of country and city occurs, often very dramatically, within the colonial and neocolonial societies. This is strikingly reflected in the intensely overcramped cities which developed as a direct result of the imposed economic order and its consequences.[44]

Thus, in spite of almost general decolonization, the process of artificial urbanization which started in colonial times and was characterized by industrialization based on capital, equipment, and technicians from abroad and an export trade arising partly from this industrialization (including mining) and partly from the introduction and generalization of cash crops is by no means at an end in most of independent Africa. Development goals begun during the colonial era were carried forward into the independent period. Despite import substitution, industrialization in Africa has not kept pace with the growth of the labor force. This situation has been aggravated by the importation of advanced technology which permits high output worker ratios. As a consequence, those lucky enough to find employment are absorbed mainly in small-scale enterprises and service occupations. Today the African continent provides less than 5 percent of the world industrial output.

The employment of migrants was perhaps the clearest expression of the difference of capitalist development in Europe and Africa. The primary industries for which African migrants were recruited required an entirely different set of assumptions about African labor. Among the most basic was that which held that the African was a target worker.

> When migrants come to town it has been said that they
> have a definite sum in view, and that they hope to earn
> that amount and then go home again. The sooner that
> can be done, therefore, the quicker the worker's return
> to his village. . . . This accounts for the statement
> frequently made that the offer of a higher wage means
> less work and not more.[45]

A sociological interpretation of this assumption is that the labor power of Africans was abstracted from the full potential of its carriers as humans. The Africans simply became a piece of machinery which was discarded to the reservations when no longer of use. Most studies of urban migration never studied how government policies together with the colonial ideology of African workers as temporary sojourners served to justify this end.

Three interrelated trends can be identified in an indigenous and integrated process of urbanization. First, there is growth of primary production, agriculture, forestry, and mining. Second, there is the expansion of secondary production, manufacturing and communication. Third, there is proportionally greater expansion of tertiary production trade, transportation, services, and communication. At particular times and in various societies these trends stand in differential relation to each other. The tragic but determining fact for African societies is that the industrial development that forms the economic basis of the towns and cities was—and to a large extent still is—based on primary production and processing of raw materials.

This development was reflected in the class structure of the colonial city in which prevails a transplanted, alien managerial class whose interests in the development of African resources—both human and natural—are limited to the requirements of the extraction of immediate superprofits. The colonial situation also fostered the development of a tiny, indigenous petty bourgeoisie comprised of comprador and low echelon bureaucratic elements. This class remains dependent upon foreign exploitation for its existence even after the dismantling of the formal empire. They have no independent role in the development (or underdevelopment) of their country. Removed from the process of capital accumulation by the export of capital to the metropolis, this class turns to the conspicuous consumption of foreign commodities. [46] The consequences of imperialist penetration is most evident in the underdeveloped proletariat who reside in the urban slums and whose existence was demanded and whose character continues to be determined by the requirements of foreign capital. Thus, the development of technology and skills was not related to the material needs of African political economy in these cities.

Even more significant for the long-run development, in Africa, industrialization was never undertaken, because it would have led to the local accumulation of capital, which might in turn have produced a real increase in the salaries and rights of African laborers. Local industrialization would have challenged the colonial monopolies. [47] African urban economies operate within a system which was organized to extract raw materials for foreign industries. City growth, including the aberrant relationship between the country and the city, expressed the illogic and imbalance of the colonial economy as a whole. [48] The failure of colonialism to complete the task of social transformation it had begun, indeed the pauperizing dynamic of the colonial system, produced the most profoundly distorted and skewed urban societies.

Comparing the European and African experience, Basil Davidson points out,

> The first [industrialization] destroyed, but also after its fashion, mightily rebuilt afresh, the second, having gone far to ruin what if found, could only leave for Africans the task of making a new society. No such new society came into being during the colonial period. Little was left behind but an utter impoverishment of the old society, a chaos of ideas and social relationships. . . . When the principal colonizing powers eventually withdrew, everything of basic social meaning remained to be begun or rebuilt afresh. [49]

Though the early development of the bourgeois city was, in many respects, comparable to the destructive invasion of the colonial world, urbanization in Africa was not a recapitulation of the earlier experience in the development of European capitalism. It was, on the contrary, the articulation of its final contradictions. The structure of the city in Africa reflects the fact that these societies' economies were conditioned by the development and needs of the European economies to which they were subjected as producers and processers of raw materials. Their industrialization increases their dependence upon the industrialized nation; it does not contribute to strengthening the internal market in the country in which it takes place and, because of modern, capital-intensive technologies, it hardly contributes to an expansion of the industrial labor force. Thus industrialization based on alien technology undoubtedly figures among the most important processes that alter traditional class structures and provoke the development of new social classes, but it does so within the general framework of dependent and underdeveloped capitalism. [50]

CONCLUSION

The comparative study of urbanization raises questions regarding the relationship between urbanization and industrialization. The co-occurrence of these two processes in the development of Western Europe, in particular in England, and in the United States, contrasts sharply with the urbanization that has occurred without industrialization in Africa and elsewhere. The problems of African urban life are conceived to be what Daniel Lerner calls the "decoupling" of the twin processes. [51] The solution frequently posed is the promotion of industrialization and the delaying of urbanization in order to return the two processes to harmonious relation. The implementation of such a mechanical proposal usually takes the form of population control programs and "foreign aid" which aids not the industrial development of the recipient but the transfer of social surplus to the donor.

Those who try to draw parallels between the urbanization and industrialization of Europe and that of Africa fail to recognize that these processes are aspects of the development of the capitalist mode of production at a given point in history for Africa. Failing to recognize this, social scientists are frequently at a loss to account for the combination of burgeoning urban centers and limping industrial development in Africa. One need only examine the relation between Europe and the United States on the one hand and Africa on the other to discover why advanced industrial development has taken place in the former countries while the basis of industrialization has never been firmly established in Africa.

Africa does not suffer from a mysterious decoupling of urbanization and industrialization but rather from imperialist penetration which creates forced, shanty urbanization in the colonies and industrial development in the metropolitan countries. The exaggerated influx of masses of people from rural areas into urban centers was precipitated by indiscriminate policies designed to create a surplus labor force as quickly as possible without regard for future consequences. Towns sprung up in mining regions from which raw materials were extracted and shipped to the metropolitan country without material benefit accruing to these towns. These raw materials contributed to industrial development and growth in Europe, not Africa. Murray and Wengraf note, "The leading towns [in Africa] were not the creation of industrialization and inherent technical progress, but were rather the product of an export-directed colonial agriculture [and mining], whose rents and profits found an urban outlet in consumption and speculations."[52]

In Africa the urbanization of the population was not accompanied by diversification of the urban economy and alteration in urban-rural economic relations. In fact, there were few ties between one sector of the economy and another so that in any single colony there could be no beneficial interaction between the various sectors let alone organic development.

Foreign investment is incapable of solving Africa's underdevelopment and skewed urbanization. The high level of contemporary technology means that foreign companies will continue to use labor-saving machinery rather than labor-intensive methods. It should be quite obvious by now that intensely overcrowded cities in Africa are a direct result of anarchic and unplanned economic development and its internal consequences. Having begun as centers of colonial trade and administration,

these cities have drawn in, the surplus people and the uprooted labourers of the rural areas. This is a long-term
and continuing process, intensified by rapid rises in general population. Familiar problems of the chaotically expanding city recur, across the world, in many of the poorest countries. People who speak of the crisis of cities with
London or New York or Los Angeles in mind ought to think
also of the deeper crises of Calcutta or Manila or a hundred other cities across Asia and Africa and Latin America.
A displaced and formerly rural population is moving and
drifting towards the centres of a money economy which is
directed by interests very far from their own. The last
image of the city, in the ex-colonial and neo-colonial world,
is the political capital or the trading port surrounded by the
shantytowns, the barriadas, which often grow at incredible
speed. In Peru, . . . a few acres of desert have become,
in a fortnight, a "city" of thirty thousand people, and this
is only a particular example, in the long interaction between altered and broken rural communities and a process
of capitalist agriculture and industrialization sometimes internally, more often externally directed. 53

The study of the city and the social processes unleashed in the form
of urbanization raises fundamental questions about the colonial legacy
in Africa and elsewhere. What was the nature of the colonial economy?
For whose benefit did commerce and industry invade Africa, and what
were its implications for industrialization? The trajectory of urban
development in Africa was based on extractive capitalism which created urban complexes exemplified in the Katanga region of the Congo,
the copper belt of Zambia, and Witwatersrand of the Transvaal in
South Africa. Each one of these urban complexes was contingent on
the demands of the dominant system.

It was John Stuart Mill who said that the trade between England
and the West Indies in the eighteenth century was like trade between
town and country. In present-day Africa, the links are even closer,
and it is "more marked that the town (Europe) is living off the countryside (Africa)."54 And the towns in Africa are simply the nodal
points in the chain of urban-rural interconnections and the world division of labor.

African urbanization presented an eloquent, if tragic, example
of the process that created abstracted urban centers and broken communities. The towns and cities were abstracted from their environment and more organically and closely related to the metropolitan
countries than their own hinterland. With no steady growth in the

secondary and manufacturing sector of the economy, no expansion of the internal market was possible. The position of the urban work force itself was unsteady with its fortunes dependent on the oscillation in the demand for raw materials in the world markets. The uncertainties attendant on all raw material-producing countries were reflected in the urban structural instabilities and the unresolved contradictions between town and country.

NOTES

1. David Harvey, Social Justice and the City (Baltimore: The Johns Hopkins University Press, 1973), pp. 313-14.

2. Max Weber, The City (New York: Free Press, 1958), p. 66; and Arnold Toynbee, Cities on the Move (New York: Oxford University Press, 1970), p. 8.

3. Raymond Williams, The Country and the City (New York: Oxford University Press, 1973), p. 7.

4. Karl Marx, Capital, vol. I, Trans. Ben Fowkes (New York: Vantage, 1977), p. 472.

5. Karl Marx, Genesis of Capital (Moscow: Progress, 1969), p. 52; and Williams, op. cit., p. 304.

6. Perry Anderson, Passages from Antiquity to Feudalism (London: New Left Books, 1974), pp. 19-20.

7. Karl Marx, Pre-Capitalist Formations, quoted in Ibid., p. 150.

8. Ernest Harsch, "Cities in Decay," International Society Review 34, no. 6 (1973): 137.

9. Williams, op. cit., p. 292.

10. Ibid., p. 48.

11. J. W. Thompson, An Economic and Social History of the Middle Ages. (300-1300) (New York: The Century Company, 1928): 792-93.

12. Frederick Engels, Anti-Duhring. (New York: International Publishers, 1939), p. 318.

13. Murray Bookchin, The Limits of the City. (New York: Harper and Row Publishers, 1974), p. 59.

14. Walter Rodney, How Europe Underdeveloped Africa (Dar es Salaam: Tanzania Publishing House, 1972), p. 254.

15. Frantz Fanon, The Wretched of the Earth. (New York: Grove Press, 1963), p. 32.

16. Ibid.

17. Ibid., p. 39.

18. Henry Kamm, "The Last Days of the Empire," New York Times Magazine (August 18, 1974), p. 58.

19. Karl Marx and Frederick Engels, On Britain (Moscow: Foreign Language Publishers, 1964), p. 97.

20. Ibid. , p. 147.

21. Ibid. , p. 59.

22. Lewis Mumford, The City in History (New York: Harcourt, Brace & World, 1961), p. 44.

23. Peter Wilsher, "Everyone, Everywhere is Moving to the Cities," New York Times, June 22, 1975.

24. Ibid.

25. Harvey, op. cit. , p. 232.

26. Bookchin, op. cit. , p. 64.

27. Marx and Engels, op. cit. , p. 42.

28. Eric Williams, Capitalism and Slavery (London: Andre Deutsch, 1964), p. 68.

29. Ibid. , p. 279.

30. Leonard Reissman, The Urban Process: Cities in Industrial Societies (New York: The Free Press of Glencoe, 1964), p. 153.

31. Phillip Hauser, "Urbanization: An Overview," in The Study of Urbanization, ed. Phillip Hauser and Leo Schnore (New York: John Wiley and Sons, 1967), p. 34.

32. Daniel Lerner, "Comparative Analysis of Processes of Modernization," in The City in Africa, ed. Horace Miner (New York: Praeger, 1967), pp. 21-38.

33. Ruth Simms Hamilton, Urbanization in West Africa: A Review of Current Literature (Evanston, Ill. : Northwestern University Press, 1965), pp. 5-8.

34. Ibid. , p. 25.

35. Valdo Pons, Stanleyville: An African Urban Community Under Belgian Administration (London: Oxford University Press, 1969).

36. Ellen Hellman, Sellgoods (Johannesburg; Oxford University Press, 1953).

37. Republic of South Africa, Report of the Local Government Commission, Stallard Commission (Pretoria: Government Printer, 1922), p. 42.

38. Arthur Wina, quoted by B. Magubane, "Pluralism and Conflict Situations in Africa: A New Look," African Social Research 7 (June 1969): 5.

39. Great Britain, Colonial Office, Report of the East African Royal Commission (London: His Majesty's Stationery Office, 1955), p. 201.

40. V. S. Naipaul, In a Free State (Middlesex: Penguin Books, 1973), pp. 103-04.

41. Phillip Mayer, Townsmen or Tribesmen (Capetown: Oxford University Press, 1961), p. 94.

42. Harvey, op. cit. , p. 262.

43. Alejandro Portes, "Comparative Urbanization and National Development" (Paper presented at the 71st Annual Meeting of the American Sociological Association, 1968), p. 5.

44. Jean-Paul Harroy, "The Politician, Economic, and Social Role as Urban Agglomeration in Countries of the Third World," Civilizations 17 (1967): 167.

45. Robert F. Baldwin, Economic Development and Export Growth. A Study of Northern Rhodesia 1920-1960 (Berkeley: University of California Press, 1966), p. 114.

46. S. Nwosu, "Obstacles to Economic Development," Africa 22 (June 1973): 48.

47. Rodolfo Stavenhagen, Social Classes in Agrarian Societies (New York: Doubleday, 1975), p. 60.

48. Roger Murray and I. Wengraf, "The Algerian Revolution" New Left Review 22 (1963): 14-65.

49. Basil Davidson, Africa in History (New York: Macmillan, 1968), p. 277.

50. Stavenhagen, op. cit. , p. 54.

51. Lerner, op. cit. , p. 25.

52. Murray and Wengraf, op. cit. , p. 19.

53. Williams, op. cit. , p. 279.

54. Quoted in Rodney, op. cit. , p. 194.

Part Two

NORTH AFRICA:
EVOLVING STRATEGIES

Unlike most of the rest of the African continent, the countries of North Africa have had a long history of urbanization predating most of their numerous successive colonial experiences. They are relatively more urbanized, with well-established, though rapidly evolving, national urban systems. They have recently experienced accelerating rates of both population and urban growth which are helping orient their urban patterns in new directions.

These directions vary significantly among the countries of North Africa, partly because of differences in their geographical and spatial systems, historical developments, and colonial experiences and partly because of the recent divergences in their economic fortunes and political systems. The following chapters trace the evolution of some basic issues of national urban development in Morocco, Algeria, Libya, and Egypt, and offer an assessment of the responses and opportunities of their post-independence national development strategies.

Janet Abu-Lughod offers some important insights into the colonial impact on the rather unique precolonial urban pattern in Morocco. She indicates how colonial partition and subsequent conscious colonial urban policies have fragmented what had been a relatively balanced urban system. The resulting rifts between North and South, between the indigenous and superimposed urban systems, and between the European and Moroccan quarters is when centers contributed to the transitional nature of postcolonial urban development in Morocco. Their consequences (disintegration, inequality, discontinuity, and dependency) continue to provide Morocco's planners with their most challenging tasks for the future.

Unlike Morocco and Tunisia, Algeria had little continuity in its urban system. Colonial settlements replaced or obliterated precolonial towns, according to Richard Lawless, rather than coexisting with them side by side. The traditional economy and social structure were disrupted and relegated to the fringes of the modern economy. Thus, massive and sudden population shifts and the ruralization of towns were the immediate reactions to independence. The functional transformation of the towns was not, therefore, accompanied by a consonant morphological change. Duality in the economy prevented the development of an internal market, the tertiary sector and unemployment were both inflated, and the previous ethnic segregation was replaced by economic (class) segregation in the towns.

Gerald Blake analyzes the planning efforts in Libya, which had no national strategy to guide the development of individual towns until the mid-1970s. The long-range plans for towns, primarily by Western planners, were isolated and unrealistic exercises in the face of rapid national transformation. Such plans may have in fact strengthened preexisting trends of spatial disintegration and conflicted with recently formulated national goals of creating a balanced urban system.

Egypt, on the other hand, has had a well-established and integrated urban system. The challenges facing its national development stem, in effect, from the need to prevent the unbalanced redistribution of urban population within the confines of its present urban hierarchy. Extreme population pressures (unique to Egypt among the North African countries) and a shortage of arable land have literally forced development efforts in directions unfamiliar to Egypt's planners and its population, according to Salah El-Shakhs. Egyptians, by nature, are not desert dwellers, and the success of the new desert cities and development regions will tax the planners' ingenuity and the government's ability to diversify and expand the national economy.

The North African countries are thus facing the challenges of reorienting their long-established urban systems in new directions. Unlike many other African nations, they are in a process of transition proceeding from a well-established base of national urban networks, but like most they have to cope with several urban imbalances that resulted from their colonial experiences.

4

MOROCCAN URBANIZATION: SOME NEW EQUATIONS

Janet Abu-Lughod

THE PRECOLONIAL ROOTS OF URBANISM

Morocco had the distinction of evading direct colonial control during the nineteenth century when the spoils of much of the Third World were being parcelled out among the competing yet complicitous European states. Whereas Algeria had fallen, at least nominally, into French hands by 1830, and Egypt and Tunisia were made official parts of the overseas empires of Great Britain and France, respectively, by the 1880s, Morocco survived as an "autonomous" state until 1912, when it was finally subdivided between Spain (which took the northern rim) and France (which took the much larger and richer southern section). Granted, much of her autonomy had already been undermined in the nineteenth century by economic imperialism, but

The research on Morocco has been made possible by grants from the Ford Foundation and the Center for Studies of Metropolitan Problems, National Institute of Mental Health, Grant 1-R01-MH21551. I am grateful to Mohammed Guessous of Mohammed V University and the successive directors and staff of the census office of the Moroccan government for educating me about Moroccan urbanization and making available some of the data utilized here. After this chapter was written I had occasion to see an article by R. Escallier, "La Croissance urbaine au Maroc," in <u>Villes et sociétés au Maghreb</u>: <u>Études sur l'urbanisation</u> (Paris: Centre National de la Recherche Scientifique, 1974), pp. 145-73, which utilizes similar data in a parallel analysis. Our interpretations, however, are often at variance.

political imperialism was to introduce very different factors into Moroccan patterns of urbanization.

Morocco was also rather unique in having constituted a powerful and relatively independent regional entity throughout the long history of Islam. Indeed, on occasion her dynasties extended their core hegemony eastward to encompass Algeria and even Tunisia, northward to include large portions of Spain, and southward to the sub-Saharan centers. Even when these political links were weak, trade connections remained strong, for Morocco also constituted a central node in the long distance trade which extended south to Timbuktu and east to Tunis and then Cairo. These trade routes linked the major cities of Morocco to one another and gave the country a well-balanced urban hierarchy focused around the chief interior axes.

Given the technology of the time, the urban linkages necessary for dynastic control and long distance trade were sufficiently loose and functionally specific to permit considerable provincial autonomy on a smaller, coexisting scale. Significant provincial cities linked to their immediate hinterlands ran on a momentum of their own, independent in many respects from the larger system of regional and imperial integration at the top. This multiplicity of semi-independent urban subsystems was strengthened by Morocco's unique custom of capital system rotation. The ruler followed a semi-nomadic circuit over the year, alternating his court from Marrakesh in the South, to Fez in the East, to Meknes, and then to Rabat in the West. Such an egalitarian treatment of the four largest cities in the country helped to prevent too great disparities in their size and significance from developing.

These factors resulted in Morocco's unusual precolonial urban pattern, namely, an impressive hierarchy of urban, peri-urban, marketing, and weekly market places scattered regularly over much of that vast country. The 1912 partition of the country into Spanish and French zones had the paradoxical effect of further increasing the hierarchy's fullness since partition required a virtual duplication of functional hierarchies. Furthermore, the coastal regions, which had hitherto been quite tangential to the major urban system of the interior (partly because the coastal cities were so frequently in the hands of outsiders) became the major zones of foreign settlement, thus spawning a rival hierarchy related to trade, export, and extraction of wealth from the countryside.

Because of these somewhat special circumstances, Morocco today differs from many other developing excolonial countries in that it does not have a single predominant primate city.[1] It has not suffered as dramatically as have other less-developed countries from the effects of pure allometric growth. Overconcentration of wealth

and decision making there may be, but the urban population has not
been concentrated exclusively within a single giant city whose growth
inevitably outstrips that of its potential rivals. Had France's dominating colonial power not been short-lived, the situation might have
been quite different for, during the French Protectorate period
(1912-56), Casablanca took on all the functions and monopolistic
tendencies one associates with the extractive capital city of colonialism. While this evolution has not been entirely reversed during the
postcolonial period, its force and inevitability have been undermined
by counter pressures which would not have developed had direct
colonial rule persisted.

Continuity is another striking feature of Moroccan urbanism.
The names of many of Morocco's cities reverberate deep into history.
Of the earliest towns that had populations of 20,000 or more as early
as the tenth century—Sijilmasa, Meknes, Fez, Salé—three remain
important centers. (Only Saharan Sijilmasa never really recovered
from its destruction by the Fatimids in 958 A.D.) By the twelfth
century Marrakesh and Rabat had been added to the urban hierarchy.
Later, the ports of Mogador (now Essaouira), Tangiers, Mazagan
(now Al-Jadidah), Safi, Tetouan, and so on, assumed visibility, and
these are still found on lists of Morocco's cities in the present century. Only the primate city of Casablanca, having been a mere fishing
village called Anfa before the French selectively developed it, and
some new or newly important towns linked to French rule, such as
Khouribda (a mining center) and Kenitra (originally called Port
Lyautey), are conspicuously absent from the historic record.

COLONIAL TRANSFORMATIONS IN THE URBAN SYSTEM

Urbanism, therefore, was scarcely a new import to Morocco
during the modern period, nor were the cities merely foreign-
instigated impositions upon a traditional agrarian base. Nevertheless,
there were major transformations in the urban system of Morocco
during the twentieth century. These changes prepared the ground for
the present situation which, in turn, sets limits to the modifications
which the future can bring.

It is difficult to establish accurately the precolonial bench mark
from which to estimate the changes introduced by the French and
Spanish protectorates, since accurate data do not go back far enough
and indeed remain incomplete for the Spanish zone. However, we
can reconstruct part of the situation as it existed in 1921, based upon
a French census. In that year, the French zone of Morocco contained
15 places which had been constituted as municipalities. These
places had a combined population in excess of 600,000, of whom

TABLE 4.1

Moroccan Municipalities in the French Zone, 1921

Municipality	Number of Residents	Percentage of Residents by "Nationality"			
		Muslims	Jews	French	Other Foreign
Marrakesh	145,000	90	9.0	1.0	0.0
Fez	124,500	90	7.2	2.2	0.6
Casablanca	110,934	46	15.8	22.3	15.8
Meknes	38,159	73	15.7	7.9	3.0
Rabat	33,714	59	10.1	21.4	10.0
Safi	25,806	83	12.6	2.7	2.0
Salé	24,300	85	10.7	2.7	1.4
Oujda	22,280	51	6.4	19.7	23.1
Mazagan (Al-Jadida)	22,093	76	15.2	5.6	2.8
Mogador (Essaouira)	19,503	50	45.7	3.2	1.2
Azemmour	13,967	93	5.5	1.0	0.0
Kenitra (Port Lyautey)	10,074	57	2.0	27.4	13.4
Sefrou	8,332	58	39.4	1.0	0.0
Taza	7,500	73	1.4	18.3	6.9
Settat	6,825	75	17.6	5.9	1.8
Total	612,987	74	12.0	8.5	5.5

Note: The arrangements and computations are ours. The term "nationality" to refer to religious communities is admittedly peculiar, but we have simply followed French usage here.

Source: Raw data presented in Table 1 of the statistical appendix in, de la Casinière, Les municipalités marocaines (Rabat: Government Printer, 1924).

one-fourth were either foreign (mostly French) or Moroccan non-Muslim (almost all Jewish). If we assume that the foreigners arrived on the urban scene chiefly after the protectorate began, we can estimate that half a million Moroccans (including Jews) might have been "urbanites" in the French zone at the time the protectorate was established.

Not included in Table 4.1 are such cities in the Spanish zone as Tetouan, Larache, Ceuta, and the international city of Tangiers. Also omitted are such places in the French zone as Beni Mellal and Berkane, which had not been accorded municipality status, despite their size. Their absence from this list and their appearance on later lists should not be taken to indicate first appearance in the hierarchy.

Certain peculiarities which were to characterize Morocco's urban pattern during colonialism are already evident in the data presented in Table 4.1. Thus, even by this early date one notices a bifurcation in the urban system between the preexisting hierarchy (the indigenous precolonial urban system) and a new overlay of foreign-sparked urbanization which intersected only intermittently with parts of the indigenous hierarchy.

In the pre-French hierarchy, Marrakesh and Fez occupied prime positions, followed by Rabat-Salé (twin cities on opposite banks of the Bou Regreg River, now considered a single urban prefecture), and then Meknes. These four royal cities dominated the picture; they were all linked to the former interior system. (Except for Rabat-Salé, all are inland cities, and even Rabat-Salé by that time was not an important functional port.) Beneath them in the indigenous hierarchy were several coastal towns and additional interior towns along the east-west axis of the Taza Gap.

On top of this preexisting hierarchy was a second set of urban linkages representing the superimposed colonial system. The kingpin of that system was Casablanca, which in those early days contained a population that was two-fifths foreign and less than one-half indigenous Moroccan Muslim. Rabat (but not neighboring Salé) constituted the second point in that system. An early French decision had established Rabat as the political capital of the protectorate, independent of the port and economic capital of nearby Casablanca. Oujda was the third member of the French system. This border post along the Taza Gap became critical to France once it took over Morocco, for it linked the latter with Algeria. Oujda assumed importance both for military control and, because of its location along the railroad, for break-in-bulk functions. Along the same route were the intermediary points of Meknes and Taza, both partially integrated into the French system. The final member of the new system was the French-built town of Kenitra (originally called Port Lyautey), a military port designed to take some of the pressures off Casablanca.

FIGURE 4.1

Growth Rates of Moroccan Cities, 1921–71

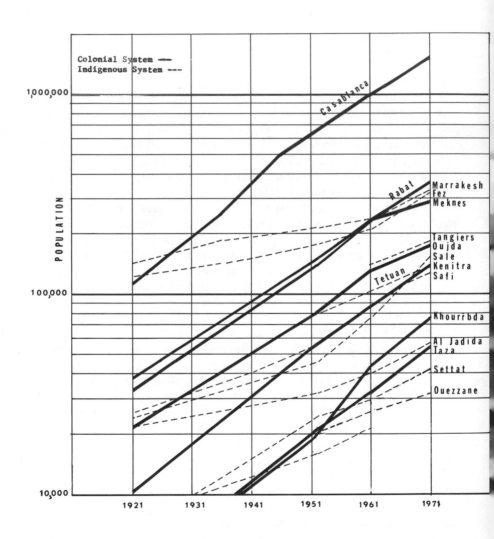

This system was focused on the coast via the chain of Casablanca-Rabat-Kenitra (all within 100 miles of one another), through which Morocco maintained its lifeline to the Metropole. In turn this coastal enclave was connected to France's more important holdings in Algeria via the lifeline of the Taza Gap (served by rail) to the border post of Oujda. While these coastal towns were a superficial imposition, they were so critical to the colonial economy that they eventually reoriented the urban system around a coastal focus.

The trends which had thus been established as early as the first decade of French rule intensified during the new few decades. Cities in the French system grew at the fastest rate, both through immigration from abroad and by attracting a disproportionate share of the rural Moroccans who were being displaced from the interior by French settlers and their agriculture. By 1936, Casablanca's population had increased to 250,000, for the first time outstripping the largest Moroccan city, Marrakesh, which had grown only to 190,000. Casablanca continued to expand even more in the years that followed, reaching 500,000 by 1946, close to 700,000 by 1952, almost 1 million in 1960, and 1.5 million by 1971. Rabat's population followed a similar trajectory of growth, albeit of lower magnitude, increasing from 33,000 in 1921, to over 150,000 in 1952. By 1960 it had almost 250,000 inhabitants, and, by 1971, it topped 368,000, making it the second largest city of the country. Indeed, all cities in the French system grew at similar high rates, as can be seen from Figure 4.1, which shows the semi-log graph of population increase for cities in the colonial system, as compared to those in the indigenous hierarchy.

Annual growth rates exceeded 5 percent, and cities doubled in size every ten to fifteen years for cities in the colonial system. In marked contrast, the slope of population increase for cities in the neglected Moroccan urban system remained flat indeed. During the thirty-year period of maximum colonial control (between 1921 and 1952), the most important centers in the Moroccan system, Marrakesh and Fez, grew very slowly and along perfectly parallel trajectories. Both grew by less than 50 percent during that period when power and control had shifted to the superimposed colonial system. Nor did the smaller towns of the Moroccan hierarchy fare much better. Al-Jadida had as flat a growth rate as the giants, while up to the end of the colonial period Safi, Salé and Sefrou had rates of growth only slightly more vital. (Among the more traditional towns, only Meknes was partially linked to the French system and therefore had a growth rate comparable to others in that system.)

Not only was there a bifurcated urban hierarchy during the colonial period, there was a dual pattern of urban-rural distribution for the two populations; so cities played a very different role in the

life of Moroccans than of foreigners. Essentially, the Moroccan
Muslim population served as the rural base, while the Europeans and
Moroccan Jews lived chiefly in the urban superstructure. Thus, in
1952 some 22.8 percent of the population of Morocco (French zone
only) lived in the 19 municipalities of the country, while 77.2 percent
still lived in areas classified as nonurban. Moroccan Muslims were
underrepresented in the cities (18.5 percent lived in the 19 municipalities, while 81.5 percent lived in nonurban places), whereas
Europeans and Jewish Moroccans were concentrated overwhelmingly
in urban areas. About 80 percent of each of these two groups lived
in the 19 municipalities, while only 20 percent lived in nonurban
parts of the country. [2]

It was this overconcentration of the European and minority
Moroccan populations in the major cities that enabled the development of the bifurcated system of cities, which reached its fullest
expression in Morocco in a handful of cities in the French hierarchy.
Each of the Moroccan cities incorporated into the French urban system (plus the two major Moroccan cities of Fez and Marrakesh which
remained tangential) was self-consciously designed as a "dual city"
by the French plans promulgated to guide urban growth in the early
protectorate period. [3] Each city was divided into a set of native
quarters (including, but not confined to, the preexisting "medina")
and a set of European quarters. Segregation of the two populations
was extreme. Europeans could not live in the "native quarters," and
the exclusion of natives from the European quarters was remarkably
complete.

As late as 1951-52, de facto apartheid was pervasive in the
largest cities. In Casablanca, for example, 96 percent of the Muslim
Moroccan population lived in the so-called native quarters (the original medina, the new medina, the bidonvilles, etc.). In Fez, close
to 99 percent of the Moroccan Muslims lived in their own section—in
this case, the ancient medina and its extensions. In Marrakesh, the
percentage was over 95; in Meknes it was 97; in Oujda, 94 percent;
in Rabat, 95 percent. [4] In short, toward the end of French rule, fully
96 percent of the 1,353,300 Moroccan Muslims living in the six
largest cities in the country (who by then constituted some 78 percent
of their total populations) were segregated into quarters assigned
exclusively for their use. Only 4 percent lived in the European quarters (which often occupied the largest proportion of the land available
for urban building), and many of these, presumably, were servants
who received housing as part of their wages.

The enormous inequalities and differential developments of
these segregated quarters, which so complete a system of urban
apartheid made possible, are difficult to imagine. Despite the fact
that tax revenues were raised substantially from the native quarters,

urban expenditures for municipal improvements and public services (utilities, streets, hospitals, schools, etc.) were allocated largely to the exclusively foreign quarters.

A similar pattern of European concentration in cities had taken place in the Spanish zone of Morocco, although the statistics are less adequate. In Tetouan there was a very large Spanish population which was segregated in the new city, and, even after legal decolonization, Moroccan Muslims constituted only three-fourths of the population. Tangiers was even less indigenous. As late as 1960, only about 70 percent of Tangiers's 142,000 inhabitants were Moroccan Muslims, while close to one-fourth were Europeans. These percentages are even higher than those which prevailed in French Morocco after decolonization, for the Spanish residents did not repatriate to the extent that French settlers did after independence. After 1956, only Oujda and Casablanca retained a sizable European minority, and only Rabat and Meknes kept a modest proportion of foreign residents.

DECOLONIZATION AND NEW EQUATIONS FOR CHANGE

Thus, when Morocco became independent and reunited in 1956, it inherited a complex urban system fragmented along multiple lines of cleavage, the sources of which have been traced above. Let us recapitulate them here, before moving on to the new equations and policy problems which Morocco now faces in bridging these cleavages and reuniting these fragments into a single national system within which Moroccan development can take place.

First, there was the rift between the northern coastal rim and the southern bulk of the country. While this rift was based upon a natural barrier (the lateral chain of the Rif Mountains), it had been intensified by the political partition. The Spanish Protectorate had imposed its own economic and judicial system, its language, and its cultural forms of urban building on the cities of that zone. The French had done likewise in at least major subregions in the South. Few lines linked the North with the South, and these had been increasingly abandoned as colonial partition persisted.

Second, there was the rift between two urban systems, one preexisting—culturally and historically rooted in the country and tightly entrenched with surrounding rural hinterlands and trade routes of ancient significance—the other superimposed by colonialism and its extractive economy which used the urban "bases" in Morocco as part of a chain of economic linkages to the Metropole. These two systems meshed only imperfectly and incompletely, with large portions of each system not integrated with others.

Third, within those parts of the urban system which had been more or less integrated into the colonial structure (and which therefore contained high proportions of foreigners), there was the rift between the European and Moroccan quarters. The former increasingly took on the appearance of protected and defensive islands dwarfed by the rapidly growing and increasingly predominant "native quarters" which had been largely ignored in the elaborate plans made by the French and bypassed by the urban improvements lavished on the numerically small but geographically expansive European quarters. Apartheid, coupled with the great economic and political power monopolized by the colonists, had resulted in highly disparate fragments in the internal structure of the cities.

The present urban situation in Morocco is highly transitional. It is a hybrid of diverse trends, some of which predate colonialism, some of which were set in motion by the colonial experience, and some of which represent counter trends which have been initiated only since decolonization in 1956. Developments in the coming decades will take place according to a new set of equations in which one can expect the first and third cleavages created under colonialism to assume greater policy importance while the second issue will continue to decline in significance. However, the continued involvement of Morocco with the "world system" through neocolonialism may temporarily give strength to the last vestiges of "dying colonialism."

The base line for tracing contemporary developments is the period just after 1956. Between that date and the taking of a complete census in 1960, there was a substantial exodus of European residents and some movement of the Moroccan Jewish population out of the country. In 1950, there had been 85,000 Spanish residents in the northern zone and over 267,000 Frenchmen in the southern zone. Another 27,000 Spaniards lived in the southern zone at that time. By 1960, there were only 175,000 Frenchmen and 93,000 Spaniards left in the country,[5] and this number dropped considerably lower by 1971. On the other hand, there was an internal migration of Moroccans during the post-independence period which, coupled with heightened rates of natural increase, led to rapid growth of cities and even more rapid "nativization" of the urban hierarchy.

The striking result was that, in general, during the postcolonial period, cities in the "colonial" hierarchy grew somewhat more slowly, whereas those in the "Moroccan traditional" hierarchy experienced rates of growth considerably higher than before. There has been, therefore, a certain equalization between the earlier discrepancies. While it is still too early to predict trends from the two data points available to us (the censuses of 1960 and 1971), it appears that a considerable amount of unification has already been achieved in the short period that has elapsed since independence. Table 4.2

TABLE 4.2

Major Urban Centers of Morocco, Populations 1936–71

Prefecture, Municipality, or Town	Population (in thousands)				Percentage Increase in Intercensal Growth[a]		
	1936	1952	1960	1971	1936–52	1952–60	1960–71
Casablanca	247	682	965	1,506	176	41	56
Rabat–Salé	115	203	303	523	77	55	73
Rabat only	83	156	227	367	88	46	62
Salé only	32	47	76	156	47	62	105
Marrakesh	190	215	243	333	13	13	37
Fez	144	179	216	325	24	21	50
Meknes	75	140	176	248	87	26	41
Tangiers	—[b]	—	142	188	—	—	32
Oujda	35	81	127	176	131	57	39
Kenitra	18	56	87	139	211	55	60
Tetouan	—	81	101	139	—	25	38
Safi	25	57	81	129	128	42	59
Khouribda	8	20	41	74	150	105	80
Mohammedia	10	25	35	70	105	40	100
Agadir	—	30	17	61	—	—	*[c]
Al–Jadida	24	35	40	56	46	13	40

(continued)

TABLE 4.2 (continued)

Prefecture, Municipality, or Town	Population (in thousands)				Percentage Increase in Intercensal Growth[a]		
	1936	1952	1960	1971	1936-52	1952-60	1960-71
Taza	15	22	32	55	47	31	72
Beni Mellal (NAM)[d]	10	16	29	54	60	81	86
Kasr el Kebir	—	32	34	48	—	6	41
Larache	—	42	31	46	—	—	*e
Settat	18	25	30	42	39	17	40
Berkane (NAM)	—	—	20	39	—	—	95
Oued Zem (NAM)	6	—	—	33	—	—	—
Ouezzane	16	21	26	33	—	—	27
Nador	—	22	—	32	—	—	—
Jerada (NAM)	—	—	19	31	—	—	63
Essaouira	15	22	26	30	—	—	15
Sefrou	12	17	21	29	—	—	38
Fkih Ben Salah (NAM)	—	—	—	27	—	—	—
Sidi Kacem (NAM)	6	15	19	27	—	—	42
Khenifra (NAM)	—	—	—	26	—	—	—
Youssoufia (NAM)	—	—	—	22	—	—	—
Taroudant (NAM)	9	—	—	22	—	—	—

Kehmisset (NAM)	—	—	—	22	—	—	—
Azrou (NAM)	—	—	—	21	—	—	—
Sidi Slimane (NAM)	—	—	—	20	—	—	—
Berrechid (NAM)	—	—	—	20	—	—	—
Total population in places with 20,000+				4,647 (i.e., 30% of total population)			

[a]The percentage increases were computed merely as a straight-line, rather than a geometric, annual rate of increase. My concern was not to estimate the rate of increment (particularly since the period includes a drop in population and then an increase in those communities having had large numbers of foreigners before decolonization) but merely to present relative average rates of net increase.

[b]Census for 1936 and 1952 numbers available.

[c]We have not computed a rate of growth for Agadir since the town was essentially destroyed by an earthquake and rebuilt.

[d](NAM) next to a place name means that despite its population size the town does not have municipality administrative status. It should be noted further that some communities that do have municipality status were not populous enough to appear in our list, although they appear on earlier lists of Moroccan cities compiled solely on the basis of administrative criteria (i.e., Ifrane, Al-Hoceima, Asilah, Azemmour, and Chechaouen).

[e]I have not computed the growth rate for Larache because of the sharp drop in population between 1952 and 1960 due to the exodus of foreigners.

Sources: Population figures for 1971 have been taken from preliminary returns of the Census of Population and Housing for 1971. Those for the largest 25 communities in any of the census years (going back to 1936) can be found in Ralph Thomlinson, "Les relations entre les rangs des villes et leurs populations au Maroc: 1936-1971," in As-Soukan (Centre des Recherches et d'Études Démographiques, Rabat) 1, no. 2 (June 1973). These were checked against figures for 1936, 1952, and 1960, which appear in Royaume du Maroc, Recensement démographique, Juin 1960, volume I of Population légale du Maroc (Rabat: Service Central des Statistiques, June 1961), p. 99, particularly.

presents information on the populations of urban prefectures and municipalities (plus other urban-sized places) of unified Morocco for 1960 and 1971, with earlier figures included where readily available.

The major fact to be noted from Table 4.2 is that the gap between the growth rates of the fastest growing cities and the ones increasing most gradually narrowed considerably in the generation spanning the colonial and post-colonial periods. Between 1936 and 1952, when colonialism was the dominant entry in the urbanization equation, the range was extremely wide. During that interval Casablanca experienced an average annual rate of growth of 11 percent; Kenitra's average annual growth rate was 13 percent; and Oujda grew at an average rate of 8 percent annually. These are to be contrasted with average annual growth rates of .8 percent and 1.5 percent, respectively, for Marrakesh and Fez, and those in the vicinity of 5 percent for Meknes and Rabat-Salé (mixed system participants).

These gaps narrowed considerably during the eight-year 1952-60 period straddling decolonization. Computing the net population change and averaging this over the eight-year period (an illegitimate operation, see note a to Table 4.2), we find that the average annual growth rates range from highs of 6.9 percent (Rabat-Salé), 7.1 percent (Oujda), and 6.8 percent (Kenitra) to lows of 2.6 percent (Fez) and 1.6 percent (Marrakesh). While the same cities fall in the high and low portions of the distribution, the range is substantially narrower.

By the period 1960-71, the gap had virtually closed, with Rabat-Salé's average annual growth rate the highest (at 6.6 percent) and Marrakesh's the lowest (with 3.4 percent). Most values fall between 4 and 5 percent. In general, those urban communities which had previously experienced abnormally low rates of growth have increased their rates, whereas those which experienced abnormally high rates of growth during the colonial period have experienced sharp declines in those rates in recent years.

These observations are still clouded by the recency of the departure of the foreign population; one cannot simply project them into the future. However, avowed policies of national planners in Morocco do stress the importance of deflecting growth from the areas privileged during colonial rule to those which had been temporarily bypassed. These plans envisage massive infusions for Fez and, to a lesser extent, Marrakesh. Indeed, there has even been talk of relocating the country's capital from Rabat to Fez in order to strengthen the indigenous urban system once again.

The repair of the rift between North and South has not yet made as much progress. Since independence and unification, the cities in the northern zone have been growing only modestly; they are relatively less important at the end than at the beginning of the period

1960-71. One of the major public projects undertaken in recent years was construction of the so-called Unity Highway designed to link North with South across the Rif Mountains. While portions of this road were substantially completed by 1974, some parts remained unimproved, and there was still little traffic over it.[6] This is in marked contrast to coastal routes connecting the "French" system of cities or even the coastal north-south axis between Tangiers and Rabat. Obviously, more than roads will be required to integrate these two sub-areas of the country.

Somewhat more progress has been made in bridging the rift between the ex-European (so-called modern) quarters and the ex-native zones (both central medina and periphery). But the ecological structure has changed surprisingly slowly, despite the rapid succession of population which occurred as members of the Moroccan bourgeoisie and upper working class moved into the places vacated by Europeans.

While the magnitude of the foreign population was not that great, its concentration in the cities, in a limited number of them, and, within that limited number, in highly specialized zones, meant that the impact was sharp where it occurred and unnoticed elsewhere. In 1960, there were some 400,000 foreigners and 162,000 Jewish Moroccans in the country. According to an official intercensal estimate, these numbers had dropped to 190,000 and 100,000, respectively, by 1965. At the same time, the Moroccan Muslim population increased by 2 million (or about 18 percent over the five-year period).[7] According to the census taken in 1971, there were only 112,000 foreigners and 31,000 Jewish Moroccans left in the country, although the total population had risen to almost 15 million. By then, clearly, foreigners and Jews constituted less than 1 percent of the population. Even in the largest cities of the "French system," which had previously derived so much of their character from the Metropole, the percentage of foreigners had shrunk to 3 percent in Casablanca, 2 percent in Kenitra, 3 percent in Larache, and 3.5 percent in Rabat. Even alien Tangiers, with the highest proportion of foreign residents, had only 5 percent.[8]

The housing formerly occupied by almost half a million emigrants, almost all of them resident in only a handful of cities in the country, was therefore available for Moroccan occupancy. As this housing stock changed hands, the caste-like cleavage between "foreign" and "native" quarters, so carefully nurtured and defended during colonialism, was converted to a class cleavage between "modernized," French-speaking, educated, and well-to-do Moroccans and all the rest who have not yet partaken significantly of the fruits of independent development.

This phenomenon is easy to ascertain impressionistically but unusually complex to study scientifically. I have completed a factorial ecology for only one city in Morocco, the twin prefecture of Rabat and Salé, the former having been drawn into the French system, the latter having always remained within the traditional Moroccan system.[9] From my findings it is clear that there exists fairly rigid class segregation between Rabat (higher) and Salé (lower) and between the "European-originated quarters" (both central and suburban) and the Moroccan-Muslim quarters (both the medina and the peripheral squatter settlements and public housing projects) which occupy entirely different niches in the city's ecology. The previous caste segregation based upon class/nationality has given way during decolonization to a segregation according to class/cultural differences. Rabat-Salé is at the initial stage of homogenization of the social structure, and until the social gaps are closed, the ecological gaps in the urban structure are not likely to be bridged. While I do not have data for the other "dual cities" of Morocco, my own guess is that Rabat-Salé is not an atypical case. Very similar changes have been occurring in Casablanca, Kenitra, Oujda, Tetouan, Tangiers, and so on.

Urban planning can do much to reduce the inequities and discontinuities that exist between the two ways of life in these cities. Policies are called for that will treat the poorer quarters preferentially, in order to make up for long years of neglect under colonialism. Thus far, Moroccan policy has aped on a larger scale those techniques the French tended to follow on a small scale, at least when they thought about it. The government has continued to build massive housing projects (trames sanitaires), to clear squatter settlements (bidonvilles), and to replace them with uniform minimum housing. This is perhaps the most costly way to solve the problem. Recently, however, there has been a rethinking of this approach and a more sympathetic attitude toward the bidonvilles. Punitive and prohibitory approaches have been replaced by benign neglect. Even this easing of tensions has resulted in substantial conversions to rather attractive permanent housing in these large quarters. Work and financing are clearly at the initiative of residents. If more land were allotted to settlers and if minimum sites and services rather than housing were provided, even more significant progress could be made.

Upgrading the most neglected quarters is one strategy for closing the gap. Relative neglect of the most privileged quarters is probably a necessary corollary, although that policy is not likely to receive support, given the fact that the policy makers now live in these zones. To some extent, however, this has perforce been happening. Again, although my data here are quite impressionistic, I have observed some deterioration of the "colonial quarter" districts

closest to the medina, at least in Rabat. For about two blocks deep
into the ex-colonial quarter, land uses and marketing techniques
appear to be undergoing "medinization." Gone are the French-type
department stores; now appearing are street stalls, smaller shops,
and vendors. A transitional zone now seems to be growing up to
mediate the formerly wide contrasts between the "old" and the "new,"
the "native" and the "foreign." This process is likely to become even
more important in the future.

The current issues in urban development in Morocco are thus
the same ones that surround Moroccan development itself. Can a
pattern of development be found that combines growth with equity
(distributive justice), that unifies the country internally while reducing
dependent ties to Europe, and that yields a modern yet Moroccan
nation which is authentically based on the past but tied to the future?
This pattern will certainly require attention to the still glaring gaps
in urbanism which have been Morocco's legacy from colonialism.

NOTES

1. Ralph Thomlinson, "The Primate City in Morocco: Casablanca or Rabat or None?" Population Review: Demography of Developing Countries 19, nos. 1 and 2 (January-December 1975): 24-33.

2. Annuaire statistique de la zone française du Maroc, 1952
(Rabat: Gouvernement Chérifien, Service Central des Statistiques,
1952), p. 13.

3. Details can be found in Janet Abu-Lughod, "Moroccan
Cities: Apartheid and the Serendipity of Conservation," in African
Themes, ed. I. Abu-Lughod (Evanston, Ill.: Northwestern University
Press, 1975), pp. 77-111.

4. I have compiled data from various tables in volumes 1-4 of
Recensement général de la population de la zone française de l'Empire
Chérifien, April 1951 (Rabat: Services Central des Statistiques,
1953-1955) to obtain these estimates.

5. Royaume du Maroc, Service Central des Statistiques,
Nationalité, Sexe, Âge, volume 1 of Resultats du recensement de
1960 (Rabat: Service Central des Statistiques, 1965), pp. 17-18.

6. Author's observations, July 1974.

7. Royaume du Maroc, Division du Plan et des Statistiques,
La situation économique du Maroc en 1965 (Rabat: Service Central
des Statistiques, 1966), p. 16.

8. Tables 1 and 2, in Royaume du Maroc, Direction des Statistiques, Population legale du Maroc d'après le recensement général
de la population et de l'habitat 1971, series E, volume 1 (Rabat:
Direction des Statistiques, December 1971), pp. 1-6.

9. Janet Abu-Lughod, "Urban Structure under Decolonization: The Factorial Ecology of Rabat-Salé, Morocco" (Report prepared for the Social Science Research Council Conference on North African Urbanism, New York, June 1976) (Princeton, N.J.: Princeton University Press, 1979).

5

ALGERIA: TRANSFORMATION OF A COLONIAL URBAN SYSTEM UNDER A PLANNED ECONOMY

Richard I. Lawless

The town is the heritage of a colonial past. The Algerian town does not exist.[1]

Algeria, like the rest of the Maghreb, has urban traditions stretching back to classical times. Yet, until the advent of colonial rule in the early nineteenth century, the country remained weakly urbanized compared with its neighbors, Morocco and Tunisia. Phoenicians, Romans, Byzantines, Arabs, and Turks each established their own urban networks according to their separate cultural traditions and economic and political aims; consequently, there was little continuity of urban occupation from one period to another. Only ruins mark the sites of cities founded by the Romans and Byzantines, and outside the southern oases few centers established by the Arabs survive to the present day. Indeed, one writer has described the urban history of Algeria as "a succession of fallen cities."[2]

PRECOLONIAL URBANIZATION

When the French conquered Algeria in 1830, the urban system created by the Turks was already in full decline. Only about 5 percent of the country's population—some 150,000 people—were urban dwellers. Algiers, the most populous city, contained only 30,000 inhabitants; Constantine 25,000; and Tlemcen 10-12,000. Usually characterized by high, fortified walls, these precolonial towns contained a dense complex of dwellings separated by an intricate maze of narrow winding streets and dead-end alleyways which reflected the absence of wheeled traffic. Few buildings were more than one story

79

tall, and only the slender minarets of the numerous mosques broke the monotony of the townscapes. Around the great mosque were areas of intense commercial activity—the souks with the various trades and crafts localized in different streets. These public places existed in sharp contrast to the residential quarters where the houses of rich and poor alike invariably presented a bare exterior, the private life of each extended family being focused on the interior courtyard concealed from the eyes of strangers.

Towns existed in isolation one from another. They exercised political and administrative control over a limited area of the surrounding countryside and contained flourishing handicraft industries, while the middle classes prospered through commerce and the ownership of gardens and olive groves in the intensively cultivated zones immediately outside the city walls.[3] The vast majority of Algerians, however, lived in the rural areas, in the tribal hinterland, jealous of the wealth of the town dwellers and yet despising them for their lack of manly qualities. The centuries-old hostility between town and countryside, moreover, was accentuated because many of the urban dwellers were Muslims of foreign origin—Andalusians, Turks, and Koulouglis—or Jews.

COLONIAL URBANIZATION

The French conquest and the establishment of colonial rule introduced a new phase of urbanization in Algeria. New extensions were built to the precolonial centers; the traditional quarters were restructured and parts even destroyed to allow the the construction of new roads, squares, and public buildings. Such was the fate of the lower part of the medina (casbah) in Algiers, where the existing urban structure was obliterated to make way for new military and port installations.[4] Due to the paucity of urban centers, many new towns were created by the French—Philippeville (now Skikda) in 1838, Sidi bel Abbès (1843), Tiaret (1843), and Sétif (1846); later some colonization villages and garrison stations in the interior became flourishing small towns. Unlike Morocco and Tunisia, where European towns were constructed alongside Arab medinas, in Algeria the new colonial foundations effectively replaced the existing urban network, and the precolonial towns were either destroyed or submerged by the numerous new European constructions. The French occupation resulted in the dominance both spatially and visually of colonial style townscapes. Early European towns were characterized by a particular layout, a grid with streets crossing each other at right angles and at roughly equal intervals. Each town had a central square, a town hall, and a Catholic church—notable only for the monotonous architectural styles adopted—and pavements lined with carefully pruned trees. In addition there were vast barrack complexes, railway sidings, grain silos, and wine caves. Later, new residential quarters were added characterized by villas set in walled gardens, while after World War II large complexes of high-rise apartment blocks grew up on the urban fringes. The functions of these new European foundations reflected the structure of the colonial economy. Towns in the interior became the intermediaries between the rural areas around and the capitalist market, the instruments by which the colony's agricultural and mineral products were collected for export to metropolitan markets. As elsewhere in Africa, this new orientation of the economy towards European markets led to the spectacular growth of a number of ports, notably Algiers, Oran, and Annaba (formerly Bône), at the coastal termini of the new rail and road networks which tapped the wealth of the interior. The creation of a modern communications network resulted in the emergence for the first time of a city system as we now understand the concept. A series of scattered precolonial towns, each with only a limited sphere of influence existing in comparative isolation and having little contact, were replaced by towns with distinct economic linkages. With interaction and competition, some centers acquired higher order services by virtue of their nodality, and a new hierarchical structure gradually emerged. Interaction was almost exclusively between the inland centers and the large coastal cities. The result was a typically "colonial" urban hierarchy.

Algeria was the most intensively colonized country in the Maghreb and received the bulk of the settler population. Throughout the colonial period the vast majority of settlers were urban dwellers. In 1959, for example, of the 1 million Europeans in Algeria (11 percent of the total population), 85 percent lived in towns, and until the 1930s the total urban population was predominantly European (see Table 5.1). The settlers were mostly administrators, bankers, technicians, traders, professional men, and skilled workers, though some had lesser jobs. They formed a privileged minority economically, culturally, and socially distinct from the Muslim population; but not all were wealthy, and there was a significant group of poor whites. The indigenous Jewish population, who were granted French citizenship in 1870 and who rapidly identified with the privileged European community, were also a strong urban minority. They were shopkeepers, traders, and artisans, and the majority were working-class.

In sharp contrast, the Muslim urban population actually declined during the first decades of colonial rule. Massacres, expulsions, and the disruption of the precolonial economy depopulated the cities, and most of them did not regain their Muslim population of

TABLE 5.1

Population of the Principal Algerian Towns
in the 1931 and 1960 Censuses

Towns	1931				
	Europeans and Jews	Percent of Total	Muslims	Percent of Total	Total
Algiers and suburbs	223,658	66.4	112,920	33.5	336,578
Oran and suburbs	135,799	78.7	36,667	21.2	172,466
Constantine	51,142	48.7	53,760	51.2	104,902
Bône	38,064	55.4	30,714	44.6	68,778
Philippeville	23,773	49.8	23,977	50.2	47,750
Tlemcen	12,164	26.4	33,896	73.6	46,060
Sidi bel Abbes	30,497	66.4	15,405	33.5	45,902

Towns	1960				
	Europeans and Jews	Percent of Total	Muslims	Percent of Total	Total
Algiers and suburbs	312,000	35.9	558,000	64.1	870,000
Oran and suburbs	212,000	49.3	218,000	50.7	430,000
Constantine	36,000	16.6	181,000	83.4	217,000
Bône	44,000	30.5	100,000	69.5	144,000
Philippeville	26,000	30.6	59,000	69.4	85,000
Tlemcen	11,000	13.7	69,000	86.3	80,000
Sidi bel Abbès	35,000	34.7	66,000	65.3	101,000

Sources: J. Ganiage, Les affaires d'Afrique du Nord de 1930 à 1958 (Paris: Centre de Documentation Universitaire, 1972), p. 2; and J. Despois, L'Afrique du Nord (Paris: Presses Universitaires de France, 1964), p. 211.

1830 until the twentieth century (Tlemcen in 1891, Algiers and Constantine in 1911, and Miliana not until 1962). Algiers, the capital, suffered a particularly harsh fate. Immediately after the conquest, the occupying power took over many public habous properties whose income traditionally supported mosques, schools, and charities. In his famous parliamentary report of 1847, Alexis de Tocqueville lamented,

> Everywhere we have put our hands on these revenues
> . . . we have ruined charitable institutions, dropped
> the schools and dispersed the seminaries. Around us
> lights have been extinguished, and the recruitment of
> men of religion and men of law has ceased. In other
> words we have rendered Muslim society much more
> miserable, disorganized, ignorant and barbaric than
> it was before knowing us.[5]

Substantial remnants of the traditional Muslim bourgeoisie survived only in Tlemcen and Constantine.

Algerian society remained overwhelmingly rural but did not escape the destructive impact of colonial rule and settler colonization. The Senatus-Consultus of 1863 hastened tribal disaggregation in the countryside by permitting tribally owned land to be broken into privately owned pieces, thus undermining tribal cohesion and the authority of the chief. The Warnier Law of 1873 completed the destruction of the tribe by permitting property sales to Europeans. In one way or another the settlers appropriated vast tracts of land in the coastal plains totaling more than 7 million acres, or 27 percent of Algeria's arable land. Squeezed off their traditional lands and experiencing population pressure as a result of galloping demography, a growing number of Muslims were forced to seek jobs as laborers on European farms or in mines. Later, particularly after the crisis that hit the colonial agricultural sector during the 1930s, Muslims also invaded the new European cities (see Tables 5.1 and 5.2). From 1936 to 1948 alone these centers received a net influx of half a million Muslims. Meanwhile the impoverished rural population continued to increase in absolute numbers despite the massive exodus.

The towns were economically and socially ill-equipped to absorb this continual influx from the countryside. By 1948 the rate of growth of the colonial economy could no longer keep up with the growth of the Muslim population, and many migrants were unable to find steady jobs. There was little industrialization, and with a large settler population many poor whites occupied urban jobs open to Muslims in neighboring Tunisia and Morocco. In 1955, only 12.5 percent of Algerian Muslims were employed in the secondary sector and

TABLE 5.2

The Muslim Population of Algiers, 1866-1954
(in thousands)

Year	Total Population	Muslim Population	Percent of Population Muslim
1866	65	13	20.00
1886	103	22	21.36
1906	174	40	22.99
1926	266	73	27.44
1936	348	118	33.91
1948	474	226	47.68
1954	570	293	51.40

Source: P. Marthelot, "Les bidonvilles encasernés: contribution à l'étude du surpeuplement à Alger," in Les influences occidentales dans les villes Maghrébines à l'époque contemporaine, no. 2 (Algiers: Etudes méditerranéennes, 1974), p. 124.

9.5 percent in the tertiary sector, demonstrating the difficulties which Muslims experienced in becoming integrated into the modern urban economy. The rate of urban unemployment among Muslims was high, ranging from 25 to 33 percent.[6]

Poorly integrated into the colonial urban economy, the new Muslim proletariat lived apart from the European residents—separate as well as unequal. Some of the early migrants found accommodation in the traditional Muslim quarters, the medinas, which rapidly became dangerously overcrowded. Densities of 200,000 inhabitants per square kilometer were recorded in the Haute Casbah district of Algiers in 1954. But the majority were forced to make their homes in the miserable shantytowns (the so-called bidonvilles, or towns made out of tin cans) that mushroomed in and around all the major cities. In 1955, two-fifths of the Muslim population of Algiers lived in bidonvilles, and although none of them achieved the dimensions of the bidonvilles of Casablanca and Rabat (the largest, Mahieddine, had 10,000 inhabitants), they emerged as a major new element in the urban landscape of the capital and of Algeria's other urban centers.[7] Attempts to rehouse some of the occupants of the bidonvilles during the last decade of colonial rule as part of the counterinsurgency measures adopted by the French, represented a classic case of too little too late.

Laws enacted in 1919 and 1958 were incapable of reducing the sharp spatial segregation of ethnic-religious groups in the towns, and integration of Muslims and Europeans proved as impossible to achieve as "assimilation." A few Muslims—members of the liberal professions and prosperous traders—succeeded in moving into some European districts occupied by low to middle-income groups (such as the so-called mixed areas of Bologhnine, Mustapha, and Belcourt in Algiers). But most Muslims who worked in the European quarters during the day returned to their own quarters at night. The town remained essentially alien to the Muslim citizens. R. P. H. Sanson accurately summarizes their position: "There were few Muslim Algerian families among the urban bourgeoisie. In the alien towns most Algerians were servants, labourers, minor civil servants, poor craftsmen and middlemen. Muslim Algerians did not feel at home in the town."[8]

Rural to urban migration accelerated rapidly after the outbreak of the war of independence in 1954, as Muslims fled from the insecurity of the countryside. This movement was also undoubtedly stimulated by the harsh regroupment policies adopted by the French army in the face of revolutionary guerrilla warfare. These military activities are estimated to have affected half the rural population—some 3,525,000 people—with permanent effects on the Algerian settlement pattern.[9] Without a doubt this represents one of the most brutal population displacements in history.

POSTCOLONIAL URBANIZATION

The violence and chaos immediately preceding and following Algerian independence in July 1962 had an equally traumatic impact on the country's urban population. Within the space of a few months the bulk of the Europeans and Jews, the vast majority of whom were townsfolk, left Algeria for France.[10] The scale and pace of this exodus was unequalled in Africa until the dramatic flight of white settlers from the strife-torn Portuguese territory of Angola in 1975. The departure of the settlers was accompanied by a massive influx of Muslims from the traditional quarters, bidonvilles, and regroupment centers into the European quarters of the towns, where they rapidly occupied the numerous houses and apartments abandoned by European residents. In a period of less than six months Algeria's towns were transformed in size and in ethnic composition as they experienced a veritable transfusion of population. The scale of

FIGURE 5.1

Towns and Cities with More Than 10,000 Inhabitants in Northern Algeria in 1966

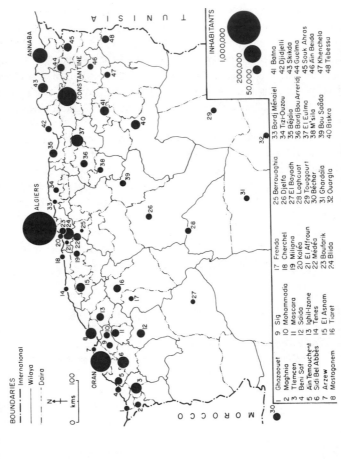

Source: Commissariat National au Recensement de la Population, Villes Recensement de la Population et de l'Habitat en 1966, serie B, vol. 3 (Algiers: Government Printer, 1966).

urbanization and of the "Algerianization" of the towns was given statistical confirmation by the 1966 population census (see Figure 5.1).

Definitions of Algeria's urbanized population vary, but the Commissariat National au Recensement de la Population (CNRP) in publishing the official results of the 1966 Census of Population* considered as "urban" 94 chief towns or communes where more than 1,000 of the active population were in nonagricultural employment. Of these they distinguished 64 "urban" communes (where at least 1,000 of the active population were in nonagricultural employment and represented more than 75 percent of the total active population) and 30 "semi-urban" communes (where at least 1,000 of the active population were in nonagricultural employment and represented between 50 and 75 percent of the total active population). These two categories included 4,699,200 inhabitants, or 38 percent, of Algeria's total population. At the previous full census in 1954, only 26.9 percent of the population, 2,563,489 people (Muslims and Europeans), were urban. Thus, in spite of the departure of some 800,000 European townsfolk, the number of urbanized Algerians had more than doubled during the intercensal period. Algiers lost 315,000 European colonists yet grew from 449,929 inhabitants in 1954, to 943,551 in 1966, and if its suburban ring of communes is included it now forms a metropolis of over 1.5 million inhabitants. Constantine and Batna experienced even more rapid urban growth during this period (Table 5.3).

The exodus of white settlers and the Algerianization of the colonial urban system eliminated the conflicts and tensions of ethnic dualism. But the massive transfer of population from the countryside to the towns provoked severe economic and social problems which the newly independent republic was poorly equipped to solve. In spite of an urban history stretching back to classical times, independent Algeria possessed few living urban traditions that were authentically Algerian. As a result of brutal urbanization, the majority of the urban dwellers were recent rural migrants—new urbanites[11]—poor, illiterate and with few skills or resources. Consequently, some writers speak not of the urbanization of the Algerian population but of the ruralization of the towns. An important part of the urban population remained poorly integrated into the urban economy, already seriously disrupted by the economic dislocation of a harsh decolonization. This phenomenon expressed itself in a high rate of urban

----

*A new census was conducted in February 1977. The preliminary results by commune were published at the beginning of 1978, but as of June 1978 no statistics had been released for urban centers.

TABLE 5.3

Algeria: Population of Towns with More Than 50,000 Inhabitants in 1966, and Percentage Growth 1954–66

Towns	1954	1966	Annual Growth Rate, 1954–66	Percentage Growth, 1954–66
Algiers	449,929	943,551	6.4	110
Oran	274,772	325,807	1.4	18
Constantine	111,315	245,621	6.8	121
Annaba	88,920	152,395	4.6	71
Sidi bel Abbès	65,267	88,514	2.6	36
Sétif	40,168	88,212	6.8	120
Blida	38,067	85,823	7.0	125
Tlemcen	53,233	71,872	2.5	35
Mostaganem	56,446	63,744	1.0	13
Skikda	48,773	61,157	1.9	25
Batna	18,504	55,751	9.6	201
Biskra	52,511	53,851	0.2	3
Bejaia	29,748	50,467	4.5	70

Source: Fiche documentaire, Annales algériennes de géographie 2, no. 4 (July/December 1967): 122.

unemployment and underemployment (in 1966, 31 percent of the active urban population were unemployed), the proliferation of degraded forms of precapitalist craft industries, and an inflated tertiary sector with numerous street traders, small shopkeepers, barbers, public writers, shoeshine boys, and others serving a clientele with an extremely low purchasing power.[12] In addition, the houses and apartments inherited from the European residents were poorly adapted to the social organization and economic resources of the new urbanites and rapidly became overcrowded and fell into a state of disrepair. These acute problems of employment and housing were intensified by the continuous influx of rural migrants and by high rates of natural increase among an urban population still strongly influenced by rural customs and values. Predictions suggest that by 1986 the urban population of Algeria could reach 14.53 million,

TABLE 5.4

Algeria's Urban Population, 1830-1986
(in millions)

Year	Total Population	Urban Population	Percent Urban
1830	3.00	0.15	5
1886	4.00	0.60	15
1948	7.60	2.00	26
1966	12.00	4.70	38
1986	23.70	14.50	61

Source: J. Le Coz, "De l'urbanization 'sauvage' à l'urbanization intégrée," Bulletin de la Société Languedocienne de Géographie 6, no. 1 (January-March 1972): 5.

61 percent of the total Algerian population (see Table 5.4). Thus the major tasks facing the urban planners in independent Algeria were those of absorbing "the continuous flow of migrants, and integrating them into the urban economy in order to transform the uprooted peasant into a citizen with a place in the social system based on the efforts of his labour."[13]

In the early years of independence the fight for political survival dominated the new Algerian government's attention. During the revolutionary war the National Liberation Front (FLN) had evolved no real economic strategy for an independent state. The modern sector of the Algerian economy had been created to serve the needs of the metropolitan power, not the Algerians themselves, and the new republic remained heavily dependent on the former colonial power for its economic survival—as indeed the Evian Accords, which gave Algeria independence, had intended. The economy remained "colonial" in its orientation and continued to display the characteristic dualism of colonial territories, that is, an unbalanced and unintegrated economy characterized by the coexistence of a dynamic "modern," export-oriented sector of production, and a "traditional" sector of subsistence agriculture inhibiting the development of an internal market. At independence, agricultural produce made up 80 percent of all exports, wine alone representing 53 percent. Almost all exports went to France, which in turn supplied the bulk of Algeria's imports.

The new republic inherited an important technical, industrial, and agricultural infrastructure, and its economic potential was considerable, but there was a serious shortage of trained cadres. As Samir Amin put it, "the national government inherited the material foundations laid during the colonial period but with no one to man them and no one to serve."[14] Under President Ben Bella there was a brief flirtation with worker self-management but no real attempt to make it an organized political and economic force. By 1968, however, the new regime of Colonel Houari Boumedienne, which came to power in a swift and bloodless coup d'état in June 1965, was more secure. With a newly found political stability and growing revenues from oil and gas exports, the government embarked on an ambitious program to reorient and restructure the Algerian economy.

As a preliminary to planned economic development, the Algerians set about regaining control of the country's natural resources through a program of nationalization affecting lands owned by settlers, banks, industries, mines, and transport services. With the nationalization in February 1971 of the French oil companies operating in the country, all key sectors of the Algerian economy passed under the control of large state companies. Algeria was transformed into a highly planned, centrally controlled economy. By means of the pre-plan (1967-69) and the ambitious First and Second Four-Year Plans (1970-73 and 1974-77), Boumedienne's government, composed mainly of technocrats, has set out to change the whole structure of Algerian economy from one based essentially on agriculture—with the modern sector tied to vulnerable markets in Western Europe—to one in which industry plays a dominant role. Their development strategy is based on a model developed by the French economist G. Destanne de Bernis of Grenoble University. At the center of this economic model is the concept of "industrializing industries" based on Algeria's own natural resources (oil refineries, gas liquefaction plants, petrochemical complexes, and steelworks), producing raw materials to supply other sectors of industry engaged in the production of vehicles, farm machinery, pumps and irrigation equipment, electrical goods, and plastics. The products of these industries are then to be used to transform traditional agriculture so that this sector can produce raw materials for industry and food for Algeria's rapidly expanding population. Of central importance, therefore, is the concept of linkages between different sectors of the economy and, in particular, between agriculture and industry. The traditional agricultural sector is to be modernized and integrated into the national economy. This sector still contains the majority of the population, and the aim is to raise incomes so that these peasant families can afford the goods produced by Algerian industry. The agricultural sector is to be integrated with the new industrial sector to provide

not only an internal market for industrial products but also a source
of new raw materials for industry. By the early 1980s Algerian
planners believe that industry will be able to absorb the urban unemployed, while the "agrarian revolution" launched in 1972 is intended
to modernize the traditional agricultural sector, increase agricultural production, reduce under- and unemployment in that sector,
and slow down rural to urban migration.

Thus, under the new planned economy, the urban network
inherited from colonial rule was not to be abandoned; there was to
be no brutal deurbanization in the name of cultural purification on
the scale experienced in Cambodia. Rather, rapid urbanization was
to be reinforced by industrialization. During the colonial period,
what industry that existed—mainly service and processing industries,
such as oil and flour mills, bottling plants, breweries, and pasta
and biscuit factories—was heavily concentrated in the main coastal
ports, particularly in Algiers. A leading principle of the new industrialization, however, is the decentralization of industrial plants.
Following the massive investment in the industrial sector since 1967,
three centers are emerging as the country's major industrial development poles, Arzew, Skikda, and El Hadjar. The key "industrializing
industries" are located here. Arzew, 40 kilometers east of Oran,
and Skikda in eastern Algeria, formerly small fishing ports, have
become major oil and gas terminals possessing huge oil refineries,
gas liquefaction complexes, and petrochemical plants. The former
colonization center of Duzerville (now El Hadjar) near Annaba, the
third industrial development pole, has been entirely transformed by
the establishment of a massive iron and steel complex and, close by,
a phosphate fertilizer plant. Other industries have been established
in the chief towns of the wilayate (departments), daïrate (arrondissements), and communes. So far the eastern part of the country, a
poor, overpopulated mountainous region where colonization had only
a limited impact, has been particularly favored and, through industrialization, is gradually becoming integrated into the modern economy.[15] Several factories have been set up at Tizi-Ouzou, Sétif,
Constantine, Annaba, and Batna, including mechanical engineering,
electrical equipment, plastics, and textile industries. Many smaller
towns in the east have also been chosen for the location of new industries, among others, Guelma (pottery, cycles and motor cycles,
sugar refining), Bejaïa (textiles), Souk Ahras (cellulose), Biskra
(cement, date processing), El Kala (paper and canning), Azzaba
(pharmaceuticals), and Hadjar Soud (cement).[16] An even more ambitious plan envisages the creation of a new industrialized area in the
interior steppelands, stretching from the west to the east of the
country between Maghnia and Tebessa. The locations for some of
the key elements in this industrial belt have already been selected.

They include aluminum production at M'sila, an engine manufacturing complex at Ain Oussers, a plant producing light trucks at Tiaret, a foundry and a pump and valve factory at Berrouaghia, and a high quality and special steel plant at Ain Mlila. A whole series of light industries in all the urban centers of the region (textiles, food, and construction materials) are to be added to these nuclei of heavy industry. In this way industrialization is expected to play a major role in regional development.

In addition to these new industrial functions, growing state control of the Algerian economy has greatly strengthened the administrative functions of the town, particularly the capital, Algiers, and the chief towns of the thirty-one wilayate.* Since independence, state capitalism has replaced the private capitalism of the colonial period, and forty-five state companies and sixteen national agencies dominate the Algerian economy. With their head offices in Algiers, these companies control industry, mining, imports and exports, marketing and distribution of goods as well as tourism and many other economic activities. Most have established regional offices in the chief towns of each wilaya, and these towns now function as the key regional centers through which the state directs the economy. The influence of the chief towns on the economic life of the wilayate is now very extensive.[17] The postcolonial period has therefore seen the emergence of a new urban hierarchy in Algeria in which linkages between Algiers, the capital, and the regional administrative centers—the chief towns of the wilayate—are gradually replacing an essentially colonial urban system in which the inland towns, functioning as marketing and collecting centers, were linked to the large coastal ports.

A further major new development has been the strengthening of the educational functions of the towns as a result of a massive expansion of the school system and the creation of new universities and technical institutes. Since independence, when the vast majority of the population was illiterate, spectacular progress has been made in primary and secondary education, and since 1971 practically all children born after 1962 have attended school. New universities have been established at Constantine, Oran, Annaba, and Tlemcen, and others are planned. A number of specialized institutes (École Supérieure de Chimie, Institut National Agronomique, Institut de

---

*The chief towns of the wilayate are Algiers, Annaba, Batna, Constantine, El Asnam, Médéa, Mostaganem, Ouargla, Oran, Saïda, Béchar, Sétif, Tiaret, Tizi Ouzou, Tlemcen, Adrar, Laghouat, Oum el-Bouagui, Béjaïa, Biskra, Sidi bel Abbès, Blida, Bouira, Tebessa, Tamanrasset, Djelfa, Jijel, Skikda, Guelma, M'sila, and Mascara.

Psychologie appliquée at Algiers, Institut de Technologie Agricole at Mostaganem, Institut National des Hydrocarbures et de la Chimie at Boumerdès) have been set up, and many more will be created in the future in order to train the administrative, scientific, and technical cadres essential to the success of Algeria's development strategy.[18]

These profound functional changes which have affected Algeria's towns and cities during the last decade have not been accompanied by dramatic morphological change. Of course, the three major industrial development poles—Arzew, Skikda, and El Hadjar—have been entirely transformed. In addition, vast industrial zones are beginning to appear on the outskirts of many of the principal northern towns, bright new administrative complexes affirm the key role of the chief towns, and new school buildings are a striking feature of all towns, large and small. Nevertheless, with absolute priority accorded to productive investment, relatively little residential building has taken place since independence (only 5 percent of total plan allocations have been devoted to housing); so that the urban fabric inherited from the colonial period remains substantially unaltered. Even at Arzew and Skikda no new residential quarters have been constructed, and while Oran continues to act as a convenient dormitory center for Arzew, at Skikda squalid, unhealthy, and overcrowded bidonvilles (containing 35–40,000 inhabitants) have mushroomed around the colonial town.[19]

As a result, many of the former European quarters of Algeria's towns as well as the traditional Muslim districts have become seriously overcrowded and degraded, merely aggravating the problems of social adaptation for the new urbanites, and if some of the old bidonvilles have been destroyed, new gourbis and tents have appeared on the urban fringes. Perhaps inevitably Algiers with its strong powers of attraction exhibits the worst examples of these features, though they are present in all the northern towns.[20] In the first and second arrondissements of Algiers (Bab-el-Oued and Casbah-Oued Kourin) densities exceed 40,000 inhabitants per square kilometer and in two quarters, El Kettar and Belcourt, reach 100-150,000 inhabitants per square kilometer, or 4-5 people per room.[21] New bidonvilles have sprung up on the urban fringes, opposite the Renault factory on the Baraki road, along the edges of the Oued El-Harrach, and around Fort l'Empereur, Barberousse, El Kettar, and Frais Vallon, replacing the much larger squatter settlements of the late colonial period which penetrated into the very heart of the city and were demolished by the government after independence. Bidonvilles now contain an estimated 40,000 inhabitants,[22] not only new arrivals from the countryside but also migrants from other quarters of the city.[23] However, probably the most acute and urgent problem is that of the vast complexes of high-rise apartment blocks where some

40 percent of the population of Greater Algiers live and where densities are substantially higher than those recorded in the most overcrowded quarters of the city. Rapidly submerged by an influx of poor new urbanites, these complexes, originally built for Europeans in the lower and middle-income groups, are hopelessly ill-adapted to the needs, resources, and social organization of their new occupants. Everywhere shutters remain permanently closed and windows are even bricked up in the search for some privacy. Deprived of adequate maintenance, some complexes no longer possess electricity, while poor conditions of hygiene seriously threaten the health of the occupants. These blocks have in effect become vertical bidonvilles. Marthelot describes conditions in two complexes, Diar es Saada and Diar el Mahçoul, in the following terms: "They appear run down, lacking maintenance, the approaches defiled and washing hanging from the windows. . . . Large numbers of children play in the entrances, on the stairs and in the corridors of these once impressive buildings."[24]

Furthermore, in most towns and cities the spontaneous occupation of the European quarters was quickly followed by the spatial segregation of the new Algerian population according to socioeconomic rank. Little research has been carried out on this phenomenon,[25] but the broad patterns of residential segregation can be easily identified. The tensions of ethnic segregation have merely been replaced by new tensions resulting from socioeconomic segregation. In Algiers, for example, the higher income groups—members of the liberal professions, directors of state companies, and the former minor functionaries newly promoted to the upper ranks of the civil service—are strongly concentrated in El-Biar, Hydra, and El Mouradia, formerly high-class European residential areas. These quarters, situated on higher land, are well maintained, and, in the spacious villas, now surrounded by high walls, the occupants can enjoy the benefits of modern urban life without losing the traditional privacy required for family life. At the other end of the socioeconomic scale, the lower income groups and the numerous unemployed inhabit the lower parts of the city, Casbah, Bab-el-Oued, Belcourt, and El Harrach, with their overcrowded tenements and bidonvilles.[26] Increasingly, among a population transplanted from rural areas to the anonymity of the towns, place of residence rather than family links determines the individual's membership in a particular social group.

CONCLUSION

In recent years, the attention of Algeria's economic planners has been firmly focused on the depressed rural areas where over half of the population still gain their livelihood. The implementation of the agrarian reform aims to raise agricultural production, increase rural incomes, regroup the population in 1,000 new villages, and reduce rural-urban drift. the reality is somewhat different. At most the reform will probably affect 10-15 percent of privately owned land, and only about 10 percent of the total agricultural labor force will acquire land. The reform program is behind schedule and has met with considerable resistance from the peasants, many of whom are reluctant to join the new cooperatives because of fear of excessive bureaucratic control. There are some examples of beneficiaries actually abandoning their newly acquired land.[27] Thus, the reform's success in eradicating rural under- and unemployment and reducing the rural exodus is likely to prove limited. Net migration, moreover, is only one component of urban growth, and high rates of natural increase are likely to emerge as the dominant factor insuring continued rapid urban growth. Family planning programs as a means of restricting urban growth as well as population growth have been rejected by the Algerian government, and strong reliance is placed on economic development to raise the standard of living and to reduce fertility.[28] Some success has been achieved in creating jobs in the nonagricultural sectors (some 163,000 between 1973 and 1975), but urban unemployment remains a problem. Almost all the new jobs available are for skilled workers and managers, and there are few openings for the poor, unskilled urbanites. Price subsidization of basic commodities has helped the least privileged urban groups, but their standard of living and consumption levels remain low.

Because of the high priority given to industrialization, investment in urban development, especially new housing and public services, has been seriously neglected since independence. Algerian planners believed that the urban infrastructure inherited from the colonial period would support at least the early stages of industrialization. These assumptions have proved false, and acute housing shortages, high rents, and overcrowding have become major problems for the urban population. In 1977 there were 9.3 persons for every housing unit, compared with only 6.11 persons in 1966. Even though the minimum industrial wage was raised to 600 dinars* per month at the end of 1977, the monthly rent for a small apartment in Algiers can range from 1500 to over 3000 dinars. Furthermore, these housing problems have begun to exert a negative effect on the industrial sector itself. There are many examples of management

---

*One Algerian dinar equals approximately U.S.$0.25 (as of June 2, 1978).

and supervisory staff and even skilled workers who have been forced
to turn down job offers in new factories because they were unable to
find housing close by. The housing problem has also been identified
as the major constraint restricting the reintegration of Algerian
workers from France into the national economy.[29]

The government is now acutely aware of the deteriorating
urban situation and is poised to take action. The year 1978 became
a year of assessment during which the Secretariat of State for Planning attempted to adjust the direction of planning policies. Algeria's
aim is still to industrialize quickly, but the authorities are anxious
to deal with urban problems before they become too difficult to
handle. Consequently, housing, community development, and urban
modernization received the highest allocations in the 1978 development budget, and investment in these sectors will rise more quickly
than other investment during the new development plan to be announced
at the beginning of 1979. A program to build 100,000 new houses a
year over the next five years has already been announced. There
will also be more emphasis on developing light industries to help
provide jobs and meet the growing demand for consumer products.
The program for these small and medium-scale industries will be
initiated by the wilayate, the basic units for regional planning in
Algeria. Their planning departments must be strengthened if implementation and effective supervision of local, urban, and commune
plans are to be achieved without the long delays that have weakened
Algeria's regional development policy in the past.

The next decade should reinforce and consolidate the profound
functional changes that have occurred in Algeria's urban economy
since independence and witness a marked improvement in the quality
of urban life for at least some of the citizens. Unfortunately, present
economic planning policies offer little help or hope to the urban poor
who lack the skills needed to enter the new urban economy. Access
to education has been greatly improved, but the way to the top is
inevitably easier for those who start with an educational advantage,
which in turn depends on social class. Urban modernization may
transform the outward face of Algeria's towns, but without a radical
redistribution of wealth the sharp divisions in urban society will
prove more difficult to erase.

NOTES

1. J. Franchet, "La formulation de l'espace algérien," in
Villes et sociétés au Maghreb—études sur l'urbanisation (Paris:
Centre National de la Recherche Scientifique, 1974), p. 46.

2. R. P. H. Sanson, "La symbolique rurale et la symbolique urbaine du néocitadin algérien," in Les influences occidentales dans les villes Maghrébines à l'epoque contemporaine (Algiers: Etudes méditerranéennes, no. 2, 1974), p. 140.

3. On precolonial towns in Algeria, see D. Sari, Les villes précoloniales de l'Algérie occidentale—Nédroma, Mazouna, Kalâa (Algiers: Société National d'Edition et de Diffusion, 1970).

4. COMEDOR (Comité Permanent d'Etudes, de Développement, d'Organisation et d'Amenagement de l'Agglomeration d'Alger), Les transformations du tissu de la Casbah pendant la période coloniale, vol. 4 in Etude pour la rénovation de la Casbah d'Alger (Algiers: Government Printer, 1970).

5. A. de Tocqueville, Oeuvres complètes, vol. 3 (Paris: Gallimard, 1962), p. 323.

6. C. H. Moore, "Old and New Elites in North Africa: The French Colonial Impact in Comparative Perspective," in Les influences occidentales dans les villes Maghrébines à l'époque contemporaine (Algiers: Etudes méditerranéennes, no. 2, 1974), p. 30.

7. R. Descloitres, J. Cl. Reverdy, and Cl. Descloitres, L'Algérie des bidonvilles. Le tiers monde dans la cité (Paris: Mouton, 1961).

8. R. P. H. Sanson, "Prise de la ville, prise du pouvoir," in Villes et sociétés au Maghreb—études sur l'urbanisation, ed. R. P. H. Sanson (Paris: Centre National de la Recherche Scientifique, 1974), p. 24.

9. M. Cornaton, Les regroupements de la décolonisation en Algérie (Paris: Les editions ouvrières, 1967).

10. The events leading up to the massive exodus of Europeans are vividly described in P. Henissart, Wolves in the City—The Death of French Algeria (London: Rupert Hart-Davis, 1970).

11. On the "new urbanites" see Sanson, "La symbolique rurale," op. cit., pp. 135-41.

12. C. Bardinet, "Problèmes démographiques de l'urbanisation en Algérie dans la période 1962-1972," Bulletin de la Société Languedocienne de Géographie 6, no. 1 (January-March 1972): 14.

13. Bardinet, op. cit., p. 12.

14. S. Amin, The Maghreb in the Modern World (Harmondsworth, England: Penguin, 1970), p. 243.

15. D. Sari, "La restructuration des centres urbains en Algérie," in Villes et sociétés au Maghreb—études sur l'urbanisation, ed. R. P. H. Sanson (Paris: Centre National de la Recherche Scientifique, 1974), pp. 56-59.

16. For a detailed discussion of the location of Algeria's new industries, see "Première carte industrielle de l'Algérie," Industries et Travaux d'Outremer 22, no. 247 (June 1974): 546-62.

17. R. I. Lawless, "Centrality and the evolution of a central place hierarchy in western Algeria" (Paper presented at the Developing Areas Study Group Meeting on Marketing and Central Place Systems in Less Developed Countries, Annual Conference, Institute of British Geographers, Oxford, January 1975).

18. Sari, op. cit., pp. 60-63.

19. "Skikda: les retombées du boom industriel," El Moudjahid (August 6, 1974): 2.

20. P. Y. Péchoux et al., "La part des quartiers d'habitat précaire dans la croissance récente de Mostaganem," Bulletin de la Société Languedocienne de Géographie 6, no. 1 (January-March 1972): 91-103. R. I. Lawless and G. H. Blake, Tlemcen: Continuity and Change in an Algerian Islamic Town (London: Bowker, 1976).

21. P. Marthelot, "Les bidonvilles encasernés: contribution à l'étude du surpeuplement à Alger," in Les influences occidentales dans les villes Maghrébines à l'époque contemporaine (Algiers: Etudes méditerranéennes, no. 2, 1974), p. 129.

22. COMEDOR (Comité Permanent d'Etudes, de Développement, d'Organisation et d'Amenagement de l'Agglomeration d'Alger), Équipe bidonvilles—Report no. 1, Exploitation de l'enquête bidonvilles—enquête réalisée par la wilaya d'Alger 1972 (Algiers: Government Printer, 1973).

23. This is a phenomenon also identified at Rabat by Professor Janet Abu-Lughod. Oral communication, July 1975.

24. Marthelot, op. cit., p. 132.

25. AARDES (Association algérienne pour la recherche démographique, économique et sociale) Algiers, has carried out an interesting survey of household expenditure which provides some valuable indications of segregation according to socioeconomic rank in Algeria's towns and cities: Enquête sur les budgets familiaux auprès des ménages algériens, 7 vols. (Algiers: Government Printer, 1970).

26. Sanson, op. cit., p. 26.

27. N. Abdi, "Réforme agraire en Algérie," Maghreb-Machrek 69 (1975): 34-35.

28. R. J. Lapham, "Population policies in the Maghreb," Middle East Journal 26, no. 1 (Winter 1972): 9.

29. Amicale des Algériens en Europe, "Nouvelle perspectives pour l'émigration algérienne," Report of the 8e Assemblée Générale des Cadres, Nancy, February 12-13, 1977, p. 90.

6

URBANIZATION AND
DEVELOPMENT PLANNING IN LIBYA

Gerald H. Blake

URBAN GROWTH

Unlike many other parts of the African continent, North Africa
has had a long and distinguished record of urbanism going back to
pre-Roman times. Despite the changing fortunes of individual towns
and cities, urban life somehow has always managed to retain its
vitality. In recent decades, like the rest of the African continent,
the region has experienced accelerating rates of urban growth. Between 1965 and 1975, North Africa's urban population grew at 5.9
percent per annum, and the rate is expected to increase during the
next decade.[1] The causes of this urban explosion, as elsewhere,
may be found in the combined effects of high rates of natural increase
and migration to the towns. North Africa has registered some of the
highest rates of natural increase in the world in recent years (3.2
percent per annum from 1970 to 1973),[2] and natural increase is
therefore a more significant component of urban growth than in
many other parts of Africa.

According to the 1973 Census, Libya's population increased at
any average annual rate of 4.2 percent between 1964 and 1973 (see
Figure 6.1 and Table 6.1).[3] Substantial immigration of foreign labor
occurred during this period, while rapid population increase formed
the base for rapid urban growth. Unfortunately, there are widely

The author is greatly indebted to the University of Benghazi,
and to the Centre for Middle Eastern and Islamic Studies at the University of Durham, England, for enabling him to visit Libya on a
number of occasions.

FIGURE 6.1

Urban Centers in Libya

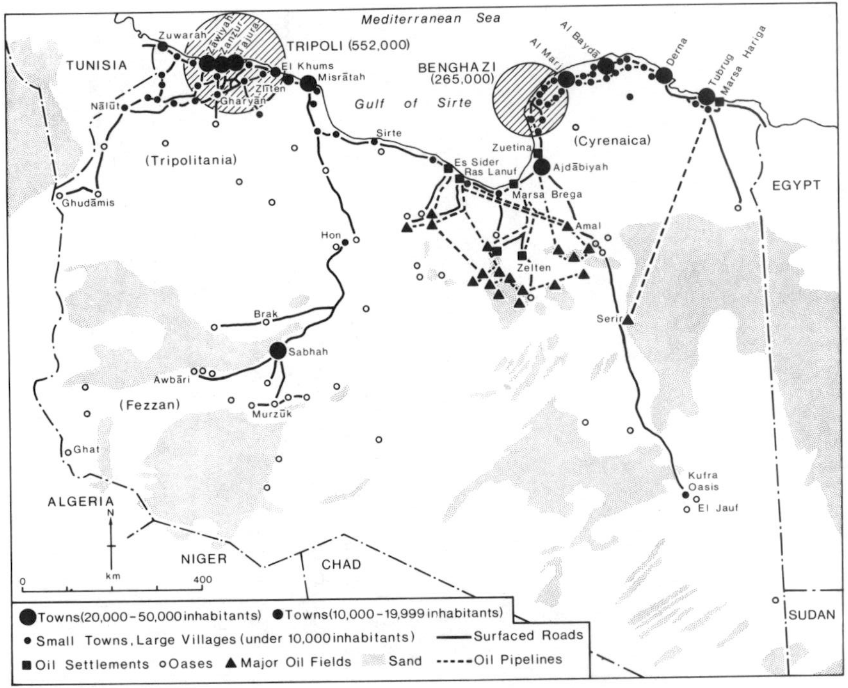

Source: Compiled by the author.

TABLE 6.1

Settlements with over 5,000 Inhabitants in 1973

Settlement	Rank	Population Size, 1973	Population Size, 1966	Growth Rate, 1966-73
Tripoli	1	551,443	300,448	9.1
Benghazi	2	264,491	160,000	7.4
Misratah	3	50,000	32,930	6.1
Al Baydā	4	39,831	12,600	17.9
Derna	5	37,097	22,700	7.3
Zāwiyah	6	35,653	19,700	8.8
Tobrug	7	34,407	16,350	11.2
Ejdabiah	8	34,198	18,000	9.6
Sabhah	9	32,169	13,600	13.1
Tajura	10	26,000	12,000	11.7
Al Marj	11	21,986	11,222	10.1
Zanzur	12	15,000	10,000	6.0
Zlīten	13	14,240	4,500	17.9
Zuwarah	14	14,037	14,618	(0.6)
Homs	15	11,296	5,000	12.3
Kufra El Jof	16	8,336	3,500	13.2
Sirte	17	8,000	3,900	10.8
Tarhuna	18	8,000	2,400	18.8
Ben Gashir	19	8,000	2,640	17.2
Gharyān	20	7,451	4,700	6.8
Sorman	21	7,000	2,000	19.5
El Ajelat	22	7,000	—*	—
Nālūt	23	6,724	6,566	0.3
Shahat	24	6,405	2,328	15.6
Sabratah	25	6,000	—	—
Beninah	26	5,409	3,750	5.4
Hon	27	5,347	2,970	8.8
El Abiar	28	5,000	3,400	5.7
El Gusbat	29	5,000	3,200	6.6
Ez Zahrah	30	5,000	2,000	14.0

*Dash indicates data not available.
Source: S. El-Shakhs, "Urbanisation and spatial development in Libya," Pan-African Journal 7, no. 4 (1975): 378.

differing estimates as to the rate of urban growth in Libya, largely
because of different definitions of "urban." The official Libyan definition of "urban" (quoted in United Nations publications) is "the total
populations of Tripoli and Benghazi plus the urban parts of Al Baydā
and Derna."[4] According to this definition, the degree of urbanization
in Libya is still quite modest, having risen from 19.4 percent in
1950 to 30 percent in 1977. Similarly, the urban growth rate between
1965 and 1975 is given as 5.8 percent, below both Algeria and Morocco.[5] This definition, however, considerably underestimates the
true proportion of urban dwellers, since it excludes some small
urban centers in the 10,000 to 20,000 range, and even more in the
5,000 to 10,000 range. In a country with a small, scattered population such centers clearly perform urban functions of considerable
importance. That the official definition underestimates Libya's
urban population may be further borne out by some interesting figures
for the number of "agricultural holders" in Libya given in the 1973
census, which numbered them at 180,000. Assuming an average of
5.8 persons per household (the national average), this would represent just over 1 million people dependent on agriculture, or about
48 percent of the population.[6] Even allowing for a substantial number
of nonagriculturists in nonurban settlements, the rural population
seems surprisingly small.

A more realistic basis for analysis of Libya's urban population
is to consider all settlements with populations of over 5,000 (see
Table 6.1). While these figures undoubtedly exaggerate the true
urban populations of several settlements by including rural dwellers
within ill-defined municipal boundaries, the overall results are probably little affected. On this basis, in 1973, 55.9 percent of Libya's
population lived in settlements with over 5,000 inhabitants, 51.6 percent in settlements with over 10,000 inhabitants, and 49.2 percent in
settlements with over 20,000 inhabitants. Moreover, comparison of
1966 and 1973 populations revealed an astonishing average annual
urban growth rate of 16 percent.[7]

The urban hierarchy in Libya has long been dominated by the
capital city of Tripoli, the natural focus of the country's most populous and productive area, and the chief port. Tripoli's population
increased from 130,000 in 1954 to 552,000 in 1973, or from 12 percent to 25 percent of the total population. Even more remarkable,
however, has been the growth of Tripoli Muhafada, the administrative
district embracing Tripoli and a number of small settlements within
its sphere of influence; here the population increased by 79 percent
between 1964 and 1973. Although the area of the Tripoli Muhafada
represents little more than 1 percent of Libya, it now accommodates
over 31 percent of the total population. In reality, a number of other
growing urban centers within 50 to 60 kilometers of Tripoli (including

Zāwiyah) lie outside the boundaries of the Muhafada, and the enormous social and economic importance of the Tripoli region is, if anything, underestimated by these figures. An urban region is thus emerging whose attraction is already powerful and gaining momentum. The problems raised by such regions are familiar enough in the developing world, but in a country the size of Libya, with an average density of 1.3 persons per square kilometer, overconcentration raises particularly acute problems for national economic and social development.

The degree of primacy exercised by Tripoli is not, however, as complete as in some African states,[8] because of the existence of a second important urban center in Benghazi, whose population increased from 70,000 in 1954 to 264,000 in 1973. At one time it seemed that Benghazi might rival Tripoli when it became the administrative headquarters of the oil industry, a growing port, and the natural regional focus for Libya's second most populous region in northern Cyrenaica. From 1951 until 1963 (when Libya became a unitary state), Benghazi was also the joint federal capital with Tripoli. For a short period in the early 1960s, Benghazi actually grew more rapidly than Tripoli.[9] But between 1964 and 1973 the Muhafada of Benghazi recorded only 46 percent increase in population compared with 79 percent for the Muhafada of Tripoli. There are also a number of smaller towns in the eastern provinces which act as quite important local alternatives for rural migrants, including Derna, El Marj, Tubrug, and Al Baydā. Nevertheless, Benghazi remains incomparably the most important city in Libya after Tripoli, with about 12 percent of the national population and 18 percent of the country's "establishments," defined as buildings where some kind of economic activity is conducted.[10] The high degree of spatial imbalance created by the two coastal regions around Tripoli and Benghazi is graphically illustrated by the fact that with less than 10 percent of the area of Libya, between them they account for 92 percent of the people, 14 of the 15 towns with over 10,000 inhabitants, and 86 percent of agricultural production.[11]

NATIONAL URBAN DEVELOPMENT STRATEGY

In spite of the implications of rapid urban growth and the continuing domination of Tripoli and Benghazi, no integrated plan for the development of Libya's network of urban centers was given serious consideration until the mid-1970s. Government intervention was largely confined to the commissioning of a series of physical master plans for individual towns and to a policy of equitable distribution of services and development benefits throughout the country. In recent years this policy has been manifested in attempts to locate manu-

facturing industries in a large number of towns. The physical master
plans themselves were instrumental in bringing modern services,
such as sewerage, fresh water, and electricity, to even the smallest
towns, and attempts were made to rationalize road systems and urban
land use and to build modern housing. On the other hand, they failed
to examine the different growth potential of towns in a national context
and to give positive encouragement to those most favorably located.
The increasing domination of the country by Tripoli also constituted
a strong argument for some overall national urban strategy, which
was largely ignored. Thus the master plan for Tripoli published in
1969 rejected the idea of developing a series of satellite growth centers around the city that would limit congestion but allow future economic development to enjoy the advantages of proximity to the metropolitan core. The master plan envisaged some growth in centers such
as Azīzīyah, Zanzur, Tagiura, and Zāwiyah, but in the main provided
for the continued expansion of Tripoli. [12]

A costly example of the absence of a decisive policy towards
urban growth was the abortive attempt to establish a new national
capital at Al Baydā between 1954 and 1969. The chosen location had
some significance for the Libyan people since it was near a famous
Sanussi zawiya or religious school,* but in other respects Al Baydā
was a most unsuitable place from which to administer a disunited
population in a vast territory. Although this became clear early on,
the pretense was maintained and for several years Al Baydā somehow
grew with the location of some (but not all) government departments
and other services in the town. Much inefficiency and frustration
resulted in the division of responsibilities between Tripoli, Al Baydā,
and sometimes Benghazi. At the time master plans were being prepared for the towns of Libya, Al Baydā was still struggling to become
the national capital. In 1969, the Revolutionary Council finally declared
Tripoli the capital of Libya, leaving a town of some 40,000 people
at Al Baydā.

A further example of this absence was the process by which oil
exporting terminals became established in Libya between 1961 and
1968 (see Table 6.2). A network of pipelines was constructed, not
all of which took the shortest route to the sea, and five loading terminals were built. This extraordinary pattern was the result of
rivalry among the seven original producing groups of companies and
may also have had something to do with an attempt to distribute

---

*The Sanussis played an important part in resisting the Italian
conquest of Libya, and their exiled leader became king after independence in 1951.

TABLE 6.2

Oil Exporting Terminals in Libya

Year	Terminal	Established by
1961	Marsa Brega	Esso
1962	Es Sider	Oasis/Panam
1964	Ras Lanuf	Mobil/Gelsenberg/Amoseas
1967	Marsa el Hariga	British Petroleum/Hunt
1968	Zuetina	Occidental

Source: Data compiled by the author.

revenues between the two provinces of Tripolitania and Cyrenaica, whose boundary then passed between Marsa Brega and Ras Lanuf. It is true that the four terminals in the Gulf of Sirte practice offshore loading by underwater pipelines and therefore represent relatively little capital investment. In the absence of natural harbors, offshore loading was probably the best initial arrangement since permanent harbors would have been extremely costly and taken a long time to construct. The four terminals, however, represent a wasted opportunity to concentrate activities and create a potential pole of development which might have been more relevant to the needs of the country. Today, Marsa Brega is emerging as a small town with some 4,000 inhabitants, and a proper artificial port is being completed. A petrochemical complex is also being added to the existing oil refinery and the liquefied natural gas plant. Marsa Brega is not likely to grow very large, but with explicit plans to encourage its development in every possible way, it could grow into a lively new town in a part of Libya which was almost empty 15 years ago. A fifth oil loading terminal was established at Marsa el Hariga near Tubrug because direct inshore loading of tankers was essential for oil from the Serir field due to its high viscosity, which made offshore pumping problematic. By 1967, there was thus a strong argument for building a large artificial oil port on the Gulf of Sirte, but no decision has yet been made to build one.

TOWN PLANNING

In 1966, five years after the first oil had been exported from Libya, the Ministry of Planning and Development initiated an extensive urban planning program designed both to regulate urban expansion and to make the benefits of the country's new found wealth accessible to as many citizens as possible. A number of Western consultants were commissioned to prepare master plans for all the major urban centers in the country, including, notably, Tripoli and Benghazi. Most of the plans were published in the following three years, accompanied by inventory reports which still provide a valuable source of data on the urban scene in Libya in the early 1960s; the inventory reports on the Tripoli region, for example, ran to 11 volumes.[13] The planning horizon for the master plans extended some 20 years into the late 1980s. Considering the detailed nature of the plans and the spectacular rate of change brought about by oil revenues such a time span was probably too long.

A complex range of interrelated factors had to be considered when Libya's urban master plans were devised. Assumptions had to be made concerning the social implications of oil revenues with regard to future ownership of motor vehicles and the demand for recreational space and leisure amenities. Government policy was to develop manufacturing industry as a means of diversifying the economy and creating employment opportunities. At the same time agriculture was to be encouraged in an attempt to check migration to the towns. Every citizen was to be provided with adequate services in the fields of education, health, housing, and transport. In this there was great emphasis on modernization, yet the Islamic cultural heritage of the country was to be somehow reasserted. The production of a physical plan for the next two decades or so would have to take account of the development potential of each urban center in its regional context, bearing in mind local resources of soils, water, manpower, and raw materials, all of which tend to be scarce in Libya. In general, the data for such assessments was inadequate and was further complicated by the problem of forecasting changes in the national economy that might affect the level of demand for goods and services in the future. The proper evaluation of all these factors offered plenty of scope for errors of judgment, even among the most skillful planners. It is not surprising, therefore, that the original plans have been drastically modified in many cases and sometimes effectively abandoned. Even so, most Libyan towns today show some evidence of the planning ideas of the 1960s, for example, in the form of industrial estates or neighborhood schemes. Without the broad guidelines laid down in the master plans, the physical expansion of Libyan towns would have been uncontrolled and chaotic in the 1960s and 1970s.

It seems regrettable that the master plans of 1967-69 appear to have largely overlooked the possibility of adapting traditional urban styles to the needs of the modern world. With substantial oil revenues to spend, the Libyans might have insisted on the exploration of new ways of combining old and new, as some imaginative architects and planners have attempted in other parts of the Islamic world. One exception was the plan for Sabhah, which recognized the value of traditional building styles in a desert environment, and recommended their continuation.[14] Elsewhere, however, Western ideas appear to have been introduced wholesale and local forms abandoned uncritically, particularly with respect to residential buildings. Other features of the master plans reflected universal planning techniques for coming to terms with motor vehicles—ring roads, straight, wide streets, car parks, and private garages. As a result, the distinctive townscapes and vibrant ethos of the Libyan-Arab town is being replaced by the dull but functional layout characteristic of the motor age all over the world. The master plans of 1967-68 were not, in fact, the first major urban plans attempted in Libya since independence. In February 1963, the town of Barce (El Marj) in Cyrenaica had been devastated by an earthquake, and a comprehensive plan for the reconstruction of a new town, four kilometers to the west of the ruined site, was published in 1964.[15] The new town of El Marj was subsequently built, closely following the master plan. A Libyan agency, the Barce Reconstruction Organisation, instructed the planners to incorporate a number of concepts in the new town that were fundamentally Western in origin, such as detached houses with front gardens wherever possible, neighborhood centers with a range of facilities, and a grid network of wide roads.

In spite of certain other weaknesses, the 1960s master plans introduced some important ideas regarding the old city cores, or medinas, particularly in Tripoli and Benghazi. The question of what to do with these ancient quarters, many of which are the inheritors of noble urban traditions, is being faced by planners throughout North Africa. While Libyan cities do not possess the cultural and aesthetic richness of many Islamic cities in the Maghreb, such as Fez, Marrakesh, Tlemcen, or Kairouan, their ancient medinas unquestionably incorporate some structures well worth preserving. In certain North African cities, conservation of old quarters is proceeding in a self-conscious attempt to preserve a tourist amenity, but in Libya conservation may be justified on different grounds. First, the old quarters represent a stock of housing eminently suited to the social needs of their inhabitants, and, second, they provide a rare link with Libya's precolonial past. Thus the street pattern of part of old Tripoli shows basic alignments laid out by the Romans, while the funduks, or inns, and the traditional suqs are relics of a magnificent commercial past. The problem is that such areas are generally congested (with densities of between 600 and 700 persons per hectare), and much of the housing is below standard. Narrow streets and alleys prevent the circulation of motor vehicles and make it difficult to provide services such as electricity and sewerage. Furthermore, facilities such as playgrounds, schools, and clinics are generally inadequate. The condition of such areas deteriorated during the Italian administration (1912-43), when they were largely ignored. The largest and most problematic medinas are in Tripoli and Benghazi, but, in both, the master plans recommended selective preservation of certain "positive features," such as squares, pedestrian precincts, and neighborhood life, [16] together with some form of controlled urban renewal. [17] The solution proposed is thus a sensible compromise between the "living museum" approach and total demolition.

MANUFACTURING INDUSTRY

Besides its involvement in infrastructural development and town planning, a second broad area in which government activity is affecting urbanization in Libya is in the development of manufacturing industry. Before the Revolution of September 1969, the Libyan economy was primarily a services economy dependent upon foreign trade sustained by large oil revenues. In the large cities in particular, a vast tertiary sector continued to expand. Although the government tried to encourage industry it had no policy of major direct involvement. The usual subsidies and tax exemptions had failed to create large-scale industries; in 1970 there were only 213 firms, out of a total of 2,000, with over 20 workers. Furthermore, the majority of these enterprises were in Tripoli and Benghazi. Their activities were largely confined to processing food, drinks, and tobacco, furniture making, and some traditional manufactures, such as carpets and leather products. Altogether, capital investment in industry was modest compared with investments in commerce, services, and construction. Between 1962 and 1969, the total investment in manufacturing industry amounted to $U.S. 143 million, of which the private sector contributed $U.S. 128 million. [18] These figures may be compared with some $U.S. 300 million allocated to the industrial sector in 1974-75 alone. [19]

Since 1969, the revolutionary government has embarked upon a vigorous policy of industrial development, with a view to reducing the country's dependence on foreign trade and oil revenues. Progress has been impressive, and manufacturing industry now accounts for 10 percent of the national income and employs more than one-sixth of the active population. A large number of foreign consultants from all over the world have been engaged to establish manufacturing units, often using some of the most advanced production techniques available. In the First Five-Year Plan, 1963-68, some $U.S. 22 million was allocated to industry, or about 3.5 percent of the budget. In the 1976-80 Plan of Economic and Social Transformation, over 15 percent of total investment is allocated to industry, amounting to $U.S. 3.634 million.[20] It is important to appreciate that this enormous industrial program is still in its infancy, and its impact on urban growth has yet to be fully felt. Obviously, when the 1960s urban master plans were devised, industrial development on this scale was not foreseen, while the emphasis on heavy industry is relatively recent.

Table 6.3 indicates the location of some 40 new industrial plants known to have been completed or under construction in 1971-74. Of these, about half were in or near Tripoli and Benghazi. One estimate suggested that 40 percent of the increase in employment between 1972 and 1975 would be concentrated in these two regions.[21] The projects listed represent an unknown number of jobs, possibly about 6,000. There are in addition a number of other projects currently under discussion or being actively planned in Libya, some of which are extremely ambitious. These include plans for a huge iron and steel works near Misratah, tractor and truck assembly, fertilizer, tire, and heavy chemical works, and electric goods manufacturing plants. Several of these might be located outside the two major urban areas, but some are already earmarked for location in Tripoli and Benghazi. Although the government is committed in principle to locating industry elsewhere, the existence of such large markets is bound to provide strong economic arguments against the small towns. Also, the ports of both Tripoli and Benghazi are being currently expanded and modernized. As industry expands in Libya it is likely to reinforce the dominance of Tripoli and Benghazi and the coastal zone in general. Alternative poles of development might be encouraged by vigorous planning, for example, around the new ports of Misratah, Derna, and Marsa Brega, but they will always be overshadowed by their powerful neighbors.

A major problem facing Libya is the shortage of manpower of all kinds, and expansion of the industrial sector, together with the attendant infrastructure, is exacerbating the shortage. In recent years, Libya has recruited guestworkers from Egypt, Tunisia, Morocco, and Chad. At the same time, the well-paid opportunities in the new factories are continuing to attract young men from the rural areas into the towns. Since about 1964, the government has made strenuous efforts to improve agriculture and raise living standards in the rural areas, but the measures have not been wholly successful in checking migration. Far more attention needs to be given to the provision of good housing and services in rural areas—at least as

TABLE 6.3

Examples of Industrial Projects Completed or under Construction
in Libya, 1971-74

Location	Industrial Project
Western provinces	
Tripoli	Dairying
	Flour milling
	Fish canning
	Fruit and vegetable canning
	Leather tanning
	Shoes
	Prefabricated housing
	Scrap iron smelting
	Dry batteries
Azīzīyah	Glassware
Gharyān	Ceramics and pottery
Homs	Sardine canning
	Cement
Misrātah	Shoes
	Carpets
Zanzur (near Tripoli)	Asbestos
	Fish canning
	Textiles
Zāwiyah	Oil refining
Zlīten	Flour milling
	Date syrup processing
Zuwārah	Sardine canning
	Desalination plant

(continued)

good as those available in the small towns. As far as services are
concerned, the district center concept proposed for the oasis of
Misrātah may prove workable where a dense rural population is
located in close proximity to a town. In this plan, Misrātah municipality embraces town and country alike, and services are provided
for rural dwellers in five district centers and in 15 neighborhood

TABLE 6.3 (continued)

Location	Industrial Project
Eastern provinces	
Benghazi	Dairying
	Bricks
	Cement
	Lime
	Prefabricated housing
	Electric cables
	Steel pipes
	Pipe fittings
	Paper bags
Derna	Clothing
El Marj	Flour milling
	Wool spinning and weaving
Marsa Brega	Petrochemicals (ammonia, ethylene, methanol)
Zuetina	Desalination plant
Hon	Date processing
Sabhah	Flour milling
	Tomato processing

Source: Middle East Economic Digest (London weekly, various dates, 1971-74).

centers at the village level. District centers will include primary schools, post office, police station, shops, and market.[22] Some of these amenities would clearly have convenience value, but it is doubtful whether the shops and market in the district centers would ever provide an acceptable alternative to Misratah itself, which was visited frequently by the inhabitants of the oasis even in the pre-oil era. On the three market days a week, about one in ten of the entire population of Misratah's hinterland appear to have entered the town.[23] Such intensive interaction between town and country probably characterized certain other Libyan urban centers, but with the gradual disappearance of traditional periodic marketing local interaction is giving way to social and economic contacts with other centers farther afield, often with the two major cities themselves.

CONCLUSION

The absence of a coherent overall policy for urban growth in Libya has resulted in costly mistakes and, above all, in missed opportunities for national development planning. With fewer than 100 settlements with more than 2,000 inhabitants, and only 30 with over 5,000 inhabitants, there was a real possibility of drawing up an integrated national plan for settlement in Libya. Such a plan might have gone some way towards reconciling various government attitudes towards the urban sector both before and after the Revolution of 1969. There was a desire to achieve balanced growth between Tripolitania and Cyrenaica, in the interests of national unity. The growth of Tripoli in particular at the expense of the rest of the country was deplored, at least, in theory. At the same time the importance of market forces were recognized in the drive to enlarge and diversify manufacturing industry. The benefits of oil revenues were to be taken to the people in the form of improved urban amenities and modern housing and services in towns of all sizes. No doubt the chief reason why no national plan was adopted to coordinate these objectives was that it did not seem necessary. The rate of urban growth and change was nearly always underestimated, as was the potency of the geographical and economic forces favoring the Mahafadas of Tripoli and Benghazi.

The need to take some of the pressure off Tripoli and Benghazi and move in the direction of decentralization can best be met by encouraging the growth of satellite centers. These should be those existing settlements that are already experiencing strong growth as a result of proximity to the major cities and other geographical advantages. Throughout the Middle East, certain axes of development can be identified where the forces of growth are powerful.[24] In the case of Tripoli, the coastal highway eastward is clearly such an axis, and planned development in this direction would enjoy the advantages of proximity to the coast, good communications, and a productive agricultural hinterland. In time, an almost unbroken low density linear city might develop between Tripoli and Misratah (over 200 kilometers). Misratah is today the third city in Libya; it has grown remarkably since 1966 and is likely to continue to do so as the new iron and steel works is built and the port at Casr Ahmed comes into full operation. The Misratah region has also been the scene of large-scale agricultural development projects. The problems associated with Benghazi are less acute, but the region of strongest growth

potential again lies towards the east, along the main road as far as
Derna. A possible corridor of development lies between Al Bayda
and Derna, and eventually the Benghazi-Derna axis might evolve as
a populous urban region.[25] Several towns along this axis have high
growth potential and enjoy one of Libya's most favorable environments. The deliberate encouragement of growth along the Tripoli-
Misratah and Benghazi-Derna axes would accelerate a trend which
is probably inevitable in the very long term. Properly planned and
controlled, such growth could alleviate congestion around the two
major cores and provide an ideal context for proposed industrial
expansion. It has been suggested that the central zone along the Gulf
of Sirte should become the focus for future urban development efforts
because of the increasing intensity of interaction between the two
metropolitan cores.[26] Sirte or Marsa Brega would presumably become
the foci for urban growth. Superficially, this is attractive from a
national viewpoint, but in the absence of any evidence of growth
forces in the region at present it would be unlikely to have much
success.

As to the smaller towns away from the coastal development
axes, a great deal of preliminary work is necessary before the formulation of an integrated plan. There is particular need to understand
the functions of small urban and semi-urban centers in the 5,000-
10,000 population range. Municipal boundaries should be devised to
permit the collection of meaningful statistics relating to urban areas
so that the role of migration can be properly analyzed even in the
smallest towns. The provision of services and local administration
are likely to remain the chief functions of most small towns. Some,
however, could be revitalized by their integration into agricultural
development schemes providing a range of high quality services and
light agro-based industries, such as mechanical engineering and food
processing. A few small towns might specialize in tourism if the
government of Libya ever decided to encourage a tourist industry. It
is important to realize that very few of the small urban centers are
destined to grow. Libya, in common with many developing countries,
will never evolve what was once regarded as a "normal" or "balanced" urban hierarchy.[27] The pattern for the future seems already
established in the emergence of two dominant metropolitan regions
and a scattering of rather small urban centers. The consolidation
and survival of these small towns should be given very high priority
in any future national strategy for urbanization.[28]

NOTES

1. United Nations, Statistical Yearbook 1972 (New York:
United Nations Publication, 1973), p. 60.

2. United Nations, <u>Demographic Yearbook 1973</u> (New York: United Nations Publications, 1973), pp. 82-84.

3. Libyan Arab Republic, <u>1973 Population Census Preliminary Results</u> (Tripoli: Ministry of Planning, Census and Statistical Department, 1973), p. ii.

4. United Nations, <u>Demographic Yearbook 1976</u> (New York: United Nations Publication, 1977), p. 161.

5. United Nations, <u>Statistical Yearbook 1972</u>, op. cit., p. 60.

6. Libyan Arab Republic, op. cit., pp. 2-11.

7. S. El-Shakhs, "Urbanisation and Spatial Development in Libya," <u>Pan-African Journal</u> 8, no. 4 (1975): 373.

8. J. I. Clarke, "The Growth of Capital Cities in Africa," <u>Afrika Spectrum</u> 2 (1971): 33-40.

9. J. I. Clarke, "Oil in Libya, Some Implications," <u>Economic Geography</u> 39, no. 1 (1963): 40-59.

10. Libyan Arab Republic, <u>Housing and Establishment Census Preliminary Results</u> (Tripoli: Ministry of Planning, Census and Statistical Department, 1973), p. v.

11. El-Shakhs, op. cit., p. 371.

12. Whiting Associates International, <u>Tripoli Master Plan Final Report</u> (Tripoli: Ministry of the Interior, Libyan Arab Republic, 1969), pp. 143-48.

13. Whiting Associates International, <u>Tripoli Inventory Report</u>, 11 vols. (Tripoli: Ministry of Planning and Development, Kingdom of Libya, 1967).

14. Whiting Associates International, <u>Master Plan for the City of Sebha</u>, Southern Region Preliminary Report, no. 2 (Tripoli: Ministry of Planning and Development, Kingdom of Libya, 1967), p. 7.

15. Lublin McGaughy (Libya) Ltd., <u>Planning Report for the New Town of El Marj</u> (Benghazi: Barce Reconstruction Organisation, 1964), pp. 6-9.

16. Whiting Associates International, <u>Benghazi Master Plan Final Report</u> (Benghazi: Municipality of Benghazi, 1967), recommendation 4, n.p.

17. Whiting Associates International, <u>Tripoli Master Plan Final Report</u> (Tripoli: Ministry of the Interior, Libyan Arab Republic, 1969), pp. 143-48.

18. Central Bank of Libya, "The Post-Revolution Industrial Situation in the Libyan Arab Republic," <u>Economic Report</u> 14, nos. 7-12 (1974): 31-32.

19. Central Bank of Libya, op. cit., p. 32.

20. "Libya," in <u>The Middle East Yearbook 1978</u> (London: I. C. Magazines Ltd., 1978), p. 28.

21. M. Prasad, Provisional Projection of Population and Labour Force of Libyan Nationals 1972-1976 (Tripoli: International Labour Organisation, 1973), p. 4, quoted by Dilip K. Pal, "Urban Development Potential in Libya: A Speculation in Form and Structure" (Paper presented at the Faculty of Arts International Geographical Conference, University of Benghazi, March 1975), pp. 7-9.

22. McGaughy et al., Master Plan for the City of Misratah 1968 (Tripoli: Ministry of Planning and Development, Kingdom of Libya, 1967), pp. 17-21.

23. G. H. Blake, Misurata: A Market Town in Tripolitania Research Paper in Geography, no. 9 (Durham: University of Durham, 1968), p. 24.

24. J. Abu-Lughod, "Problems and Policy Implications of Middle Eastern Urbanisation," pp. 42-62, in Studies on Development Problems in Selected Countries of the Middle East, United Nations (New York: United Nations, 1972), p. 54.

25. Pal, op. cit., pp. 9-10.

26. El-Shakhs, op. cit., p. 384.

27. Abu-Lughod, op. cit., pp. 51-52.

28. A "National Settlement Pattern" study, completed in 1976, has been undertaken for the Libyan Government by Italconsult of Rome to provide the basis for future settlement planning.

7

URBANIZATION IN EGYPT: NATIONAL IMPERATIVES AND NEW DIRECTIONS

Salah El-Shakhs

INTRODUCTION

Egypt, the second most populous country in Africa after Nigeria, has had a long history of settlement patterns and urbanization. It was a birthplace of civilization long before any written history, when great cities and kingdoms grew up along the banks of the Nile River. Alexandria, now a metropolis of 2.5 million people, was established around 332 B.C. It was the second ranking city of the Roman Empire and, for a long time, a chief Mediterranean port. Cairo, the largest metropolis in Africa, with over 8 million people, has been the capital of Egypt for over 1,300 years.

During this long history, Egypt has been subjected, until recently, to a succession of foreign rule—Greek, Roman, Arab, Turkish, French, and British. Its population, which had its ups and downs in the Ancient and Medieval periods, has continued to grow rapidly in modern times; it has more than quadrupled since the first census was conducted in 1897, increasing from 9.7 million people then to around 40 million at present. Yet, throughout its history, Egypt's settlement pattern has been dictated largely by the Nile River. With very few exceptions, the population has clung to the river and settled within the narrow confines of its valley and delta.

Today, more than ever before, Egypt is faced with extreme pressures on both its spatial and economic systems. Such pressures are shaping recent policies on urbanization and national development in Egypt in relatively new directions, so as to break out of its historical spatial confines, expand the economy and its employment base, increase the urban system's capacity to absorb expected urban growth, and reduce the pressures on Cairo and Alexandria. This chapter reviews recent urbanization trends in Egypt and current government strategies on spatial development and discusses some of their potential impacts on the future of the urban system.

RECENT URBANIZATION TRENDS

Egypt's number one problem has often been cited as the rapid growth of its population.[1] Indeed, the population is estimated to have totaled only 2.4 million at the beginning of the nineteenth century. Since then, it has roughly quadrupled twice, once during the nineteenth century and again over the last seventy-five years. The fastest growth occurred during the last four decades, following an earlier period of relative stability, and is wholly due to natural increase. Immigration was almost negligible during that period. Except for a few temporary fluctuations, the birth rate has been stable, with a gently declining long-range trend. However, rapid improvements in public health, particularly in infant care, have caused a sharp decline in the death rate (Table 7.1). Both of these trends are expected to continue with further social improvements. The population is currently growing at an annual natural rate of increase of 2.6 percent, and, depending on the set of assumptions used, is projected to reach between 60 and 75 million by the end of this century (Table 7.2).

The impact of Egypt's rapid population growth on overall development is particularly acute in view of the inelastic supply of cultivated land and land suitable for settlement. The settled portion of the country represents only a fraction of its area (less than 5 percent). While the cultivated area is estimated to have expanded by less than 50 percent between 1875 and 1975, the population is estimated to have grown more than sixfold (Figure 7.1). Thus, the cultivated land per capita has dwindled from 0.8 to 0.16 feddan over that period. Such imbalance between land and population has resulted in the decline of per capita food production as well as the serious overpopulation of the Nile valley and its delta. With an estimated 1042 persons per square kilometer in 1975, this area has become one of the most densely populated in the world.[2]

Overpopulation in rural areas was partly responsible for the ever increasing migration to cities. Egypt's urban population (in towns of 20,000 people or more) has consequently grown eightfold, and its proportion to the total population has more than doubled since the turn of the century (Table 7.2). Currently, the annual rate of urban population growth is 4 percent.

This rapid shift towards urbanization has taken place with no major additions to the systems of settlements. "Not a single city has been established in Egypt since the opening of the Suez Canal (in the

TABLE 7.1

Selected Vital Statistics for Egypt, 1906-64
(per thousand)

Period	Birth Rate	Death Rate	Natural Increase	Infant Mortality per Thousand Live Births
1906-09	43.0	25.5	17.5	289
1910-14	42.0	26.2	15.8	352
1915-19	39.8	31.6	8.2	262
1920-24	42.8	25.8	17.0	140
1925-29	43.9	26.5	17.4	153
1930-34	42.7	27.0	15.7	163
1935-39	42.8	26.9	15.9	163
1940-44	39.6	26.8	12.8	160
1945-49	42.4	23.0	19.4	139
1950-54	43.6	18.7	24.9	134
1955-59	40.0	17.4	22.6	132
1960-64	42.5	16.0	26.5	117

Sources: Ministry of Housing and Construction, The Planning of Sadat City: Status Report No. 1 (Cairo: The Ministry, 1976), pp. 1-6; as compiled from the Arab Republic of Egypt Annual Yearbooks, Vital Statistics; and Clyde Kiser, "Demographic Studies of Selected Areas of Rapid Growth," Milbank Memorial Fund Quarterly (1944).

late nineteenth century) and the construction of its three cities."[3] Past urban growth has thus been primarily absorbed by existing cities and by previously nonurban settlements, which represented the only horizontal expansion of the urban system. Although 23 such settlements were added to the urban system between 1960 and 1975, the proportion of the urban population in the small and medium-size cities (under 100,000 population) has declined from 21.9 percent to 19.8 percent over the same period (Table 7.3). This means that the urban population continued to concentrate in the larger cities with over 100,000 population and, more specifically, in the two largest urban areas of Cairo and Alexandria. The share of these two areas of the total urban population increased from 59.6 percent to 61.5 percent over the same period.

TABLE 7.2

Population and Urban Growth, 1907-2000
(in millions)

Year	Total Population	Urban Population	Percent of Total	Rural Population	Percent of Total
1907	11.300	2.100	19	9.200	81
1927	14.200	3.800	23	10.400	77
1947	19.000	6.400	31	12.600	69
1967	30.600	12.900	42	17.700	58
1975	37.100	16.300	44	20.800	56
2000 (Estimates)[*]					
Low	60.000	35.000	58	25.000	42
Moderate	65.948	34.293	52	31.655	48
High	75.000	45.000	60	30.000	40

[*]The range of projected population represents the lowest and the highest estimates made for Egypt in a variety of sources, the figures most often used are the moderate estimates projected in the source document.

Source: Ministry of Housing, Report on Human Habitat in the Arab Republic of Egypt (Cairo: The Ministry, 1975), p. 15.

This trend towards urban concentration or primacy in the urban hierarchy is nothing new to Egypt. However, for a brief period between 1960 and 1966 it did seem that smaller towns and cities were growing faster than either Cairo or Alexandria.[4] One may speculate that the decentralization process which seems to have started in 1960 was temporarily disrupted by the migrations forced by the 1967 Middle East war. A look at the data, however, does not bear such conclusion. Cities under 100,000 population were not adversely affected by the war; indeed, some of them have been recipients of migrants from the Canal's three large cities. A more likely explanation of the short-lived trend towards urban deconcentration in the early 1960s lies in the temporary impact of an aggressive industrialization program on small cities, particularly in upper Egypt, and the building of the Aswan High Dam.

FIGURE 7.1

Population/Land Relationships, 1850–1974

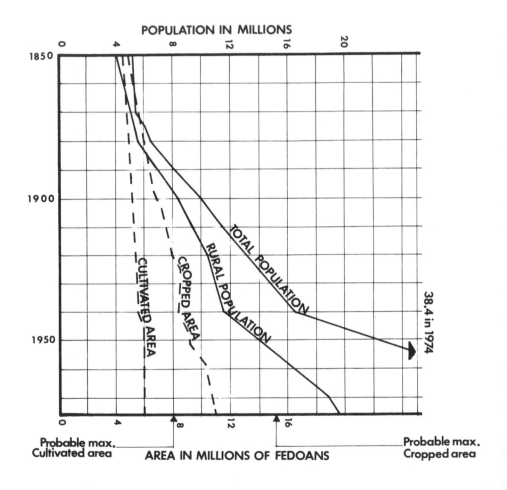

TABLE 7.3

Distribution of Urban Population and Urban Settlements, by Settlement Size, 1960–75

Settlement Size	1960		1966		1975	
	Number of Cities	Percent of Urban Population	Number of Cities	Percent of Urban Population	Number of Cities	Percent of Urban Population
20–50,000	44	15.2	53	18.3	53	11.3
50–100,000	9	6.7	10	5.7	19	8.5
100–250,000	10	18.5	10	13.3	9	9.6
250–500,000	0	0.0	2	4.5	5	9.1
500–1,000,000	0	0.0	0	0.0	0	0.0
1–2 million	1	17.2	1	14.7	0	0.0
Over 2 million	1	42.4	1	43.5	2	61.5
Total	65	100.0	77	100.0	88	100.0

Source: Data taken from several population census and estimate publications of the Central Agency for Mobilization and Statistics.

FIGURE 7.2

Urban Pattern and New Development Regions, 1976

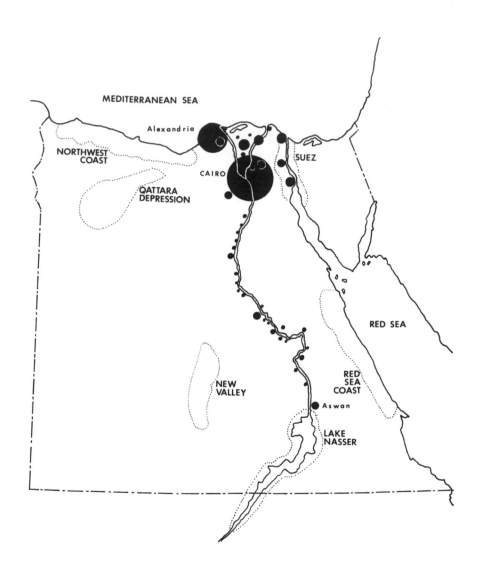

Source: Compiled by the author.

The distribution of urban growth continues its primate pattern by being skewed in favor of the two largest urban areas (Figure 7.2). The development of large regional urban centers to fill the gap between the two primate cities and the rest of the urban system has been conspicuously lagging behind national urbanization and industrialization trends. Not only did the regional centers' share, as a group, in the urban population decrease, but their individual population sizes have generally declined relative to that of Greater Cairo, with the notable exception of Aswan (Table 7.4).

This trend, however, is unlikely to continue indefinitely. The urban population is expected to reach between 35 and 45 million by the end of this century (Table 7.2). The capacity of Cairo and Alexandria to absorb a major part of this growth is very limited. Even if the populations of these two cities could grow to 17 and 5 million, respectively, the current projections for the year 2000,[5] there would still remain some 5 to 15 million additional urbanites who would have to be absorbed elsewhere within the urban system.

NATIONAL IMPERATIVES

It would, thus, be no exaggeration to say that Egypt is practically bursting at the seams. Its foremost spatial as well as economic problem can be characterized as the rapidly shrinking per capita supply of usable land resources. Inevitably, this has resulted not only in increasing migration to urban areas, as indicated earlier, but also in increasing fragmentation of agricultural land holdings and the creeping transfer of fertile land to nonagricultural uses, both urban and rural, particularly housing.

The majority of the present urban centers are located either in the midst of or near agricultural land. As a result of their growth, this vital resource is being eroded by urban uses almost as fast as new lands are being reclaimed at great expense and effort. The latter amounted to less than 1 million acres since 1952, including the major contribution of the Aswan High Dam. From this perspective, it could be argued that it is in a sense fortunate that urban growth has not been evenly distributed. While unequal distribution has created major problems in Cairo and, to a lesser extent, in Alexandria, it may have been a blessing in disguise. It syphoned most of the urban growth away from the smaller urban centers located in the midst of rural areas. In fact the planners for Greater Cairo took this into account in their recommendations for policies on migration and projections of Cairo's growth in 1966.[6]

Encroachment on agricultural land has therefore become a taboo in Egyptian development planning, at least at policy-making

TABLE 7.4

Comparative Growth of Large Cities and Regional Centers, 1960-75

Urban Centers	1960			1975			Percent Growth 1960-75
	Rank	Population (thousands)	Percent to Greater Cairo	Rank	Population (thousands)	Percent to Greater Cairo	
Greater Cairo	1	3,747	100.0	1	7,272	100.0	94
Alexandria	2	1,516	40.5	2	2,383	32.7	57
Port Said	3	245	6.5	3	328	4.5	34
Ismailiya	4	221	5.9	11	182	2.5	-17
Tanta	5	184	4.9	5	280	3.8	52
Mahala Al-Kubra	6	178	4.8	6	267	3.6	50
Mansurah-Talkhah	7	171	4.5	7	257	3.6	87
Suez	8	159	4.2	4	301	4.1	89
Asyut	9	127	3.4	10	188	2.6	48
Damanhur	10	126	3.3	12	176	2.5	39
Zagazig	11	124	3.3	9	211	2.9	70

El-Faiyum	12	102	2.7	13	167	2.3	63
Al-Minia	13	94	2.5	14	136	1.9	44
Beni Suef	14	79	2.1	16	107	1.5	36
Dsmietta	15	72	1.9	15	113	1.5	57
Zifta-Mitghamr	16	71	1.9	17	98	1.3	37
Suhag	17	62	1.7	20	85	1.2	37
Qena	18	57	1.5	21	83	1.1	44
Shibin El-Kom	19	55	1.5	23	81	1.1	47
Benha	20	53	1.4	18	94	1.3	79
Mallawi	21	52	1.4	24	73	1.0	38
Aswan	22	48	1.3	8	226	3.1	368
Kafr El-Dawar	23	43	1.2	32	53	0.7	22
Girga	24	42	1.1	35	51	0.7	20
Minuf	25	41	1.1	29	59	0.8	40

Source: Adapted from Ministry of Housing and Reconstruction, The Planning of Sadat City: Status Report #1 (Cairo: The Ministry, 1976).

levels. Enforcing such policy at the village levels, and even at the level of small urban centers, is quite a different matter. Egypt's 5000 or so villages, many of which are over 20,000 in population, are currently not subjected to building permit requirements or any other land-use controls, except crop regulations by the ministry of agriculture. Farmers continue, in large numbers, to allow new housing to be built on farm land for a variety of reasons. Primarily a change in the extended family structure (a break-up of a family or new family formations with children's marriage, etc.) or the desire of a prosperous urbanite member of the family to build a modern home and maintain roots in the village are responsible for such activity. Occasionally, tiny parcels of land, usable only as building sites, are sold outside the family in cases of extreme financial distress. In urban centers, the regulations, and severe penalties for violators, are frequently not enforced. Inadequate municipal planning, corruption, and most of all extreme housing shortages are responsible for the violations and the laxity of government reaction to them. Amendments to building laws have been passed frequently since 1960, in Cairo and elsewhere, exempting previous violators from the prescribed penalties, which included the demolition of the illegal structures. (The maximum penalty is currently limited to the payment of stipulated fines.) As long as extreme population pressures and housing shortages exist in the valley and the delta, it is impractical to expect the implementation of farm land preservation policies.

In the late 1960s, a strategy of "promoting the growth of those urban communities located on the fringes of agricultural areas, of which Cairo is one, and directing their expansion into the close-by desert areas" was implicitly followed in order to relieve population pressures on farm land.[7] Since then, however, Greater Cairo has added over 3 million people to its population (a growth of almost 60 percent in the last ten years), and its urban problems have reached crisis proportions. The area's infrastructure is so badly overloaded that in 1976 some prominent Egyptian architects and politicians attempted to promote a movement to abandon Cairo in favor of a new capital to be built in the desert.[8] Clearly, the long-term implications of current population and urbanization trends, were they allowed to continue, could be detrimental to Egypt's development goals. At best, the rate of population growth is expected to slow down only minimally in the foreseeable future.[9] Short of large-scale out-migration from Egypt, spatial reorganization and expansion become national imperatives in dealing with overpopulation and its consequences in both rural and urban areas.

SPATIAL DEVELOPMENT STRATEGIES
AND IMPLICATIONS

In the government's view, effective spatial reorganization means that "the life of the Egyptian people cannot remain confined to the Delta and the narrow valley of the Nile."[10] At least five new, primarily desert, "development regions" and three totally new desert cities (with expected ultimate population sizes of over half a million each) are presently at different stages of planning and development (Figure 7.2). Of the five regions, the Suez Canal was given top priority because of its existing urban infrastructure and apparent potential. The other regions include Aswan (and Lake Nasser), the New Valley, the North-West Coast and the Qattara Depression.[11]

Such direction may represent a compelling rationale for the future development of Egypt, in view of its spatial and economic imbalances. Indeed, policy makers and planners alike perceive these new developments as the symbols and face of the "new" and "modern" Egypt. They are conceived as a required "breakthrough" in the development process intended to transform the space-economy through:

preservation and expansion of the scarce supply of available land resources;

expansion of the industrial base of the economy with an increasing reliance on foreign technology and capital investment, as embodied in President Sadat's 1973 "open door policy"; and

moderation of the mounting population pressure on the almost dysfunctional national capital and the rapidly growing second city, Alexandria.[12]

Thus, one of the major explicit objectives of these strategies is to redirect future urban growth away from the two primate cities and other urban centers in the densely population rural areas. It is questionable, however, even if the new developments succeed in achieving their projected growth, that the normal growth of existing centers (through natural increase) could be affected. The combined total absorption capacity of the new developments has been estimated at 5.3 million, which could go up to 11.5 million people at best. This includes 5 million in the Suez Canal region, 1 million in the northwest coast, 4 million in the other regions, and 1.5 million in the new cities.[13] This leaves an estimated 10 to 20 million new urbanites to be absorbed primarily by existing urban centers, including Cairo and Alexandria.

Whatever spatial distributional characteristics are finally achieved, however, it seems clear that the nature of future urban

development in Egypt will be forced into nonconventional directions
as a result of

extreme conditions of crowding and higher densities, not only in large
      cities but in smaller towns and villages as well;
radical departure from the traditionally close and symbiotic ties be-
      tween urban and rural areas;
altered environmental conditions in new desert developments unfamil-
      iar to the bulk of Egyptians and Egyptian planners; and
the increasing economic and technological orientation to the West in
      general, and the consequent reliance upon Western advisers,
      architects, and planners.

    It is virtually certain that the population and economic pressures
in Egypt, combined with a Western approach to development and modernization, will likely conspire to accentuate the differences among
the ecologically distinct but coexistent communities within the mosaic
of large Egyptian cities.[14] Visible and glaring disparities in wealth
and conspicuous consumption patterns between the majority of the
urban poor (including the middle classes who are squeezed between
runaway inflation and virtually fixed incomes) and the lucky few
(Western and Arab businessmen and tourists as well as Egyptians who
have benefited from the open door policy) have already precipitated
the "food riots" of January 1977. Only a blind optimist would lightly
dismiss the future potential for further social and political stresses
inherent in the new development equation. Such implications, however, are largely beyond the scope of this chapter.
    What interests us here are the implications of the new develop-
ment conditions on living patterns. Traditionally, Egyptians are not
desert dwellers, and the majority of urban settlements grew in close
proximity to bodies of water and rural hinterlands. Such proximity
has, traditionally, served several important functions in Egyptian
urban life. It has moderated the harsh environment, provided a
readily accessible substitute to public open space and recreational
activity (which is in short supply in urban areas), nurtured close ties
between urbanites and their rural origins, and provided opportunities
for income support and sources of cheap food supplies (particularly
for new migrants and the poor).[15] While the location of new development regions and desert cities will minimize such opportunities, the
demand for them is likely to be intensified as a result of increased
densities and housing occupancy ratios as well as new "modern"
construction standards.
    The open courtyards and private rooftops characteristic of
single-family rural and traditional urban housing in Egypt have all
but disappeared in new developments. Single-family housing consti-

tutes only a fraction (less than 5 percent) of the urban housing supply. Additionally, housing standards, in terms of space requirements, ceiling heights, and so on, have been on the decline in face of mounting shortage and escalating cost. In effect, the extent of activities that could be accommodated at home is decreasing, thus increasing the need for outdoor or public space.

This shift of activities from private to public space, in reaction to reduced space standards, will likely be further strengthened by increasing occupancy ratios. The expected excess growth in urban population without corresponding increases in the supply of housing, employment, and urban services will lead to a higher frequency of doubling-up and tripling-up of families in the same dwelling unit. The occupancy ratio is already as high as four persons per room in some parts of Cairo and Alexandria. This phenomenon is no longer limited to the low-income population, and its impact is felt by new migrants as well as newly wed couples.

Construction methods also raise many questions about the adequacy of new housing, particularly in a desert environment. Economy, technology, modernity, and the rapid pace of development all point to mass-produced multi-story structures of reinforced concrete and burnt brick, with minimal capacity for heat insulation. Economically produced prefabricated units of similar materials are now gaining a foothold in new development in Helwan and elsewhere. This type of construction could only add to the forces that tend to drive the families outside their home for more and more activities.

Traditionally, the crowded urban population tended to maintain close relationships with their home villages or those of their relatives and ancestors. Aside from its social aspects, such close interaction provided access to more open and more natural environments, particularly for children, and compensated for the shortcomings of urban environments. Its frequency, however, is greater when these villages are parts of the city's hinterlands and within easy access from it. The population of new desert cities and regions, which spring out of no such populated hinterlands, are likely to lose the benefits of similar interaction. This is particularly true when settlements are located away from the valley and the delta.

A large number of people in the traditional cities and towns also derive economic income support from their proximity to rural hinterlands. This could take many forms ranging from access to cheap or free food supplies from their villages to actually engaging in subsistence agricultural activities. Such support will be hard to come by in desert cities, at least in their formative stages, and will cause hardships for the poor and new rural migrants.

In conclusion, planners must recognize that the rapidly growing urban population in Egypt will increasingly face radical changes in their traditional living patterns, both in old and new developments. Inevitable increases in densities and rates of occupancy, coupled with declining space standard and reliance on modern construction technology and design, will tend to force the population to shift more of their activities from private to public space. However, such public accommodations (both existing and planned) are also in short supply. Thus, people will increasingly be faced with the choice of either curtailing their activities to the extent that private and public accommodations can sustain or adapting their use of any available public space to suit their needs. Experience shows that the latter alternative is more likely.

New developments in the desert will impose some additional constraints on their prospective populations by virtue of their isolation from a well-developed rural hinterland, their inhospitable climate, and their modern design and construction techniques. Although normally such conditions may discourage their growth, desert cities will likely exceed their planned densities as a result of the sheer magnitude of urban growth. It is the populations of these new developments, therefore, that will face the greatest challenge to the traditional patterns of urban living in Egypt.

NOTES

1. CAPMAS, Population and Development (Cairo: Central Agency for Public Mobilization and Statistics, 1973).

2. Ministry of Housing and Reconstruction, The Planning of Sadat City: Status Report #1 (Cairo: The Ministry, 1976), pp. 1-5.

3. President Anwar El-Sadat, October Working Paper (Cairo: Government Press, 1974).

4. S. El-Shakhs, "National Factors in the Development of Cairo," The Town Planning Review 42, no. 3 (July 1972): 236.

5. R. J. Watkins, "Metropolitan Cairo and Alexandria," projection memorandum on Cairo's growth, Ministry of Housing and Reconstruction, September 1976.

6. Greater Cairo Planning Commission, General Plan for Greater Cairo (Cairo: G.C.P.C., 1970).

7. El-Shakhs, op. cit., p. 247.

8. For problems of transportation, housing, etc., in Metropolitan Cairo, see John Waterbury, Egypt: Burdens of the Past, Options for the Future (Hanover, N.H.: The American Universities Field Staff, 1973).

9. Watkins, op. cit.

10. El-Sadat, op. cit.

11. General Organization for Physical Planning, Suez Canal Regional Plan (Cairo: G.O.P.P., 1976), p. 4.

12. Advisory Committee for Reconstruction, Terms of Reference for the Planning of Sadat City (Cairo: Ministry of Housing, August 1975), pp. 5, 6.

13. G.O.P.P., op. cit., p. 47; and Ministry of Housing and Reconstruction, op. cit., pp. 1, 16.

14. For an account of such multiplicity of communities within large Egyptian cities, see Janet Abu-Lughod, "Developments in North African Urbanism: The Process of Decolonization," in Urbanization and Counter-Urbanization, ed. B. J. L. Berry (Beverly Hills: Sage, 1976), pp. 202-05.

15. S. El-Shakhs, "New Cities in the Desert: Pattern of Forced Urbanization and Modernization in Egypt" (Paper delivered at the Middle East Studies Association's annual conference, New York City, November 1977).

Part Three

WEST AFRICA—
URBAN TRANSFORMATION

Planning as an approach to the process of development and transformation is not without its problems, particularly in countries that until recently were dependent on colonial administrations and that constituted elements in much larger systems. Aside from the shortages in experienced manpower, lingering dependency on expatriates, and the organizational difficulties of institutionalizing the planning function, the issues to be addressed are quite complex. Furthermore, there is a paucity of tested experiences and research results that may help in determining choices among alternative development strategies.

The chapters in this section provide important insights into the process of spatial and economic transformation in a number of West African nations: Upper Volta, Ivory Coast, Ghana, and Nigeria. The focus is on evaluating a number of development approaches at both the national and local levels. They all point out the crucial role of institutions, political development, and the role of government in the planning process.

Political development plays a crucial role in the process of transformation, not only nationally but also at the local levels of individual communities, as Wunsch indicates in his study of Ghana. Micropolitical development focused on indigenous African institutions can help evolve such traditional institutions in such a way as to better serve continuity and conflict resolution. Too rapid a shift to modern institutions may result in fragmentation and discontinuity, particularly in countries with diverse populations, like those of West Africa.

Population diversity and potential social conflicts are not the only issues to be addressed by political development. The West African nations share many imbalances and inequities which resulted partly from the nature of the development process itself. Sectional imbalances, interregional inequalities, and intraurban inequities, while not unique to West Africa, are all important issues of transformation which require major political decisions and planning strategies.

The Ivory Coast attempted to deal with such imbalances (reluctance of Ivorians to stay in low-income agricultural jobs, disparity between the north and the south, excessive urbanization, etc.) through a novel growth center approach. This approach involved the alternating infusion of concentrated doses of investment in infrastructure in connection with revolving National Independence Festivals among designated cities. In Nigeria, the political decision to divide the country into 19 states may yet prove to be the most effective approach to creating a more balanced urban hierarchy and to mitigating interregional disparities. Approaches designed to deal with urban imbalances range from the establishment of a new national capital in Nigeria to squatter upgrading schemes in Ouagadougou.

All of these approaches represent the West African nations' political and planning responses to their inherited development problems and to their rapid pace of urbanization. They represent experiments whose results and long-range impacts on their spatial systems have not yet been finally tested. If one thing is clear, however, it is that the impact of political and planning decisions is likely to be far reaching in their formative stages. The chapters that follow provide a needed input into the evaluation process of possible alternative approaches to orderly transformation.

8

POLITICAL DEVELOPMENT AND
PLANNING IN GHANA:
A COMPARATIVE STUDY OF
TWO MEDIUM CITIES

James S. Wunsch

INTRODUCTION

Until recently, political scientists concerned with less developed states tended to focus on the macro or systemic level of public affairs. This tendency no doubt related to the central government's preeminent role in economic planning and international affairs, its control of legal sovereignty, and its apparent position at the head of national, social, and institutional modernization and political integration. It represented, however, an incomplete perspective.

Fortunately, a growing and multidisciplinary body of research and literature pertinent to micropolitical development has contributed to a more sophisticated conception of development and its problems.[1] For example, the implementation of development plans requires effective local institutions to supplement national-level expertise and personnel;[2] constraints on national government resources limit that government's ability to penetrate unilaterally to all levels and in all areas of policy implementation;[3] while central government sovereignty is a legal fact, the realities of administration in all systems lead influence to gravitate to proximate institutions and actors.[4] National modernization, integration, and social change rarely, if ever, appear

This research was carried out during 1971-72, under funding by the Fulbright-Hays Doctoral Dissertation Research Abroad Program and by the Africa Studies Program of Indiana University. Immediate supervision was provided by the Institute for African Studies of the University of Ghana, Legon.

as a unified process of steady movement along predictable dimensions which duplicate the experience of other states but will be unique to each region (perhaps to each state), and the outcome of this process will be determined by events and actors throughout developing societies rather than merely at the capitals.[5] Finally, several recent publications suggest that exclusive development of national-level institutions may impede linkage and responsiveness, sustain regional inequality, and increase vulnerability to domestic forms of colonialism.[6]

Political change has a variety of pathologies. Political institutions have, at times, simply stagnated and failed to function effectively.[7] In some unfortunate situations, political institutions have been on balance a liability for national economic growth and political integration; in some areas, political change has stimulated ethnic conflict, facilitated corruption, and wasted scarce resources.[8] Identification of variables conducive to the growth of institutions able to resolve conflict and organize collective action is a critically important task in contemporary Africa.

This chapter will focus on urbanization and political institutional development in two urbanizing areas in central Ghana. It will assess and analyze the nature and extent of political development in each city and explore a variety of urban environmental characteristics for their relationship to local political growth.

Political development will be considered in a structurally neutral perspective, emphasizing capacity rather than form.[9] With this as a general framework, modern political theory suggests several activities that all developed polities must perform. These activities include rule initiation and application, conflict resolution, organizing and implementing of collective action, and developing and sustaining public-private linkages.[10] Each town will be evaluated analytically for the extent to which its formal and informal political institutions perform these activities.

Among the urban environmental factors to be considered are each area's characteristics before rapid growth occurred; the nature and patterns of growth experienced by each area; economic base and situation; ethnic and general social characteristics; size and settlement patterns; and extent and type of central government presence. Apparent relationships among these variables will be explored for insights to scholars of African urbanization, political change, and development, and to public policy makers in areas pertinent to development planning.

TECHIMAN

Site and Situation

Techiman is a town of some 12,000-14,000 population located at the intersection of the Nkronza-Sunyani road and the Kumasi-Kintampo road, 80 miles north of Kumasi. The Kintampo road continues northward to Tamale where it meets the major southward routes of migration and trade from northern Ghana and Upper Volta. This places Techiman on one of Ghana's major north-south roads; so for many years a great deal of commerce and trade has passed through the town.

Urbanization Process

Historically, Techiman was the site of a major market. However, when the state was defeated by the Ashante Empire in 1877, the market was destroyed, and the people left the area for a self-imposed exile in Bondoukou-Gyaman State in the Ivory Coast. In 1896, after the British conquest of Ashanti, the Techiman people returned to the area.[11]

The rebuilding of the market waited, however, until 1944. Then, the new Omanhene, Nana Akumfi Ameyaw, and several elders set out to recreate the former market. After substantial preparation, including travel throughout Ghana as well as trips to Upper Volta and Mali, newspaper advertisements, and building many structures to shelter the traders, the market was reestablished. At first it grew slowly, and on many occasions during its early period the traditional council bought unsold goods to sustain and stimulate its progress. By the mid-1950s it had become the largest market between Kumasi and Tamale, and it stimulated comparable growth in the town's population, size, economy, and ethnic diversity. By 1970, the proportion born outside Techiman Traditional State's area was 49 percent, and the non-Bono proportion was approximately 40 percent.[12]

The market meets every Friday and is one of Ghana's major sites for wholesaling yams and plantain, two of its staple crops. Trucks regularly come from Kumasi, Tamale, Obuasi, and Dunkwa, with a few from as far as Accra, as well as from Upper Volta, Mali, and the Ivory Coast. On a typical market day, several thousand people arriving on more than one hundred trucks and many small buses will participate.

The market has affected Techiman dramatically in several respects. Since its reestablishment, town population has grown

TABLE 8.1

Techiman: Population and Structural Growth

Year	Population	Number of Structures
1921	878	135
1931	2,254	208
1948	2,581	253
1960	8,755	511
1970	12,068	661

Source: Dennis M. Warren, "Voluntary Associations in a Market-Agricultural Secondary City: The Case of Techiman, Ghana" (Paper presented to the African Studies Association, November 2, 1973, Syracuse, N.Y.).

nearly 500 percent, and the number of structures has nearly tripled (see Table 8.1). As the site of a major market it has drawn a large population of non-Bono people, including other Akans and a diversity of other ethnic groups from northern Ghana, Nigeria, and former French West Africa; one survey found members of sixty-five other ethnic groups living in Techiman.[13] After the market's redevelopment, Techiman expanded its hospital, became the location for a secondary school, an Amadyian Muslim mission, and several government offices, built a large new mosque, and experienced substantial economic growth.

Modern Development

In 1972, Techiman consisted of some 700 structures clustered at the Kumasi-Kintampo-Sunyani-Nkronze crossroads.

Techiman's still deep roots in the rural-agricultural economy, however, are reflected in the half of the population that still finds farming its major occupation and in the heart of the market, which is centered around agricultural commodities. Many of those living in the Zongo (generally non-Akans) have acquired land and farm at least part time, as do many others involved in the market on Fridays.

Nearly all adults in Techiman participate in the economy in some role. Unemployment is only 3.5 percent (although underemployment is a greater problem). In addition to farming and trade (72.7 percent), Techiman residents are employed by several major retailers, the schools, the hospitals, the local council, and several offices of the national government. There are also a number of laborers and semi-skilled and skilled craftsmen (including tailors and seamstresses, carpenters, masons, and mechanics), clerical personnel, drivers, bakers, and miscellaneous service workers. There are some 40 professional positions in Techiman, including schoolteachers, nurses, ministers, civil servants, and two physicians. Nearly all are filled by Ghanaians. There are, as well, some 540 students over 15 years of age.

Socially, Techiman is still somewhat of a "plural" society.[14] Although there is much economic and some political contact between Zongo inhabitants and the rest of Techiman, social contact appears to be minimal. Most interviewees in a social sample listed either Akans or non-Akans as their closest friends, but rarely both.* This may be explained in part by residential and religious patterns. Zongo residents are less likely to send their children to school than Techiman residents, and if they do so they will often send them to the Amadiyan Koranic school. Most respondents reported meeting their friends at school or church, or through their families. Finally, much social activity is centered on the palm wine, pito, akpetishi, and beer bars, where more faithful Muslims do not go. Language differences would not seem to be a factor as most Zongo residents spoke Twi well. The two communities are amicable but separate. However, with the Aliens Compliance Act of 1970, a number of the compounds in the Zongo were vacated when their owners left Ghana. These are now occupied by Brongs, and this residential integration might bring greater community mixing.

The major political institutions and actors in Techiman are the Techiman Local Council, the Techiman Traditional Council, the Techiman Zongo Council and several civil servants responsible to ministries of the national government.

The Techiman Local Council is a management committee selected by the Accra government, under the authority of the district officer at Wenchi. It has been allocated most of the responsibility for the administration of local services and government. It has authority to raise revenue, pass bylaws, propose development projects

---

*In each town a social survey was conducted by sampling at random approximately 400 households.

(with regional and district approval), and supervise local health inspections, public works, and development projects. The traditional council is headed by the Omanhene and includes approximately a dozen senior subchiefs. This council possessed all local authority in the precolonial era but has had its authority gradually reduced since. It does, however, retain a great deal of local customary authority and influence.

The third major local political institution is the Zongo Traditional Council. This includes the Zongohene (chief of the Zongo, always the chief of the Hausa community), his subchiefs, and the heads of the various Zongo communities. This council was established after the turn of the century when the town was reorganized politically into Zongo and Brong sections. While it is not an "official" traditional council (recognized by the national government) and recognizes its subordinate status to the traditional council, it has been important in Zongo public affairs and in linking the Zongo with the traditional council.

Finally, there are several offices of other Accra ministries located in Techiman that are not under the authority of any local officials. These include the police, court, secondary school, agriculture officer (produce inspector), veterinary services officer, public health nurse, and the office of irrigation, reclamation, and surveying. These administrative offices have varying levels of contact with and impact upon the local population.

Techiman, thus, is an area which has experienced in the last thirty years gradual urban growth in the context of continuing social, economic, and political "traditional" institutions and patterns. It is a precolonial town, capital of a traditional state with a well-known history dating nearly two centuries before colonial rule. It still has active and viable traditional institutions, a large proportion of its residents of the local ethnic group, and an economy still closely tied to agriculture. However, in the postwar era it has experienced steady physical and population growth, substantial immigration, growing ethnic diversity, a steadily diversifying economy, and the permanent presence of several of the national government's political and administrative agencies.

These patterns and the town's experience with political development are an example of one urbanization-development experience. As such and in comparison to other experiences, they may be a source of insights to development planners.

OBUASI

Site and Situation

Obuasi is a city of some 30,000 inhabitants, the ninth largest
city in Ghana. It lies on the edge of the tropical rain forest, 100
miles from the coast and 40 miles south of Kumasi. The surrounding
area is primarily agricultural, with some logging still occurring. It
is a district seat under the Ashanti Region administration and lies
in Adansi Traditional State, one of the states historically under the
Ashantihene.

Urbanization Process

Obuasi is not a traditional city. Until the arrival of Ashanti
Goldfields Corporation (AGC) in 1897, it was only a small settlement,
too insignificant to even justify an "adikro" (lowest chief in the Akan
hierarchy of traditional offices). It remained a small settlement
until the turn of the century and the development of the mine into a
major enterprise.

The mining company began rudimentary operations when a
large area was leased at a nominal sum from traditional rulers, and,
in 1897, machinery was brought in by porters. By 1903, a railroad
had been completed from Sekondi-Takoradi. The growth of a town
soon followed.

From the earliest period, Obuasi has been highly diverse
ethnically. The railroad to the south (and later to Kumasi) increased
the flow of trade along an axis including Obuasi and funneled migration
by southern ethnic groups (Fantis, Akwiapims, Nzimas, Anlos) into
and through Obuasi. Additionally, the reluctance of the Ashanti to
forego generally prosperous farming to do the heavy underground
labor meant that labor from the north was in demand. And the demand
was not denied.

Laborers came from the "Northern Territories" of Ghana as
well as from former French West Africa generally. Many Nigerians
were also attracted, though they generally traded or engaged in semi-
skilled and skilled crafts. The diverse ethnic panorama included
Moshies, Grunshies, Walas, Dagombas, Frafras, Kousais, Hausas,
Yourbas, Sisalas, Kanjagas, Kusasis, Busangas, Kados, Fulanis,
Ibos, Ewes, Kotokolis, and many others. In 1964, the district commissioner had registered 35 ethnic heads. In 1972, after the Aliens
Compliance Order, thirty were registered.[15]

As Table 8.2 illustrates, Obuasi has grown rapidly, and it has
grown into a highly diverse community. However, gradually the

TABLE 8.2

Obuasi's Growth

Year	Population	Percent Locally Born	Percent Born Outside Ashanti Region
1948	15,724	20.0	52.0
1960	22,818	30.4	48.3
1970	31,005	40.1	38.1

Source: 1970 Census of Ghana, vol. 2, pp. 560-61; William and Judith Hanna, Urban Dynamics in Black Africa (Chicago: Aldine, 1970), p. 119; Gold Coast Census Office, Census of Population, 1948; Report and Tables (London: Published on behalf of the Government of the Gold Coast by the Crown Agents for the Colony, 1950), p. 366.

proportion born outside this region is declining, and Obuasi's population is stabilizing somewhat. Even so, many of the younger generation reported as born in Obuasi were born of non-Ashanti; so these figures somewhat understate its ethnic diversity.

Modern Development

Today Obuasi lies cradled by a series of scenic hills in a valley some three miles long and from one-half to one mile wide. It is located on the paved east-west road connecting the partially paved Kumasi-Sekondi road with the paved Kumasi-Cape coast road. Adjacent to but slightly removed from the town, is the mining "compound," which includes the administration office block, warehouses, a motor pool, machine shop, several shafts, miscellaneous other buildings, and the gold ore refining complex. Among the various departments and facilities, the mine occupies as much area as the town itself and includes several residence areas for most of the senior staff.

Obuasi, unlike Techiman, includes a variety of housing styles. There are rudimentary mud compounds in the Zongo and in Obuasi's suburbs, larger and more substantial cement-coated or cement-block compounds in the central neighborhoods and an adjacent township, single-family electrified "estate houses" in the two government housing estates, and mine-owned barrack-like structures for the "junior" staff. There are as well a few comfortable mine-owned single family bungalows with electricity and water for Ghanaian "senior" staff in several locations.

There is little association between ethnicity and residential area. Even though the Zongo is primarily inhabited by Muslims, it includes a diversity of ethnic groups and some scattered non-Muslims. There is, however, clear if not great, economic variation among neighborhoods. In general the closer one gets to the central area, the more substantial the housing becomes. Exceptions to this are the scattered Ghanaian senior staff quarters and the two government housing estates. Most compounds are occupied by their owners, who let extra rooms at five to ten cedis monthly to corporation workers and sometimes the worker's dependents.* Most inhabitants have no fewer amenities (usually more) than in rural areas, but they suffer from severe overcrowding. One young junior staffer shared a small office-sized room with three others, a common occurrence. It is not unusual for a husband, wife, several children, and a younger brother, for example, to share one medium-sized room (15' by 10').

Economically, the heart of Obuasi is the Ashanti Goldfields Corporation. It employs some 80 percent of those employed in wage labor and currently has a "senior staff" (professional-supervisory) of some 300, which is approximately 50 percent Ghanaian and 50 percent expatriate and includes the vast majority of professional positions in Obuasi. [16]

The "junior staff" (blue collar) numbers around 7,500 African workers. Since the Aliens Compliance Act, the foreign African proportion has, however, been reduced to about 800. Most underground workers are now from northern Ghana and are Dagarti, Wala, Mamprusie, Dagomba, or Grushie. The average take-home pay of an unskilled miner is 50 cedis monthly, and the company provides medical care and some housing, the latter grossly insufficient. Few workers stay with the corporation their entire working lives but, like many Dagartis, come and work for six to eight months and return home to do their heavy farm work. Many of them return to Obuasi, when they must begin again in the lowest paying jobs and often wait six to twelve weeks for work at all. There is a yearly

---

*During the period of field research the Ghanaian new cedi was exchanged at a floating rate of approximately U.S.$1.00.

turnover of some 1,200 workers, and most unskilled workers tend to work five to seven years and then leave permanently.[17]

Obuasi, unlike Techiman, has had little unused farm land to allocate to non-Adansis. For this reason, relatively few adults (19 percent) consider agriculture their primary employment. While another one-fifth (21 percent) of the adult population is employed in petty trade, the remainder (60 percent) is employed in wage or salaried occupations.[18] Along with the mine, there is employment in the government offices, the secondary and other local schools, construction, logging, general services, as agricultural laborers, in the several major retailing establishments, and in skilled crafts, such as carpentry, goldsmithing, and seamstressing and tailoring. Unemployment is moderate (10 percent by labor office estimates) but alleviated by the regular turnover in junior staff positions at the mine.

Social patterns in Obuasi fit those typical of Africa's "new-towns" much more closely than do those in Techiman.[19] While the average adult Techiman resident has 6.0 biological relatives living in town locally, the average adult Obuasi town dweller has only 3.0 such relatives living locally. Nearly 40 percent of Obuasi's adult residents have zero or one biological relative living in Obuasi, while only 19.6 percent of Techiman's residents can be so characterized.

Residential patterns in Obuasi also fit the new-town model more closely. Most individuals in Obuasi live in either a single-family dwelling or in one or two rooms of a compound otherwise occupied by nonrelations. Even those with relatives in Obuasi often find it impossible to share a building with them (aside from spouse) because of limited vacancies.

One should not, however, assume Obuasi's residents have remained isolated. Of Obuasi's adult population, 71.6 percent reported they were living in Obuasi with their spouse. Some 90 voluntary associations, including ethnic associations and unions, occupational and trade associations, diverse recreational associations, "friendly" associations, funeral associations, religious groups, and lodges and secret societies, are active in Obuasi. These provide their members with friendship, recreation, moral support, and tangible economic aid and social services.[20]

Obuasi is an important center of government activity. It is the seat of the District Council as well as the Magistrate's Court. Also located in Obuasi are the district social welfare office, education office, police headquarters, administrative office, prison, and several agricultural offices. There is no effective traditional Adansi presence in Obuasi, however. This is in part because of the disagreement between the Adansi Omanhene and his subchief, the Akrokerrihene, regarding authority over the Obuasi area. The dispute was temporarily settled under the Nkrumah government, which elevated the Akrokerrihene to his own Omanhene-ship and placed Obuasi under his rule. During this time the Akrokerrihene nominated an Ashanti resident of Obuasi to be the Obuasihene and also selected a queen mother. This arrangement was terminated shortly after the first coup in 1966, when all stools were returned to their pre-independence status.

The only major local political institution in Obuasi is its urban council, comparable in size and function to Techiman's local council. It has been responsible for the health department (the personnel for which was recruited, trained, posted, evaluated, and paid by the District Health Office at Bekwai); maintenance of schools, drains, the market, and roads; and collection of the basic rate. The council is responsible for developing and administering local development projects. However, it has never attempted any. It also is empowered to pass bylaws pursuant to these matters, which are subject to approval by district, regional, and national officials. The only area of the above in which the town council has been at all active is in supervising health services. Public works (i.e., maintenance of government property) has been supervised and actually completed by the works superintendent based at Bekwai.

Obuasi thus developed from an unimportant, small settlement to a major city in merely a few decades. This rapid growth overwhelmed the traditional social and economic patterns and institutions of the area, and the influx of non-Ashanti along with Adansi internal division overwhelmed traditional political institutions. With an industrial-wage labor system as the heart of the economy, with great ethnic diversity and the majority of the population immigrants, and with sustained urban physical and population growth, Obuasi is as "new" a town as Techiman is an "old" town. Just as Techiman offers an observer urbanization-development in continuity, Obuasi offers the observer urbanization development in discontinuity.

POLITICAL DEVELOPMENT

The remainder of this chapter will explore the levels of political institutional development of each town. Each town will be analyzed according to how well its formal and informal political institutions perform these activities, these institutions including the Techiman Local Council, the Obuasi Urban Council, the Techiman Traditional Council, the Techiman Zongo Council, and the chiefs and heads of the many ethnic and voluntary associations in the two towns.

The "modern" town councils in Techiman and Obuasi are weak institutions. In Techiman, the council plays virtually no role in any

political activity. The few rules it has promulgated are of little significance and have never been seriously applied. It has taken almost
no role in conflict resolution (although before and during the field
work period several local conflicts and controversial issues developed), has never taken a major role in organizing collective action,
and has developed no independent linkages with the Techiman
population.

Obuasi's town council, an "urban" council because of the town's
larger population, has performed little better than Techiman's. It
has, on a few occasions, initiated and applied rules pertinent to matters of some importance. For example, after a fire destroyed the
market's structure, open fires were prohibited in the market. Similarly, after several traffic accidents, incidents of personal property
damage, and numerous complaints, the urban council began to regulate livestock in town. However, over several years of activity, these
were the only actions of any significance the council took, aside from
determining local tax rates. The Obuasi urban council, furthermore,
has never organized any collective action nor had a significant role
in resolving any major communitywide conflict.

Urban Councilors in Obuasi, however, have played some role
in linkage. While their lack of activity in formulating municipal
statutes led to a corresponding lack of interest in their meetings,
both councilors and civil servants reported several instances when
complaints pertaining to public sanitation (both nonenforcement and
enforcement) were conveyed from private citizen to inspector by
urban councilors.

Several factors may explain these moribund local councils.
First, neither council has participated in an election in more than a
decade. While electing members is not a certain means of assuring
activity and responsibility, it stimulates some interest in the institution concerned and assures members will be at least well known,
if not always well qualified.

Second, Ghanaian local government is, like most systems
growing from parliamentary experience, allocated only minimal
authority, and that under the supervision of the national administration. Lacking more than rudimentary authority, local councils have
tended to draw less influential individuals as members, have received
little public attention, and have not developed into bodies accepting
and responding to responsibility for local problems and affairs. In
no activity could either local council be regarded as developed.

Techiman's political arena, however, also includes two important "traditional" bodies: the traditional council and the Zongo council.
Each has been active to varying degrees in all four political activities;
both have been very active as agents of conflict resolution, have

developed strong linkages with the population at large, have organized several collective actions, and have initiated and applied rules.

Probably the most important function for each of Techiman's traditional councils is conflict resolution. This has, however, tended more often to be in individual conflicts than in issues of community-wide importance. This conflict resolution function operates through a highly developed structure. Within each family, the head is the first arbiter of disputes. When he is unable to resolve the issue, it is carried to the chief of his division or quarter (if non-Bono, to the chief of his ethnic association). In the Zongo, if it still cannot be resolved, it is taken to the Zongohene and his council, then to the Techiman Gyaasehene, and finally to the Omanhene and his traditional council. In Techiman proper, if a divisional chief cannot resolve a dispute, it is taken to the Omanhene and the council. The "queen mother" is effectively chief of the town's women and hears cases pertaining to children, marriages, and affairs among women.

All these appeals and the acceptance of the bodies' decisions are, of course, extra-legal and voluntary. Considering this, it is significant that few civil disputes ever go to the formal court system; most are brought to this structure and resolved by it. While there certainly is substantial social pressure to utilize and accept these authorities, this fact in itself suggests that there is substantial continued popular support for the traditional council. Critical to this is the successful integration of the non-Bono communities into this system.

While most of the conflict resolution is of individuals involved in civil disputes, in several instances the traditional council has arbitrated disputes between the local council or government administrators and townspeople. These have pertained to such problems as tax increases, resistance to payment of the tax rate, location of a septic tank latrine, registration of voters, and medical innoculations.

The traditional structures are active as well in rule initiation and application, organizing collective action, and sustaining linkages with the population. Of these, rule initiation is perhaps the least significant in the councils' functioning. It is here that the absence of formal, legal authority most clearly affects the traditional councils. For here the councils' actions are limited essentially to applying and modifying customary rules and reacting to problems brought to them that can be interpreted as falling in areas of traditional authority.

For example, a large proportion of the civil cases brought to the council deal with agricultural boundary disputes. Compensations developed for awards in noncash cropping have been modified and remodified to take account of several cash crops, with new ones still being introduced (during 1971-72, the agriculture ministry stationed a development officer in Techiman to encourage cotton growing;

coffee growing has recently expanded rapidly). In one situation, the hierarchies of two unions were competing to organize members of that occupation in Techiman. Conflict developed, and the Omanhene, using his authority as head of the market, arbitrated the dispute and issued rules regulating local union organization generally. During the field research period, the traditional council reacted to rapidly escalating costs for customary general observations by placing a limit on contributions and expenditures. A particularly interesting instance of customary rule modification occurred when rules regulating sexual conduct were revised to take account of the number of girls now going on to school instead of into marriage.

While many local problems are brought to the traditional council as disputes, or can be resolved by initiating rules justified by customary authority areas, some critical ones cannot. The traditional council cannot raise revenues. It cannot employ or dismiss administrative personnel. Administration of schools, public sanitation, public health, and all criminal matters are beyond its authority and direct influence. For this reason, the inadequate development of "modern" political institutions seriously hampers local development in areas requiring "new" administrative structures, personnel, or activities.

Finally, anyone choosing to ignore the social pressure and able to ignore the economic pressure which can follow, can ignore nearly all rules and decisions of the traditional council without fear. But they are exceptions, for as the Omanhene observed,

> After I have settled a case, the one who fails to accept my judgement can appeal to the Magistrate's Court. Because we have time to sit on the cases properly, few do appeal to the court. And when they do go to the court, generally our judgement is still endorsed.[21]

The highly developed structure that penetrates into each family via its divisional or ethnic chief has also worked well in Techiman in organizing collective action and in insuring popular-official linkages. On several occasions communal labor for development projects has been organized by and through the traditional structure. These projects have expanded the hospital, built a new school, constructed a water cistern, and improved local roads. In another instance, basic-rate collection was temporarily transferred from the local council, which had little success, to the traditional council. The latter explained, justified, and collected the rate via the traditional communication structure, dramatically improving the town's rate collection.[22]

Upward linkage is also provided by this structure. An individual has access via his family head, divisional chief, or by addressing the council in its fortnightly session. Many, as well, have access via one or more of the many associations and unions found in the community. Public opinion has been expressed to the council on such matters as the basic rates, special levies, desired development projects, and other problems including those mentioned above.

Overall, the Techiman traditional political structure constitutes a well-developed political system. It has allowed for continuous and structured input and output via the traditional chiefly hierarchy, has facilitated special interest representation via the access it allows the many market, occupational, and ethnic unions and associations, is accessible as well to individuals at its open meetings, has well integrated the non-Bono people by replicating its structure in the Zongo and linking that with the Techiman council (the Zongohene sits on the Techiman Traditional Council), and has successfully resolved most civil disputes and many of the general controversies in the locality.

A variety of factors may explain its success. First, the town is still a relatively small community; such a personalized structure may depend on all individuals having personal contact with members of the political elite. Second, the Bono traditional system, with its dispersed, hierarchical structure and ties into every area and family in the community, seems particularly well suited to perform these political functions and has had seventy-five years to integrate gradually the near 40 percent of the local population that is non-Bono into Techiman's political system. Third, ethnic heterogeneity has been overcome by an effective application of federalism: each ethnic community has its own head who hears cases pertaining to its internal affairs. On more widespread issues, they represent their community on a larger body. While the reach of the Techimanhenc into the Zongo is weaker than into Techiman proper, his influence via the Zongohene and Zongo council has been sufficient to settle interethnic disputes, maintain order in a multi-ethnic market, and take effective communitywide collective action.

Undergirding these three factors is probably a critical fourth: the actions of the traditional council are accepted because it appears to have been successful in the past in resolving conflict, sensitive to public feeling, and a reliable source of information to the public. What sustains it is the same force that ultimately sustains all non-coercive associations. It retains a public support that accepts most decisions and restrains by social and economic pressure those who might not.

Obuasi, as noted earlier, lacks any community-wide traditional institutions. The only attempt to institute such a structure, made during the 1960s, failed. The chiefs so established were unable to perform any major political functions. Considering their lack of a juridical-communication structure such as Techiman's, the absence of a tradition of effective decision making by a community-wide traditional body, and the attempt to integrate in one act such an ethnically diverse community as Obuasi, this is perhaps not surprising.

Still, the large number of ethnic group and association chiefs are, in Obuasi as in Techiman, important in resolving some conflicts. In Techiman, of course, their actions are sanctioned by and partially integrated into the townwide traditional structure.

In Obuasi, however, they must perform these functions without this benefit. Furthermore, the substantially larger number of individuals in Obuasi, their higher incomes, and the population's greater dispersion (Techiman is perhaps one square mile; Obuasi is several times larger in area) seem to have weakened the chiefs' influence over their communities. Additionally, the relatively large professional community in Obuasi is only rarely involved with these structures and unlikely to look to them for leadership.* Still, disputes are brought to the Obuasi chiefs from within their communities, and occasionally chiefs of two communities will meet together to arbitrate a civil dispute between members of different communities. Thus, some conflict resolution is performed by Obuasi traditional institutions.

On a few occasions, attempts have been made in Obuasi to resolve neighborhood problems, and the heads of several ethnic communities have met. These have generally been unsuccessful, as neighborhoods are too ethnically heterogeneous and/or skeptical of traditional leadership to accept and enforce the chiefs' decisions. Only once, when a substantial and abrupt tax rate increase was threatened, did an effective coalition form. This, of course, was based on an obvious and shared interest, and the coalition included many nontraditional and prominent individuals as well as several ethnic group chiefs.

The absence of effective, general institutions has severely hurt the Obuasi community in general rule making as well as collective action and linkages. To some extent, purely administrative questions

---

*A few educated, white-collar individuals held leadership positions among several southern Ghanaian ethnic groups or benevolent associations. In most situations, however, higher status (corporation senior staff or other local professional) individuals had little to do with ethnic or ethnically linked associations. A major communication gap locally seemed to be between southern, usually Christian, Ghanaians and northern, usually Moslem, Ghanaians and non-Ghanaians. Few institutions, associations, or situations of shared status brought them in contact beyond the market place or areas of mixed housing.

in such areas as sanitation, utilities, public health, and policing are handled by the large number of national government civil servants present. But in collective action and linkage, Obuasi suffers. For in spite of the town's many needs and relative prosperity, it has been unable in the last decade to organize any successful self-help development project. Linkage weaknesses as well are evident in problems cited by the public sanitation personnel in enforcing sanitary regulations. The weak linkages were also manifested in the Obuasi disturbances of 1969, which appear in part to have been caused and amplified by inadequate communications.23

Market unions in each town have been active resolvers of conflict and initiators of rules. Among their tasks have been physically organizing the markets, regulating prices and measurements, settling disputes regarding competition for customers, enforcing standards, assuring supplies, distributing goods from wholesalers, and regulating retailing privileges. In Techiman they are authorized and supervised by the Omanhene; in Obuasi there is no overall authority, though the unions appear nonetheless to function effectively. In each town, market unions regulate hectic and busy markets.

DEVELOPMENT STRATEGY

Considering these aspects of political growth, Techiman is clearly the more politically developed of the two cities. This is largely a product of the continued viability of its "traditional" institutions. In the two cities, the Techiman Traditional Council and Zongo Council were the only institutions with popular linkages and the only ones capable of initiating rules, resolving conflict, and taking collective action. In spite of the absence of official (national government) authority, they had retained sufficient legitimacy, support, and power to perform these functions.

Their effectiveness may be explained by the gradual and moderate growth of the town, the early establishment of political institutions for non-Bono peoples, and their early and continued integration into Techiman's political system. Along with these factors, Techiman's traditional leadership visibly supported and encouraged several innovations and development projects and continued successfully to resolve such disputes as land ownership, bad debts, civil suits, and contention over marital obligations.

In contrast, in both towns "modern" political institutions have remained largely moribund. This may be explained, at least in part, by their inability to build popular support and the reluctance of the national government to allocate to them any real and substantial power. Lacking such power, more often nominated than elected, and facing either a highly diverse, politically inchoate populace or a populace already supporting alternate institutions, the local councils never began to develop into effective political bodies. Without formal power or popular support they were without function. And as Obuasi was also without community-wide traditional institutions, it has remained politically fragmented.

Public policy makers in developing countries face crucial choices. In many circumstances, past economic decisions and demographic patterns will project patterns to the present which are, essentially, beyond modification. But future economic choices, such as the improvement and building of roads, the location of markets, and the location of new industries, are amenable to rational planning.

While economic considerations must be weighed to avoid irrational decisions, such as locating industries without reference to labor force, infrastructure, or markets, it must be remembered that there are no "purely economic" decisions. The location of an industry will have an impact on local political and social patterns, which in turn will affect the cost and viability of operating this industry. Furthermore, even if some of these costs can be externalized to the national government, the society as a whole still must pay them.

The effectiveness and viability of Techiman's political institutions suggest that urbanizing-developmental policies that sustain and help existing institutions to evolve may be of merit. Gradual growth in many areas may avoid the concentration of social problems and political instability in the largest cities, take advantage of existing institutions' potential for growth and development, and spread general development more widely across the society. Together, these achievements ought to facilitate greater social, political, and economic integration of states composed of a diversity of nations within a single boundary. Finally, administrative costs are among the highest costs all systems face, both in economic terms and perhaps in terms of lost human initiative and creativity. A multi-center policy of national development is one strategy development planners should pay more attention to in future choices.

NOTES

1. Several disciplines have contributed excellent works to an expanding literature emphasizing African microdevelopment patterns. Major works include Abner C. Cohen, Custom and Politics in Urban Africa: A Study of Hausa Migrants in Yoruba Towns (Berkeley: University of California Press, 1969); Maxwell Owusu, Uses and Abuses of Political Power (Chicago: University of Chicago Press, 1970); Richard Sklar, Nigerian Political Parties: Power in an Emergent

African Nation (Princeton, N.J.: Princeton University Press, 1963); C. S. Whitaker, The Politics of Tradition: Continuity and Change in Northern Nigeria, 1946-1966 (Princeton, N.J.: Princeton University Press, 1970); and Howard Wolpe, Urban Politics in Nigeria (Berkeley: University of California Press, 1974).

2. Julius Nyerere, Ujamaa: Essays on Socialism (London: Oxford University Press, 1968); Warren F. Ilchman and Norman T. Uphoff, The Political Economy of Change (Berkeley: University of California Press, 1971), pp. 208-55; and D. R. F. Taylor, "The Role of the Smaller Urban Place in Development: The Case of Kenya," in Urbanization, National Development and Regional Planning in Africa, ed. Salah El-Shakhs and R. A. Obudho (New York: Praeger, 1974), pp. 143-60.

3. In an analysis of obstacles to agricultural development, Guy Hunter, Modernizing Peasant Societies: A Comparative Study of Asia and Africa (London: Oxford University Press, 1969), details several problems such a strategy might ease.

4. Owusu, op. cit.; and Aristide Zolberg, Creating Political Order: The Party States of West Africa (Chicago: Rand McNally, 1966).

5. C. S. Whitaker, Jr., "A Dysrhythmic Process of Political Change," World Politics 20 (1967): 190-207.

6. Henry L. Bretton, Power and Politics in Africa (Chicago: Aldine, 1973), pp. 93-158; M. B. K. Darkoh, "Toward a Planned Industrial Reallocation in Ghana," in Urbanization, National Development and Regional Planning in Africa, ed. El-Shakhs and Obudho, op. cit., pp. 110-29; Charles Elliot, Patterns of Poverty in the Third World: A Study of Social and Economic Stratification (New York: Praeger, 1975); and, Justice N. Mria offers a balanced view of this issue in "National Urban Development: The Issues and the Options," in Urbanization, National Development and Regional Planning in Africa, ed. El-Shakhs and Obudho, op. cit., pp. 75-92.

7. S. N. Eisenstadt, The Political Systems of Empires (New York: Free Press, 1963), pp. 300-60.

8. Fred Riggs, Administration in Developing Countries: The Theory of the Prismatic Society (Boston: Houghton-Mifflin, 1964), and Cohen, op. cit., explore the relationship between political and social change, ethnic conflict and ethnic competition.

9. Defining political development to hold cultural bias constant is not simple. Perhaps the best definition is found in Alfred Diamant, "The Nature of Political Development," in Political Development and Social Change, ed. Jason Finkle and Richard Gable (New York: Wiley, 1966), pp. 91-96.

10. Gabriel Almond and G. Bingham Powell, Jr., Comparative Politics: A Developmental Approach (Boston: Little, Brown, 1966);

and Karl Deutsch, Nerves of Government: Models of Political Communication and Control (New York: Free Press, 1963).

11. Dennis M. Warren, "Voluntary Associations in a Market-
Agricultural Secondary City: The Case of Techiman, Ghana" (Paper
presented to the African Studies Association, November 2, 1973,
Syracuse, New York); and James S. Wunsch, Voluntary Associations:
Determinants of Associational Structure and Activity in Two Ghanaian
Secondary Cities (Ph.D. diss., Indiana University, 1974).

12. Warren, op. cit., pp. 16, 17.

13. Ibid.

14. Leo Kuper and M. G. Smith, eds., Pluralism in Africa
(Berkeley: University of California Press, 1969).

15. E. Ampene, "Obuasi and Its Miners," Ghana Journal of
Sociology 3, no. 2 (1973): 73-80; G. W. Eaton-Turner, "A Short
History: Ashanti Goldfield Corporation, Ltd. 1897-1947" (Ashanti
Goldfields Corporation, Ltd., 1947).

16. Personal communication, Obuasi District Labour Officer;
Personal interview, Assistant Personnel Officer, Ashanti Goldfields
Corporation.

17. Personal communication, Obuasi District Labour Officer.

18. Ghana Census Office, 1970 Population Census of Ghana,
Volume II: Statistics of Localities and Enumeration Areas (Accra:
Government Printer, 1972), pp. 560-61.

19. International African Institute, Social Implications of Industrialization and Urbanization in Africa South of the Sahara (Paris:
UNESCO, 1956), passim.

20. This parallels the role of voluntary associations elsewhere
in West Africa. See Kenneth Little, West African Urbanization: A Study
of Voluntary Associations in Social Change (Cambridge: Cambridge
University Press, 1965).

21. Personal interview, Nana Kwachi Ameyaw II, Techiman-
hene.

22. James S. Wunsch, "Central Government Penetration and
Traditional Institutions in Two Ghanaian Cities" (Paper presented at
the Midwest Political Science Association, April 26, 1974).

23. Government of Ghana, Report of the Commission of Enquiry
into Obuasi Disturbances, 1969 (n.p.: Government of Ghana, n.d.).

9

URBANIZATION, RURAL TO URBAN MIGRATION, AND DEVELOPMENT POLICIES IN THE IVORY COAST

Garland Christopher

INTRODUCTION

The problem of the rural exodus in the Ivory Coast is inextricably related to the problems of urban unemployment and agricultural labor shortage. Even though the Ivory Coast has enjoyed an exceptionally high rate of economic growth since independence in 1960, there has been growing urban unemployment. This is directly related to the unwillingness of young Ivorians to pursue careers in agriculture and to the structure of capital investment. Typically, investments have been capital intensive and thus have not favored the only resource that is in abundant supply: labor.

It has been predicted by the Planning Ministry that from 1970 to 1980 there will be 841,000 new entrants to the labor force with only 819,000 new openings available during this period. The shortage of 22,000 jobs is not on the surface disheartening, and many less developed countries (LDCs) would like to be in a similar situation; however, the distribution of new employment between the rural and urban sectors aggravates the deficit. There will be 288,000 new jobs available in urbanized areas versus 610,000 requests, and 531,000 new jobs in the agricultural sector matched against 231,000 requests. The task then of economic planning in the Ivory Coast for the 1970s has been (and continues to be) the equalization of labor supply and demand in these two sectors.

It is evident from the above distribution that the Ivorian agricultural sector will call increasingly on a foreign labor force to insure its functioning. Thus, the problem of rural-urban migration and urban unemployment and their consequences for economic planners are vastly different from that in other developing countries. Elsewhere in

the developing world there is a flight from agriculture because jobs
are simply not available, and, if they are, the wage is at a subsistence
level.[1] Hence, the Ivorian unemployment problem lies in the Ivorian
economy's inability to provide desirable, modern sector jobs in relation to the number of its citizens opting for modern sector employment,
either in the agricultural or urban sectors.[2] Only when agricultural
and urban incomes are more similar will rural youth have more lati-
tude in making their migratory decision. All in all, the lack of adequate extension efforts and the increasing rarity of choice agricultural
land literally push rural youth to the cities.

The associated problems of unemployment and excessive urbanization are of concern to Ivorian policy makers, and programs have
been initiated to combat them. This chapter will analyze the planning
of growth centers in the interior, centers which are supposed to aid
the process of decentralization of economic activity and give meaningful employment opportunities to the inhabitants of the interior. It is
also hoped that the decentralization of economic activity will alleviate
the congestion in the two principal cities of the Ivory Coast, Abidjan,
the capital, and Bouake, the second largest city. Also given that the
maximization of gross national product has been the major goal of the
Ivory Coast, it is particularly interesting to review the Ivorian plans
for both urbanization and rural development. It is clear that a mix of
policies to promote modern sector employment invariably has ramifi-
cations with respect to urbanization plans, and, conversely, plans for
rural development have ramification with respect to urbanization. The
most obvious goal of all these plans is that of creating a suitable rural
environment so that the propensity to migrate need not arise or, if it
does, that its impact on rural communities be less severe than it is
presently. A longitudinal study of rural youth conducted in 1967-69
found that the percentage of educated rural youth who remained in
their villages varied from 36 percent in the north to approximately
15 percent in the central region. Most economists would agree that
whenever a rural community loses a significant proportion of its educated population the effects are bound to be devastating from the viewpoint of potential economic progress.[3]

Throughout this chapter, the focus will be on economic policies
in the Ivory Coast and how they affect its citizens. It is vital, at least
from the perspective of manageability, to narrow the focus of this
chapter because the urbanization problem in the Ivory Coast is inti-
mately related to various external, political, and economic developments over which the Ivory Coast has little control. One could cite
the case of political refugees from Guinea and that of the Voltaics
whose country, the Upper Volta, is one of the poorest in the world.

THE PROCESS OF URBANIZATION

Urbanization in the Ivory Coast is a recent phenomenon. As recently as 1900, the ancient capital of Grand-Bassam had only 7,000 inhabitants, and Abidjan was only a village of fishermen situated in the now fashionable neighborhood of Cocody. Man, the principal central-western city, barely contained 7,000 inhabitants in 1952, and in 1965 its population totaled 27,000 inhabitants. Much the same could be said for other cities.

In the national census of 1965, it was found that based on the definition of an urban area as one containing a central city with a population of at least 10,000, the Ivory Coast had 19 urban areas. It was also found that the population of Abidjan accounted for 34 percent of the urban population, a share which had increased to 37 percent by 1974. Of these 19 urban areas, eight were located in the southern prefecture, and, if other forest regions were excluded, only four urban areas were located in the savannah zone. Thus, a clear urbanizing tendency exists in the Ivory Coast: a greater growth rate for the urban population in the southern forest zone. This tendency is due to the southern zone's ability to produce the cash crops of cocoa and coffee.

The definition of an urban area as one containing more than 10,000 inhabitants may be somewhat strict and mask underlying urbanizing tendencies in a developing country such as the Ivory Coast. If we define a secondary urban area as one containing at least 4,000 but less than 10,000 inhabitants, then there were 270,000 inhabitants in such "secondary" urban centers in 1965. [4]

Because of the Ivory Coast's expanding agricultural production and its generally favorable economic performance since independence, urbanization has contributed to the present economic cleavage between the country's northern and southern departments. In 1970, there was only one additional city in the northern savannah zone with a population of at least 10,000 added to the four that existed in 1965. This city was Odienné, which is located in the extreme northwest of the savannah zone.

Combining the population of primary and secondary urban centers, we find that in 1970 the urban population accounted for about 28 percent of the total population. Table 9.1 shows that the urban population quadrupled over a period of 12 years. The Ivory Coast has had vast movements of population which have significantly contributed to the process of urbanization since independence. The flow of migrants, both domestic and from other countries, to urbanized areas has been at least as large as the urban population's natural growth rate. In

TABLE 9.1

Urban Population in the Ivory Coast

Year	Number of Cities	Urban Population	Percent of Total Population
1958	27	447,000	15
1965	62	946,000	22
1970	69	1,438,000	28

Source: "Plan quinquennal de développement économique, social et culturel 1971-75," Abidjan, Ministère du Plan, 1970, p. 30.

some cities, net migration has accounted for most of the population growth experienced. A few examples will illuminate the dynamics of the migration process. During the period 1960-65, the population of Abidjan increased by 12 percent, an increase that was almost entirely due to net migration. Abengourou, another forest zone city, regis- tered an 11 percent increase in its population, with net migration accounting for over 70 percent of that increase.

However, the Ivory Coast is a relatively small country, both from the perspective of physical space as well as total population. Due to its size, it is interesting to look at the dynamics of the migra- tion process. In particular, what are the factors attracting large numbers of people, both citizens and foreigners, to the urban areas of the Ivory Coast and, more specifically, to the cities in the southern forest zone? The answer must include the domestic as well as the international dimension of migration because there are at least 1 mil- lion foreigners in the Ivory Coast. In 1974 they accounted for 20 per- cent of the total population. In 1963, the percentage of foreign-born to the total population of Abidjan was greater than that of people born there, and even this percentage was biased downwards because no account was taken of the children born in Abidjan of migrant parents (see Table 9.2). With respect to the presence of foreigners in the Ivory Coast, one cannot disregard European dominance in certain sectors of the Ivorian economy. Due to various cooperation agree- ments that the Ivory Coast has concluded with France and the high rates of economic growth—in which the demand for skilled and tech- nical labor has exceeded the local supply—the situation is such that several occupations are dominated by French nationals. For instance,

TABLE 9.2

Place of Birth of Citizens and Noncitizens in the Ivory Coast
(percentage)

City	Year	Born in Ivory Coast	Born Elsewhere	Foreign-Born	Total
Abidjan	1963	29	38	33	100
Abengourou	1962	30	38	32	100
Agboville	1958	37	33	30	100
Man	1958	70	21	9	100
Bouake	1958	37	31	32	100
Grand-Bassam	1963	47	28	25	100
Dabou	1966	32	35	33	100
Dimbokro	1958	50	32	18	100
Korhogo	1962	32	42	26	100

Source: "Bilan et perspective de la population de la Côte
d'Ivoire," Bulletin de l'Afrique Noire (Dakar) (March 1967): 9, 757.

in 1974, 80 percent of all teachers in the secondary school system
were French nationals. However, it is recognized by Ivorian policy
makers that the "Ivorianization" of high-level occupations is crucial,
and, accordingly, the Ivory Coast has expended a significant proportion of its current budget to education. Indeed, the Ivory Coast
devotes a proportion of its current budget to education that is larger
than that of any other country, developed or less developed.

Rural-Urban Income Inequality

Abidjan's extraordinary economic growth rate can be attributed
to various economic factors. Largely because of its favorable rates
of economic growth since independence and a favorable balance-of-
payments position, and despite the quadrupling of oil prices in 1974,
the Ivory Coast's economic performance has been termed an economic
"miracle" by many observers. In 1976, its trade surplus was 80,894
billion francs African Financial Community (CFA), which represented
a rate of import coverage of 125.9 percent. In 1969, the rate of import coverage was 139.6 percent. Preliminary economic statistics

TABLE 9.3

Distribution of Yearly Salaries, by Region for 1974
(in francs CFA)

Department	Average Yearly Salary	Estimated Population (1975)
Abidjan	442,000	921,687
Abengouro	345,000	175,891
Bouake	333,000	632,111
Guiglo	314,000	135,252
Korhogo	282,000	276,846
Gagnoa	266,000	256,000
All departments (Excluding Abidjan)	386,000	

Source: Françoise Achio, "Le secteur public et semi-public: physionomie de l'emploi 1973," premiere partie, Abidjan, Ministère de l'Enseignement Technique, March 1974.

lead one to believe that 1979 will be another good year for the Ivory Coast. Abidjan's growth has been due primarily to its favorable location along the Ivorian Coast and the construction of a port in the Vridi Canal. The Vridi Canal was opened in the 1950s to oceangoing shipping, and, concomitant with the need to export agricultural products and import consumer and capital goods, massive investments in urban infrastructure and port facilities have been made. Even though Abidjan is favorably located on the coast, it was favored during the colonial era because of its location in the southern forest zone.

The logic of colonial economic policy was to stress exports and cash crop production, albeit to the detriment of food crops. Food crops are perhaps favored climatically in the northern zone. Thus, left with the institutional structures inherited from the colonial era, the Ivory Coast has continued to stress the promotion of export crops. Present policy, however, continues to stress the necessity of cash crop production and the benefits of foreign exchange earnings, but with the provision that cash crop exports must be diversified and the fruits of the Ivorian economic "miracle" be equitably distributed

TABLE 9.4

Average Monthly Salary of Various Sectors
of Public Employment
(in francs CFA)

Department	Average Monthly Salary
Abidjan	30,000
Interior	16,000
Primary	13,000
Secondary	28,000
Tertiary	38,000

Source: Françoise Achio, "Le secteur
public et semi-public: physionomie de l'emploi
1973," premiere partie, Abidjan, Ministère de
l'Enseignement Technique, March 1974.

throughout the country.[5] Presently, as a result of uneven development
in the Ivory Coast, there is a distinct economic cleavage between the
country's southern and northern zones. The extent of this uneven
development can be seen from Tables 9.3 and 9.4.

The extent of excessive urbanization in the Ivory Coast in general
and in Abidjan in particular can also be seen in Tables 9.3 and 9.4.
Abidjan has the highest average monthly income, while in terms of
income and social mobility, the cities in the interior are infinitely
less desirable as a living place than Abidjan. It can also be seen that
the occupations of a service nature, included in the "tertiary" category, have the highest average income of any occupational grouping.
It is clear that the vast majority of the employment in any service-
related category will be located in an urbanized area, and probably
at Abidjan, since Abidjan alone has both population and income levels
to support significant amounts of service activities.

Researchers from various disciplines have studied the causes,
consequence, and dynamics of migration and produced various models.
Perhaps the most interesting economic model was developed by Harris
and Todaro; in it they postulate that individuals base their decision to
migrate on income or utility maximization.[6] The logical conclusion is
that the difference between income available in urban areas as opposed
to rural areas is the main attraction to the individual migrant and that

this behavior is perfectly rational as far as the individual migrant is concerned. Hence, there are possible diseconomies arising from the migration process due to the difference in the total social and private costs of migration. The individual migrant undoubtedly does not calculate the social cost of his migration.

In the simplest of cases that can be hypothesized from the Harris-Todaro model, if industrial wages are double the wages in agriculture, rural-urban migration will continue until the probability of finding a job in the urban sector declines to one-half. Godfrey has shown that Todaro's model is not generalizable and, at least with reference to Ghana, does not fully characterize the decision to migrate and that migration can continue to exist in equilibrium—defined in the Todaro sense.[7] For example, a strong negative preference for rural life among the educated young is a cause of migration into urban centers where the average income, weighted by the urban unemployment rate, is perhaps lower than the average wage in agriculture. Moreover, with explicit reference to the Ivory Coast, rural out-migration is highly differentiated; by no means do all rural migrants move to urban areas. Indeed the bulk of rural migration in the Ivory Coast is rural-rural.

If the Todaro model were applied to the northern region, with its low per capita income, the question of why this region has the lowest rate of out-migration could not be answered. On any socioeconomic scale, the northern region is much worse off than the southern forest region. It thus appears that the restrictive social structure in the northern region has restrained migration and, because of land shortage there, when migration does occur it is usually to an area where land is available and the problem of overpopulation is nonexistent. In such a situation, we typically have a family which has no income, yet following the strict application of the Harris-Todaro model would force the using of the average "expected" urban income as the expected income of the departing family member. Yet what the migrant is fleeing from in our hypothetical example has nothing to do with an expected urban income but rather with a need for greater liberty and more personal freedom.

Past research on migratory patterns in the Ivory Coast has clearly shown that, where there is a land shortage in a rural area, the usual destination is an area of land availability; however, in areas where the aspect of land shortage does not pose itself and where the social structure is rigid and traditional, the departures are usually to an urbanized area. In this latter case, the individual expects to find a greater degree of personal freedom. Thus, it appears, rural-urban migration does not become critical for any agricultural society until it has reached a certain degree of integration into the market economy and is unable to fulfill the aspirations of its younger members.

It is not a question of disregarding the search for higher income as a very important variable in the migratory decisions, but to preclude other variables is unwarranted. We do not know why a certain member of a village migrates to Abidjan and another village member goes to another locality. Yet, somehow the simple explanation of an urban-rural income difference clouds the differences of these two individuals' economic behavior. It is perhaps best to approach the problem of migration in the Ivory Coast in a multidisciplinary manner with emphasis on various push and pull mechanisms in the migratory decision. The question of motivational factors and the perception of life in another locality is complex, and unfortunately the shortage of space here precludes a detailed analysis.

Conventional Economic Theory
Applied to Excessive Urbanization

According to conventional economic theory, the trend toward excessive urbanization in the Ivory Coast is but short-term. In theory, when economic growth such as the Ivory Coast has experienced continues over a sufficiently long period, regional income inequality is inevitably reduced. Growing regional income inequality carries the seeds of its own destruction.

The dynamics of the conventional theory are as follows: Since the bulk of modern-sector employment is located in Abidjan, other things held constant, the average worker in the modern sector has a greater quantity of capital to work with. Thus, because of this and other market imperfections, his average wage is higher than his counterpart's in the interior of the country. He is more productive because he is equipped with more modern technology than his counterpart in the interior.

Given a prolonged fiscal or monetary expansion, be it by direct government intervention or indirectly by a rise in the world price for a principal Ivorian export, we have the case where certain industries would be priced out of the high-income area of Abidjan into lower-income regions. Particularly hard hit would be industries whose location was not optimal in the sense of their being located outside the areas of primary production. Growing restlessness and the resulting increased wage demands of the labor force would be but one cause of this outflow of industries. Such a trickle-down effect, if carried to its logical extreme, will have the industries of high-labor productivity shifting into regions of lower income, and the low-wage industries of these regions will be forced into even more isolated regions. Such a theory coincides perfectly with the wishes of Ivorian planners who believe that if strong enough impulses of economic growth are

diffused toward the interior of the country, growing urbanization of
the Ivory Coast and the excessive urbanization of Abidjan can be
arrested. In any case, this scenario may be consistent with the views
of Ivorian policy makers, but it is vastly inconsistent with economic
reality. Even though the Ivory Coast has achieved high rates of economic growth, its industrial structure is weak and highly fragmented.
In the Ivory Coast, one cannot really talk about an industrial structure
in the sense of there being active, inter-firm relationships, with one
firm's output as another's inputs; such is the exception rather than
the rule. On the other hand, the Ivory Coast, with its population of
nearly 7 million, is simply too small to permit the installation of a
large number of integrated industrial complexes.

The logical conclusion of such a trickle-down effect is that if
economic growth is sustained over a sufficiently long period, it leads
to the disappearance of regional income and welfare inequalities. The
impulse to economic expansion in such a dynamic system has to be so
intense that a central city in each region becomes necessary (the
term central city is used here as an economic and commercial center,
not solely an administrative center). Then the rural-urban migration
decision of the individual migrant is complicated. He now has the
possibility of migrating either to Abidjan or to one of the central
cities in the Ivory Coast. In the typical case he will migrate to the
central city of his area of origination. Such a scenario is evident in
the regional economic development plans and policies of the Ivory
Coast, to which we shall now turn.

REGIONAL ECONOMIC PLANS

The scenario described in the preceding section is explicit in
the Ivorian plans of regional development. Regional developmental
policy is based on a particular region's developmental potential. Irrespective of whether a particular project is going to pay for itself in
the short or long run, Ivorian policy makers seem willing to funnel
resources from one sector to another in order to maximize the economy's long-term growth potential. The goal is to create regional
growth poles in hitherto neglected regions. Because the growing urbanization of Abidjan is perhaps inevitable in the short run, we shall
ignore the question of Abidjan and concentrate the discussion on Ivorian
plans for the urbanization of the interior cities of the Ivory Coast. We
shall begin this discussion with an analysis of the principle of revolving Independence Day celebrations in the Ivory Coast and conclude
with summaries of various regional development plans. Since the
formulation of both regional development plans and independence

festivals were designed to develop the Ivory Coast's interior hinterland, our discussion will stress this point and the possibilities of achieving this goal.

Revolving National Independence Festivals

Soon after independence, it was decided that one of the best ways to forge a nation was to motivate people to think in terms of national rather than tribal terms. It was decided that the festivities celebrating the nation's independence would be regularly held in the interior. A major spin-off of this decision is that once a city is allocated the festival for a particular year, the city is also allocated a budget to carry out minor and major development projects.

These projects may vary from the building of a new hospital, high school, or modern market place, to the electrification of a neighborhood or the paving of major arteries in the city. Whichever project the funds are spent on, the purpose is to make the chosen city a better place to live. The hope is to decrease the cleavage in terms of social infrastructure between Abidjan and the interior. It is felt that if the cities of the interior are equipped with modern infrastructure, an adequate level of medical facilities, and schools, the migratory stream toward Abidjan can be slowed.

One problem with the concept of revolving festivals is that the budget allocated for development purposes is often too small to create a significant impact on the region or city concerned. In terms of pure economic efficiency it is better to invest the monies into projects in Abidjan or Bouake, where the rate of return is surely higher.

Another problem is that the infrastructural facilities, if they are provided, are either poorly maintained—as is the case with paved roads or marketplace—or undersupplied, as in the case of a medical dispensary. No follow-up studies have been conducted to analyze the benefits of having revolving festivals aside from political considerations. It should be clearly understood that when a city is allocated the independence festivities, projects that are to be funded should have a continuing viability. For example, if it is proposed to pave the major arteries of a city, then there should be adequate recurring revenues for the maintenance of such a project. All too often once a project has been approved there are no plans for the maintenance, especially the projects involving the creation of social infrastructure. Such policies (I believe the better term is oversights) have led to real economic losses. If the government had no long-term interest in maintaining the local social infrastructure created, the monies could have been invested profitably in other sectors of the economy.

A related issue involves the yearly occurrence of these festivals in terms of real structural change in the cities or regions concerned. Typically the monies for the improvement of the habitat and the development of the city are granted one year before the event, forcing city officials to concentrate on projects that have a one-year life span. Some projects cannot be conceptualized and completed within a span of one year, as was apparent in the cancellation of the 1977 festivities at Sequela and their rescheduling for Abidjan. Evidently, the completion of the projects was not in sight during the final months of 1977, and the unveiling of the projects were rescheduled for the Independence Celebration of 1979, which belatedly will be held at Sequela. Perhaps these events will lead to the occurrence of the festivals in the interior on at least a biannual basis, so as to unveil significant accomplishments in the regions concerned. Such a policy may give pleasure to the regional elites, but in terms of structural transformation the result is nil. Thus, due to the tendency to concentrate on projects with an incubation period of one year or less, no structural transformation has occurred. It should be noted that when any project excludes job creation, which in turn means factories and government bureaus, the end result will be marginal and contrary to what was originally intended.

Since various problems associated with the festivals have been outlined, it would be proper to discuss at least one benefit of having the festivities in the interior. One external economy from the exercise of promoting regional festivals in the interior has been the decentralization of the day-to-day public management functions associated with these projects from Abidjan to the regional city concerned. It should be clear that although the projects may be conceptualized by public officials, the final product has a significant input from private enterprise which, of course, is charged with the actual implementation or the proposed projects.

This decentralization has given regional officials the opportunity to exercise and improve their managerial and technical skills, and this has incalculable benefits to the region concerned and also to the country. Simply speaking, the awarding of these festivals to cities in the interior can also be seen as an effort to increase human capital. It is only when the managerial skills and technical awareness of government officials are of a sufficiently high level that the Ivory Coast can gain full advantage from these investments.

The main obstacles in the path of economic development are often encountered in low levels of productivity. Backward communities usually remain backward until they are deliberately aided by the central government or until there is a discovery of a precious resource beneath its soil. However necessary such a discovery may be to economic development, it is not sufficient. I tend to believe that as the productivity of government officials and workers of the interior increase, it then becomes more profitable to introduce more productive techniques and combinations, without increasing the physical capital involved, or, in common jargon, getting more for less.

We shall now turn to a few of these projects, which are massive in scale and have great potential for transforming the areas and cities concerned. These projects may be called the projects of a grand scale because their goal is the creation of regional "growth poles."

The Port of San Pedro

One such grand-scale project is the creation of a growth pole at San Pedro. The creation of the Port of San Pedro was in response to the lack of development of the southwestern region, a region rich in forests and national resources. Such a project has necessitated the creation of 400 kilometers of road and feeder arteries. Before the creation of the Port of San Pedro, the immense resources of the southwest were not exploited due to the lack of means to move the products out. A regional development authority ARSO) was created in 1971 and charged with the coordination of development plans for the southwest.

The choice of the site for the port in deep water inevitably meant the choice for the then future city of San Pedro. The goal of Ivorian planners was to create a growth pole in the southwest that would permit the development of a relatively neglected region and thereby allow the southwest, with its immense national resources, to play a pivotal role in the development of the Ivory Coast. Such a project could only end by reducing regional disparities between Abidjan and the rest of the country, augmenting dwindling forest resources elsewhere in the country, easing the congestion of the Port of Abidjan, and creating a favorable economic environment so that rural out-migration from the southwest would be directed toward the city of San Pedro.

Construction of the port began in 1968 and was completed in 1971. Before construction began there were only 51 people censused as being born in San Pedro. The vast majority of the residents were migrants, domestic and international. As soon as the port was officially opened, there was immediate congestion due to the inadequacy of the existing infrastructure; however, within a span of nine months, the Port of San Pedro had reached an estimated monthly tonnage of 75,000 metric tons. However, as is apparent from Table 9.5, traffic in the port has exceeded initial expectations, but the vast majority of the tonnage of the timber exported is unprocessed and therefore does not permit the capturing of various external economies necessary for balanced growth in the southwest.

TABLE 9.5

Freight Traffic at San Pedro, Selected Years
(in tons)

Type of Freight	1972	1973	1974[*]
Imports	11,103	27,173	18,950
Exports	854,812	991,031	511,589
Total	865,915	1,018,204	530,489

[*]Refers only to the first semester of 1974.

Source: Emmanuel Dioulo, "Le pari raisonable de San Pedro," unpublished document, prepared for the Republic of Ivory Coast, January 1975.

Undoubtedly, the Port of San Pedro has great potential as a regional pole of development, but its real economic significance can only be determined in the years ahead. Since the Ivory Coast has an extremely limited industrial infrastructure, any type of massive industrial relocation scheme, for the moment, will have a zero-sum result; the employment loss of Abidjan will be the employment gain of San Pedro, but no overall change in employment will result.

The real value of San Pedro lies in the possibility of exporting agricultural produce at a lower unit cost than possible elsewhere. Its greatest benefit for the 1980s undoubtedly lies in its role enabling rapid evacuation of the iron ore that has been discovered some 200 kilometers from San Pedro at Man. As the iron ore industry develops along with the timber industry, and providing that the Ivory Coast is able to engage in some processing of these resources, a program of viable, integrated regional development could be envisaged.

Ostensibly, one could foresee a paper pulp company and an industry of explosives, the latter to exploit the iron ore resources in Mont Klahoyo, near Man. In anticipation of the future economic growth of San Pedro, public investment in the development of the southwest will increase by over 33 percent in the second half of the 1970s (see Table 9.6).

The development of the southwest is heavily dependent on two resources, timber and iron ore, the former renewable over a very long period and the latter nonrenewable. So the future of the Ivorian gamble is dependent on how successful it is at creating value added in

TABLE 9.6

Planned Public Investment in the Southwest
(millions of francs CFA)

Investment Sector	1971–75	1976–80
Agriculture	9,000	16,000
Economic infrastructure	13,700	16,100
Cultural infrastructure	1,300	1,600
Sanitary infrastructure	500	450
Social infrastructure	200	400
Administrative infrastructure	1,000	1,500
Consulting services and studies	800	800
Total	26,500	36,850

Source: "Plan quinquennal de développement économique, social et culturel 1971–75," Abidjan, Ministère du Plan, 1971, p. 437.

these industries and also at internalizing that value. This is the first task of the industrialization of the southwest. If the Ivory Coast is not successful in creating and capturing the value added in these industries, it is possible that the long-term private profitability of these investments will be higher than its long-term social desirability. Indeed, in the period 1975–77, the economic development of the southwest was of such high priority that the monies allocated to economic development were larger for the southwest than for Abidjan (see Table 9.7).

The second task of industrialization is to provide training and transferability of skills acquired by the workers of the industries proposed. This will be needed because as mechanization proceeds in Ivorian agriculture, the excess agrarian population will increase. Perhaps, in most cases, the best policy is to proceed from a complete absence of mechanization to nonmotorized mechanization, and only at a later stage to motorized tractation. In this way, the economic bases would have been laid for mechanization, and displaced agricultural workers would be more able to find work in ancillary industries. Even though the southwest accounted for 4.9 percent of the gross national product in 1972 and 6.3 percent in 1975, the growth has not been even in the sense that villages are losing their land to timber companies

TABLE 9.7

Percentage Distribution of Planned Public Investment, by Major Program, 1975–77

Program	North	East	South	West	Center West	Center	South-west	City of Abidjan	Total Allocated	Grand Total
Economic development	57.8	0.0	18.8	28.2	11.9	23.2	39.2	10.9	26.9	26.9
Economic infrastructure	27.0	58.4	76.2	68.6	34.0	39.7	41.8	26.4	41.1	39.6
Social development	9.2	30.8	2.8	0.4	31.6	18.6	14.9	41.5	20.2	19.6
Cultural development	5.4	5.1	2.0	2.9	22.5	17.2	3.7	11.3	8.3	7.8
Central government	0.7	5.7	0.2	0.0	0.0	1.2	0.4	9.9	3.4	6.1
Total (percent)	17.8	0.4	18.2	2.8	1.7	14.8	14.0	30.3	100.0	100.0
Total (CFAF billion)	46.9	1.0	47.8	7.4	4.5	38.8	36.9	79.6	263.0	378.7

Source: Loi Programmes 1975–77; Ministry of Planning.

owned by both nationals and nonnationals. However, they have not been able to work in the timber industry in appreciable numbers. Indeed, the timber industry employed only 3,500 individuals in 1975, a drop of 200 from 1972.

The timber industry is characterized by a high capital-labor ratio and does not generate any significant linkage effects, which could increase investment in other sectors. The replacement capital needed in this industry is highly specialized and, save for the use of local labor to transport the logs to port, the involvement of African is presently weak.

As industry is planned and developed for the southwest, a policy of promoting food crops and export crops will be needed. Ostensibly, the region is rich enough to permit a significant increase in the acreage allocated to the cash crops of coffee and cocoa, both of which could be transported by boat or truck. If transport is by the latter, excess capacity in the trucking industry should not be allowed to increase, as would happen if trucks return empty to their home base in the southwest. Perhaps cement would be one of the principal products used as return freight.

The Dam of Kossou

Another project involving the creation of a regional development authority (AVB) was the building of the Dam of Kossou on the Bandama River in the Bouake forest zone. A massive hydroelectric complex was constructed at Kossou in order to alleviate the expected deficiency of hydroelectric power in the 1980s in the Ivory Coast. At peak efficiency the dam produces 500 million kilowatts, nearly equal the power production of the entire country. Due to the rise in water level caused by such a massive project it was necessary to displace upwards of 50,000 people. The Regional Authority for the Bandama Valley (AVB) was charged with the resettlement of these displaced people, the development of tourism around the man-made lake, the development of a fishing industry around the Kossou Lake, and the construction of new villages for the migrants. It should be noted that the city of Bouake lies within the boundaries of economic influence of the Kossou Project.

The agricultural program developed by the AVB includes the development of rice (3,500 hectares), maize, livestock, cocoa, cotton, and peanuts, all of which are now possible through the irrigation of a large expanse of land. It is expected that the value added in the industrial structure will pass from 4.4 billion francs (CFA) in 1970 to more than 19.5 billion francs (CFA) in 1980. This increase will generate 9,200 new industrial jobs. The realization of these goals, how-

ever, will depend on the creation of industries drawn by the electric
generating power of the Kossou Dam, and the development of peripheral cities in the Bandama Valley.

Regional Development in the Savannah Zone

The last major regional development plan concerns the northern
region of the Ivory Coast, although no regional authority has been created to coordinate the development plans. The development plans for
this area center around the creation of a growth pole at Korhogo, the
most important city of the northern region in terms of population and
commercial activity. Similar to the program at San Pedro, the policy
is to develop an integrated development program in order to create
structural interdependence among the industries of this region, capture and internalize external economies associated with the agglomeration of industry, and create a skilled labor pool.

The urbanization program revolves around the creation of industrial jobs and labor productivity increases in the agricultural sector
through increased mechanization. Ivorian policy makers stress heavily
the importance they attach to the development projects in this region,
ostensibly because of the poverty of the region and also because the
Senufos, the predominant tribal group in the north, have not exhibited
high rates of out-migration. Conventional economic theory suggests
that areas such as the north should have high rates of out-migration
but, due to the Senufos' restrictive social structure, regional out-
migration has yet to become a major problem.

The strategy opted by the government for the northern savannah
region seems to be one of gradual technological change and innovation,
with large sums expended on technical and agronomic research in
order to ascertain this region's needs and capacities. Industrialization
plans include a sugar complex—already completed at Ferkessdougou,
50 kilometers from Korhogo—rice, cotton, and livestock development
plans. It is expected that the value added in agriculture will increase
to 20.5 billions (CFA) in 1890, from about 12.3 billion in 1970, thereby
increasing the incomes of the plan's beneficiaries. For instance, the
Cotton Areas Rural Development Project goal is to increase the incomes of the land-poor groups in the savannah. The production of
cotton is to be promoted and expanded in a crop rotation system with
maize, rice, and groundnuts. Ultimately, the goal of the projects in
the northern region is to make the north a principal reservoir of food
crop production. If the Ivory Coast is not successful in this endeavor,
the north will be a recipient of permanent economic assistance and a
drain on the resources of the more prosperous regions of the Ivory
Coast.

CONCLUSION

Since independence, the major cities of the Ivory Coast have nearly all trebled in size. Although there are differences in growth rates between the cities of the southern forest zone and the northern savannah zone, generally urbanization is increasing throughout the Ivory Coast. Indeed, if the expected economic growth realizations of the savannah zone should become a reality, there will be increased urbanization in that zone also.

The cause of the urbanization "crunch" in the Ivory Coast is due to its favorable post-independence economic performance and political restrictions in various countries of West Africa. Presently it cannot be said definitely if the aspect of international migration is more important than internal migration in the population expansion of Ivorian cities. However, we do know that foreigners constitute, in some cities, a larger proportion of the population than does the native-born population. A simplistic policy prescription for the control of urbanization is the restriction of international migration, but presently the question is not one of control for a variety of reasons. First of all, the dynamic sectors of the economy, including agriculture and the timber industry, are dependent on foreign labor to fulfill certain menial tasks in their processes of production. Native-born Ivorians have shown a negative preference for these tasks, and it is the foreigners whom certain industries have come to rely on.

The Voltaics are the largest group of foreign Africans, and historically the Upper Volta has always had a special relationship with the Ivory Coast. For a certain period during their colonial history they were administratively attached as one nation. Economic growth has been minimal in the Upper Volta since independence, and due to the Sahelian drought, many Voltaics, along with other Sahelian nationals, were forced to seek their fortunes in the Ivory Coast. They have, however, met with long periods of unemployment if they migrated directly to urban areas and especially so if they were relatively well educated. A stated goal of the Ivory Coast is the Ivorization of employment in the modern sector of the economy.

Ivorian officials have sought to combat the excessive urbanization of Abidjan and Bouaké through various development plans. Some of the most ambitious are the development of the Port of San Pedro, the development of the Bandama Valley, and various programs for the savannah zone. The goal of all of these programs is the creation of a favorable economic environment so that the need to migrate does not arise, and, if it does, that it be minimal in its impact on the societies involved. A favorable economic environment must be created because with few exceptions rural-urban migration in the

Ivory Coast can be viewed as a rational response to changing economic conditions.

NOTES

1. For a critical examination of the subsistence wage controversy, see Deepek Lal, "Disutility of Effort, Migration and the Shadow Wage Rate," Oxford Economic Papers 12 (April 1973): 112-26.

2. An interesting discussion of the problems of defining the modern and informal sectors of a developing economy can be found in Louis Emmerig, "A New Look at Some Strategies for Increasing Productive Employment in Africa," International Labor Review 110 (September 1974): 199-218.

3. "Une analyse de mobilité: exode rural des jeunes," Abidjan, Ministère du Plan, 1969.

4. Detailed analyses and summary reports of regional surveys done in 1965 may be found in "Population: Côte d'Ivoire, 1965," Abidjan, Ministère du Plan, 1967.

5. The economic performance of the Ivory Coast has elicited words of praise from some quarters and criticism from others. Space here does not allow for a discussion of these responses, but the interested reader is referred to Samir Amin, Le développement du capitalisme en Côte d'Ivoire (Paris: Les Éditions du Minuit, 1967), for the viewpoint of a Marxist economist; and to J. Dirck Stryker, "Exports and Growth in the Ivory Coast: Timber, Cocoa, and Coffee," in Commodity Exports and African Economic Development, ed. Scott R. Pearson (Lexington, Mass.: Ballinger, 1974), pp. 10-66.

6. J. R. Harris and Michael P. Todaro, "Migration, Unemployment and Development: A Two-Sector Analysis," American Economic Review 60 (1974): 126-42.

7. See E. M. Godfrey, "Economic Variables and Rural-Urban Migration: Some Thoughts on the Todaro Hypothesis" (Paper presented to the East African Agricultural Economics Society Conference in Kampala, June 1972).

10

TRANSITIONAL URBANIZATION IN UPPER VOLTA: THE CASE OF OUGADOUGOU, A SAVANNAH CAPITAL

Gary Bricker
Soumana Traoré

INTRODUCTION

Situated south of the Niger Bend and north of the West African rain forest, the savannah region of the Mossi Plateau has long been the natural crossroads of Sudanic trade between the Sahara and the Guinea Coast. In about the twelfth century, the invading Mossi conquered the indigenous peoples and established a system of rural aristocratic households ringing the palace compound of their paramount chief, the Moro Naba. Their settlement thrived and bore the name of one of its more prominent chiefs, Ouaga. Hence, the meaning of Ouagadougou—the village of Ouaga. Since the medieval society was largely rural-based and was supported primarily by royal taxation in the market place, the settlement remained limited in size to about 5,000 inhabitants.[1]

After a few peaceful trading encounters with the Mossi, the French coastal administration found resistance among the chiefs to the proposal that Mossi lands of the upper Volta tributaries be annexed to the humid coastal territories. Consequently, the French took the village by force in 1896. While the French military expedition was chasing the deposed Moro Naba into the hinterland, the town residents rose up in protest over the occupation. Voulet, the French commander in charge, was so angered by this public display that he ordered most of the village burned to the ground.

This show of force was formalized in early 1897, when Voulet accepted the surrender of the remaining lesser chiefs and assumed the administration of the town.[2] After a rural "pacification" campaign ending by 1904, Ouagadougou and its hinterland became one of many chef-lieux in the new French colony of the Upper Senegal and

Niger. During World War I, the city was the main military recruitment center for the savannah. After the war it became an administrative center in its own right. Modest public work projects begun in Ouagadougou at the turn of the century were expanded in 1919 as Upper Volta became a distinct colonial entity. Most of this construction took place east of the original Mossi village. This trend in modernization has not changed; the eastern quarters of today's capital are still the fastest developing and most prestigious areas of Ouagadougou.

Cotton was the first cash crop introduced primarily as a source of revenue to support the young colony's French administration. [3] However, during the Depression, Upper Volta was demoted from full colonial status because its financial frailty could not support a resident colonial administration. By 1938, the territory had been integrated into the Ivory Coast, which encouraged Voltaic laborers to migrate extensively towards the coast to seek employment which might compensate for the falling world demand for cotton fiber.

At the close of World War II, the more vocal politicization of local dissatisfaction with the status quo in French West Africa probably led the foreign administrators to consider the reestablishment of Upper Volta as a separate territory. The Mossi chiefs' desire to regain control of outmigrating manpower and the need for laborers to complete the northern stretch of the Abidjan-Niger Railway also persuaded French officials to designate Ouagadougou as capital of a new Upper Volta in 1947.

SETTLEMENT PATTERNS IN UPPER VOLTA

Today's urban pattern in Upper Volta has been dictated primarily by colonial transportation networks and poor climatic conditions not conducive to human settlement. Thus, the average density of 15 persons per hectare varies enormously due to two factors, one, manmade, the other, natural. Unfortunately the most fertile lands south and southeast of Bobo-Dioulasso are inhospitable because of infestation by disease-carrying insects such as the tsetse fly (Glossina morsitans) and the black fly (Simuliidae family). The far eastern reaches of Upper Volta are so arid as to restrict the population to very low densities. The same holds true for northern Upper Volta. Thus, much of the population is semi-nomadic. Due to natural phenomena the relatively healthier areas contain a large portion of the population. This population centers on their former capital, Bobo-Dioulasso, and the central Mossi Plateau, dominated by Ouagadougou. It is thought that the more inviting Mossi Plateau region may be straining its capacity to hold safely such a large rural farming population, which is concentrated at a density of about 23 persons per hectare. [4] Given the quality of the soil and the persistent risk of drought, densities greater than 23 persons per hectare might result in inadequate local food production. In fact, densities approaching 100 persons per hectare are recorded in some semi-rural, peri-urban settlements near Ouagadougou.

Historically, Upper Volta's major trade link with the modern world has been the Abidjan-Niger Railway. Though the railroad never reached Niger, as its name would imply, it has been Upper Volta's major gateway to international trade markets on the coast. This influence has lessened during the past 20 years since trucks now successfully negotiate the wide variety of lateritic road conditions in Upper Volta. For some time, the Abidjan-Niger Railway terminated at Bobo-Dioulasso. Consequently, this town grew to be the colony's most active commercial and administrative center. When the railway line was eventually extended to Ouagadougou, the new terminal city naturally grew with the infusion of new commercial opportunities.

Prior to independence, the French administration shifted the colonial capital to Ouagadougou. However, its population did not eclipse that of Bobo-Dioulasso. With the addition of the new national bureaucracy to its residential rolls, Ouagadougou finally became the most populous city of Upper Volta a few years after independence. The next three largest cities (Koudougou, Kaya, and Ouahigouya) are all Mossi Plateau towns four to five times smaller than either Bobo-Dioulasso or Ouagadougou. Of these, Koudougou benefits from its location on the Abidjan-Niger Railway and is the largest of the three cities, with a population of some 36,000. Banfora, the smallest population center, with over 10,000 inhabitants, is considered to be the fastest growing town in Upper Volta. This is due to the arrival of migrants to fill laborer positions in the new sugar cane industrial complex located a few kilometers outside the bustling town, which is situated on the road between Bobo-Dioulasso and the Ivory Coast border.

Upper Volta continues to have serious problems of water resource management as well as inadequate infrastructure. Consequently, no more than 5 percent of the country's 5.3 million residents are urban dwellers.

UPPER VOLTA SINCE 1960

Eighteen years after independence, the young republic's economy is still based on subsistence agriculture, external aid, and wage transfers from Voltaics working in neighboring coastal nations. More than 90 percent of the people remain peasants growing grain and raising livestock. Foreign aid, of which more than half comes from France,

FIGURE 10.1

Comparative Distribution of Salaried Workers in Upper Volta, 1974–75

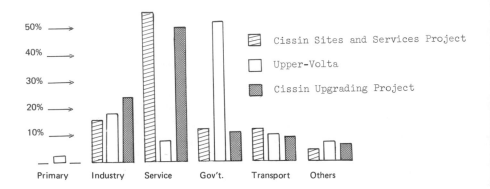

Note: This figure represents only the monetized active population. The Société Africaine d'Etudes et de Développement estimates that only 2.6 percent of economically active Voltaics are monetized, that 98 percent of the Cissin Sites and Services residents are regularly salaried, and that 60 percent of the Upgrading Project residents are either salaried or in the modern, monetized sector. (See notes 8–11 for further explanations.)

Sources: La Société Africaine d'Etudes et de Développement, A Qui Appartiendra Ouagadougou? (Ouagadougou: S.A.E.D., May 1975). U N.C.H.B.P./E.C.A., Mission Report: Upper Volta (New York: United Nations, 1971). U.N.D.P., Liste d'Attributaires– Cissin Pilote (Ouagadougou: U.N.D.P., 1974).

covers 75 percent of annual government expenditures.[5] Voltaic households with family members working outside the country receive annual wage transfers equalling about U.S.$12.2 million, an amount equivalent to total foreign aid receipts.[6] Only slightly more than 1 percent of the active population receives salaried income, and one-half of this restricted minority are civil servants.[7] (See Figure 10.1.)

OUAGADOUGOU SINCE INDEPENDENCE[8]

Migration to Ouagadougou,[9] which had been increasing since the end of World War II, accelerated considerably after independence

in 1960.[10,11] About half the population is under twenty, yet there is
not the strong imbalance in sex distribution that one might anticipate
in many Third World cities.[12] To house this rapidly growing population lateritic rubble is the only locally available building material
sufficiently durable to resist erosion during rain season. However,
the extraction and shaping of laterite can be troublesome. Therefore,
most rural and urban structures are built of sun-dried, earthen
bricks known as <u>banco</u>, which require annual maintenance. A recent
survey revealed that only 2 percent of rural homes and 10 percent of
urban homes met modern construction "standards."[12]

Thus, present-day Ouagadougou is experiencing a transitional
stage of urban development in which population growth is due primarily to young migrants. Yet, the city does not reflect the typical
coastal town's demographic cross-section disproportionately represented by male migrants. New arrivals to this single, locally accessible urban concentration must be prepared even more than their
coastal peers to eke out an agricultural subsistence as young families
in the midst of a transitional, semi-urban setting. Consequently,
farming and petty trade in farm produce remain common "urban"
activities in Ouagadougou, where actively farming peasants may
represent as many as half of the new squatters.[14]

THE SOCIAL AND NEIGHBORHOOD FABRIC
OF OUAGADOUGOU

Ouagadougou's allotted or municipally recognized neighborhoods
have over time come to bear one of two designations: residential or
traditional (see Figure 10.2). "Residential" neighborhoods, such as
Koulouba, constitute about 10 percent of the titled plots of the city
and were exclusively the residential quarters for foreign administrators.[15] Provided with most municipal services, this area is
today being slowly transformed into administrative annexes or business centers. The new locus of residence for high-level civil servants
is the Zone du Bois addition, which is similarly well equipped with
modern amenities.

"Traditional" neighborhoods are not at all reminiscent of traditional Mossi villages but are, rather, urbanized areas of adobe
homes built on a grid pattern which the post-World War I administrators provided with drainage, public standpipes, schools, and
street lighting. Most of these "traditional" quarters, such as Dapoya
or Nemnin, house primarily lower and middle-level bureaucrats,
successful entrepreneurs, and perhaps 15 percent "urban" farmers.
Homes here are rarely built of concrete, which must be imported,
as is common practice in the residential sector.

FIGURE 10.2

Municipally Recognized and Surveyed Neighborhoods in Ouagadougou, 1975, including the Network of Paved Roads

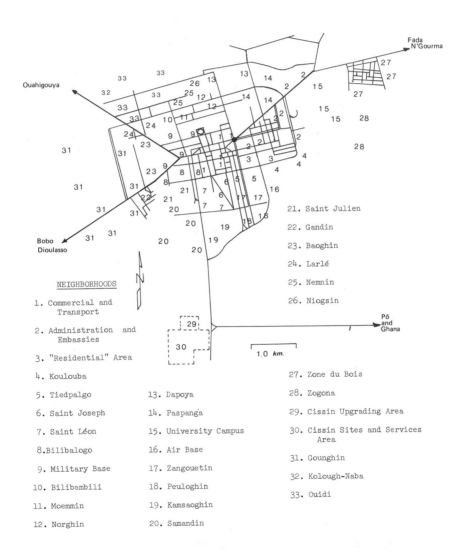

NEIGHBORHOODS

1. Commercial and Transport

2. Administration and Embassies

3. "Residential" Area

4. Koulouba

5. Tiedpalgo

6. Saint Joseph

7. Saint Léon

8. Bilibalogo

9. Military Base

10. Bilibambili

11. Moemmin

12. Norghin

13. Dapoya

14. Paspanga

15. University Campus

16. Air Base

17. Zangouetin

18. Peuloghin

19. Kamsaoghin

20. Samandin

21. Saint Julien

22. Gandin

23. Baoghin

24. Larlé

25. Nemnin

26. Niogsin

27. Zone du Bois

28. Zogona

29. Cissin Upgrading Area

30. Cissin Sites and Services Area

31. Gounghin

32. Kolough-Naba

33. Ouidi

Source: La Société d'Etudes et de Développement, A Qui Appartiendra Ouagadougou? (Ouagadougou: S.A.E.D., 1976), p. 36.

Information regarding the squatter neighborhoods now compris-
ing about half the city area and representing half the 1974 population
of 120,000 varies, it seems, almost from month to month. (See
Figure 10.3.) The oldest squatter neighborhoods frequently appear
as modern as the legally titled areas. Such would apply to Hamdalaye,
parts of Dagnoé, and Tennoghin. These older areas have fewer city-
dwelling peasants and tend to border the allotted neighborhoods. These
first "spontaneous" residents concentrated along ravines and roads
for easier access to water, <u>banco</u>, and employment opportunities
associated with the city center. The newer peripheral squatter areas
are not so densely settled, and their economic life is founded more
on the fertility of their fields nearer the genuinely rural hinterland.
Such would be the case for the young neighborhoods of Tanghin and
Sambin. These two spontaneous zones are especially progressive and
dynamic because of their proximity to the municipal water reservoir.
Also, paved road favors their direct access of the town's commercial
center.

Thus, the "spontaneous" or squatter neighborhoods may be of
several vintages. First, the areas west of the present city center
have been left untouched by public intervention and are, in fact, older
than the modern city, itself. These western neighborhoods such as
Nonsin and Hamdalaye often surpass some of the "traditional" quarters
in the relative quality of their housing stock. Second, some squatter
neighborhoods which were developed under customary land grant
agreements such as Ipelcé and Tennoghin have now grown less rural
and are more densely settled, with only occasional intervention by
often absentee traditional chiefs. Third, there are the burgeoning
peri-urban communities where new squatters construct rustic huts
as temporary shelter, sell some of their surplus garden produce in
the town markets, and have a generally precarious land tenure. Yet,
even the peripheral urban squatter is often assisted by family members already established in the city. In these peripheral zones the
newcomer must contend with the modernized urban chief who may
abuse his land-granting prerogative by soliciting a sizable honorarium
for initial usufruct privileges on undersized plots of land. Tampoui
and Kalgondé would typify such post-independence squatter areas.
Most "residential" neighborhoods are easily recognizable for having
the lion's share of paved access roads, while the "traditional" areas
have only major collector roads paved. Spontaneous or squatter
neighborhoods are noted by their dominantly "organic" patterns, an
absence of municipal improvements, and more intense agricultural
activity.

FIGURE 10.3

Squatter Neighborhoods in Ouagadougou, 1975

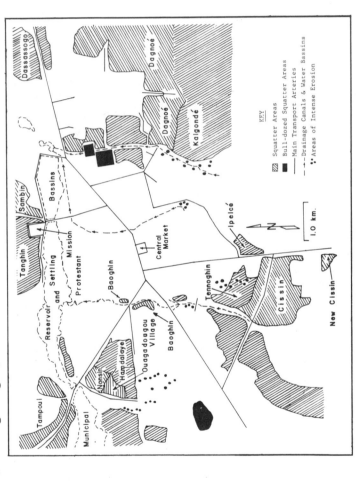

Source: Société Africaine d'Études et de Développement, A Qui Appartiendra Ouagadougou? (Ouagadougou: S.A.E.D., 1976), p. 24.

PROBLEMS FACING THE MODERN CITY

Increasingly arid conditions in Upper Volta have not favored total rural independence and may have spurred people to settle nearer the two major cities. Evidence from several sources easily confirms the view that satellite farming communities are rapidly becoming more densely settled. [16] Household water provision is increasingly mentioned as a problem. In 1972, three out of four households received water solely through privately maintained wells. In 1975, almost three out of four households purchased water at least part of the year, and one out of four Ouagadougou households bought water year-round. The aridity and increasingly dense population of Ouagadougou have lowered the water table to about 20 meters. Potable water can be obtained year-round only at a depth of 30 meters. [17]

Only a small minority of Ouagadougou residents have municipal water piped directly into their homes. In 1975, these fortunate few paid 69 CFA francs per cubic meter, as they did in 1972. [18] Yet, for those who had to pay for public standpipe water by way of intermediary watersellers, the going price rose from a maximum of 250 CFA francs per cubic meter in 1972 to an average of 550 CFA francs per cubic meter in 1975. [19]

Despite their chaotic transition, their rapid population increase, and their increasing financial burdens, the squatter neighborhoods are evolving economic institutions to answer some of their present needs as testify the very animated spontaneous marketplaces of Cissin, Dagnoé, and Tanghin. Numerous squatter neighborhoods can extend up to two kilometers before dispersing into the hinterland, due to the untenable cost of drinking water provision.

The municipally recognized city is growing, too, and seems to have a clear preference for eastward expansion. Authorities have already bulldozed two squatter areas to make way for ministerial offices, embassies, and the new Upper Volta university complex. In short, the activities of the officially sanctioned city and the rapid arrival of people who maintain traditional land tenure concepts combine to pose a serious threat to the rational management of Ouagadougou. The present trend shows an antagonistic relationship between the newcomers and the municipal authorities.

POPULATION AND SPATIAL PROJECTIONS

Projections of Ouagadougou's population growth and land use can be roughly calculated from United Nations estimates that half the city is squatter and that both squatter and allotted areas share a common density of slightly under 60 persons per hectare.. These

FIGURE 10.4

Population Projection for Ouagadougou

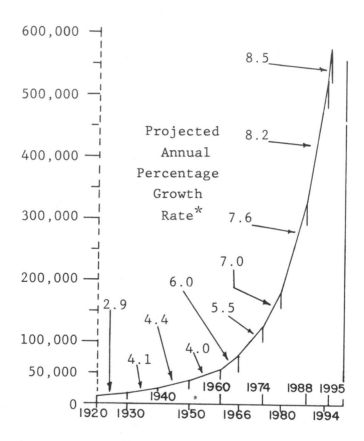

*Rate computed as "rate of return" on annually compounded investment between given dates. (See explanatory note on p. 187.)

Sources: U.N.D.P., Le Financement de l'Habitat (Ouagadougou: U.N.D.P., 1974), pp. 8-9; G. Morrison et al., Black Africa: A Comparative Handbook (New York: Free Press, 1972), p. 374; Société Africaine d'Études et de Développement, A Qui Appartiendra Ouagadougou? (Ouagadougou: S.A.E.D., 1976).

projections are posited upon two assumptions: first, the squatter population is growing at a constant rate between 10 and 20 percent per annum, and, second, the allotted areas of the city have a constant

growth rate of 3.4 percent per annum.* If the city maintains its
present average density of 60 persons per hectare and allows for
public infrastructure to grow as a function of the land-use requirements presently serving today's allotted neighborhoods, then two
projected results can be envisioned (see Figure 10.4): the city's
overall growth rate will approach that of the squatters, and major
land use will eventually be typified by squatter neighborhoods.[20]

These future estimates are optimistic in that only the minimal
squatter growth rate of 10 percent is computed. Nevertheless, in
20 years, because of the great disparity in growth rates, four out of
five city dwellers may be squatters. Spatially this projection implies
that by 1995 the city may be four times larger than today and seven
out of every ten hectares may be located in squatter areas. Only
3 percent of the land would be equipped with the complete set of
standard amenities now typical of only "residential" neighborhoods.
(See Figure 10.5.)

The schematic drawing of projected city size is probably exaggerated because squatter neighborhoods are known to be experiencing
densification above 60 persons per hectare. Also, the local agricultural productivity needed for the livelihood of perhaps 25 percent of
the city's residents is directly linked to the amount of yet undeveloped
"urban farmland." Another unknown that will influence population
growth and dispersion is the increasingly difficult provision of potable
water and the exorbitant transportation cost of water from public
standpipes. Scarcity and price inflation will foster overcrowding
which will, in turn, reduce the amount of open land supplying the city
with produce and providing subsistence jobs to a large sector of the
active population.

ALTERNATIVES TO URBAN DETERIORATION

It appears that Ouagadougou is destined to test the natural limits
of its urban holding capacity. Increased dryness would only aggravate
the present urban migratory drift. Bulldozing undesirable areas has
proved ineffective as a squatter removal policy. Yet, the vast majority of Voltaics are too poor to finance modern municipal facilities.

Since in the end authorities can only make threatening pronounce-
ments about squatter "illegality" (as did the mayor of Ouagadougou
in an open air harangue to the squatters of New Cissin), what practical answer is there to improve the situation?[21] Given Upper Volta's

---

*Populations projected as $1.0 + \text{rate}^{(t+1)-t}$ x population at t.

FIGURE 10.5

Land-Use Impact of Squatter Settlement Growth
in Ouagadougou

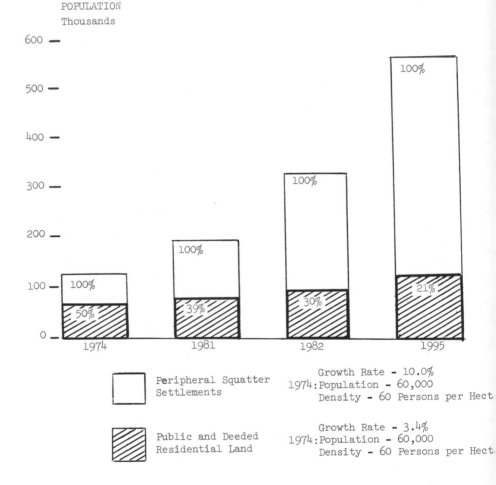

Sources: U.N.D.P., Le Financement de l'Habitat (Ouagadougou: U.N.D.P., 1974), pp. 8-9; Société Africaine d'Études et de Développement, A Qui Appartiendra Ouagadougou? (Ouagadougou: S.A.E.D., 1976).

constraints, proven options are few. The most adaptive individual response to the dilemma has been for Voltaics to disperse and seek more viable coastal locations of employment (typically Ivory Coast or Ghana) from which to send home voluntary transfers. New policies regarding residential shelter must be coherent to the public at large and feasible in the immediate future if impending social and economic deterioration are to be avoided.

THE CISSIN HABITAT OPTIONS

One feasible alternative to improve the transition of Ouagadougou has recently been revealed by the United Nations' Development Programme's Habitat Project on the southern outskirts of the capital. Known as Cissin, this neighborhood was divided into two distinct zones for community development experimentation: the Sites and Service Area and the Settlement Upgrading Area. In the Sites and Service Area, lots were parceled out to city residents needing shelter but also having a steady income stream to finance their own housing construction loan at the National Development Bank. Public response to this opportunity was so strong, particularly among civil servants, land speculators, and those already housed, that the Habitat staff reallocated the parcels to favor those candidates with lower incomes. However, conservative banking regulations excluded from loan consideration applicants without regular, year-round incomes. Thus, the Sites and Service Area did not typify the average Voltaic household nor the average financial circumstances of Ouagadougou residents despite efforts to reach the lowest income levels. An independent survey of the Sites and Service Area's residents revealed that their community cohesion was quite weak due to conflicting ethnic and neighborhood allegiances nurtured during earlier residence in various quarters of the main city.

The second phase of the Cissin Habitat experiment entailed the gradual improvement of a ten-year-old squatter area adjacent to the Sites and Service Area. The system used in this second zone, known as the Upgrading Area, was to set social goals with local leaders and to offer advisory assistance in modernizing or improving residential structures and community sanitation procedures. The incentive for participation was the city authorities' guarantee of stable land tenure for the squatters. The Upgrading Area acquired no bank loans for construction and only contributed a fee to repay the city for the installation of summary drainage, roads, and public standpipes, which residents could not provide themselves. The social effect of minor spatial restructuring and the hope of stable home tenure proved to be far more encouraging than the ambiance of isolation prevalent in the Sites and Service Area. A positive response has been far more generalized and rapid among Upgrading Area residents. The Sites and Service Area has lagged behind in housing completion because of bottlenecks in loan financing, cost overruns by hired construction teams, and absenteeism of owners employed full-time in town. Many future title holders of the Sites and Service Area have also refused to take up residence until the city pipes water to the area, which in 1975 was only served by a combination of wells and water venders.

On social and economic grounds, the Upgrading Area residents offer a more authenic picture of Ouagadougou and a more feasible manner of self-financing in a nation of such limited financial resources. Psychologically, the Upgrading model is important in that it does not require residents to uproot themselves from a familiar environment. Likewise, it offers community leaders, either elected or self-appointed, a dignified role to play as catalysts for change within the reach of even the humblest of neighbors.[22] Alternatives for a generalized, incremental improvement of Ouagadougou residential conditions during the next twenty years are few, if one wants to propose immediately feasible action in a country where GNP per capita is estimated at $100 per year.

If one were to estimate the cost of a vulgarization of the two Cissin models on purely financial grounds, one might approach the accounting in the following manner.

The average 1974 cost to rationalize infrastructure and provide construction loans in the Sites and Service Area was 4,272,440 CFA francs per hectare, or 71,207 CFA francs per person. The average 1974 cost for self-help infrastructure improvement in the Upgrading Area of Cissin was only 418,750 CFA francs per hectare, or 6,979 CFA francs per resident. The projected final density of the Sites and Service Area and also of the Upgrading Area was about 60 persons per hectare in both cases. This figure fortunately is also similar to both titled and squatter area densities in the present city. To upgrade existing squatter areas including those areas projected through the year 1995, approximately 2,360 hectares would have to be treated, that is, 118 hectares per year.[23] Finally, one should bear in mind that the total 1974 Ouagadougou municipal budget was 493.6 million CFA francs, of which 147.0 million supported New Operations.[24]

With these figures one can estimate the comparative annual burden of residential improvement using each scheme of community development. The economic realities of the Cissin Sites and Service Area model correspond to a residential standard to which the city does not yet have the good fortune to aspire. It is not infrastructure cost and the government contribution that render the program unrealistic. Rather, what makes the Sites and Service Area scheme unfeas-

TABLE 10.1

Annual Comparative Cost of Ouagadougou Squatter Zone Improvement, 1974–95
(118 hectares per year)
(in millions of CFA francs)

Scheme	Cost	Cost as Percentage of 1974 City Budget	Cost as Percentage of 1974 New Operations
Cissin sites and service			
Government's grant	36.9	7.5	25.1
Resident funds for infrastructure	36.3	7.4	24.7
Loans for housing	431.0	87.3	293.2
Total	504.1	102.1	342.9
Cissin upgrading area			
Government community redevelopment funds repayable by residents	49.4	10.0	33.6
Construction funds for housing improvements	self-financed	self-financed	self-financed
Total	49.4	10.0	33.6

Source: Compiled by the author.

ible is tying up 431.0 million CFA francs in associated housing construction every year. This model would require that publicly funded loans from the National Development Bank be spent every year. These funds would be equivalent to the entire city budget for 1974. Not only would such skewed allocations be of questionable value for the public at large but would tend to become a political liability. The Sites and Service Area scheme is an unrealistic response to the impending Ouagadougou shelter crisis.

Even by simple comparison of infrastructure costs, the Sites and Service model would cost 23.8 million CFA francs more than the Upgrading model to provide associated infrastructure for the same 118 hectares. In Table 10.1, the column "Government's Grant" covered primarily a community center, a health clinic, a marketplace, and a school. These items are included in the infrastructure costs cited above. If they were funded by the eventual residents of the Sites and Service scheme, their infrastructure repayments would have been larger on a per capita basis.

The application of the Redevelopment Area scheme, basically a rudimentary squatter upgrading approach, seems a financially viable model for urban improvement in the harsh economic climate of Ouagadougou.

In short, for twenty years the city could pay the highest estimated cost to improve substantially the infrastructure of all present and future squatter neighborhoods through the year 1995 by advancing 10 percent of its 1974 municipal budget to newly titled residents who would collectively arrange to reimburse the city. Final granting of the land title or lease could be predicated upon the eventual "standardization" of the housing stock from the residents' own savings. Such home improvements willingly undertaken with infrastructure repayment might require five to ten years depending on the financial resources of each household and community. The Upgrading Area experiment does not require unreasonable financial sacrifices from the residents, nor does it disrupt the evolving social allegiances and institutions in the community. The incremental improvements of the Upgrading Area do not represent a financial risk to its periodically unemployed or underemployed residents. The self-financed housing improvements do not constitute a burden on the country's capital development budget. Those private funds which are spent in upgrading would engender entrepreneurial crafts and skills within the community and have a multiplier effect throughout the entire city economy.

Furthermore, the sale to better-off central city residents of choice parcels created during the restructuring and replotting of squatter areas such as Cissin would serve to integrate gradually the city's diverse cultural groupings and cause income levels to mix. Sales proceeds could also defray infrastructure costs or underwrite additional community services. As long as such modest upgrading programs are based on government loans at economic or near economic interest rates with a well-executed repayments collections system via a combination of taxation and user charges, one need not anticipate that squatter upgrading per se will encourage more urban migration. This "pay-as-you-go" approach is the only logical format for Ouagadougou community improvement except for the most essential of public needs: security, health, and education. Thus, local participatory development would take hold by the initiation of a modest infrastructure improvement scheme relying largely on self-help and motivated by the security of land tenure.

CONCLUSION

Even though the Upgrading Area's model of housing and community facilities improvement is not a prestigious realization, it is authentically Voltaic and not open to the vagaries of foreign assistance programs. If the 200 families of the Cissin Upgrading Area give any indication of the anticipated city-wide response to such a plan, one can easily assert that similar programs could unleash a shelter upgrading movement based on grassroots participation with a minimum drain on scarce government resources. Such an accelerated transition within the Ouagadougou squatter communities would rely partially on traditional village contagion to attain a community goal. Yet, it would also duly recognize those individual households which were particularly eager to contribute personal funds and labor in response to the title granting mechanism. Though Ouagadougou would naturally continue to reflect the general austerity and modesty of scale mandated by a chronically weak national economic base, the capital city of Upper Volta could be "turned around" in a few years.

Only popular participation can save Ouagadougou from its precarious future. This new policy requires a rapid expansion in the number of social workers in the field and better access to modern banking institutions for scarcely monetized residents. Without the development of formalized savings and larger investment opportunities for long-term projects, community infrastructure and genuinely low-cost shelter may be jeopardized. These two changes, the nurturing of community development through active social intervention and forming habits of modern investment-oriented savings, constitute a partial decentralization of the municipal decision-making process. This reform is required so that more residents will become willingly involved in the operation of their city and will have a personal stake in its successful management.

The primary cause of the presently unfavorable situation in Ouagadougou is neither technical, physical, nor even the absence of some "key" resource for developmental "take-off." Rather, the present impasse is both institutional and cultural. Civil servants, bankers, and appointed officials who manage the city are slowly recognizing that their own aspirations and modern values acquired largely through European training have little rapport with the objectives that the average Voltaic can hope to attain in the near future. By diminishing their social role as a guiding minority and by directing this transitional society toward goals which only they themselves can realistically hope to achieve, the municipal authorities may risk undermining the support of the population at large.

The upgrading model of city improvement remains a coherent, modest, and proven method to begin community modernization now so as to go farther in the future. Whether to nurture or ignore the Cissin experiment is a choice both political and cultural in nature. With the demonstrated enthusiasm of the population and the renewed support of its municipal leaders, there is no reason why Ouagadougou must continue on the treacherous path so typical of the modern history of many other African cities.

NOTES

1. Elliott P. Skinner, African Urban Life: The Transformation of Ouagadougou (Princeton, N.J.: Princeton University Press, 1975), p. 19.

2. Ibid., p. 23.

3. Ibid, pp. 32-33.

4. Ibid.

5. L'Année politique africaine, 1973 (Paris: Société Africaine d'Editions, 1974), pp. 11-62.

6. "Upper-Volta," in Africa South of the Sahara, 1974 (London: Europa, 1975), p. 927.

7. Data as of 1969 from United Nations Centre for Housing, Building, and Planning/Economic Commission for Africa (U.N.C.H.B.P./E.C.A.), Mission Report. Upper Volta (New York: United Nations, June 8, 1971).

8. Given that the U.N.C.H.B.P./E.C.A. Mission Report, op. cit., claims that the active population has only 1.1 percent wage earners, and knowing that Upper Volta is about 5 percent urbanized, The Société Africaine d'Études et de Développement has estimated that of monetized employment, 1.1 percent would represent primarily civil servants and hired workers in private business and industry. The remaining full-time, small-scale entrepreneurs and traders have been excluded from this 1.1 percent figure. Assuming that these excluded individuals are city dwellers and constitute about 30 percent of the active urban population, the S.A.E.D. estimates that the national population receiving a regular, monetized income is $1.1\% + (5.0\% \times 0.30) = 2.6\%$.

9. According to the United Nations Development Programmes (U.N.D.P.)'s Liste d'Attributaires—Cissin Pilote, only 2 percent of the registered Sites and Service Project households were designated as full-time subsistence farmers, thus leaving 98 percent to represent the monetized sector of wager earners and entrepreneurs.

10. According to the S.A.E.D.'s May 1975 survey of the Cissin Sites and Services Area, 40 percent of the households declared their

principal economic activity to be subsistence agriculture in which all produce was consumed domestically without sale.

11. U.N.C.H.B.P./E.C.A., Mission Report, op. cit.

12. Skinner, op. cit., pp. 39-40.

13. U.N.C.H.B.P./E.C.A., Mission Report, op. cit.

14. Marie-Thérèse Manchotte, Les Quartiers Spontanés de Ouagadougou (Ouagadougou: Ministry of Public Works, Transportation, and Urbanism, March 1973), p. 29.

15. United Nations Development Programmes, Le Financement de l'Habitat (Ouagadougou: U.N.D.P., June 1974), pp. 8-9.

16. Manchotte, op. cit., table no. 7, and S.A.E.D., "Questionaire Définitif du Projet Cissin," May 1975, questions iv.2.1 through iv.2.8.

17. Author's conversations with chief well digger working in Cissin Upgrading Area, June 1975.

18. S.A.E.D., A Qui Appartiendra Ouagadougou? (Ouagadougou: S.A.E.D., 1976), draft p. 34. Sixty-nine CFA francs per cubic meter is equivalent to $0.274 per 100 U.S. gallons; 250 CFA francs per cubic meter, $0.4616 per 100 U.S. gallons; 550 CFA francs per cubic meter, $1.0156 per 100 U.S. gallons. (The exchange rate of the CFA franc is fixed at 50.0 CFA francs to 1.0 French franc. In the summer of 1975 the floating exchange rate averaged 205.0 CFA francs to the U.S. dollar.)

19. U.N.D.P., Le Financement de l'Habitat, op. cit., pp. 8-9.

20. Geometric calculations for the original schematic rendering of the city's projected spatial growth are found in S.A.E.D., A Qui Appartiendra Ouagadougou?, op. cit., Appendix II-4.

21. As reported to authors by Emile Ouédraogo, head social worker at the Cissin Sites and Service Area dispensary and community center. Report corroborated by Redevelopment Area chief to have taken place in early August 1975.

22. The broad conclusions about the social impact and implementation feasibility of the Cissin Project models are supported by "Preliminary Survey Results," S.A.E.D., A Qui Appartiendra Ouagadougou?, op. cit., Appendix I-9. This appendix is the quantitative analysis of a six-category interview conducted in 113 households within the two areas of the Cissin Project.

23. Detailed financial calculations and complete sources are offered in S.A.E.D., A Qui Appartiendra Ouagadougou?, op. cit., pp. 48-49, 51-52.

24. "La circulation routière à Ouagadougou," Le Développement Voltaique 25 (1975): 9-10.

11

URBANIZATION, PLANNING, AND PUBLIC POLICIES IN NIGERIA

Ademola T. Salau

INTRODUCTION

The current rapid rate of urbanization is an important index of change in Africa. This process is relatively recent, being primarily a post-World War II phenomenon. Most governments are now very concerned with its increasing tempo because of the concomitant adverse effects. There is an increasing urgency for the formulation of effective strategies to cope with the negative effects of urbanization as well as to utilize its potential generative influences.

In the black African context, Nigeria is remarkable for its high level and long history of urbanization. The country also has one of the fastest rates of urbanization at present. For example, while the annual growth rate of the total population between 1952 and 1963 was estimated at 3 percent, the urbanization rate was 12 percent during the same period.[1] The number of urban centers with 20,000 or more in population jumped from 29 in 1921 to 180 in 1963, and the proportion of the total national population concentrated in these cities rose from 7.2 percent in 1921 to 19.1 percent in 1962.[2]

Urbanization has been perceived at times as a self-generating phenomenon. However, an understanding of its relationship to governmental actions is crucial to the formulation of an urban policy. The question is how much and what form of urban growth in Nigeria can be attributed to governmental actions or have resulted from deliberate policy decisions and/or neglect?

This chapter seeks to address this issue. It is divided into three sections. The first summarizes the evolution of the Nigerian urban system from the precolonial period to the present. Particular attention is paid to the role of government in this process. This study's contention is that public decisions play a major role in urban growth and development in Nigeria. This is followed by a section dealing with the issues of urban planning in Nigeria. Finally, some suggestions are advanced for a national strategy of urbanization.

EVOLUTION OF THE URBAN SYSTEM

The Nigerian urban system had evolved to some degree before the advent of British colonialism. This "traditional" urban system corresponded to the sociopolitical organization. With over 200 linguistic groups in what was later to become Nigeria, urbanization was greatest among those groups which had developed large central- ized and complex political systems. Prominent among these groups were the Fulani, Hausa, and Kanuri (Bornu) in the northern part and the Bini and Yoruba in the southern part of the country. Each of these groups had a well-established hierarchy of administrative units with corresponding centers of appropriate rank and size.[3] To a great extent, the involvement of both the Bornu and Hausa states in inter- national commerce across the desert and forest areas to the south contributed to the importance and growth of some of their towns. Kano is perhaps the best-known city that benefitted tremendously from the trans-Sahara trade.

In the north, therefore, an urban hierarchy had evolved before British penetration. At the top of this urban system was Sokoto, which had emerged by the end of the nineteenth century as the most populous town, largely due to its political importance rather than its commer- cial function. Below Sokoto were the metropolitan centers, the head- quarters of the various emirates, whose population by the early twentieth century varied between 30,000 and 60,000.[4] Some of these towns, such as Kano and Jukawa, served as major trade termini and craft centers; others, such as Koolfu in Nupe, Gumel, and Baebaegie, were the trade centers on various trade routes.[5] In the south, towns were less commercial in nature. Yoruba towns, especially, arose in the nineteenth century not only as administrative centers but as fortresses or places of refuge. These towns also served as points for imperial expansion or from which a conscious attempt to control the aborigines found in the region could be made.[6] By the mid-nine- teenth century, some Yoruba towns were estimated by early European visitors to have reached over 60,000 population for Abeokuta and Ilorin and about 100,000 population for Ibadan.[7]

The advent of British rule marked the beginning of another phase in the country's urban development. The two aspects of British policy that contributed most to this urban development were the pro- motion of the country's early economy based on agricultural and mineral products and the introduction of a transport superstructure basically designed for the exploitation of these commodities. The British established an export-oriented economy based on the exploitation of the resources of the hinterland and requiring a north-south axis of commercial traffic. The introduction of a transportation superstructure (in this case, the railroad) was therefore essential to the realization of these colonial objectives in Nigeria. The three principal motives for building lines of penetration, thus, were (1) to connect an administrative center on the seacoast with an interior area for political and military control; (2) to reach areas of mineral exploitation; and (3) to reach areas of potential agricultural production.[8] These were obviously the motives behind the coast-to-interior railway lines completed at the close of the nineteenth century to link the ports of Lagos and later Port Harcourt with the hinterland.

The introduction of the railways led to the emergence of new towns and the increasing growth of the population of towns on the transportation lines. For example, Kano grew to an estimated population of over 130,000 by 1950 compared to its 30,000 population of 1850. Kaduna, Enugu, Aba, Umuahia, Port Harcourt, and Jos were among the towns that arose or grew as a result of the network. However, the new transportation network also had an adverse effect on the traditional, precolonial towns. Sokoto, for example, declined from an estimated population of 120,000 in the 1850s to 52,000 in 1952, and Maiduguri, Oyo, and Katsina also experienced a rapid decline in importance and population as a result of being bypassed by the new railway system. Mabogunje vividly summarized this process:

> Irrespective of their size, traditional urban centers which were not on the rail-line or any other major routeways found themselves shunted into the backwater of economic decadence, losing many of their virile young men to centers now better favoured locationally. To make the situation more serious, the new type of trade, based on export and import, exposed traditional manufacturers to competition from better finished articles. The result was the undermining of traditional craft and a worsening of the position in the decadent urban centers.[9]

The result of British colonial policy, therefore, was the drastic alteration of the country's existing hierarchy of towns and the emergence of a new spatial pattern, an institutional framework facilitating the development of certain urban centers which persist to the present.

THE EMERGING NATIONAL URBAN HIERARCHY

The products of new economic orientation, administrative expansion, and infrastructural development effected during the colonial period were the establishment of new urban centers and the transformation of the national spatial economy. By 1963, as Green and Milone have pointed out, the hierarchical urban system had emerged in Nigeria.[10] At the apex of this hierarchy stood the city of Lagos with its population expanding at about four times the national rate of growth. At the bottom of this hierarchy lay the two urban complexes, the cities of Kano, Kaduna, and Jos in the north and Enugu, Aba, and Port Harcourt in the east. This hierarchical pattern conformed to the three main growth centers that have been accumulating population since the end of World War II.

The federal military government divided the country into a twelve-state political structure in 1967; this structure was further subdivided into 19 states in 1976. Although radical changes in the present spatial structure will be long in coming, it is inevitable that the administrative reorganization has introduced a new element with potential for effecting a far-reaching transformation of the national settlement pattern. The cities designated as capitals of the new states have the potential of becoming—as some already are—interregional and intrastate foci of production and commerce. Together, they constitute an emerging national urban hierarchy which in time will replace the traditional unidirectional spatial structure focusing on the core areas of the south. The new state capitals thus become the pivotal centers necessary for a national system of cities with the capacity both to mobilize local resources for local needs within the individual states and to articulate interregional exchanges for specialized products and services.

The newly created states have acquired political and administrative power that has led to the increased growth of their capital cities. These cities are becoming increasingly important as employment centers for civil service and private firms and are assuming the role of dominant urban centers by capturing many regionally oriented services and functions, especially branches of firms in service industries being set up and manufacturing activities. There is a general agglomeration of local consumption activity at these centers, and regional universities, technical colleges, and other institutes of higher learning are being located there. Finally, these cities are becoming recipients of the major share of investment in public infrastructure, for example, low-cost housing, hospitals, energy, highways, and so on.

The emerging national urban hierarchy can therefore be recognized as consisting of five grades or levels of urban centers.[11] First are those cities which are presently functioning effectively on a national level. These cities are the most important in many respects as they are the focus of the nation's political, economic, and transportation networks. These cities are Lagos, Ibadan, Kano, Kaduna, Enugu, and Port Harcourt.

The second grade consists of those cities functioning on interregional levels. These cities are the capitals of their respective states. Regionally oriented services and functions emanate from these centers. They include cities such as Sokoto, Benin, Calabar, Ilorin, and Owerri. The third tier of urban centers are those operating mainly on the intrastate level, such as Akure, Minna, Abeokuta, Yola, Bauchi, and Makurdi. The fourth group are major provincial urban centers, such as Kafanchan, Sapele, Shagamu, Mokwa, Nnewi, and Oron; the fifth consists of the much smaller towns functioning mainly on a local level, including Ejinrin, Lame, Effium, Osi, and Itu.

At the same time, the rapid rate of urbanization also portends the development of urban complexes in some parts of Nigeria. Already we are witnessing the merging of some close and sprawling urban centers, especially those located on major transportation systems. For example, all cities on the Lagos-Ibadan corridor (about 80 miles in length) will likely merge together in the not too distant future to form one giant megalopolis. Other potential conurbations are the Enugu-Onitsha-Aba-Port Harcourt axis, the Kano-Zaria-Kaduna axis, and the Benin-Sapele-Warri axis.

Another government decision that will have a far-reaching effect on the national spatial system is that of relocating the federal capital from Lagos to another site in the center of the country.[12] Centrally located, the new capital has the potential of reorienting the national spatial economy in a direction different from that designed by the colonial rulers, a direction which was more suitable for mobilization of resources for overseas markets than for development of internal markets. In the long run, the growth rate of the old capital city of Lagos will at least be reduced if not completely arrested, and thus some of the city's immediately pressing problems will be alleviated.

URBAN PLANNING: ISSUES AND CHALLENGES

The major challenge to planning is how to utilize the urbanization process in a way that conforms to and enhances the overall goal of development. The history of planning in Nigeria to date has not been enviable. Urban planning has been neglected at the national and regional levels for a long time. Before the creation of states in 1967, there were no distinct ministries responsible for urban planning per se; the only ministries close to such a function were the Ministries of Work and Housing. These, however, were invariably involved only with the supervision of the construction and building projects undertaken by the governments. The first legislative framework in which laws governing urban and regional planning were formulated was the Town and Country Planning Acts of the United Kingdom. Under this ordinance, the federal and state governments were empowered to initiate "planning schemes with respect to any land . . . with the general objective of controlling the development and use of land."[13] This ordinance led to the establishment in some regions of Town Planning Authorities, but these authorities concentrated on building control, estate development, and road layouts in towns, without taking advantage of the exceptionally wide provisions of the ordinance empowering the promotion of an integrated and comprehensive development program for the areas. There was also a lack of coordination among these authorities, the local administrative councils, and the housing corporation set up by the governments to develop housing estates and low-income buildings for urban areas.

Despite the variations in planning approaches from state to state in Nigeria, there are certain problems and handicaps common to all. Planning in many parts of the country has long been crisis-oriented and biased towards physical aspects. It is not uncommon that "planning" stops at the issuing of housing occupancy permits, building inspections, and land allocation. Many states had recently engaged the services of foreign consultants in preparing master plans which they hope will help in their planning efforts. However, these master plans are sometimes shelved, or, if implemented, it is in a haphazard way which defeats their comprehensiveness and long-range objectives. In some cases, the plans turn out to be mere exercises out of tune with daily life.

One of the important planning issues is how to correct the existing imbalances between urban and rural areas and among different parts of the country so as to effect the goal of a "just and egalitarian society" envisioned in the Second National Development Plan. Although these new urban growth areas capture an inordinate amount of resources, their performances so far have not been enviable.[14] The first main problem is how to integrate isolated communities into the state and national communications system. The existing transportation network was more conducive to colonial exploitation of agricultural and mineral products of the interior than it is to the present development needs of the country. The pressing need now is for a network linking the more backward parts with the growing and prospering areas and, in general, one that extends economic linkages across the whole country, east to west as well as north to south. The system should link not only all the state capitals but must evince a vertical integration with the smaller towns and rural villages.[15] The lack of effective integration of rural areas into the national spatial and economic system is evidenced by the fact that the booming condition of the Nigerian economy has not reached the rural areas as well as it should. The rural areas are being bypassed because the urban centers are not, in the words of Mabogunje, "adequately serving the rural population. . . . the emphasis on import-substituting industrialization has meant that with few exceptions, industries in our cities do not derive their raw materials from the rural areas . . . (but) increasing amount (being) spent on the food imported from abroad."[16] Many of the measures taken so far to tackle the overwhelming urban problems have been criticized for being "at best short term in their conception and ad hoc in their application."[17] Government decisions and actions play a crucial role in the urbanization process. The role of the transportation network in the evolution of the Nigerian urban system is a good example of the impact of governmental actions.

The decision on where to locate major industries is another issue that influences the urbanization process. In the past, the locations of industrial plants or other major manufacturing projects by the governments had often been decided purely on the basis of political expediencies rather than on how these would fit in the overall development goal.[18] The location of industrial projects and governmental institutions is of critical importance to urban growth and development. Most private industrial establishments choose the administrative centers as locations due to the presence of governmental institutions and a highly developed infrastructure. The presence of the federal and state government offices is thus of utmost importance for these urban centers. It is advantageous for most private enterprises to locate in administrative centers, as L. L. Schatzl aptly sums up: "The trend towards increasing government interference in private enterprise coupled with the inefficient administration and communication characteristic of developing nations seemed to favor a permanent, direct contact with the public administration."[19] Perhaps more important is the fact that governments are the single largest employers; this encourages labor migration to the administrative centers or state capitals in search of employment. A good example of this is Kaduna, a state capital, where in 1969, 95 percent of all industrial employees worked in enterprises with public participation.[20] The federal government has become concerned about the distribution of industrial activities equitably all over the country. It is obvious that absolute equitableness in distribution cannot be achieved nor warranted either at the national or state level because external economies of scale, transport, and manpower supply would continue to favor the old and economically strong core areas and the various state capitals as the most profitable locations. However, the creation of more states in February 1976 will likely help equalize development in the long run, considering the fact that there are now many more growth points (in the form of seats of federal and state governments) compared to less than five as late as 1966.

There are several other planning issues to be addressed. Among these is the fact that successful comprehensive planning (rather than mere physical planning) requires skilled planners, basic information or data systems, adequate funding of planning efforts, and a capable and honest administrative bureaucracy. Planning has been hampered to a great degree by the paucity and, sometimes, unreliability of data. This shortcoming has long been recognized by many planners, but they always have seemed to stop at decrying this gap without doing much about it. It will be beneficial in the long run if substantial attention is paid to the collection of data on the local level (metropolitan and provincial) without waiting for a national census or relying too heavily on it. Attention has been focused lately on the lack of manpower, and this is more obvious in the need for professional planners.

It is almost impossible to effect planning without an adequate control on the use and ownership of land. Urban planning can be obstructed by powerful land owners who can frustrate a planning effort by legal maneuvers or even by downright noncompliance with any master plan. Planning powers can be employed to regulate the nonuse or misuse of land through a system of taxation to enforce development or by restraining owners of occupied dwellings from discontinuing their use. The abuse and misuse of land should be prevented so as not to injure the public interest.

The federal government has declared itself to be unequivocally committed to urban and regional planning. The challenge is how to proceed in this effort so as to accomplish maximum and effective results. [21]

ON A NATIONAL STRATEGY OF URBANIZATION

The most serious indictment against the government has been its failure in formulating a coherent and well-articulated urban policy for Nigeria. Although there is a paragraph entitled "Urban Policy" in the Third National Development Plan, this topic was treated in a rather off-hand, glib sort of way, in general statements. [22] There is no doubt that there is a need for a deliberate urban policy rather than policies for cities to be inferred from the actions and decisions of the federal and state governments having reference to the cities. However, there are several conceptual issues that need to be clarified and recognized before a viable urban policy can be formulated. [23] Until now, no consensus has developed on optimum city size, although it is important to know when our cities have reached a point yielding decreasing returns. What are the private costs and benefits as a function of city size and economic composition? We need to know the distribution of city sizes in a national system as a function of the national economy, technology, incomes, consumer preferences, and transport costs, and the costs of producing and distributing overhead services as a function of city size. The fact that there are no specific answers to these conceptual issues is perhaps partly to blame for the lack of effective urban policies even in many developed countries.

In the Nigerian context, an urban policy must address itself to many other issues. Among these are whether the accelerating rate of urbanization is good. If so, how does it fit within the national social objectives, especially when the urban residents have access to more modern amenities than those of the rural areas, which still constitute more than 70 percent of all Nigerians? If the rate or urbanization is deemed too fast, how can the migration and urban growth be curtailed? What is the best pattern of urban-rural spatial development to maximize economic growth and the states' goal of "a land of bright and full opportunities for all citizens"?

A national urban policy must include at least population and migration policy, national land-use plan, rural development, and ecological programs. An analysis of these elements is warranted in order to show their importance and how they can be incorporated in an urban policy for Nigeria.

Population and migration policy is a sine qua non of any national urban policy. The basic question is what rate of population increase is appropriate to the national economy. One school of thought believes that the current rate of population growth in Nigeria is too high and that efforts should be made to reverse the trend. However, the government does not share this view and has asserted that "emphasis of policy is therefore being deliberately placed on accelerating the rate of growth of the economy rather than on direct action to achieve a drastic or immediate reduction in the overall birth-rate."[24] Perhaps more important is also the spatial distribution of the population. What role should the government play in changing the pattern of migration? It is easy to exaggerate the migration of people from one area to another, especially when seen in the rural-urban context. However, the fact remains that geographical mobility of people and resources is not as free or widespread as it should be due to many factors, not the least of which are connected to the basic attachments of Nigerians to their villages or towns of birth and an element of ethnic suspicion or rivalry. The creation of more states is not likely to weaken this barrier, and it may have the opposite result. The challenge, therefore, is how to achieve and improve the access to all parts of Nigeria by all citizens without fear or hindrances. Seen in a rural-urban

context, the objective here should be "improving access of all producing and consuming areas to one another through a linked system
. . . giving all populated areas access to the social capital that has
been invested in central places, whether in form of education or
health facilities or of other urban services."25

The process of urbanization has sharply accentuated the inherent
weaknesses of the present system of land tenure and land transactions.
The question of land ownership and control can no longer be treated
with levity. In bemoaning the ill effects of rapid urban growth, the
contribution of the use, ownership, and marketing of land is often
neglected. Since urban growth entails the conversion of rural land to
urban use, it is inevitable that the price of land should rise. Therefore, an immediate problem is how to control the inflation of land
prices, especially to curb the activities of speculators. Several projects in the Second Development Plan were reportedly frustrated because of the difficulty of obtaining land at reasonable prices. An
integral part of the problems is the land tenure system. The question
is whether the land tenure system and the nonuniform character of
land transactions in different parts of the country need a total over-
haul. There is a consensus that there is a need for reform in the
present system, but the extent of reform is the bone of contention.
Whereas the customary land tenure system precludes cash payment
for an alienation of interests in land, the pace of urbanization and
development has triggered excessive demand for land and its alienation through the market system. Therefore, "conveyances" patterned
after the British legal system were being drawn to mark transactions
that could then be registered with the governments. The acquisition
of land through this system, however, has not solved the problem of
land ownership, an issue which never arose under the customary
system because land is held for "use" rather than owned, and rights
to land were either an integral part of citizenship or of membership
in a kinship group.26 There are now differences in the systems of
land ownership in different parts of the country. In the north, the
colonial period brought along with it a system whereby absolute rights
in land belong to the state by law, whereas to the south the system is
still one of communal ownership with variation from place to place.
The present system invites confusion. A reappraisal and probable
modification of the customary land tenure system is appropriately
called for. A decree was recently promulgated nationalizing all land
in the country. There had been much opposition to this decree, and
it may be nullified when a civilian government comes into power. It
is also doubtful that the present bureaucracy could evolve a fair and
quick process of alienation of land so invested in the governments to
the citizens.

One of the constraints to effective mobility of people and resources throughout Nigeria has been the fear, indeed hostility, of the local people to citizens from different parts of the country. As a result, many skilled people have often refused to work in other parts of the country, except among their own ethnic groups. This has led to shortages of personnel in some parts and overconcentration in others. The hostility shown by the local people is due to many factors. Among these is the fear that migrants may take over the land, thereby depriving the local people of what they consider theirs or that the migrant may meddle in or dominate local politics. This problem must be resolved, perhaps through residency requirements whereby a migrant is qualified, after a certain period of time, to vote and participate in local politics. A citizen should not be deprived of his rights just because of his movement to another part of the same country. A system must also be devised whereby migrants are guaranteed tenure on land within a specific period of time.

As pointed out earlier, many of the cities owed their phenomenal growth to the migration of people from rural areas. For example, about 644,000 people were estimated to have migrated to metropolitan Lagos within the decade 1952-63. Unless a concerted policy of rural development is effected, the migration from rural to urban areas will continue unabated. It is not sufficient to provide basic amenities such as electricity, pipe-borne water, education, and health facilities. Rural areas need to be effectively integrated into the national economy. Agricultural productivity has been declining at an alarming rate in recent years due to the neglect of the rural areas and of farming. The recently launched program of "Operation Feed the Nation" is a dramatic gesture emphasizing the concern over the deterioration of agriculture in the economy and the need to turn the situation around. The federal government has also rightly committed itself to increase rural productivity and income and to diversify the rural economy.

A policy to grapple with the incipient problems of air and water pollution being generated by accelerated development efforts and to alleviate the concomitant problems of urban growth is also called for. The conservation of Nigerian resources, such as the wilderness, and preservation of architectural and historic places of interest and buildings must be an integral part of such a program of ecological and environmental preservation.

CONCLUSION

A consensus now exists that there is a relationship, however ill-defined, between urbanization and economic development. This fact must not be forgotten in our indictments of the ill effects, indeed hazards, of the sudden and phenomenal increase of urbanization in Nigeria. Rather, the question must concern our ability to harness and guide the process of urbanization for the benefit of the country's development. The government's role in this process cannot be over-emphasized. The creation of more states in Nigeria is an example par excellence of the effects of governmental decisions and policies on the process and pattern of urbanization. When Nigeria was divided into 12 states in 1967, the largest towns or commercial centers were chosen as the capitals for the new states. The effect of this action was to make these new seats of governments attractive to migrants. As Imoagene succinctly observes,

> eleven of the twelve states, the capital town is also the town with the greatest percentage share of industrial and trading enterprises located in it. This is both a cause and effect of the primate status of these towns . . . the additional administrative functions created more opportunities which in turn caused further expansion and demographic and otherwise. The third point . . . is the disproportionately small percentage of the States' industrial and trading enterprises located in the second industrial center. Only two of the twelve states have up to one quarter of all their enterprises in the second industrial center.[27]

The creation of more states is not being indicted here. In fact, I believe that this action will be very beneficial in the long run in that it will reorient the country from the excessive concentration of people, industries, and other social amenities in a certain few locations to a more hierarchically diffused spatial distribution. The point here is to stress the view that urban patterns and growth in Nigeria result from many public policies, whether deliberate or not. The government, therefore, must recognize this fact and tailor its policies and decisions to conform to overall national objectives and goals. I agree with the view that "instead of looking upon urbanization as a process of urban growth causing a number of problems to be solved . . . (we must not forget that it is also) a process or instrument of social change and development."[28]

NOTES

1. L. Green, <u>Nigeria: Population Models for National and Regional Planning 1952-67</u> (Ibadan: National Institute of Social and Economic Research, 1969).

2. A. L. Mabogunje, "Cities and Social Order," University of Ibadan Inaugural Lecture, 1974.

3. U. I. Ukwu, "Urbanization and Socio-economic Development," in Management of Rapid Urbanization in Nigeria, ed. A. Adedeji and L. Rowland (Ile Ife: University of Ife Press, 1973), p. 212.

4. A. L. Mabogunje, Urbanization in Nigeria (New York: Africana, 1968), p. 68.

5. Ibid.

6. Ibid., p. 76.

7. W. R. Bascom, "The Urban African and His World," Cahier d'Études Africaines 4, no. 4 (1963): 172.

8. E. J. Taaffe, R. L. Morrill, and P. R. Gould, "Transport Expansion in Underdeveloped Countries: A Comparative Analysis," Geographical Review 53 (October 1963): 503-29.

9. A. L. Mabogunje, "The Economic Implications of the Pattern of Urbanization in Nigeria," Nigerian Journal of Economic and Social Studies 7, no. 1 (1965): 16.

10. L. Green and V. Milone, Urbanization in Nigeria—A Planning Commentary (New York: Ford Foundation, 1973), p. 8.

11. This is similar to that of H. I. Ajaegbu's "Grades of Urban Centers." See his Urban and Rural Development in Nigeria (London: Heinemann, 1976), p. 55.

12. A. T. Salau, "A New Capital for Nigeria: Planning, Problems and Prospects," Africa Today 24, no. 4 (1977).

13. Cap. 155 of the Nigerian Law, Nigeria Town and Country Planning Ordinance No. 4 of 1946, quoted in A. L. Mabogunje's "Toward an Urban Policy in Nigeria," Nigerian Journal of Economic and Social Studies 16, no. 1 (1974): 89.

14. It had been calculated that the country had over 80 percent of its nonagricultural public capital investment in the urban areas. See S. A. Aluko, "Resource Allocation and Overall Strategy in Nigeria's Second National Development Plan 1970-74: A Symposium," The Quarterly Journal of Administration 5, no. 3 (1971): 267-84. Some scholars have asserted that Nigerian cities are parasitic, with few urban dwellers making positive productive contribution to the economic growth, and many have reached a stage where increasing investments may be yielding decreasing returns. See A. L. Mabogunje, "Urbanization in Nigeria, A Constraint on Economic Development," Economic Development and Cultural Change 13, no. 4 (1965): 413-38.

15. For a good and insightful analysis of this issue, see M. I. Logan, "Key Elements and Linkages in the National System: A Focus for Regional Planning in Nigeria," in Planning for Nigeria, ed. K. M. Barbour (Ibadan: University of Ibadan, 1972), pp. 16-39.

16. Mabogunje, "Towards an Urban Policy in Nigeria," op. cit., p. 87.

17. Ibid., p. 85.

18. The wrangling on where to locate the proposed iron and steel mill operation by the Balewa regime was the most famous case. See O. Aboyade, "Industrial Location and Development Policy," Nigerian Journal of Economic and Social Studies 10 (1968).

19. L. L. Schatzl, Industrialization in Nigeria: A Spatial Analysis (Munich: Weltforum Verlag, 1973), p. 91.

20. Ibid., p. 101.

21. See, Republic of Nigeria, Nigeria: Guidelines for the Third National Development Plan 1975-80 (Lagos: Government Printer, 1974), p. 34.

22. Republic of Nigeria, The Third National Development Plan 1975-80, vol. 1 (Lagos: Federal Ministry of Economic Development, 1975), p. 291.

23. See L. Wingo, "Issues in a National Urban Development Strategy for the U.S.," Urban Studies 9, no. 1 (1972): 16.

24. Republic of Nigeria, The Third National Development Plan, op. cit., p. 293.

25. A. L. Mabogunje, "Regional Planning and the Development Process: Prospects in the 1970-74 Plan," in Planning for Nigeria, ed. K. M. Barbour, op. cit., p. 10.

26. S. Famoriyo, "Land Transactions and Agricultural Development in Nigeria," Eastern African Journal of Rural Development 7, nos. 1, 2 (1974): 179-88.

27. O. Imoagene, "The Impact of Industrialization and Urbanization on the People of Nigeria," Presence Africaine 96, no. 4 (1975): 579.

28. See, International Union of Local Authorities, Urbanization in Developing Countries (The Hague: Martinus Nijhoff, 1968), p. 7.

Part Four

EAST AFRICA: DEVELOPMENT PERSPECTIVES

Historically the urbanization process in East Africa is in many respects different from that of the countries already discussed. Although unique variations exist among the East African nations, the region's development history embodies several common attributes. Prior to the arrival of non-Africans, the region's settlement patterns were characterized by pastoral and nomadic societies and isolated precolonial kingdoms. Except for the coastal strip and the core settlements of these kingdoms, there were few compact settlements in East Africa. The articulation and integration of spatial urban systems in the region were largely a result of the development of caravan routes and of colonial trade and administrative networks.

Such networks were largely superimposed upon and distinct from indigenous settlements. Africans were either excluded or restricted in terms of migration and urban residence during the colonial era. Such restrictions and the sparse pattern of settlement over the years partly explain the generally low level of urbanization in most of East Africa. This bifurcation of the urbanization process presented the recently independent nations with a host of planning and development problems.

The chapters in this section place current problems of urban development and planning within their proper historical perspectives. In Ethiopia, a deep-rooted feudal heritage and urbanization without development (largely in response to foreigners) left their unmistakable stamp of disintegration, confusion, and conflict on urban development patterns and processes. The Koehns analyze such problems and their impact on recent planning experiences in Ethiopia both at the national and local levels. They point out the lack of a comprehensive planning orientation and the absence, particularly with respect to land, of the institutional, political, and legal frameworks necessary to bring it about.

Kenya presents a good example for the duality in settlement systems. R. A. Obudho traces the development of this anomaly in the urban system and its impact on spatial development processes and policies. His conclusions point out the need to emphasize the role and potential of the smaller indigenous central places in regional development.

Colonial policies on residential development, and on housing in general, are quite evident in the historical development of both Dar es Salaam and Lusaka. Racial separation of populations in essence created a physical structure parallel to the colonial political and economic order. Such disparities in housing and among neighborhoods are obviously being exacerbated by rapid urbanization and the growth of squatter settlements. Since independence, both countries have been attempting approaches to deal with their housing problems. In Tanzania, however, the potential of the Ujamaa concept, with its emphasis on creating a new social system, is yet to be realized in urban areas, according to Edwin Segal in his chapter on Dar es Salaam. In Zambia, the favored approach is to break the rigid connection between employment and housing which has been created in an effort to evade responsibility for housing labor in the colonial period.

Urban patterns in East Africa are largely the recent creation of colonial powers. Unlike North or West Africa, indigenous urban settlements or urban systems did not exist in East Africa in precolonial periods. As such, despite subtle diversities in their experiences, the East African nations share a generally low level of urbanization and an alienation of most of their urban populations in their cities.

12

URBANIZATION AND URBAN DEVELOPMENT PLANNING IN ETHIOPIA

Peter Koehn
Eftychia F. Koehn

HISTORY OF URBANIZATION

The northernmost provinces of Ethiopia have been the locus of some measure of urban life for at least 18 centuries. However, until recently few urban settlements had emerged in the south, and the history of urbanization in the northern highlands is characterized by abrupt ebbs and flows.

Prior to the twentieth century, the major factors responsible for the establishment and growth of towns were the caravan trade, the proliferation of regional capitals ruled by feudal lords, constant shifting of the location of the capital city of the Empire until the founding of Addis Ababa by Emperor Menelik in 1887, and the establishment of military garrisons in conquered southern provinces. Since the beginning of this century, towns have grown up in response to the Italian occupation (1936-41), around important natural resource centers, and along the Addis Ababa-Djibuti railway line. The towns of Nazreth, Mojo, Debre Zeit, and Akaki, along with the capital city of Addis Ababa, form an industrial region which encompasses most of Ethiopia's largest enterprises.[1]

Ethiopian cities and towns can be divided into those established in response to indigenous pressures and those which trace their origin to the economic or political activities of foreigners. The indigenous Ethiopian town owes its nature and early development principally to political and military considerations. The ghebi (palace compound) of the king or emperor provided the central locus of highland towns. Around the ghebi one would find the residences of military chiefs and the Orthodox Church hierarchy.[2]

Addis Ababa is the last capital city of the Ethiopian Empire founded in this fashion. In its formative period, Emperor Menelik

FIGURE 12.1

Ethiopia: Urban Centers

Source: Compiled by the author.

distributed land among ranking officers of the court and other favored individuals. Quarters were separated from each other by stretches of unoccupied land in order to reduce the possibility that conflicts would break out between armies loyal to different nobles. [3] As a result, Addis Ababa looked like a cluster of villages. The central city grew up as a series of quarters, or sefers, of irregular size and shape surrounding important landmarks, such as a palace, that still are evident today. The later growth of Addis Ababa took in villages that remain unplanned enclaves, surrounded by modern residential and commercial edifices. Poor and wealthy urban dwellers have always lived in close proximity in Addis Ababa, and not in quarters segregated along class and racial lines.

Harar, capital of the southeastern province of Hararghe, constitutes an Islamic city of indigenous origin. The mosque is the central structure. Remnants of the ancient city's protective wall and gates still encircle residents of the old section of Harar. Industrial development has not occurred in Harar, and the city's net population has remained relatively stable over the past 40 years. [4]

The promotion of foreign interests lies at the heart of most of the urban growth experienced by Ethiopia in the last century. The sixty-year Italian colonization of Eritrea and its five-year occupation of the rest of Ethiopia stimulated the expansion of towns, where expatriates dominated manufacturing and commerce. [5] Asmara, the second largest city in the country, provides a pertinent illustration. In the early nineteenth century, a small indigenous village with a population of about 150 occupied the site of the present urban area. Asmara began to expand rapidly when it became the administrative capital of the Italian colony of Eritrea in 1889. The estimated population of the city reached 5,300 in the 1890s and 98,000 in 1937. Just over 200,000 persons lived in Asmara in 1972. [6]

In the case of Dire Dawa in the east, the need for a depot and repair station at a midway point along the French railway line connecting Addis Ababa to the Red Sea led to the establishment of a completely new urban settlement in 1902. Dire Dawa's residential development occurred along racial and class lines. Most engineers and skilled workers employed by the Franco-Ethiopian Railway Company, as well as other Europeans, lived in the central section of town, known as Gazira, while non-Europeans resided in the densely populated Magala area. [7] The town grew from 20,000 inhabitants in the late 1930s to more than 60,000 today. Dire Dawa, Addis Ababa, and Asmara are the only cities that have attracted a number of large manufacturing establishments.

Distribution and Growth of Urban Settlements

Although there is a long history of urban settlement in Ethiopia, the country is far from highly urbanized. Its current population of about 28 million people is overwhelmingly rural. According to the National Sample Survey conducted in the mid-1960s, only one-twelfth of the country's total population lived in the 185 towns of more than 2,000 inhabitants. Although this proportion is relatively small for the continent of Africa as a whole, urban growth in Ethiopia is occurring at a rapid rate (almost 7 percent annually). An estimated 6.5 percent of Ethiopia's total population resided in urban areas of more than 20,000 inhabitants in 1972. [8] The 14 provinces vary considerably in terms of the proportion of the population living in cities and towns,

TABLE 12.1

Estimated Urban and Rural Population in 1967, by Province (in thousands)

Province	Total Population	Rural Population	Urban Population	Percent Urban
Arussi	1,110.8	1,069.4	41.4	3.7
Bale	159.8	139.8	20.0	12.5
Begemder	1,348.4	1,277.9	70.5	5.2
Eritrea	1,589.4	1,324.1	265.3	16.6
Gemu Goffa	840.5	818.5	22.0	2.6
Gojam	1,576.1	1,506.3	69.8	4.4
Hararghe	3,341.7	3,189.2	152.5	4.5
Illubabor	663.2	637.9	25.3	3.8
Kaffa	688.4	635.1	53.3	7.7
Shoa	3,970.3	3,115.4	854.9	21.5
Sidamo	1,521.9	1,430.9	91.0	6.0
Tigre	2,307.3	2,200.4	106.9	4.6
Wollega	1,429.9	1,376.0	53.9	3.8
Wollo	3,119.7	3,021.1	98.6	3.2
Total	23,667.4	21,742.0	1,925.4	8.0

Source: Ethiopia, Central Statistical Office, Survey of Major Towns in Ethiopia, Statistical Bulletin No. 1 (Addis Ababa: C.S.O., December 1968), p. 1.

ranging from a low of 2.6 percent in Gemu Goffa in 1967, to highs of
16.6 percent in Eritrea and 21.5 percent in Shoa (see Table 12.1).
Addis Ababa accounts for more than 18 percent of the population of
Shoa and thus the high urban population of Ethiopia's most populous
province.

The primate city of Addis Ababa accounts for one-third of the
total town population of Ethiopia. Addis Ababa is the most populous
city in East and Central Africa, and one of the consistently fastest
growing cities in the world. Its present size probably approaches 1.5
million inhabitants, and this population is increasing by roughly 8
percent per annum.[9] The combined population of Addis Ababa and
Asmara accounts for 43 percent of Ethiopia's total town population.
In 1970, only 15 percent of the urban population lived in the 109 towns
with less than 5,000 inhabitants, while over 60 percent resided in the
14 cities and towns with populations in excess of 20,000 (see Table
12.2). In addition to Addis Ababa, Asmara (estimated population

TABLE 12.2

Distribution of Towns, by Size, January 1970

Size of Town	Number of Towns	Population	Percent of Total Population	Percent of Town Population
2,000–5,000	109	363,130	1.4	15.5
5,000–20,000	62	544,840	2.1	23.3
20,000–100,000	12	415,630	1.6	17.8
100,000 and more	2	1,014,260	4.0	43.4
Total urban population	185	2,337,860	9.1	100.0

Source: Jean Comhaire, Urbanization in Ethiopia, Dialogue 1
(October, 1967), p. 27.

218,360), Dire Dawa (59,420), and Harar (49,580), more than 20,000
people lived in the following urban areas in 1970: Dessie (Wollo),
44,810; Jimma (Kaffa), 39,790; Nazreth (Shoa), 37,620; Gondar
(Begemder), 34,630; Keren (Eritrea), 30,000; Mekele (Tigre), 27,100;
Debre Zeit (Shoa), 26,880; Debre Markos (Gojjam), 26,320; Agordat
(Eritrea), 24,000; and Bahr Dar (Gojjam), 20,480.[10]

Urbanization in Ethiopia either has not been accompanied by industrialization or has exceeded the economic growth rate of the few industrial centers. [11] Manufacturing only contributed 5.4 percent of the country's gross domestic product in 1969 and employed about 5 percent of the economically active urban population. Foreigners owned and/or managed most of the largest industrial enterprises. [12] About half of the manufacturing industries operating in Ethiopia and 60 percent of their fixed assets were concentrated in the Addis Ababa metropolitan region. [13] The complete absence of large-scale economic activity characterizes smaller towns and a number of urban settlements with populations exceeding 10,000. The vast majority of towns serve as administrative and educational centers, with small-scale trade constituting the principal economic activity. Many of the southern towns trace their origin to military or administrative activities of the central government rather than favorable economic conditions. In the latter years of imperial rule, the commercial base of older northern urban centers (Gondar, Axum, Dessie) stagnated or declined, while town populations continued to increase. Economic growth tended to be concentrated in Addis Ababa, Dire Dawa, and a few smaller, rapidly expanding southern towns (particularly Shashamene, Gore, Awasa, and Dembi Dolo). The latter towns became major marketing centers where imported goods and local agricultural produce are loaded and unloaded, distributed, and stored. [14]

The rapid population growth of small and intermediate-size urban areas in Ethiopia results primarily from rural-urban migration. The relative paucity of rural social services and economic opportunities, the promotion of commercial agriculture by the imperial legal order, the mechanization of agricultural production and attendant eviction of tenants and marginization of the peasantry, as well as recent famines and political unrest all have contributed to the "push" or repulsion of people from rural areas. [15] Many of the migrants to Addis Ababa come from the north where pressure on the land is the greatest. Unrealistic expectations regarding employment opportunities exert a powerful influence "pulling" rural residents to towns. [16] Moreover, the large-scale exodus of the most intelligent school-aged young people from the countryside and small towns is induced by the concentration of educational facilities in urban areas. [17]

Intermediate and smaller urban areas attract roughly equal numbers of rural migrants (see Table 12.3). Urban areas of more than 20,000 inhabitants experience a higher degree of population mobility than Addis Ababa and towns with less than 20,000 residents. People are more likely to move into and out of the larger towns. The movement of people from north to south in pursuit of economic gain and public service employment represents a major component of inter-urban migration. [18] The overwhelming majority of migrants into Addis

TABLE 12. 3

In-Migration and Out-Migration in 1970, by Size of Town
(in thousands)

Area	Gross In-Migration		Gross Out-Migration		Net In-Migration	
	Size	Percentage	Size	Percentage	Size	Percentage
Rural	0	0	99	0. 4	-99	-0. 4
Town (2,000–20,000 inhabitants)	53	5. 8	13	1. 4	40	4. 4
Urban (20,000 and above inhabitants, excluding Addis Ababa)	44	7. 0	22	3. 5	22	3. 5
Addis Ababa	45	5. 6	8	1. 0	37	4. 6
All towns	142	6. 0	43	1. 9	99	4. 1

Source: Jean Comhaire, Urbanization in Ethiopia, Dialogue 1
(October, 1967), p. 14.

Ababa resided in smaller cities and towns before coming to the capital
city. [19] The relatively small population exodus from Addis Ababa indicates that interurban migration trends continue to support expansion
of the primate city. Moreover, 1973–74 survey data indicate that less
than 40 percent of the Tigre, Gurage, Amhara, and Oromo migrants
to the capital intend to return to their provincial birthplace or home.
The Oromo are most inclined to abandon their rural ties and make
Addis Ababa their permanent home. [20]
    The Central Statistical Office estimated the annual rate of
natural increase for urban and rural areas at 2. 5 percent in 1970.
Annual net rural-to-urban migration contributed the remaining 4.1
percent (nearly two-thirds) of the total town population growth rate.
Using 1970 estimates of the net overall annual rate of urban and rural
population growth (i. e. , 6. 6 and 2. 1 percent, respectively), the number of Ethiopians living in settlements of 2, 000 or more persons would

TABLE 12.4

Estimated Rural, Town, Urban, and City Populations and
Number of Towns and Cities in 1970, 1975, and 1980

	1970		1975		1980	
	Number	Population	Number	Population	Number	Population
Rural	n.a.*	22,579,000	n.a.	25,051,000	n.a.	27,756,000
Towns (2,000–5,000 inhabitants)	109	363,130	77	289,000	39	132,000
Towns (5,000–20,000 inhabitants)	62	544,840	88	805,000	118	1,149,000
Urban Settlements (20,000–100,000 inhabitants)	12	415,630	18	704,000	26	1,157,000
Cities (100,000 and more inhabitants)	2	1,014,000	2	1,422,000	2	1,995,000

*Not applicable.
Source: Jean Comhaire, Urbanization in Ethiopia, Dialogue 1 (October, 1967), pp. 8, 11.

nearly double in ten years, reaching 16 percent of the total population by 1980 (see Table 12. 4). In fact, the proportion of the population living in urban areas will be even higher, as this projection fails to include villages that will pass the 2,000-person mark and be classified as new towns.

Urbanization and Material Conditions of Urban Life

Life is difficult for most urban dwellers in Ethiopia. [21] Unemployment is widespread. Housing units are scarce and of substandard construction. Most towns lack piped water and electricity. In large cities, densely populated areas may be completely inaccessible by road; the inhabitants of such settlements are denied water outlets, refuse collection, and fire and police protection. Asmara is the only urban area where some residents are served by a sewage disposal system. [22] Poor sanitary conditions prevail. An exceptionally high proportion of Ethiopia's urban population is infected by serious communicable diseases. The urban infant mortality rate is extremely high. The staff of city clinics and hospitals cannot provide adequate medical treatment and health education to most of those in need of these services. Problems of urban service provision in the areas of transportation, housing, sanitation, public health, and welfare have been compounded by the rapid rate of rural-urban migration. Moreover, the urban population increased so dramatically from 1957-72 that no per capita increase in urban income was realized during this period. [23]

The significance of planning is underscored by the magnitude of the task that would be required to halt or reverse urbanization trends. [24] Rapid growth in Ethiopia's urban population will continue to constitute a characteristic demographic feature in the foreseeable future. Thus, the objectives and strategies embodied in urban development plans and the way in which they are fashioned and implemented will be of far-reaching consequence for the quality of life experienced by urban dwellers.

DEVELOPMENT PLANNING IN URBAN AREAS

Urban planning in Ethiopia has been limited to the physical features of towns. Social planning for the development of human abilities through urban education, training, employment, and health and welfare programs has been practically nonexistent. [25] Only a few towns outside of the capital city possess master plans; none actively engage in comprehensive planning. Moreover, metropolitan area

planning and integrated rural–urban regional planning are not attempted. [26] The remaining sections of this chapter analyze urban development planning during the reign of the conservative monarch Haile
Selassie I and evaluate future planning prospects in the wake of radical
changes introduced by the new military rulers in 1975 and 1976.

Urban Planning under Emperor Haile Selassie I

Government authorities and foreign consultants prepared town
plans during Haile Selassie's rule without involving or consulting the
mass of urban residents and recent migrants in the formulation and
execution stages of the planning process. In the largest cities, employees of the municipality's technical department participated in the
drafting of master plans. The Municipalities Department of the Ministry of Interior provided this service for a few other cities and towns.
Unrealistic goals and limited legal authority and resources prevented
municipalities from realizing the objectives set forth in these plans. [27]

Plan Preparation

Only 47 of the 210 municipalities in Ethiopia possessed master
plans. With funding secured from the Ministry of Interior, an Italian
consulting firm prepared plans for 40 towns during the 1960s; the
Municipalities Department completed seven additional plans in the
early 1970s. [28] Although the plans utilized a narrow and suspect data
base, they introduced ambitious zoning controls[29] and development
goals. Most of the development objectives embodied in the master
plans (e.g., paved roads) bore little relation to the social and economic needs of Ethiopia's urban masses. [30]
In the case of Addis Ababa, foreign consultants generated three
plans for the capital city over a ten-year period. Sir Patrick Abercrombie completed a basic master plan in 1956. The Abercrombie
plan divided the capital into commercial, central business, government, industrial, recreational, and residential zones. [31] Consultants
prepared two substantial revisions of the basic master plan—the Bol-
ton-Hennessey plan and the French Mission plan. [32] All three plans
emphasized road construction and improved traffic patterns.
Ethiopia's town plans share a number of common attributes.
Although the plans incorporated broad development goals and zoning
controls, their authors did not consult public opinion or elected local
officials during the formulation process. In any event, "old regime"
plans constituted perfunctory administrative exercises and stood no
chance of successful implementation given the urban context in which

they were introduced. Lack of legal backing, political support, and local administrative and financial capacity undermined the implementation of urban master plans. In short, urban development planning in Ethiopia did not progress beyond the drawing board. [33]

Barriers to Plan Implementation

Numerous barriers to the implementation of urban development plans can be identified. The broad definition given to plan goals and the uncertainty of political support attached to objectives identified by foreign planners with little local input generated serious administrative problems. Municipal officials did not operationalize plan objectives through capital improvements budgeting. Without multi-year capital improvement budgeting to set specific plan priorities, even the short-term objectives of urban development planning became the subject of confused and extended debate. In larger municipalities, officials also failed to institute administrative procedures requiring review of projects initiated by operating departments for conformity with approved long-range development plans. [34] The unintegrated and highly personalized nature of the prefectoral system of Ethiopian local government guaranteed that problems of inter-agency coordination and of sustaining commitment by local officials to the pursuit of plan objectives would arise in provincial towns. Thus, the Dire Dawa municipal director and the Awraja governor clashed over the allocation of resources and the sale of municipal land for urban instead of rural development purposes, while in Dessie the national police arrested municipal guards when they attempted to demolish houses built contrary to the local master plan or without the municipality's approval. [35] In Addis Ababa, newly built roads typically did not provide for bus stops and had to be torn up and rebuilt several times for laying underground cables, drainage ducts, and water pipes. Finally, Emperor Haile Salassie's arbitrary insistence on undertaking unplanned projects, shifting development priorities, and transferring funds created additional confusion. [36]

Even the wealthiest municipalities in Ethiopia did not possess sufficient resources to permit pursuit of major development projects without supplemental assistance from the central government. Yet, the central government only issued major grants in aid to a few municipalities. [37] In fact, the Municipalities Department often did not approve increased municipal expenditures during budget review and then attempted to collect "surplus" municipal revenues at the end of the fiscal year. A municipality could not seriously entertain the idea of carrying out the ambitious proposals set forth in its master plan in light of such financial constraints. For instance, the master plan for Harar (1966) calls for expansion of the road system and construction of a sewage and drainage system. A conservative estimate of the cost of the two projects is $8 million. [38] Harar is a relatively wealthy city. Yet, as late as 1974, the total annual budget (including recurrent expenditures as well as new capital investment) of the Harar Municipality amounted to E$500,000. [39] As these figures starkly reveal, Ethiopian municipalities lacked the basic financial capacity needed to implement the master plans designed by Italian consultants.

Other obstacles, legal and political in nature, thwarted implementation of the land-use provisions contained in urban master plans. Under the imperial regime, municipal officers and city councilors proved to be more concerned with and adept at protecting and furthering the interests of the landed urban elite and the nobility and with seeking material advantages for themselves than with addressing the pressing needs of the majority of city and town dwellers. [40] Municipalities lacked effective zoning authority because master plans had not been legally adopted in accordance with procedures mandated by section 1536 of the Civil Code of Ethiopia. The absence of legal authority forced municipalities to rely on voluntary compliance by developers with land-use guidelines and subdivision regulations. [41] Thus, developers laid out plots, built dwelling units, and provided or failed to provide improvements entirely at their own discretion. In practice, they rarely complied with plan guidelines. Even in Addis Ababa, subdivision usually took place without prior knowledge or approval by the municipality. Developers typically made no provision for schools, clinics, parks, or paved streets of a minimum width to allow fire-fighting and sanitation trucks to gain access into the settlement. [42]

The extensive construction of unauthorized housing units in Ethiopian cities created additional problems for planned physical development. Dwellings suddenly appeared in places designated for recreational or educational use, or in the route of planned thoroughfares. Increasingly, buildings that did not meet minimum construction and sanitary standards were crowded onto 80 to 90 percent of the land area of settlements found on the periphery of cities and in certain central city locations. In Addis Ababa, "illogical housing developments have rendered the installation of a modern sewer system impossible in many areas. "[43] Although between 40 and 60 percent of the housing units found in the capital had been constructed without a building permit, Addis Ababa municipal officials rarely tore down substandard, unauthorized dwellings and never endeavored to upgrade squatter settlements. [44]

Confusion, conflict, and corruption in municipal expropriation proceedings further retarded urban development planning under the imperial regime. Extensive urban road construction projects brought municipalities into direct conflict with land and property owners, particularly in Addis Ababa. Article 1463 of the Civil Code of Ethiopia vaguely stated that expropriation of property may be undertaken when competent authorities determined that it would "serve the public interest." This broad standard encouraged municipalities to attempt the expropriation of urban land and buildings at will. No other municipal activity embittered urban residents as deeply as its handling of expropriation proceedings. Renters are not pleased to be evicted from their homes in cities such as Addis Ababa, where alternative housing is extremely difficult to locate.

Confusion over urban land ownership rights obliged municipalities to become embroiled in long-standing and protracted disputes in order to determine which party to compensate for expropriated land or property. This situation can be clearly illustrated with reference to the capital city. The Addis Ababa Municipality encountered great difficulty making land ownership determinations. In places, the same land had been given away, sold, or bequeathed to different people by Ethiopian government officials, the Italian occupation forces, and/or initial and subsequent owners. In other cases, district chiefs failed to distribute land as expected, or land allocations consisted of imprecise verbal descriptions. Adequate geodetic and cadastral survey data did not exist for most of the city. The stones and other field reference makers used as boundary indicators in the past had been lost or destroyed over time. [45] The municipality never completed the city-wide cadastral survey needed to settle urban land ownership disputes—principally because officials acceded to pressure from those who stood to lose the most from any move to redistribute land. [46] Moreover, the manner in which municipal officials handled land and property expropriations outraged many less influential Addis Ababa landowners. Officials flagrantly violated legal expropriation proceedings and frequently ignored the requirement that the municipality pay fair compensation for expropriated land and property. Local government officials attempted to justify their action on the grounds that municipal authorities could not afford to compensate land owners at the highly inflated rates brought about by urban speculation. In 1971, the Vice Mayor of the Addis Ababa Municipality complained that "if urban land is expropriated and compensation paid at these rates, there is little or no money left for development financing itself." [47] In some cases, however, the Addis Ababa Awraja Court would intervene on behalf of small landlords and house owners adversely affected by municipal expropriation practices. The conflicts and judicial actions that resulted from municipal expropriation practices generated lengthy delays in the execution of planned municipal projects. [48] Finally, municipal officials used process irregularities and confusion to except the land and houses of influential and favored individuals from expropriation. Accusations of favoritism in land and property matters dominated the charges that led to arrest of the Lord Mayor of Addis Ababa in 1974. [49]

Speculation in land posed a further barrier to urban development in accordance with master plan objectives that became increasingly troublesome toward the end of Emperor Haile Selassie's reign. A dearth of attractive domestic investment alternatives for surplus wealth spurred urban land speculation. The demand for land that accompanied rapid urbanization and was inflated by speculators who withheld land from development pushed prices into an upward spiral. Uncontrolled land speculation perpetuated gross inequities in distribution patterns. A small number of wealthy estate holders held most urban land. In Addis Ababa, according to Mesfin Wolde Mariam's calculations, 5 percent of the population owned 95 percent of the privately owned land in 1966. [50] In a number of areas, particularly on the urban fringe, land speculation produced a mixed tenure system. Absentee landlords owned the land, while tenants leased land and "owned" any dwelling units they erected. Among the housing occupants surveyed in two of the capital city's ten districts in the early 1960s, only 8.3 percent owned the land upon which their dwelling had been built, while about 30 percent of all occupied private housing units in Addis Ababa were owned by their occupants in 1967. [51] Urban tenants behaved much as their rural counterparts did. Most leasers were not highly motivated to improve their property or join self-help projects in communities they would not reside in permanently. [52]

Furthermore, vast tracts of urban land passed back and forth among a few speculators without being occupied or utilized for development purposes. Recent estimates of urban population distribution in Addis Ababa indicate that one-third to one-half of the city's land is underutilized, supporting only 10 percent of all inhabitants. At the same time, urban land speculation fostered overcrowding in the central market area, growth pressures in squatters settlements, and leapfrog development. [53] Finally, the inflated price of urban land made it impossible for municipalities to purchase large tracts of centrally located land for planned development purposes.

Urban Planning under the Provisional Military Government*

Whereas it is necessary to build our urban areas on the basis of careful planning and study in order to utilize our

---

*Material for this section was collected in Ethiopia during the summer of 1975, under a research grant from the University of Montana.

resources in an economical manner, to improve the conditions of cities, to protect urban dwellers from diseases
and prevent illegal activities now prevalent in urban areas.

Preamble to Proclamation No. 47 of 1975, "Government Ownership of Urban Lands and Extra Houses Proclamation."

In 1974, representatives from most of Ethiopia's military units
formed an Armed Forces Coordinating Committee (called "Derg")
and gradually assumed political power in the wake of widespread urban
unrest. By September, the Derg had suspended Parliament and the
Constitution, arrested Emperor Haile Selassie, and established a
provisional military government. [54] The Derg included noncommis-
sioned officers who had principally been recruited from the southern
peasantry and radical junior officers with ties to the country's intelligentsia. The leaders of the coup sought to secure popular support for
military rule by adopting radical measures designed to change social
and economic relations in Ethiopia in a manner that would benefit the
impoverished and landless rural and urban classes. [55]

The Provisional Military Administrative Council (PMAC) drastically altered urban planning norms during the first year of its rule.
The PMAC nationalized all rural and urban land, large firms, and
rented dwellings and shops. By late 1975, central government officials
stressed the importance of social planning and argued that urban development must no longer occur in isolation from rural considerations.
The Ministry of Urban Development and Housing (formerly the Ministry of Public Works and Housing) staff had begun work on a new structural arrangement designed to institutionalize integrated regional planning in Ethiopia. Along with other measures, the PMAC moved to cen-
tralize the function of preparing regional and urban development plans
under the ministry in July 1975. All municipal personnel possessing
technical skills needed in planning were transferred to the central
ministry. [56] In short, the new government's initial actions indicated
a commitment to comprehensive planning and social change.

The PMAC removed many firmly entrenched barriers to planned
urban land use. Urban planners no longer need struggle to resolve
complicated land ownership disputes. Speculation in land ceased
abruptly with the abolition of private ownership. The government
shifted sizable tracts of urban land to its direct control, with the
stipulation that persons or families could secure possessory (or pre-
sumptive) rights to use no more than 500 square meters of land. Proclamation No. 47 of 1975 also allows the government to retract possessory rights whenever urban land is not utilized within a specified
period. Finally, the government retained broad authority to expro-
priate "for public purpose" any urban land or house. These measures

greatly strengthened the ability of the Ministry of Urban Development and Housing (MUDH) to control land use and to direct construction and general physical growth in conformance with the objectives of comprehensive urban plans. [57]

The capacity of many African governments to resolve problems of the urban environment is impaired by the absence of local institutions empowered to formulate and carry out urban plans and projects. [58] Upon assuming power, the PMAC swiftly established a new development structure, the urban cooperative (or urban dwellers' association), at the local level. Three to five hundred contiguous households form a local cooperative (kebele). Under Proclamation No. 47 issued in August 1975, the PMAC assigned important urban development roles to the kebele. Neighborhood cooperatives are expected to mobilize the energies of their members in support of the government's urban plans. With the advice and assistance of local and central government experts, the kebele are authorized to participate in the construction and direction of schools, clinics, roads, and other urban facilities. Proclamation No. 104 of 1976 expanded the list of kebele association duties and powers. Within their jurisdiction, urban dwellers associations are given responsibility for felling, mowing, and selling trees and grass, preserving and maintaining through afforestation trees and forests, protecting the soil from erosion, "beautifying the urban center," protecting public and government property, insuring the cleanliness of the neighborhood, conducting hygiene education activities, eradicating illiteracy, and keeping a register of the number of residents, births, marriages, and deaths. [59]

Proclamation No. 47 incorporates important provisions that allow kebele to overcome the financial barriers to implementing development plan objectives encountered by local governments and urban voluntary associations under the monarchical regime. Article 20 grants each urban cooperative access to revenues from local rents in its locality that do not exceed E $100 (U. S. $50). Rent payments are to be collected by the cooperative society and utilized for "the building of economical houses and the improvement of the quality of life of urban dwellers in the area" (Article 24). In most neighborhoods, urban cooperatives are collecting sizable sums of money in rent payments. In the city of Addis Ababa, for instance, 60 percent of the 143,000 private housing units occupied in 1967 were rented, and fully 93 percent of these units rented for less than E $100. [60] Furthermore, the largest proportions of rented housing existed in the central city districts of Arada and Tekle Haimanot (see Table 12.5).

All kebele associations within an area defined by the MUDH form a higher urban dweller's association. The policy committee of each kebele elects a delegate or delegates to the higher association,

TABLE 12. 5

Occupied Private Housing Units Rented in 1967, by District
(percentage)

District	Housing Units Rented in 1967
Arada	75. 7
Gefersa	60. 4
Gulele	57. 1
Intoto	46. 6
Mekakelegna	63. 0
Yeka	40. 2
Bole	58. 5
Lideta	50. 6
Keranio	39. 6
Tekle Haimanot	68. 0

Source: Addis Ababa Municipality, Census of 1967, Addis Ababa: Government Printer, 1967, pp. 196-98.

which is charged with numerous functions, including the study and implementation of ways to improve community service delivery "by coordinating the financial and manpower resources of the kebele associations within its boundary. " In the most populous cities, where more than one higher urban cooperative exists, such associations must jointly form a central urban dwellers' association. Under Article 21 of Proclamation No. 104, each higher association elects at least two of its executive council members to serve on the congress of the central association. In chartered urban areas, concerned ministries and government offices must each send one delegate to serve as a member of the congress. Government representatives are allowed to participate in the meetings of the congress but cannot vote or hold any office in the central association. In nonchartered urban centers, representatives of the Ministries of Urban Development and Housing and Interior serve as voting members of the congress; delegates from other ministries and government offices participate in the congress "when necessary. " Article 19 provides for the central association to "take over the administration of the urban center. " Toward this end, Article 23 confers on central associations duties and powers formerly granted to municipal governments. Section 11 states that central associations are "to perform the duties expected of municipalities" and to assume "all powers and duties" granted to municipalities by prior laws and regulations. Specifically, central urban dwellers' associations are charged and empowered to (1) lay out, close, and maintain streets, squares, bridges, resorts, parks, and public gardens; (2) insure that sewerage systems and houses are built properly and according to plan; (3) organize and prepare for public-use water and electricity supplies, large marketplaces, cemeteries, abattoirs, drainages, public baths, theaters, and public halls; (4) provide, in cooperation with the concerned government offices, adequate transport services throughout the urban center; (5) organize and supervize fire brigades, ambulance services, and garbage trucks; (6) take the necessary measures to insure public health and hygiene in urban centers; and (7) operate and coordinate social service programs in collaboration with the concerned government offices and agencies. Finally, central associations are granted broad authority to coordinate development projects operated by higher urban dwellers' associations.

Addis Ababa residents established kebele associations and elected their officers in August and September of 1975. In 1976, urban dwellers' associations had been organized and had begun to function in most, if not all, urban centers. However, Proclamation Nos. 47 and 104 had thrust immense administrative, technical, and decision-making burdens onto an unfamiliar and untested system of urban cooperatives. Most urban dwellers' association leaders lacked sufficient training to direct the administrative and technical staff of the municipal bureaucracy. On April 2, 1976, an editorial in the Ethiopian Herald charged some urban dwellers' association officials with failing to perform their duties and admitted that urban residents in some Addis Ababa localities desired "new elections to change their office bearers." Many of the overburdened cooperative associations appeared to concentrate on rent collection and house maintenance and to ignore the more technical and complex service functions that their members had not been trained to perform or supervize.

By 1977, urban dwellers' associations had been further derailed from providing urban services. The PMAC used the kebele, one of the few institutions it could count on for support, in an all-out attempt to suppress urban opposition to military rule. The military rulers pushed urban dwellers' associations into forming "defense squads," conducting house-by-house searches for "subversive literature," and even arresting or executing suspected opponents of the military regime. Anti-military groups responded by assassinating a number of government officials and kebele leaders. On October 8, 1977, David Ottaway reported in the Washington Post that "in the past nine months, 200 officials of the neighborhood dwellers' associations . . . in Addis

Ababa alone have been assassinated by one or another Marxist faction and another 200 seriously injured, according to city officials."[61]

The Future of Urban Development Planning

The PMAC removed many barriers to urban development planning in Ethiopia. However, new problems have arisen that require further attention and political or administrative action. Interorganizational coordination is likely to become even more problematic in Ethiopia as urban dwellers' associations join public enterprises, municipalities, and central government ministries in the unintegrated pursuit of development activities.[62] The PMAC endeavored to bolster the capacity of the MUDH to perform its enormously expanded duties by increasing the ministry's staff tenfold in late 1975 through the transfer of engineers and technical specialists from the Municipalities Department and city governments. Nevertheless, the MUDH still lacked the capacity to carry out the numerous activities that the PMAC demanded it perform. Ministry officials appeared to be confused and overwhelmed by the scope and complexity of the administrative responsibilities they had been burdened with under Proclamation Nos. 47 and 104. The ministry became so overworked that the Derg found it necessary in November 1975 to establish an autonomous public authority, the Agency for the Administration of Rented Houses, with authority to acquire and maintain urban houses renting for more than E $100 per month. Proclamation 59 of 1975 empowers the agency to revise rent schedules and to sell, buy, lease, exchange, or construct houses in accordance with government policy.[63]

Procedures also must be developed for aligning urban and regional plans with neighborhood needs. Training programs need to be improved and expanded. And, there already are indications that the process by which plans are prepared under the new regime places major constraints on plan implementation. Urban planning is now centered in the Ministry of Urban Development and Housing. The ministry is charged with establishing comprehensive plans and issuing land-use and building directives for all urban areas. These documents will set the direction for future urban development in Ethiopia, as Proclamation No. 47 of 1975 affirms the centrality of the comprehensive plan in the PMAC's approach. Section 3, Article 36 orders the MUDH to "ensure that the rents collected by a cooperative society are utilized for providing services to the urban dwellers in accordance with comprehensive urban development plans and directives issued by the Government."[64] To enforce this provision, MUDH officials insist on reviewing all proposals by urban dwellers' associations that would involve the expenditure of funds collected from local rents. The ministry will only authorize funding of programs that conform with the comprehensive plan and are of sound technical design. The technical design requirement allows expert staff in the Ministry of Urban Development and Housing to play a significant policy-determining role in the preparation of a cooperative's funding proposals.

In the initial stages of urban plan preparation, the Ministry of Urban Development and Housing evidenced little interest in actively eliciting input from urban dwellers. Moreover, Proclamations Nos. 47 and 104 fail to stipulate an interest-articulating role for urban cooperatives or their representatives in the process of determining and ordering the objectives that will be incorporated in the ministry's comprehensive plans. Certainly, the exclusion of urban residents from participation in the identification of alternative courses of action and in goal formulation decreases prospects for successful mobilization of the political support and collective energy needed to accomplish plan objectives. [65]

CONCLUSION

Through a series of swift, radical actions, the PMAC succeeded in overcoming many of the legal, political, administrative, and economic obstacles to urban change and planned development that prevailed during Haile Selassie's reign. The military rulers instituted new programs and policies aimed at improving the living conditions encountered by poor urban inhabitants. However, the system introduced by the PMAC implicitly operates on the principle of planning for rather than by the urban masses. In the absence of effective and continuous popular participation in the process of preparing new development plans and designing future urban settlements, it is unlikely that voluntary mass involvement in the implementation of official urban development programs will be forthcoming in Ethiopia.

NOTES

1. Jean Comhaire, "Urbanization in Ethiopia," Dialogue 1 (October 1967): 27-29; Ronald J. Horvath, "Towns in Ethiopia," Erdkunde [Bonn] 22 (March 1, 1968): 42, 45-46; Akalou Wolde-Michael, "Some Thoughts on the Process of Urbanization in Pre-Twentieth Century Ethiopia," Ethiopian Geographical Journal 5 (December 1967): 36; Richard Pankhurst, State and Land in Ethiopian History, Monographs in Ethiopian Land Tenure, no. 3 (Addis Ababa: Institute of Ethiopian Studies and Faculty of Law, Haile Selassie I University, 1966), p. 52; Richard Pankhurst, "Notes on the Demographic History

of Ethiopian Towns and Villages," Ethiopia Observer 9, no. 1 (1965): 60-83; Ronald J. Horvath, "The Wandering Capitals of Ethiopia," Journal of African History 10, no. 2 (1969): 205-19; and Wolfgang Weissleder, "The Socio-Political Character of an Historical Ethiopian Capital" (Paper presented at the Makerere Institute of Social Research Conference, Kampala, 1964), pp. 3, 12.

2. Akalou, "Urbanization in Pre-Twentieth Century Ethiopia," op. cit., p. 37.

3. Peter P. Garretson, "A History of Addis Ababa from its Foundation in 1886 to 1910" (Ph. D. diss., University of London, 1974), p. 46; Pankhurst, State and Land, op. cit., pp. 52-53, 149-50.

4. For details, see Peter Koehn and Sidney R. Waldron, Afocha: A Link Between Community and Administration in Harar, Ethiopia? (Syracuse, N. Y.: Eastern African Studies Program, Syracuse University, forthcoming).

5. Mesfin Wolde Mariam, "Problems of Urbanization," in Proceedings of the Third International Conference of Ethiopian Studies, Addis Ababa, 1966, vol. 3 (Addis Ababa: Haile Sellassie I University, Institute of Ethiopian Studies, 1970), p. 20.

6. Ethiopia, Central Statistical Office [C. S. O.], Population and Housing Characteristics of Asmara; Results of the 1968 Population and Housing Censuses, Statistical Bulletin, no. 12 (Addis Ababa: C. S. O., 1974), pp. 1, 6-7; Ethiopian Herald, October 4, 1972.

7. Henri Baldet, "Urban Study of Dire Dawa" (B. A. thesis, Haile Sellassie I University, Department of Geography, June 1970), p. 17.

8. Ethiopia, C. S. O., Urbanization, Statistical Bulletin, no. 9 (Addis Ababa; C. S. O., 1972), pp. 1, 8-9. About 13 percent of Africa's population lived in towns of 20,000 people or more in 1960. United Nations, Department of Economic and Social Affairs, Urbanization: Development Policies and Planning, International Social Development Review, no. 1 (New York: United Nations, 1968), p. 12. In 1971, Maaza Bekele and Bondestam estimated that 15 percent of Ethiopia's population will reside in towns with 20,000 or more inhabitants by the year 2000. Maaza Bekele and Lars Bondestam, "Ethiopia: A Case Study of the Interrelations of Population with Economic and Social Development" (Paper presented at the African Population Conference, Accra, Ghana, December 1971), p. 41.

9. J. John Palen, "Housing in a Developing Nation: The Case of Addis Ababa," Land Economics 50 (November 1974): 430-31; Ethiopian Herald, July 24, 1975. At its estimated annual growth rate of 8 percent, the population of Addis Ababa will reach 1.6 million in 1980. J. John Palen, "Urbanization and Migration in an Indigenous City: The Case of Addis Ababa," in Internal Migration; The New World and the Third World, ed. Anthony H. Richmond and Daniel

Kubat, Sage Studies in International Sociology, no. 4 (Beverly Hills, Calif.: Sage, 1976), p. 208.

10. Ethiopia, C. S. O. , Urbanization, op. cit. , p. 9; Ethiopia, C. S. O. , Population of Addis Ababa, Statistical Bulletin, no. 8 (Addis Ababa; C. S. O. , 1972), p. 6.

11. This common pattern of urbanization in the Third World is treated further in Hans-Dieter Evers, "Urban Expansion and Land Ownership in Underdeveloped Societies," Urban Affairs Quarterly 11 (September 1975): 120.

12. Lars Bondestam, "Notes on Multinational Corporations in Ethiopia," The African Review 5, no. 4 (1975): 538-41, 544-45, 549; Ethiopia, C.S.O. , Ethiopia: Statistical Abstract, 1970 (Addis Ababa: C. S. O. , n. d.), p. 120; and Duri Mohammed, "Private Foreign Investment in Ethiopia," Journal of Ethiopian Studies 7 (1969): 55-58.

13. Assefa Bequele and Eshetu Chole, Profile of the Ethiopian Economy (Addis Ababa: Oxford University Press, 1969), p. 53; Ethiopia, Ministry of Planning and Development, Regional Aspects of National Planning in Ethiopia, part I (Addis Ababa; Government Printer, 1967), p. 97.

14. See John Markakis, Ethiopia: Anatomy of a Traditional Polity (London: Oxford University Press, 1974), pp. 136, 160, 165-68; Assefa Mehretu, "Diffusion of Banking in Ethiopia; An Appraisal of the Process of Spatial Integration," Ethiopian Journal of Development Research 1 (April 1974): 40, 43, 64-65.

15. Peter Koehn, "Ethiopia: Famine, Food Production and Changes in the Legal Order," African Studies Review (in press); Asmarom Legesse, "The Genesis of Ethiopian Urbanism; Sociological Development and Ethnographic Context of Addis Ababa" (Paper presented at the Third International Congress of Africanists, Addis Ababa, December 1973), p. 8; Palen, "Urbanization," op. cit. , p. 218.

16. William A. Hance, Population, Migration, and Urbanization in Africa (New York: Columbia University Press, 1970), p. 404; Palen, "Urbanization," op. cit. , pp. 216-17; Lars Bondestam, "Prostitution in Addis Ababa," mimeographed (Addis Ababa, March 1, 1972), pp. 11, 12; and Asmarom, "Ethiopean Urbanism," op. cit., p. 8. Mullenbach's study of migrants to Akaki revealed that a majority of the household heads who moved to the sattelite town came in search of employment and trading opportunities. Hugh Mullenbach, "Urban Migration Research: Interim Report," in Preliminary Research Progress Report on Urbanization Problems in Addis Ababa, IDR Document, no. 13 (Addis Ababa: Institute of Development Research, Haile Sellassie I University, 1974), p. 5.

17. W. T. S. Gould, "Problems of Secondary School Provision in African Cities: The Example of Addis Ababa, Ethiopia," Working

Paper, no. 5 (Liverpool: University of Liverpool, Department of Geography, 1973), p. 8; Markakis, Ethiopia, op. cit. , pp. 169, 149-50; Mesfin Wolde Mariam, "The Rural-Urban Split in Ethiopia," Dialogue (Addis Ababa) 2 (December 1968): 11, 8; and Tekle Mariam Wolde Michael, "Progress Report on Unemployment and Migration of High School Leavers in Addis Ababa," in Preliminary Research Progress Report on Urbanization Problems in Addis Ababa, op. cit. , pp. 6-14.

18. Markakis, Ethiopia, op. cit. , pp. 134-35, 170.

19. The long-term impact of in-migration on urban population growth in Addis Ababa is revealed by data showing that over 75 percent of the adult population and 85 percent of the household heads had not been born in the capital city. Palen, "Urbanization," op. cit. , pp. 210-11, 216; Asmarom Legesse, "Addis Ababa: A Profile of Ethnicity and Occupational Structure" (Paper presented at the Fifth International Conference on Ethiopian Studies, Chicago, 1978), p. 12.

20. Asmarom, "Addis Ababa," op. cit. , pp. 20-21.

21. For details on urban living conditions in Ethiopia, see Peter Koehn, "The Municipality of Addis Ababa, Ethiopia: Performance, Mobilization, Integration, and Change" (Ph. D. diss. , University of Colorado, 1973), pp. 116-25; Peter Koehn, Ethiopian Provincial and Municipal Government: Imperial Patterns and Post Revolutionary Changes (East Lansing, Mich. : Michigan State University, African Studies Center, forthcoming).

22. International Bank for Reconstruction and Development, "Appraisal of the Addis Ababa Water Supply and Sewerage Project," (IBRD report, Addis Ababa, March 1972), pp. 2, 4.

23. Ethiopia, Planning Commission, "A Summary Assessment of Past Performance" (Addis Ababa: Planning Commission, n. d.), pp. 2-4.

24. I. J. Pauwels, "The Importance of Planned Urbanization and of the Development of the Construction Industry in Developing Countries," Planning and Administration 2 (Spring 1975): 51.

25. Lack of urban planning for social development is common throughout the world. Annmarie H. Walsh, The Urban Challenge to Government: An International Comparison of Thirteen Cities (New York: Praeger, 1969), pp. 186-87.

26. Bekele Haile, "Urban Conditions in Ethiopia" (unpublished paper, 1971), p. 13. Many studies report on the failure of other governments to integrate urban, regional, and national plan objectives. See E. O. Adeniyi, "The Institutional Framework for Planning and Managing Urban Settlements in the Developing Countries of Africa," Planning and Administration 2 (Spring 1975): 72; Richard Stren, "Urban Policy and Performance in Kenya and Tanzania," Journal of Modern African Studies 12 (June 1975): 273-74, 277, 283-84; and Khalid

Shibli, "Metropolitan Planning in Karachi: A Case Study," in Metro-politan Growth; Public Policy for South and Southeast Asia, ed. Leo Jakobson and Ved Prakash (New York: Halsted Press, 1974), p. 116.

27. See Ethiopia, Planning Commission, Ethiopia's Third Five-Year Development Plan 1968-1973 (Addis Ababa: Government Printer, 1968), chap. 18; Markakis, Ethiopia, op. cit., pp. 336-37.

28. Ethiopia, Ministry of Interior, "Municipalities Department Work Report and Development Plan" ([unpublished document translated by Seleshi Sissaye], Addis Ababa: Government Printer, 1971), pp. 9-15.

29. Malcolm W. Norris, "Ethiopian Municipal Administration and the Approach to Local Government Reform," Planning and Ad-ministration 1 (Winter 1974): 60.

30. See Addis Zemen, Ginbot 7, 1967 E. C. (1975).

31. Patrick Abercrombie, The Master Plan for Addis Ababa (Addis Ababa: Addis Ababa Municipality, 1956).

32. Bolton, Hennessey and Partners, Report on the Development Plan (Addis Ababa: Addis Ababa Municipality, 1961); French Mis-sion for Town Planning, The City of Addis Ababa: Master Plan Sur-veys (n. p.: Secretariat des Missions d'Urbanisme et d'Habitat, 1967); Francis J. C. Amos, "A Development Plan for Addis Ababa," Ethiopia Observer 6, no. 1 (1962): 5-15.

33. In 1974, the Chamber of Deputies charged that the Munici-palities Department had failed to implement town master plans pre-pared at a cost of E$6.7 million. Ethiopian Herald, September 5, 1974.

34. Public Administration Service [P. A. S.], Organization and Management of the City of Addis Ababa, Ethiopia (Chicago: P. A. S., 1970), pp. 32-35.

35. Seleshi Sisaye, "A Critical Evaluation of the Administration of Services Provided by the Municipality of Dessie" (B. A. thesis, Haile Sellassie I University, 1973), p. 31.

36. Markakis, Ethiopia, op. cit., p. 224.

37. Norris, "Municipal Administration," op. cit., p. 56.

38. Ethiopia, Ministry of Interior, General Analysis and the Report on the Master Plan for Harar (Addis Ababa, Government Printer, 1966), pp. 108-09.

39. Interview with the Head of the Finance Department, Harar Municipality, August 26, 1978.

40. In 1974, Addis Zemen (Ginbot 7, 1967 E. C.) accused "the majority of municipalities" of ignoring the needs of the unemployed, weak, disabled, and prostitutes, while spending local funds on re-ceptions and banquets whenever the Emperor visited and in celebration of his birthday. Also see Malcolm W. Norris, "Ethiopian Local Gov-ernment-Revenue Aspects," Local Finance (April 1976): 14.

41. For the same reason, industrial firms were able to locate in the midst of residential zones and government offices were scattered throughout a city. As a consequence, in parts of Addis Ababa sewage emitted by factories traverses a considerable distance through residential areas before flowing into a stream or river. Ethiopian Herald, December 19, 1974; June 8, 1975.

42. P. A. S. , City of Addis Ababa, op. cit. , pp. 90-93; Gould, "Problems of Secondary School Provision," op. cit. , p. 15.

43. Public Administration Service, Establishment of the Addis Ababa Water and Sewage Authority (Chicago: P. A. S. , 1970), pp. 118, 90; Ethiopian Herald, December 19, 1974.

44. See Addis Ababa Municipality News, Hamle and Nehassie 1966 E. C. , p. 19; and Yilma Abebe, "Personnel Administration in the Municipality of Addis Ababa" (B. A. thesis, Haile Sellassie I University, 1973), p. 48. In contrast, the Asmara Municipality engaged in planned urban renewal aimed at "demolishing slum areas and replacing them with new roads and buildings. " The municipality reported that it spent half a million Ethiopian dollars demolishing housing units in Aba Shawl in 1972 and resettling inhabitants of the district elsewhere in the city. Ethiopian Herald, October 4, 1972. Many of the Aba Shawl residents affected by the project criticized the municipality's actions on grounds that they did not desire to relocate, could not afford to build a new home with the amount of money provided by the city, and could not locate suitable rental units in other districts. The Nairobi City Council regularly demolishes squatter housing in certain parts of that city. The Tanzanian and Zambian governments have achieved limited success with programs aimed at upgrading squatter settlements in Dar es Salaam and Lusaka. Stren, "Urban Policy and Performance in Kenya and Tanzania," op. cit. , pp. 272-73, 281-82; Richard Martin, "Upgrading," in Slums or Self-Reliance ? Urban Growth in Zambia, Communication, no. 12 (Lusaka: University of Zambia, Institute for African Studies, 1976), pp. 98-101.

45. P. A. S. , City of Addis Ababa, op. cit. , p. 67; and Fikru Dessalegne, "Financial Administration in the Municipality of Addis Ababa" (B. A. thesis, Haile Sellassie I University, Department of Public Administration, 1973), p. 27.

46. Tajebe Beyene, "The Services of the Topographic Department," Addis Ababa Municipality News, no. 4 (Ginbot 30, 1967 E. C. / 1975). A complete topographical map of the city was not complete ఓ until 1973. Addis Zemen, Tikempt 2, 1967 E. C. /1975). The administrative problems that adversely affected municipal survey work are described in Koehn, "Municipality of Addis Ababa," op. cit. , pp. 180-81.

47. Bekele, "Urban Conditions," op. cit. , p. 12.

48. Seminar on Technical and Legal Aspects of Municipal Services, January 7, 17, 1972. Less than a year after the termination of monarchical rule, the court ruled that the municipality must compensate the owners of all expropriated property (including unauthorized dwellings). Addis Zemen, Hedar 14, 1967 E. C. /1975.

49. See Addis Ababa Municipality News, no. 3 (Nehassie and Hamle, 1966E. C. /1974), p. 15.

50. Mesfin, "Problems of Urbanization," op. cit. , p. 28. Also see Addis Zemen, Tikempt 2, 1967 E. C. (1975) and Ethiopian Herald, July 25, 1975. The amhara benefited disproportionately from land grant practices under the imperial regime. Of all ethnic groups, the highest proportion of land ownership in Addis Ababa existed among the Amhara (33 percent by 1973). Asmarom, "Addis Ababa," op. cit. , p. 23.

51. The lease period, or mirrit, generally extended for 20 to 30 years. Towald Akesson and Belletetch Ikakem, "Survey of Housing Conditions in Tekle Haimanot and Lidetta Districts of Addis Ababa, Ethiopia, 1962" (Addis Ababa: Ethio-Swedish Institute of Building Technology, 1962), pp. ii-iii; Addis Ababa Municipality, "Draft Report on busing in Addis Ababa: Results of the Census of 1967" (Addis Ababa, 1972), p. 192.

52. Bekele, "Urban Conditions," op. cit. , p. 15.

53. Ibid. , pp. 12, 15; Ethiopian Herald, December 29, 1974; Palen, "Urbanization and Migration," op. cit. , pp. 209-10.

54. See Peter Koehn, "Ethiopian Politics: Military Intervention and Prospects for Further Change," Africa Today 7 (May/June, 1975): 7-12.

55. John Markakis, "Social Transformation in Ethiopia: Prelude to Revolution" (Paper presented at the 20th Annual Meeting of the African Studies Association, Houston, 1977), pp. 18-19.

56. Ethiopian Herald, August 1, 1975.

57. See Proclamation No. 47 of 1975, "Government Ownership of Urban Lands and Extra Houses Proclamation," Negarit Gazeta, 35th year, no. 41 (July 26, 1975), articles 5-8, 19, 40. An increasing number of African governments are undertaking urban land nationalization schemes that involve less radical changes in prevailing patterns. See United Nations, Department of Economic and Social Affairs, Urban Land Policies and Land-Use Control Measures, vol. 1, "Africa," (New York: U. N. , ST/ECA 1167, 1973), pp. 32, 30; Nigerian Herald, April 1, 1978; and H. Jack Simons, "Zambia's Urban Situation," in Slums or Self-Reliance?, op. cit. , pp. 27-29.

58. Adeniyi, "Planning and Managing Urban Settlements," op. cit. , p. 71.

59. Proclamation No. 104 of 1976, "Urban Dwellers' Associations Consolidation and Municipalities Proclamation," Negarit Gazeta, 36th year, no. 5 (October 1976), article 9.

60. A conservative estimate of the amount of potential rent income available to Addis Ababa kebele in 1977 is E $. 7 million, based on 1967 rent figures adjusted for an increase of 5,000 new housing units per year. Addis Ababa Municipality, Census of 1967, op. cit., pp. 192-224, 231.

61. See Cohen and Koehn, Provincial and Municipal Government, op. cit.; John Markakis and Nega Ayele, Class and Revolution in Ethiopia (Nottingham: Spokesman, 1978), pp. 151-53, 162, 166-67.

62. On these points, see Walsh, Urban Challenge, op. cit., pp. 209, 215.

63. See Ethiopian Herald, August 9, 1975; Paul Brietzke, "Ethiopia," Annual Survey of African Law 9 (in press).

64. Emphasis ours. Article 24, section 1, also requires urban cooperatives "to follow and execute" the land use and building directives issued by the MUDH.

65. Albert Waterston, Development Planning: Lessons of Experience (Baltimore, Md.: The Johns Hopkins University Press, 1965), p. 465; United Nations, Department of Economic and Social Affairs, Popular Participation in Decision Making for Development (New York: U.N., ST/ESA/31, 1975), pp. 4, 14; United Nations, Department of Economic and Social Affairs, Local Government Reform: Analysis of Experience in Selected Countries (New York: U.N., ST/ESA/SER. E/2, 1975), p. 43; Martin, "Upgrading," op. cit., pp. 98-101; Adeniyi, "Planning and Managing Urban Settlements," op. cit., p. 74; and Peter Koehn, "Urban Origins and Consequences of National and Local Political Transformation in Ethiopia," in The City in Comparative Perspective: Cross-National Research and New Directions in Theory, ed. John Walton and Louis H. Masotti (New York: John Wiley & Sons, 1976), pp. 169-74. In contrast to the Ethiopian pattern, urban communes exercise primary responsibility for the preparation of social and economic development plans in Yugoslavia. Eugen Pusic and Annmarie H. Walsh, Urban Government for Zagreb, Yugoslavia (New York: Praeger, 1968), pp. 34, 82-83; Waterston, Development Planning, op. cit., p. 541.

13

URBANIZATION AND DEVELOPMENT PLANNING IN KENYA

R. A. Obudho

INTRODUCTION

The basic spatial structure of the present central place systems, however defined, has existed in Kenya from time immemorial. The earliest evidence of some spatial organization was in the form of periodic, primarily ethnic-based markets. These periodic markets formed very important nuclei for intra- and interethnic trade. However, this precolonial spatial system was very weakly organized.

With the colonization of Kenya, a new pattern in urbanization evolved such that infrastructure services were set up and new central places were gazetted all over the country. In addition to the towns established along the Mombasa-Kisumu railway and road systems, central places were created as administrative centers. Early in the process of establishing such centers, the precolonial spatial systems, mainly the periodic markets, were ignored.

The colonial administrators, however, realized the importance of periodic markets in the spatial systems of Kenya and later created more periodic markets in concurrence with administrative centers. [1] Although these two subsystems overlapped to some extent, they have never been fully integrated. The urban or modern system was initially dominated by the colonial administration, while the traditional or periodic market systems were dominated by the Africans. This dual-sector structure (modern versus traditional) has expanded further

---

into a four-sector model (urban-formal, urban-informal, rural-formal, and rural-informal). [2] While the "modernized-urban" versus "traditional-rural" model was the direct result of colonial urbanization, the rural-urban difference has been manifested and become more prominent in the postcolonial era.

PRECOLONIAL URBANIZATION

Except for the coastal strip, there were few compact settlements in Kenya that could be described as urban centers prior to colonialism (see Figure 13. 1). Although towns did not exist, central places did, and their importance varied according to which ethnic group owned them. These inland central places were the areas of initial cultural contact between the Africans and the non-African immigrants during the subsequent stages of colonization. They existed because the coastal towns required an organized hinterland. These ethnic central places developed into caravan towns which later played a very important role in the expansion of the inland trade made necessary by the demand for raw materials in Europe, the Arabian Peninsula, and Asia. Though the initial impetus for the caravan trade came from the coastal ethnic groups (especially the Nyika and later the Kamba, who took over the trade), the ties between coastal and inland trade were reinforced by the Arab caravan traders. As the caravan trade developed, a series of caravan towns emerged along the routes as places to rest and procure fresh supplies. The European involvement in the caravan trade increased the tempo of building of the caravan towns between the coast and the interior parts of Kenya. Within a year, well-fortified bomas were established at Ndi, Witu, Kiambu, Olu, Mumoni, Bura, Kikumbuliu, Ngong, Taveta, and Mumias. The purpose of these caravan bomas was "to establish some sort of understanding with the surrounding tribes in order to keep the road open and secure food for the caravans before they set out across the sparsely populated country between the fertile highlands and the lake. "[3] The last caravan town to be established during the final stage of the precolonial era was a stockade built at Kitale in the early 1890s. Until that time the caravan towns were either founded or annexed by the Imperial British East Africa Company (IBEAC) which dissolved at the beginning of 1895.

At the end of the precolonial era, there were few caravan towns and traditional centers scattered throughout Kenya. [4] The majority of the precolonial towns were concentrated in Kenya's coastal strip, with only a half dozen on the Mombasa-Uganda route. These nodal points were very important for the dissemination of ideas. To some extent, then, it is these precolonial central places which acted as

FIGURE 13. 1

Kenya Urban Geographic Regions

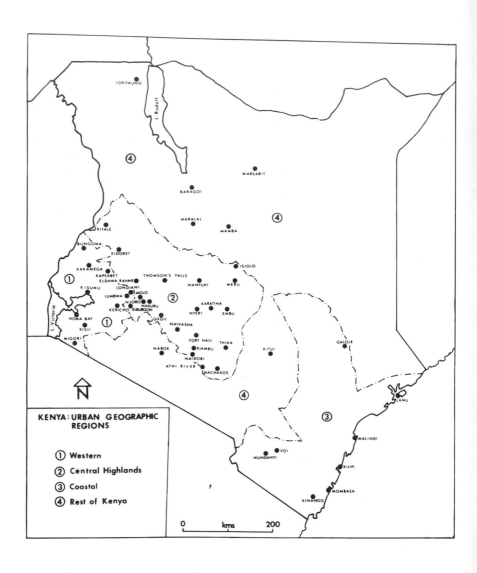

Source: R. A. Obudho, The Nature of Kenyan Urban Hierarchy
(Nairobi: East African Literature Bureau, 1979), p. 207.

244

nodes at which the colonial authorities secured a strong foodhold in various parts of the country. It is important to add that during the precolonial era, because of the undeveloped nature of the traditional centers, only horizontal organization of the centers was possible.

The precolonial central places were mainly periodic markets where the chiefs gathered from time to time to carry out the administrative functions of their respective chieftains. Residents were primarily the nonindigenous Swahili, Arab, and Indian traders. In this sense, some of the precolonial central places could be called multiracial and ethnic societies. This was particularly true of the central places in the coastal region, the majority of which were administered by the non-African population, with the indigenous ethnic groups accounting for over 90 percent of their population. The elites controlled central places, but their influence varied from region to region. The inland central places were ruled by the ethnic chiefs (then the traditional elites) while the coastal places were controlled by the exogenous elites, mainly the traditional Arab and Swahili merchants. Thus, during the precolonial era, central places were not only weakly organized but also ethnically oriented.

COLONIAL URBANIZATION

It was during the colonial period that the spatial organization of the central places in Kenya was developed and consolidated both in time and space. With the transfer of IBEAC activities to the Colonial Office, some caravan towns were developed as administrative centers required for the "pacification" and colonization process. In addition to their function as supply and resting points, they served as the political and sociocultural centers for their respective regions. In order to improve communication between the coast and interior parts of the new territory, railways, roads, and other associated infrastructures were built between 1895 and 1902. The new communication patterns helped the growth of these new administrative bomas, which were designed primarily to administer or facilitate export of raw materials and the import and sale of manufactured goods.

Non-African Settlement

By the end of 1902, the British Government was committed to the policy of non-African settlement in the East African Protectorate (EAP, now Kenya)—a move which increased the process of unbalanced urbanization in the country. The first land to be alienated for European settlement was demarcated in the buffer zone between Masailand

and the Kikuyu-Kamba region and in areas around Fort Hall. [5] With
settlement schemes concentrated mainly in the Kenya highlands, more
towns were founded in this area than in any other part of Kenya. The
actual settlement took place between 1902 and 1945, when over 300,000
settlers, mainly from the United Kingdom, came to Kenya.

The Asian and Arab communities also played a role in the urban
development by engaging in commerce. The majority of the Asians
and Arabs operated the dukas (shops), which played a strong part in
modernization at the local level. For many years during the colonial
period, the Arabs and Asians were restricted to major urban centers,
and they were only allowed to own land in the area along the railway
between Kisumu and Fort Ternan. The East African Royal Commission concluded that the Asian and Arab dukas in Kenya were "responsible for stimulating the wants of the indigenous people in the remotest
areas, by opening to them a shop window on the modern world and for
collecting for sale elsewhere whatever small surpluses are available
for disposal."[6]

The colonial period introduced a new type of economic, social,
and political development in Kenya. The economy of the country was
dominated by non-African settlers who were concentrated mainly in
the central highlands and/or in the gazetted administrative bomas.
Colonialization imposed a deliberately segregated economic, political,
and sociocultural climate in which the Europeans dominated the country, the Indians and the Asians were the "middlemen," and the Africans were overworked in low-paying jobs in urban areas or otherwise
restricted to their respective ethnic areas. Until political independence
in 1962, the urban centers were regarded more as bases for administrative and commercial activities than as centers for permanent African settlement and participation.

These policies divided the Kenya spatial system sharply into
growth nodes and lagging areas. The central highlands region, which
enjoys the highest rainfall and has the most fertile land in the country, has a high urban concentration. The resource allocation and
transport concentration there are the highest in Kenya. There is a
wide hiatus between the traditional central places and the colonial
centers. This internal polarization can be considered the main effect
of urbanization in Kenya. The fertile lands in the Kenya highland and
the urban enclaves stretching from Mombasa on the coast to Kisumu
on Lake Victoria were built as the core region of the country, where
maximum investment was concentrated. This core region was used
by colonists for the production and export of agricultural products
to the Metropole countries and the import of manufactured consumer
goods. The unbalanced development restricted the overall urbanization of the country, and, as a result, the majority of Africans have
not benefited from the process even up to the present time.

In addition to the polarized nature of urbanization, the colonization also produced peculiar urbanization traits which are worth contrasting with those of the precolonial era. The colonial central places were more racially and ethnically heterogeneous than the precolonial settlements. But it was common to find the Africans from surrounding locations accounting for the majority of the population.

Like Western Europe's preindustrial cities, where urban dwellers were stratified according to social rank, such that priests, rulers, and educators were the elite dominating the functions of the city, the colonial towns in Kenya were dominated by an expatriate elite. The African elites consisted of two groups, namely the intelligentsia and the traditional elites. The former have received a formal education in the colonial towns or abroad while the latter have risen to power through the traditional ethnic political process. Both of these groups were closely related to the colonial elites, who comprised mainly administrators and businessmen. Secondly, there were middlemen, who consisted of Asians, Goans, and Arab immigrants who did not come from the colonial country but occupied a very important commercial role in Kenya. The third and last group consisted of the mass of uneducated Africans who had migrated to the urban centers to perform semi-skilled or unskilled tasks.

An accurate analysis of urban development in Kenya was attempted after the 1948 census, the first countrywide census of its kind in Kenya. According to this census, an urban center was defined as any compact and gazetted settlement with a population of 2,000 or more inhabitants. Centers were divided into three hierarchical categories: municipalities, grade A townships, and grade B townships. Below these were trading centers. On this basis there were only 17 urban centers in Kenya by 1948. Of the non-African population of 154,846, in 1948, 73 percent resided in the 50 gazetted municipalities, townships, and trading centers.

Trading Centers

The colonizers developed three types of central places in Kenya between 1900 and 1960: towns or bomas (urban centers with 2,000 or more population), the trading centers, and the markets. Of the three, only the boma and the trading center were really established by the colonials since some form of periodic markets had existed in various parts of the country in one form or another prior to the colonization of the country. Trading centers provide a very important linkage in the urbanization of the country between the rural areas (periodic markets) and the modern, urban-based sectors. Although the trading centers are the most viable commercially, they are the untidiest and least

planned central places in Kenya. This lack of planned development is
due to several reasons. Foremost among these is the fact that land
where trading centers were built belonged to individual Africans, and
since the Indians were the only people who initially developed the trading centers, most of the land they had was on annual lease. Because
their claim to the land was not permanent, they only constructed
temporary structures, most of which have stood to this day. Second,
the colonial government did not control and regulate the planning and
building of trading centers. This uncontrolled development has therefore remained the characteristic feature of these centers up to the
present. Finally, the trading centers, like the periodic markets, have
been distributive, collecting, and bulking centers whose future existence has not been seen as secure by either Africans or non-Africans,
hence the lack of permanent investment. These conditions have been
improved with continued urbanization during the postcolonial era.
Some of the trading centers have been officially declared urban centers, thus constituting physical planning urban entities for sectorial
as well as regional planning.

POSTCOLONIAL URBANIZATION

The second national census of 1962 showed that Kenya had 34
towns with a combined population of 670,945, or 7.80 percent of the
total. This was a 100 percent increase in number of towns from 1948,
when there were only 17 towns. The non-Africans were concentrated
in the urban areas, while the Africans were concentrated in the rural
areas. This rural nature of the African population had been preserved
by colonial law which restricted African residence in urban areas.
However, in spite of these restrictions, rural to urban migration had
increased because of shortage of land with agricultural potential;
rural unemployment and underemployment; reaction against constraints
by tribal customs; the desire for better social and cultural facilities;
and the lure of the city, industrial wages, and the good life. Most of
the Africans who migrated to urban areas in Kenya created outlying
squatter rings in the peri-urban areas of the urban centers.
    As the economic and social function of these trading posts and
administrative centers increased, they were declared townships and
urban centers. As a matter of fact, most of the present townships
were gazetted during the first quarter of the present century as the
modern administration began to take shape.
    The increase of the urban population from 285,545 in 1948 to
671,024 in 1962 represented a growth of 135 percent, with an average
rate of increase of 6.2 percent per annum over the 15 years. The
third population census in 1969 showed an increase in the number of

urban centers from 34 in 1962 to 47, with a population of 1,079,908, or 9.87 percent of the total (see Table 13.1). The increase in urban population during the two census periods was 60.96 percent. The high increase in number of towns was due to a high rate of natural population increase, rural to urban migration, and the increase of township boundaries.

TABLE 13.1

Kenya: Growth of Urban Centers, 1948-69

Size of Urban Centers	Number of Towns		
	1948	1962	1969
100,000+	1	2	2
20,000-99,999	1	2	2
10,000-19,999	2	3	7
5,000-9,999	3	11	11
2,000-4,999	10	16	25
Total	17	34	47

Source: R. A. Obudho, The Nature of Kenya Urban Hierarchy (Nairobi: East African Publishing House, 1979), p. 191.

The three censuses of 1948, 1962, and 1969 adequately summarized the trend of urbanization in Kenya (see Table 13.2). The actual growth rate of the urban population for 1948-62 was 6.2 percent per annum, while for 1962-69 it was 7.2 percent per annum. By 1969, the urban population had increased to over 1 million residing in 47 urban centers. In the three censuses, over two-thirds of the urban population resided in Nairobi and Mombasa.

In considering the impact of urbanization in Kenya, it is important to note the effect of restrictive policies, which not only curbed the growth of non-African activities in the rural areas but also effectively restricted the migration to and settlement in the urban areas by the African population. Until the political independence of Kenya in 1962, the urban centers were regarded as bases for administrative and commercial activities rather than as centers for permanent African settlement and participation.

TABLE 13. 2

Kenya Urban Population, 1948, 1962, and 1969

Census	1948	1962	1969
Urban population	285,545	670,934	1,079,903
Urban population as percent of total population	5. 3	7. 8	9. 9

Intercensus period	1948-1962	1962-1969

Urban population increase	385,389	408,974
Growth in urban population, percent per annum	6. 20	7. 20
Total population increase	3,230,297	2,306,442
Growth in total population, percent per annum	3. 10	3. 40

Source: Based on the 1948, 1962, and 1969 Kenya Population Census (Nairobi: Government Printer, 1948, 1962, and 1969).

TOWARD A REGIONAL PLANNING STRATEGY

Prior to the 1960s, most of the physical planning in Kenya was carried on only within the statutory boundaries of the municipalities of Nakuru, Kisumu, Nairobi, and Mombasa, and most of it was ad hoc, with the plans usually taking the form of fully designed land-use maps. Safier recently summarized the physical planning tradition in East Africa, and therefore Kenya, when he said,

> Physical planning for urban growth in many countries including those of East Africa is a practice of long standing. In most cases it was imported by the colonial administrations and had its first application in new colonial capitals. . . . The initial concerns of town planning in East Africa were in health and hygiene and the laying out of well demarcated areas of differential land-use; these concerns

are still found enshrined in a large portion of the existing planning legislation. The majority of large urban areas in many African countries are thus today planned in a peculiar and partial manner. Both pre-existing indigenous settlement, and subsequent collections of local immigrants were for long treated outside the main design frameworks, or put into special categories for separate treatment. The properly planned areas, well laid-out and serviced to a high standard, were and are the main administrative, commercial and industrial quarters, and restricted . . . residential zones . . . all of which are closely allied with the predominantly external oriented modern urban section.
. . . The aim of traditional town planning in many African countries . . . was essentially to provide for physical accommodation of development. [7]

In discussing urbanization and development planning in Kenya, Laurenti echoed similar conclusions:

Municipal administration was handled fairly well for the modest urban centers of pre-independence days so that no serious dilemmas developed. Only in the past five years or so, as the pressures of accelerating urban growth in many Kenyan centers pushed beyond local staff and finance capacities, have problems begun to emerge with such rapidity and on such a scale that they have become visible to administrators, social scientists, technicians, and politicians. [8]

In addition to the fact that the planning of these statutory municipalities was physical in nature, almost all of it was sectorial in approach, emphasizing the economic development which would satisfy the metropolitan powers. [9] Practically all the studies on the urbanization process in Kenya were merely concerned with social surveys until 1963, when Fair proposed his oft-quoted regional approach to economic development of Kenya, in which he stressed,

It is thus necessary to establish regional as well as sectorial targets, for coordinated national planning which involves the provision not only of individual but also a combination of basic services . . . for the development often of more than one natural resource in a variety of areas of widely differing character. In all economic planning, therefore, sector analysis so that comparative development possibilities, problems, and priorities can be assessed region by region as well as sector by sector. [10]

The initial and serious attempt to bring regional planning techniques to bear on the development of Kenya was a series of studies carried out by Deutsches Institut für Entwicklungspolitik. [11] In these studies, the western Kenya region was delineated, based not on the political boundary but on an economically integrated area. Since 1960, the urban and regional Department of Physical Planning of the Ministry of Lands and Settlement has concentrated on two themes: regional research and urban planning. Between 1966 and 1978 the department published physical development plans for all provinces and urban centers. For example, since 1966 the Town Planning Department of the Ministry of Lands and Settlement has done an exhaustive inventory of physical and social planning schemes for all provinces as well as major urban centers in Kenya.

The objectives of these regional and physical plans in Kenya, according to the latest development plan, were

> concerned with the development which involves the use of
> land, studies the movement of people or goods, or modifies
> the physical environment. It deals with emerging patterns
> of production and residence, and distribution throughout the
> country of the physical infrastructure of development; roads
> and railways, power plants, shops and factories, public
> buildings, houses, schools and hospitals. Physical plan-
> ning in Kenya has two objectives. Firstly, in a national
> and regional context, to plan a national framework or strat-
> egy for the location of capital investments. Secondly, in
> the urban context to plan both large and small towns in de-
> tail, so as to produce coordinated economic land use for
> developing projects within a satisfactory environment. [12]

These objectives were accomplished in three stages. The first stage consisted of the compilation of urban and regional planning data; the second has been the analysis and projection of modernization processes, such as population growth, economic development, technical and cultural change, and the urbanization process; and the third stage was concerned with the preparation of strategic plans. Thus, most of the development planning in Kenya was concerned with the growth of major urban centers.

But despite the underdeveloped nature of all urban centers except Mombasa and Nairobi, the government has selected a "strategy of selective concentration," in which major emphasis is placed on the development of Nairobi and Mombasa. The reasons for this emphasis are several. First, these two cities have not yet reached optimum size. Nairobi and Mombasa tend to be the logical choice of industries, and these cities are well supplied with the service industries often necessary for the smooth operations of a large business. Also, Nairobi is already endowed with very good transportation routes to all parts of East Africa, while Mombasa is the major port and has natural advantages for industries, such as petroleum refining, that require large quantities of raw materials arriving by sea. Finally, Nairobi and Mombasa are necessary to attract well-qualified executive and managerial staff. Because of the economics of concentration which could accrue by the policy of encouraging development of Nairobi and Mombasa, with very limited investment in other designated "growth centers," the government has encouraged their development and at the same time emphasized rural development in the 1970-74 and 1974-78 development plans. The 1970 five-year plan stressed that

> we are now proposing that an increasing share of development plans for rural development should be directed toward the rural areas: special programs are being put together to obtain a significant improvement in the standard of rural life. Rural development is the basic strategy of this plan, for it is our aim that the fruits of development will be shared amongst the mass of people of a whole not just amongst the favoured few. [13]

As a matter of fact, the government admitted that the first two plans paid insufficient attention to programs and projects for the rural areas. Rural development was insufficiently integrated into the overall plan. It was only after this directive and after the results of the central province study were available that a detailed study of existing settlement patterns was carried out for the whole country. Of the 134 centers qualifying, 7 ranked as urban centers, 22 as rural centers, 27 as market centers, and 78 as local centers.

Regional planning strategies in Kenya have not been in harmony with the political thinking in the country. Chief decision makers and planners have ignored the abundant research and evaluation of development programs that have been done. Most of the government's stated aims and goals are in conflict, and spatial development planning has failed to recognize this problem. For example, while the Kenya government aimed at the spatial organization of rural development through the current hierarchical structure of urban, rural, market, and local growth centers, this approach has resulted in widening the gap between the modern and the traditional sectors because most of the central places designated for development were mainly in the modern sector.

If the Kenya government wants to make a significant change in reorienting the growth of the spatial system, then attention must be concentrated on the informal sector in both the urban and the rural systems. I am referring particularly to the periodic and daily markets, which provide the economic base for the majority of Kenya's Africans. If the objective of any regional development policy in Kenya is to benefit the smaller central places, such as periodic markets and the rural agricultural hinterland, then it only makes sense that selective but direct investment in these central places would be more appropriate. Urban centers in developing countries have been "nationalized" to the extent that the local tradition is now being incorporated into the urban way of life. This means that diffusion from the lower-order centers to higher-order centers is also taking place. The rural-urban linkages, though weak, are developing very quickly. Planning the periodic market subsystem will hasten the spatial development of periodic markets into fixed central places which can aid in the economies of urbanization. Planning at the local level will not only reduce the polarization and backwash effects that result when the growth centers drain rather than induce prosperity in their hinterland but will also help reorient the urban centers to their hinterland rather than to major export enclaves.

A policy of encouraging development at metropolitan levels without distributing development efforts at local or intermediate stages will only aid in increasing rural to urban migration, a situation which all regional planners are trying to correct. In addition, the major or intermediate central places will not perform their expected generative functions unless the lower centers, with the marketplace subsystems, are organized. The critical role of development planning should be that of developing towns as marketing centers rather than merely as administrative centers.

Planning in Kenya should be concentrated at the local level by developing selected local market centers in conjunction with the rural agricultural development in order to hasten their entry into the urban economy. The planning of periodic markets will reduce the problem of distance decay, increase the speed of the changing of rural markets into daily markets, and increase the pace of diffusion of traditional or rural ideas up and along the hierarchy of central places in the country. The planning of resource allocation in Kenya should be concentrated in the rural areas because it is these small central places that play a very important role in the lives of the indigenous people. The rural development of periodic markets cannot be left to the slow process of supply and demand to transform the marketplace into urban place subsystems.

The planning of spatial organization will be the only way of bridging the gap between the developed export enclaves and the underdeveloped agricultural hinterland regions of Kenya. We must emphasize the question of narrowing intraregional or intraurban inequalities as distinct from interregional inequality. The aim is to reorient central places to contribute directly to their hinterlands instead of simply collecting raw materials for internal or external export. In proposing the focusing on periodic markets as a planning strategy, we are not suggesting that all development planning efforts should be concentrated on each and every periodic and daily market in Kenya, because such a project is impossible in view of the limited resources of the country. The following are some of the suggested criteria, which have been generalized here but could be modified to meet specific regional or local conditions.

The first important basis for selecting a central place within the marketplace subsystem as a growth center for planning purposes would be the hierarchical importance of that center within the locality or region. Second, such periodic markets should be those which offer meaningful services to the people of the area. Periodic markets usually have a turnover in terms of daily business transactions that could be used as a means of measuring their importance. Third, the periodic market can be picked based on the endowment and the richness of its hinterlands for agricultural production. Since planning at the local level is to foster linking the urban areas with agricultural hinterlands, it is important that only the centers within such a region be primarily tapped for development. Finally, only centers with well-organized transportation systems should be picked for development planning. [14] Once these centers have been picked, the improvement and organization of the infrastructural services could be planned in order to improve their hierarchical organization of the spatial system.

CONCLUSION

The urbanization process in Kenya since the turn of this century can be summarized as follows. The colonial governments introduced major urban centers in the country, built roads, railways, and other forms of communication, encouraged the non-African settlements, and introduced a large-scale cash-crop economy. All these external forces were instrumental in encouraging the duality of urbanization, whereby the traditional central places helped only the indigenous Africans, while the central places artificially introduced by the colonials were externally oriented. This chapter then puts in perspective the fact that the hierarchical and spatial organization of central places in Kenya was not always conducive to the development of the country but was intended mainly for exploitation of the rich hinterlands. All the administrative centers functioned more as export enclaves than central places.

In order to reorganize and reorient the hierarchy of central places in Kenya, we have proposed a planning strategy based on marketplace subsystems. Planning at the grassroots level will help bring jobs to the rural areas where the majority of the population resides, help reorient the towns from parasitic to generative roles, and help lessen the gap between hinterland and export enclaves. The major goal in regional planning in Kenya is to lessen the disparity between rural subsystems and the urban system while at the same time retaining the specific characteristics of each.

The immediate fusion of the periodic market subsystem and the urban place subsystem can only be achieved by concentrating planning at the local level. A planning strategy should emphasize deliberately the emerging role and transformation of the numerous periodic markets, which are the modest growth poles of their respective local areas. Taking advantage of and building upon this existing structure of grassroot level centers would help to induce development in the rural areas, reorient towns toward their hinterlands, increase local participation, ease the pains of transition, and reduce the gap between the rural hinterland and the export enclaves.

NOTES

1. R. A. Obudho, "Temporal Periodicity and Locational Spacing of Periodic and Daily Markets in Kenya," Cahiers d'Études Africaines 16 (1977): 553-66.

2. D. R. F. Taylor, "Spatial Organization and Rural Development," in Freedom and Change Essays in Honour of Lester B. Pearson, ed. M. G. Fry (Toronto: McClelland and Stewart, 1975), pp. 217-14; and International Labour Organization (ILO), Employment, Incomes and Inequality—A Strategy for Increasing Productive Employment in Kenya (Geneva: ILO, 1972).

3. G. H. Mungeam, British Rule in Kenya: The Establishment of the Administration in the East African Protectorate 1895-1912 (Oxford: Oxford Clarendon Press, 1966); pp. 10-11.

4. For a detailed study of urbanization of Kenya, see R. A. Obudho, "Development of Urbanization in Kenya: A Spatial Analysis and Implication for Regional Development Strategy" (Ph. D. diss., Rutgers University, 1974); R. A. Obudho and Constance E. Obudho, Urbanization, City and Regional Planning of Metropolitan Kisumu, Kenya: A Bibliographical Survey of an East African City Council of Planning Librarian Exchange Bibliography, no. 278 (Monticello, Ill.: Council of Planning Librarian Exchange, April 1972); Andy Wachtel et al., Bibliography of Urbanization in Kenya Institute of Development Studies Bibliography, no. 2 (Nairobi: Institute of Development

Studies, 1974); R. A. Obudho, Urbanization and Development Planning in Kenya (Nairobi: Kenya Literature Bureau, 1978); R. A. Obudho, "Spatial Dimension and Demographic Dynamics of Kenya's Urban Systems," Pan African Journal 9, no. 2 (1976): 103-24; and R. A. Obudho and P. P. Waller, Periodic Markets, Urbanization and Regional Planning—A Case Study of Western Kenya (Westport, Conn. : Greenwood Press, 1976).

5. W. T. W. Morgan, "The White Highlands of Kenya," Geographical Journal 129 (1963): 149-55.

6. Great Britain, House of Commons, Colonial Office, East Africa Royal Commission 1953-1955 Report, cmd. 9475 (London: Her Majesty's Stationery Office, 1955), p. 65.

7. Michael Safier, "Urban Problems: Planning Possibilities and Housing Policies," in Urban Challenge in East Africa, ed. John Hutton (Nairobi: East African Publishing House, 1972), p. 33.

8. Luigi Laurenti, "Urbanization Trends and Prospects," in Urbanization in Kenya: An International Urbanization Survey Report, ed. (New York: Ford Foundation, 1973), p. 1.

9. For an analysis of sectorial strategy, see John Burrows, Kenya: Into the Second Decade (Baltimore: The Johns Hopkins University Press, 1975).

10. T. J. D. Fair, "A Regional Approach to Economic Development in Kenya," South African Geographical 45 (1963): 55. For later thinkings on the same concepts, see Gary L. Gailie, "Process Affecting the Spatial Pattern in Rural-Urban Development in Kenya," The African Studies Review 19, no. 3 (December 1976): 1-10.

11. For detailed analysis of these studies, see Obudho and Waller, Periodic Markets, Urbanization and Regional Planning, op. cit.

12. Republic of Kenya, Development Plan 1970-1974 (Nairobi: Government Printer, 1969), p. 81.

13. Ibid. , p. iv. Similar plans have also been made in the new Kenya Development Plan. See Kenya, Republic of, Development Plan 1974-1978 (Nairobi: Government Printer, 1973), pp. 114-47.

14. Samson Kimani and D. R. F. Taylor, Growth Centers and Development in Kenya (Thika, Kenya: Maxim Printer, 1973), pp. 15-20; see also Donald Freeman, "Development Strategies in Dual Economies: A Kenyan Example," The African Studies Review 18, no. 2 (September 1975): 17-34.

14

URBAN DEVELOPMENT PLANNING IN
DAR ES SALAAM

Edwin S. Segal

Urban development planning in Dar es Salaam is constrained by two factors: first, the existing patterns of urban and nonurban settlement and, second, national policies regarding the course of general development in the country. These are not, in themselves, unique variables. However, their specific Tanzanian forms are. The first is a function of historical patterns with a time span of several centuries, while the second dates from the effort to apply the principles of the Arusha Declaration to all aspects of Tanzanian life. Taken together, they define the context within which all of Tanzania's urban planning takes place.

HISTORICAL BACKGROUND AND DEVELOPMENT

As with the rest of Africa, much of the history of the area now known as Dar es Salaam Region* is better described as the history of population movements, rather than as that of discrete events. Such a history, by its very nature is complex and diffuse. However, some basic statements can be made delineating the major outlines of what happened.

---

*In 1974, Dar es Salaam's status was changed from that of a city within the Coast Region to an autonomous region in its own right. This change enabled a consolidation and coordination of urban and peri-urban planning. It is still too early to say what the effects of this change have been.

Although the first significant event in Dar es Salaam's history occurs in the second half of the nineteenth century, the general scope of population movements in Tanzania prior to this time is important for establishing broad patterns of migration and ethnic diversity. Unlike the founding of Nairobi at a British railhead in the heart of Kikuyu territory, Dar es Salaam's founding can be seen as a continuation of long established trends. The city did not, at first, add new patterns of migration or cultural heterogeneity as much as it provided a new focus and emphasis for what already existed.

Most of precolonial Tanzania was inhabited by groups belonging to one of two large linguistic clusters, Bantu and Nilotic. This is not to suggest any necessary cultural homogeneity among the members of these large groupings, however. As E. J. Murphy points out, the routes followed by various Bantu-speaking peoples in reaching Tanzania were many, with the migrations taking place over several different time spans.[1] Accepting Murphy's suggestion of a Bantu cradleland in central Zaire, the movements have taken place over a total period of about a thousand years.[2] The Nilotic route reconstructed by Murdock[3] is somewhat more straightforward but still occupies a period of perhaps the same length. The pattern of movements into Tanzania is further complicated by more recent events, such as the Ngoni incursions resulting from events further south and the gradual shift from Omani influence to Zanzibari influence.

The backdrop for events influencing the development of Dar es Salaam must be seen as one of ethnic and political heterogeneity in an area of many small kingdoms and chieftainships, as well as peoples less centrally organized. All in all, the area was, and still is, characterized by the lack of a dominant, ethnically based, political power. This was an area of linguistic and cultural variation, in the context of broad similarities.

The history of Dar es Salaam is, essentially, a colonial history, but unlike the history of cities like Nairobi, its roots are partially non-Western. In some senses, the founding of Dar es Salaam represents the culmination of Arabic influence on the coast and its shift to an African base. While there were earlier occasional contacts, significant continuous influence dates from at least the tenth century.

Arab presence was primarily in the form of small trading towns scattered along the coast. Up until the end of the thirteenth century, trade and its concomitant social, political, and economic influences were relatively small in scale. With the opening of the fourteenth century and the rise of Kilwa, about 250 kilometers south of Dar es Salaam, the Arab presence became stable but was still essentially isolated from the interior and had little impact on it.[4] The most significant development of this period is the birth of Swahili as a <u>lingua franca</u> and of Swahili culture.

The arrival of the Portuguese at the end of the fifteenth century begins a series of events markedly changing this pattern of coast-interior isolation. During the century in which Portugal was solidifying its ascendancy and during the following century of Portuguese control of the coast, various inland groups began a new series of movements. Some, like the Nyika, were moving south to what is now the Kenya-Tanzania border area.[5] Other movements were associated with the gradual expansion of the Maasai and related groups.[6] Finally, there were some lesser known movements, usually indicated by discussion of the northward incursions of a group known as Zimba. It seems likely that the Zimba are related to movements initiated by the growth in the last half of the fifteenth century of the kingdom the Portuguese called Monomotapa. This pattern was to be repeated in the nineteenth century by the Ngoni.

By about 1700, when the Omani began to reassert Arab influence on the coast, the state of affairs in the interior was characterized by confusion resulting from these population shifts. It was a situation not only of various conflicts but also of both the building and rebuilding of various interethnic alliances. By the end of the eighteenth century, the general state of affairs on the coast was that "of a collection of small states occupying a freer, less turbulent, and poor environment than formerly. Foreign powers had disappeared and mainland upheavals subsided, but international trade across the Indian Ocean had gone dry after two centuries of war."[7] Sayyid Said bin Sultan, the architect of Omani control, began his expansionist program around 1813. The effects on what was to become Dar es Salaam were twofold. First of all, caravan-based trade with the interior was firmly established, facilitated by the new alignments that had developed over the previous century. Caravan trade increased and solidified the movements of peoples toward and along the coast. Secondly, Said's decision in 1840 to move the center of his activities from a precarious Musquat to a more secure Zanzibar made the need for a secure base for control of the coast even more important.

THE OMANI PERIOD

Zanzibar's control of coastal trade was never unchallenged. There was always competition from other coastal towns. In addition, the nineteenth century saw the increasing replacement of ocean-going sailing vessels with larger steamships. This meant that many of the older coastal towns were less and less able to accommodate the physical requirements of ocean-directed trade. As a result of these political and economic factors, in the 1860s Sultan Sayyid Majid conceived and began the construction of Dar es Salaam near the site of the village of Mzizima, within the confines of one of the few natural harbors on the East African coast.

The new city began as a trade and administrative center and has never lost those characteristics. Dar es Salaam was, at least physically, a planned city from the start. Although few buildings from Sultan Majid's time survive, the evidence of their location and a few old woodcuts seem to indicate that the Sultan's planning gave permanent shape to what are now known as City Drive and Independence Avenue in the city center.[8]

Zanzibari interest in the city ended with the death of Sultan Majid in 1870, and with his death Dar es Salaam's directed development ended, until the establishment of a German East Africa Company station in 1887. In 1867, Dar es Salaam's population was estimated at approximately 900. By 1886-87, the population was variously estimated at between three and five thousand.[9] Two factors must have contributed to this growth of over 200 percent in 20 years: the slave trade, which experienced rapid expansion during the first six decades of the nineteenth century, and the Ngoni invasions, which took place from about 1835 to 1881.

These are both significant, not only for the movement of the peoples directly involved in them but also for their ricochet effects. There was, in this period, a constant formation and re-formation of relatively strong states, especially in the southern half of Tanganyika. These must have produced a residue of displaced people moving first coastward and then northward toward Dar es Salaam, a relatively safe, economically expanding, potential haven. The net result is that the majority of Dar es Salaam's population was, from the start, probably multi-ethnic, polyglot, and mainland African, giving increased importance to the practical development of Swahili culture and language.

THE GERMAN PERIOD

German control lasted from 1887 to 1916. The first three years of German presence in Dar es Salaam were marked by a coastal revolt. Probably because the German East Africa Company had been able to defend it, Dar es Salaam was chosen as the central headquarters for German administration when governmental control replaced that of the company around 1891. Under the Germans, a number of planned building programs took place. These are significant because they have had a lasting impact on the city and the problems it faces in post-independence Tanzania. German planning, like that of the Arabs, can only be inferred from what has survived from that period. Primarily, the planning and building seems to have concentrated on the eastern end of the harbor, producing a basically grid-patterned complex of administrative buildings and official residences in the setting of a botanical garden. Although many of the buildings have been modified, some replaced and others added, the area still retains its luxurious, upper-class garden-city atmosphere.

Two other areas also developed during this period. One is the primarily Asian commercial and residential area immediately behind the northwestern side of the harbor. The second is the large residential and commercial settlement of African workers, now know as Kariakoo.[10] There were also smaller migrant settlements, but Kariakoo was the largest. The Germans planned and began construction of Kariakoo's grid pattern shortly before World War I. By 1916, with the end of German control, Dar es Salaam had developed its basic social and physical traits as a rapidly growing, multi-ethnic, polyglot, commercial and administrative center. The population had grown to approximately 22,500 (a 1913 German estimate). An 1894 German census listed the population as 9,000 Africans, 620 Asians, and 400 Europeans. By 1913, the figures were 19,000 Africans, 2,500 Asians, and 1,000 Europeans.[11] This tripartite ethnic division was reflected in housing patterns as well as occupations. The African population tended to occupy the western and northwestern fringes of the city; the Asians were crowded into the central commercial and residential area; and Europeans occupied a bloc on the eastern end of the harbor.

THE BRITISH PERIOD

During the initial years of British control, between the World Wars, the city doubled in population. By 1943, the number of Europeans had not changed much. The African population had grown to 33,000, and the Asians to 11,000.[12] The British made few changes in the city's residential patterns, beyond opening two new residential areas for Europeans, Sea View and Oyster Bay. These both followed the German model of large, single-story houses on large plots of land. The British also completed the Kariakoo grid and imposed a similar pattern on the contiguous African settlement of Ilala.

In 1949, the British initiated overall town planning with the completion of Sir Alexander Gibb's master plan, Dar es Salaam's first.[13] The plan explicitly included provision for an ethnic and class stratification of residence. An expansion of the Oyster Bay area as a European settlement was recommended because it was close to the village of Msasani, facilitating movement of domestic servants. Expansion of the Upanga area was recommended to relieve population pressures in the dense, mainly Asian, commercial and residential area. On the one hand, the 1949 master plan recommended a European standard of one house per acre. On the other hand, in seeking to deal with a housing shortage for Africans, it explored ways of increasing density from eight houses per acre to as many as twelve. The twelve years from 1949 to 1961 saw the implementation of some of Gibb's proposals, as well as the growth of several squatter areas.[14]

Independence left Dar es Salaam with a history of urban planning of close to a century, almost all of which was directed at separating populations and creating physical parallels to political and class divisions. At the same time, to the extent that the planning activities did not recognize ethnic divisions among Africans, they also facilitated the expansion of Swahili as a language and of Swahili cultural patterns as an over-arching cultural context for the city.

In his survey, J. A. K. Leslie found areas of Dar es Salaam that were dominated by members of one ethnic group or another (Leslie was writing of the situation as it existed in 1956).[15] However, there is also evidence that this form of ethnic stratification has decreased in importance and is likely to become even less important under the impact of modern Tanzania's urban policies.[16]

NATIONAL DEVELOPMENT POLICIES

The advent of independence did not bring the immediate creation of specifically urban national policies. Neither the three-year plan developed for implementation with independence nor the first Five-Year Plan contain an explicit urban section. Of course, the concerns these documents showed for housing, power, water supply, transportation, and so on all had urban implications. Also, this is the period during which the basis for later urban policies was laid down.

From 1961 to 1967, the country gradually moved toward the development of the socialist direction explicitly announced with the publication of the Arusha Declaration of 1967. The most significant formal action of this period was the ending of freehold land tenure in 1963. The implications for control over urban development processes are clear. In addition, the concept of ujamaa as it grew and developed into a national policy, with its emphasis on creating a new social system based on traditional patterns, has a potential for affecting future urban policies that has yet to be realized.

Although there has been a Town Planning Division of the government since 1951,[17] urban development became an explicit part of national policy only with the Second Five-Year Plan of 1969-74. In addition, a new Dar es Salaam Master Plan was not completed until 1968. The result is that overall, coordinated planning for Dar es Salaam has been a reality for no more than ten years. Published materials dealing with Dar es Salaam are fragmented, and little of

it deals with the city as a unit. The most recent detailed examination
of the city is deBlij's, which deals almost exclusively with the central
core and with a period of time prior to the advent of urban planning.[18]
Most of this chapter's information dealing directly with Dar es Salaam's
efforts toward planning and implementation was gathered during the
course of field work undertaken from September 1973 to June 1974.
It is worth noting that much of deBlij's description of the central core
in the early 1960s was still essentially accurate in 1973-74.

Tanzania is primarily a rural country. No more than 6 to 7 percent of its population is urban. As a result, Tanzanian policies since
the Arusha Declaration have explicitly focused on activities whose
major goal is increasing the flow of goods and services to the rural
countryside rather than increasing the gross national product through
generation of urban wealth. This policy direction has led to an elaboration of the ujamaa concept as a central theme of development activities. President Nyerere, architect of ujamaa as a national direction,
bases it on three principles which he sees as stemming from the
nature of traditional Tanzanian societies. These involve (1) an understanding that everyone has some status (and therefore rights and obligations) in the society; (2) a societal priority on provision of at least
a minimal economic level for everyone; and (3) a basic understanding
that everyone has an obligation to contribute to the society's welfare.[19]
In more concrete terms, ujamaa refers to forms of social organization
encouraging communal, cooperative efforts and discouraging wide
differences in wealth and income. This has led to a stress on the
creation of villages with this organizational orientation as a means
of improving farmers' incomes and the quality of goods and services
they can afford.

The cooperative ujamaa villages, while experiencing some
difficulties, represent a significant new direction in national development in the Third World. Their long-term success is yet to be
proved, but the potential is clearly there. On the other hand, ujamaa
applied to urban conditions and needs is still largely unformulated.
The chief problem lies in delineating the urban analogues of the basic
village unit.

Even though city dwellers are a very small part of Tanzania's
population, the urban growth rate far exceeds that of the country as
a whole. In 1970, total population growth was approximately 2.7 percent per year; that of urban areas (towns with a population of 1,800
or more) was approximately 7 percent. Between 1965 and 1967, Dar
es Salaam's growth was estimated at 11 percent per year.[20] No matter
what the exact current figures are, it is clear that urban facilities in
general, and Dar es Salaam's in particular, are under severe pressure. Urban areas (especially Dar es Salaam, with the largest population, the greatest clustering of industries, and most of the

administrative and educational facilities) are also significant gener-
ators of the wealth and expertise necessary for the development of
the rest of the country.

The significance of rural policies for urban growth and of urban
policies for rural development has not been lost on the government.
In addition to general sections on sectors such as transportation,
education, water and sanitation, and power, the Second Five-Year
Development Plan included a specifically urban section. Its major
elements were control and direction of urban physical growth, improvement of services to city residents, improvement of the flow of
goods and services to rural areas, and, finally, "to link (rural and
urban) . . . development by planning for growth of urban communities in the outlying parts of towns as an expression of the ujamaa
concept of life."[21] Urban ujamaa, as a concept, is recognized by
both official and unofficial sources as an important component of
overall national policy. However, as already noted, it is also an idea
that has not yet been as thoroughly worked out as the notion of ujamaa
applied to rural areas.

Partly this is explained by the high priorities placed on rural
development. It is also explained by the fact that rural problems and
approaches are superficially simpler. People need to be concentrated
into villages in order to facilitate equitable and adequate distribution
of goods and services. In the cities the concentration is a central part
of the problem.

Policies directed toward developing ujamaa have a potential for
dealing with this core aspect of urbanization. The government has
experimented with housing cooperatives and has encouraged development of other cooperative societies. Most of these deal with marketing
agricultural produce; some deal with the production of artifacts for
the tourist trade (mostly wood carvings), and a few deal with transportation. However, such an approach raises fundamental policy questions
that have not yet been resolved. To what extent to small-scale, locally
controlled, neighborhood-like organizations produce a duplication of
facilities and services neither the country nor the city can afford?
How should, or could, such semi-autonomous enclaves be organized,
and what should be their relationship to larger-scale state enterprises?

If ujamaa refers to a group's activities undertaken for the benefit
of both its members and the society at large, then what level of group
is appropriate? For example, in regard to transportation, should
Dar es Salaam Metropolitan Transit, a state-owned company, have a
monopoly on urban mass transit, or should it work in conjunction with
smaller-scale transportation cooperatives? The question becomes,
What level of ownership is private and what is public? Or, again, Who
would build houses, the National Housing Corporation, individuals,
cooperative societies, or some combination of these?

The most recent available data indicate some of the dimensions of the housing problem that might be solved by implementing a well-articulated urban <u>ujamaa</u> policy. Approximately 80 percent of the city's residents have incomes under 500 shillings;[*] 67 percent of the city's residents are migrants; 56 percent of the city's residents are squatters, and 87 percent of the city's residents rent their living space.[22] In 1970-71, the National Housing Corporation saw house applications rise by about 20 percent and was able to provide enough new housing so that the net growth in unserviced applications was only 13.9 percent.[23] These are national figures, and in this Dar es Salaam represents the same housing shortage as the rest of the country, only in more extreme form. It is not surprise then that over half the city's residents are squatters.

Given the severity of the housing shortage in Dar es Salaam, the question of urban <u>ujamaa</u> has proved to be of great importance to the city, and has been of some concern to the appropriate governmental ministries.

> If it shall be possible to reach the broad masses of the population with the essential services, and with a separate dwelling for each household, it will be necessary to use higher densities . . . it will be types of houses which are not really fit for the <u>ownership form</u> where each household owns individually its own house. . . . It would . . . be in the line with the general policy of the country if many of them could be owned by housing cooperatives, which would let them to their members. This would also form a natural part of a stronger development towards cooperative living and working in urban districts, an element of urban <u>ujamaa</u>.[24]

The effort to organize and develop cooperatives has not been successful. This is largely the result of financial difficulties and the lack of experience on the part of both the organizers and cooperative society members.

The National Capital Master Plan suggested, among other things, a housing strategy that would "tackle the mass housing problem rather than providing complete homes for only a small portion of those in need. The idea in simplest terms, is to find a way to make housing build itself progressively by making maximum use of individual incen-

---

*In 1971, the time period of this study, the value of a shilling was approximately $.15. In 1978 it is approximately $.13.

tive and traditional building means."[25] The master plan called for organized, controlled, and subsidized upgrading of the houses currently being built by squatters. Essentially, this means utilizing and improving on existing patterns of urban adaptation. The basic argument is that these patterns come closer to fitting the needs of the city's residents than anything imposed by externally based advisors or consultants.

In spite of the as yet unresolved policy questions regarding the shape of urban ujamaa, urban planning in Dar es Salaam is proceeding within the broad, vaguely defined constraints of the national ideology and more immediate, practical economic and political considerations.

The directions of Dar es Salaam's efforts to relieve its housing shortage are based on a multiplicity of approaches which recognize the variations in housing situations in the city.

At the present time, Dar es Salaam contains several different types of residential area. There are villages whose historic origin is independent of the city's but which have now been absorbed by it (e.g., Msasani). There are the older, more conventional areas planned and laid out under the impact and influences of colonial administration, notions, and needs (e.g., Upanga, Kariakoo, Oyster Bay, Sea View). There are new residential areas growing entirely in the context of independent, developing Tanzania (e.g., Kijitonyama, Mikochini). There are areas, often called squatter settlements, but perhaps more accurately described as areas of spontaneous housing (e.g., Manzese, Buguruni). There are, of course, also several areas that do not nearly fit any of these categories. Mwananymala is representative of these, partially planned and laid out but undergoing considerable unplanned, spontaneous development. Such areas are analogous to areas like Msanani, but instead of being absorbed by urban sprawl, they have developed their own semi-autonomous existence within it.

The Manzese area, wholly spontaneous, is now in the process of being planned. It is characteristic of Tanzania's approach to any form of development that in this instance the planning has taken the form of regularizing what exists. The major aim is to facilitate provision of services with as little disruption of the residents as possible. The existing footpaths and roads tend to follow natural contours; those being laid out by the Planning Unit of the Ministry of Lands, Housing and Urban Development tend, as much as possible, to do no more than to replace the existing paths with wider, more stable road surfaces. The net effect is to preserve the character of the place and not impose external forms of either spatial arrangements, house ownership, or patterns of organization. There is some evidence available indicating that one of the results of such policies is to promote a merging of traditional cultural patterns with those required by urbanization.[26]

Although it is too early to be sure, it is possible that this approach to planning will result in the development of semi-autonomous units within the city approaching the structure of ujamaa villages in the rural areas. This kind of growth is also similar to the satellite communities proposed by the master plan. Of course, there is a limit to the number of such "urban villages" the city can support. If the concept of urban ujamaa is to become a reality, it needs to be adapted to various levels of urban organization.

Characteristic of Manzese, as well as more completely planned areas, is the use of unoccupied land for domestic agriculture. One informant pointed out that, given the low employment and income levels of the Manzese area, this is a necessity if the people are to maintain a reasonable standard of living and a degree of autonomy. The ministry's planning efforts here seem to be directed at preserving this aspect of urban land use.

This approach to planning can be contrasted to that found in areas formally planned and laid out prior to residential occupation. One such is Kijitonyama, Area 16 of the Dar es Salaam Master Plan. Here the whole site, some 614 acres, was planned, surveyed, and laid out, and some site facilities (e.g., water, storm drains, stabilized roads) provided first. One quadrant was then assigned to the use of a housing cooperative. This was designed as a pilot project testing the feasibility of the cooperative approach.[27] The Mwenge Co-operative Housing Society was established in 1971; by 1973-74, most of the projected housing was still unbuilt. According to informants in the ministry, Mwenge's major problem rested in its large size. In addition, the fact that the member's association with the society was based solely on the provision of housing made it difficult to maintain Mwenge as a viable organization. The extent to which these lessons can or will be applied to future efforts at developing housing cooperatives is unclear.

Another contrast in housing policy can be found in an area known as Block 45, adjacent to Kijitonyama. Like Kijitonyama, Block 45 was totally planned and laid out on paper. However, no site facilities were provided in advance. Plots were assigned on an individual basis, and the start of construction within three years was mandated. As best I can determine, plot assignments began around 1970. By 1973-74, most of the available plots contained started or completed construction.

Like Manzese, much of the unbuilt land is used for domestic agriculture. However, some of the shamba land is imperiled by new housing, and more would be if the roads were constructed as planned and the projected schools and market were built. In addition, the residents seem to have subdivided the area into smaller social-residential units than the original plans suggest would exist. In some respects, Block 45 comes close to the master plan vision of "housing building itself," but at a higher level of affluence than either originally intended or that is represented by the members of the Mwenge Co-operative Housing Society.

SUMMARY

As with the rest of Tanzania's development efforts, urban planning in Dar es Salaam exhibits a variety of experimental approaches, all of them guided by the need to provide for both the common and the individual welfare. The relatively short period of time during which there has been coordinated, goal-directed urban planning in Dar es Salaam leaves a shallow fund of relevant experience on which to build new directions.

The relatively low priority given to urban planning will probably shift somewhat over the next decade, with the construction of the new capital city in Dodoma. This will also force a reconsideration of urban ujamaa as a policy direction. Given Tanzania's dedication to deemphasizing the significance of sociocultural and socioeconomic differences, the probability is that a coherent effort will be made to develop both the concept of urban ujamaa and guidelines for its implementation.

One of the major problems in this regard is the lack of trained Tanzanian personnel, people with an understanding of both ujamaa and the requirements of planned urban growth. The creation of the Ardhi Institute, a cooperative venture involving both the University of Dar es Salaam and the Ministry of Lands, Housing and Urban Development, promises an eventual corrective. Currently the students are primarily involved in village planning; however, the Institute has no intention of ignoring the urban sector.

The net conclusion is that urban planning in Dar es Salaam has not yet reached the point where it has a clear-cut direction. Although this is frustrating for those actively involved in planning, it also seems healthy for both the city and the country. Tanzania and Dar es Salaam are not anxious simply to adopt a European, or even other African model of development planning. Instead, they are moving slowly toward an approach uniquely suited to their economic, political, cultural, and ideological requirements.

NOTES

1. E. J. Murphy, History of African Civilization (New York: Delta, 1972), pp. 178-97.
2. Murphy, op. cit., p. 184.

3. G. P. Murdock, Africa: Its People and Their Cultural History (New York: McGraw-Hill, 1958), pp. 328-41.

4. N. Chittick, "The Coast Before the Arrival of the Portuguese," in Zamani: A Survey of East African History, ed. B. A. Ogot (Dar es Salaam: Longman Tanzania, Ltd., 1973), pp. 105-13.

5. F. J. Berg, "The Coast from the Portuguese Invasion," in Zamani, op. cit., pp. 115-25.

6. C. Ehret, "Cushites and the Highland and Plains Nilotes to A.D. 1800," in Zamani, op. cit., pp. 158-66.

7. Berg, op. cit., p. 128.

8. W. T. Casson, "Architectural Notes on Dar es Salaam," Tanzania Notes and Records 71 (1970): 181-93; J. E. G. Sutton, "Dar es Salaam: A Sketch of a Hundred Years," Tanzania Notes and Records 71 (1970): 1-20.

9. Sutton, op. cit., pp. 5-7.

10. There is a tradition that the name is derived from the Carrier Corps porters who were quartered there during World War I; see Sutton, op. cit. There is an area of Nairobi with a similar name.

11. Sutton, op. cit., p. 19.

12. Sutton, op. cit.

13. Sir Alexander Gibb and Partners, "A Plan for Dar es Salaam" (London: n.p., 1949).

14. Several of the publications of the Bureau of Resource and Land Use Planning at the University of Dar es Salaam euphemistically refer to them as areas of "spontaneous housing."

15. J. A. K. Leslie, A Survey of Dar es Salaam (London: Oxford University Press, 1963).

16. Sutton, op. cit.; Joan Vincent, "The Dar es Salaam Townsman: Social and Political Aspects of City Life," Tanzania Notes and Records 71 (1970): 149-56.

17. The Editors, "Town Planning Revolves Around the People: A Record of Ten Years," Tanzania Notes and Records 76 (1975): 179-84.

18. Harm deBlij, Dar es Salaam: A Study in Urban Geography (Evanston, Ill.: Northwestern University Press, 1963).

19. Julius K. Nyerere, Socialism and Rural Development (Dar es Salaam: Government Printer, 1967).

20. L. M. Hansen et al., The Economic Development Prospects of Tanzania; Volume I, The Main Report (Washington, D.C.: International Bank for Reconstruction and Development, 1972), p. 31.

21. The Editors, "Town Planning," op. cit., p. 180.

22. These data come from a study conducted by the National Urban Mobility, Employment and Income Survey of Tanzania (NUMEIST) cited in Richard E. Stren, Urban Inequality and Housing Policy in Tanzania: The Problem of Squatting (Berkeley: Institute of International Studies, University of California, 1975).

23. J. D. Kikenya, "National Housing Corporation: Progress in Housing the Masses," Tanzania Notes and Records 76 (1975): 185-90.

24. J. V. Lwabuti, "Urban Housing Cooperatives," mimeographed (Dar es Salaam: Registrar of Cooperatives, 1973), p. 1.

25. Project Planning Associates, National Capital Master Plan Report, Dar es Salaam (Toronto: Project Planning Associates, 1968).

26. N. Georgulas, "Settlement Patterns and Rural Development in Tanganyika," Program of East African Studies, Occasional Paper no. 29, Maxwell School of Citizenship and Public Affairs (Syracuse, N.Y.: Syracuse University, 1976); Edwin S. Segal, Peri-Urban Settlement Patterns: Policy Implications, Research Report Prepared for the Ministry of Lands, Housing and Urban Development (Dar es Salaam, 1974).

27. Economic Commission for Africa, Cooperative Housing Pilot Project (Kijitonyama), Dar es Salaam (Geneva: UNESCO, 1972).

15

HOUSING AND
SERVICE PLANNING IN
LUSAKA, ZAMBIA

Norman C. Rothman

On the eve of its independence, Zambia was already the most highly urbanized country in Africa south of the Sahara with the exception of South Africa. Between 1963 and 1969, the country's total urban population increased from 747,000 to 1,188,000. As Zambia's total population was just over 4,000,000 in 1969, the urban component exceeded 30 percent. According to one recent estimate, perhaps 45 percent of the country's population may live in urban or peri-urban areas.[1]

The increase in the population of the capital city of Lusaka was even greater. The population virtually doubled between 1963 and 1969, while the incorporation of surrounding sites, which increased its area from 36 to 139 square miles in 1970, added some 80,000 additional inhabitants. The net result of migration and municipal expansion has been to increase the city's population from approximately 130,000 to over 300,000 in less than a decade.[2] This accelerated growth has further aggravated an already acute problem involving street lighting, road construction, water reticulation, and sewage for its African majority.

COLONIAL URBANIZATION

African accommodation, as it developed in Lusaka during the colonial period, evolved from existing conditions as well as official government policy. Founded as a marketing and quarrying center along a railway siding in 1905,[3] the area which gradually came to constitute the administrative entity of Lusaka was characterized by urban sprawl. The majority of properties in and around Lusaka had initially been given out in freehold. With the passage of time, the freeholder-farmers—who often were short on funds but long on land, as their realty would average upwards of 3,000 acres—arrived at tenantry agreements with Africans unable and/or unwilling to secure housing space elsewhere. Plots of these holdings were rented in return for assorted duties on the part of the plot holders. These responsibilities might include monetary payment, payment in kind through a share of the produce grown on the land, or labor commitments at certain periods, such as the sowing and reaping seasons. Services were not included in these arrangements, and tenants, for example, were expected to dig their own wells for water. [4]

Town planning decisions aggravated urban sprawl. Lusaka, in common with most European-founded urban centers in the Rhodesias (now separated into Zambia and Rhodesia), followed a pronounced spread-eagle pattern copied from the Republic of South Africa. Land was at a discount and initially sold for as little as 3 pence per acre. [5] This price factor coupled with the desire of early settlers for a measure of privacy gave the settlements that had coalesced to form Lusaka a density of less than 300 people per square mile 20 years after its foundation. At that time, an estimated 1,400-1,500 Europeans and 1,500-2,000 Africans were living in an area of approximately 14 square miles. [6]

In Lusaka, domestic and environmental services were expensive not only because of the spread-out spatial pattern but also because of underlying geophysical conditions. The town was situated on a limestone formation, the surface of which had been hollowed out. During the rainy season (November to April), these hollows would fill with water, and the water table would rise to the surface, thereby creating the danger of flooding. Drainage ditches could be dug only with difficulty for there was little protective soil coverage over the hard rock. Thus, streets would be flooded, and any aperture could collect stagnant water which might provide a breeding ground for mosquitos. [7]

The problem of accommodation-cum-services was complicated by the selection of Lusaka as the territorial capital of Northern Rhodesia in 1931. Influenced by the contemporary mania for planned capitals, such as those erected at Canberra, Australia, and Zomba, Malawi, coupled with the euphoria induced by the copper boom, the government decided to build a "generous, gracious city."[8] As both architects and government planners had been impressed by the example of Salisbury (the capital of the present Rhodesia) and other urban garden centers to the south, the pattern of racial separation was tacitly adopted. The new government center was constructed on a slight ridge two miles southeast of the old town. "Character" and "residential" zones were laid out which insured that land outside the area of drainage by gravitation to the south and east of the new capital

FIGURE 15.1   Greater Lusaka

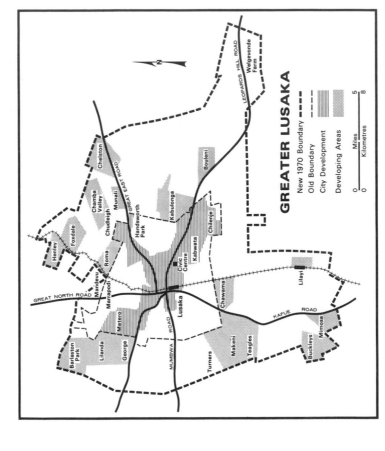

GREATER LUSAKA

New 1970 Boundary
Old Boundary
City Development
Developing Areas

Miles
Kilometres

Source: Greater Lusaka: A Guide to Residents (Lusaka: Government Printer, 1971).

area was reserved for African "locations." As the area between the new capital area and the old commercial town remained mostly unoccupied, the "central" business district was now located in the extreme northwest.[9]

World War II brought belated government recognition that African town dwellers were not just temporary interlopers working for the European employer in order to pay poll tax before returning to the countryside. The 1944 Report on the Administration and Finances of Native Locations in Urban Areas made recommendations calling for every employer to assume housing with related domestic and environmental obligations. If an employer did not provide adequate accommodation and services for his employees, the latter would be housed by the local authority, who would be paid by the employer. These recommendations were put into law by the African Urban Housing Ordinance of 1948.[10] The latter statute was completely ineffective in Lusaka, as the local authority lacked the financial base to keep pace with rising building activity, building and material costs, a rapidly increasing population, and the ever growing number of "associated" services that came to constitute part of the housing burden. The local authority received questionable help from the government and next to no help from local employers in meeting the housing obligation.

Between 1946 and 1958, the territorial government subsidized the building of temporary structures. However, the saving device of using cheaper, nonpermanent building materials proved to be very costly since temporary structures had an estimated life of five years and then had to be replaced, thus involving another capital expenditure. Temporary structures were also very susceptible to the elements, and during the 1950s collapsed periodically in the rainy season.[11] In 1958-64, the government seized upon the temporary profits shown by the Lusaka Liquor Undertaking to suspend its housing subsidy.[12] Unlike the Copperbelt towns and Kabwe, where the major employers—the mining companies—were anxious to secure a relatively permanent labor force through a sufficient wage adequate for decent housing, many of the local employers at Lusaka tried to evade their housing responsibilities. They attempted this—usually unsuccessfully—through two methods. They would sign employees on day-to-day contracts and then claim they had no obligations in regard to services for their "temporary" employees.[13] Another way was simply to house their employees in the serviceless, unauthorized compounds that had grown up on the freehold land surrounding the city and which by independence in 1964 housed at least one-third of the city's African population.[14] In the meantime, most local employers called for an "all-in-wage" for African employees, which would free employers from the housing and "ancillary" (as the assorted domestic and environmental services were now called) service burden.[15]

PRE-INDEPENDENCE

The wage structure that had come into existence in Lusaka by the early fifties helped to create an inverse wage-labor-housing ratio so that an increase in one would almost automatically have to be compensated at the expense of the other. The increasing cost of house rents, which include the costs of such services as street lighting, road construction, and sewerage, encouraged employers to compensate through wages. The cyclical character of economic development in Lusaka in the 1950s, when periods of expansion and over-employment alternated with contraction and underemployment, hardly encouraged short-term marginal employers, such as the minor building contractors, to assume such relatively long-range responsibilities as housing construction. Employers were reluctant to reduce an immediate profit margin. But even more established concerns less vulnerable to economic recession engaged in this practice. In the African suburb of Matero, built for African employees of industrial concerns and opened in 1952, for example, a "cheaper" 3.30 kwacha per month house (1 kwacha is equal to $1.40) would be filled more readily by an employer than a more expensive lodging. As a result, an employee might be forced to rent a 4 or 4.50 kwacha house even if he had only a housing allowance of 3.30 kwacha. For, if he wanted official housing and the company specified Matero, the employee would have to make up the difference from his own pocket. [16]

In the Copperbelt towns the mining companies, who were the major employers, had adopted a wage policy designed to maximize the efficiency of African labor. This not only involved relatively high wages (the lowest paid monthly wage of African mine workers in 1956 was computed to be 22 kwacha; the average monthly wage in Lusaka, 1957-58, was 14 kwacha) but a policy of improving productivity through the employment of a permanent labor force. Therefore, wages were no longer geared to the single man or to the subsistence level. Partly influenced by the African trade unions, particularly the mineworkers union, the companies developed an African advancement scheme wherein workers would undergo several weeks of intensive training with the possibility of promotion into a higher paid job. [17]

The policy of Lusaka's biggest employer, the government, was somewhat different. Employing men in diverse occupations and organized, at least theoretically, on a nonprofit basis, the government did not have a productivity incentive. It was not interested in the stimulated demand for goods and services that might result from an increase in African wage rates. It felt that this might have to come through higher taxation, which would antagonize the non-African tax-payers. As a result, the government was not favorable to increased wages. This policy was reflected in statistics compiled on nearly

70 percent of all African wage earners in Northern Rhodesia. As of June 30, 1958, the respective wages of miners, industrial workers, and Northern Rhodesia government employees along the urban line of rail was 26 kwacha per month, 13 kwacha per month, and 11 kwacha per month, respectively. The minority of government workers who possessed the secondary educational qualification to attain civil status received 22 kwacha per month. [18] These latter statistics reflect the continued differential between the largest employers of the mining towns and Lusaka.

Yet, while not encouraging wage increases, the government was tacitly encouraging the development of a type of housing that could only be met by raising wages. As a result of the use of government subsidies between 1946 and 1958 to meet deficits of recurring housing and ancillary services expenses and the offer of government loans for capital expenditure, the standard of housing soon exceeded the ability of the average African to pay for it. Employers faced with mounting rent burdens called in vain for all-in-wage increase. The wage increment needed to make this possibility viable would have been astronomical. In 1960, for instance, the computed annual expenditure in Lusaka for a two-room semi-detached house with an allowance for basic maintenance came to 70 kwacha. With ability to pay fixed at one-sixth of gross income, the yearly rent requirement of 42 kwacha would have averaged out to 3.50 kwacha a month. As salaries averaged 16 kwacha per month at this time, a per capita yearly allocation of over 10 kwacha would have been necessary in order to make up the deficit. [19]

This calculation was at the lower end of the housing spectrum. It was estimated in that same year that if the Lusaka City Council were to provide African areas with all of the ancillary services—street lighting, domestic electricity, sanitation, individual water supplies, and tarred roads—the unsubsidized cost would come to 11 kwacha per month. At that time, it was calculated at 35.5 percent of African wage earners were earning over 10 kwacha per month but less than 16 kwacha; 10.9 percent were earning over 16 kwacha but less than 20 kwacha per month; 14.2 percent were earning over 20 kwacha but less than 30 kwacha; 5.7 were earning over 30 kwacha but less than 42 kwacha; and only 3 percent were earning more than 42 kwacha per month. [20] Even presuming a 20 percent allowance of gross income, it was obvious that very few Africans could afford this outside of employment housing.

It was in this period 1958-64 that the government had withdrawn its subsidy. Nevertheless, even though it continued to encourage the provision of a good standard of housing and housing services, it refused to help the municipalities face the heavy commitment this policy entailed. When Lusaka applied for the approval of rents based on the

economic cost of a design and standard endorsed by the Northern
Rhodesia Housing Board, its proposals were rejected by the government. (Under Section 16 of the Urban African Housing Ordinance,
government approval was required for all rents charged by the municipalities.) The government had cited the liquor profits as a major
reason for canceling the housing subsidy, as an alternate source of
income was now available. During this period, this enterprise enjoyed
record surpluses. Lusaka, naturally anxious to utilize the mounting
profits in order to meet its increasing housing deficit, could only get
a conditional approval which was subject to renewal every year.[21]

The gulf between the standard of housing available and the
ability of a potential African tenant to rent it on an "untied" basis
continued to widen and had become unbridgeable by 1964. In that year,
an arbitrary attempt to match house types and families according to
pay highlighted the situation. Sixty-seven percent of all families
made 5 kwacha per month or less, while merely 20 percent of all
available houses fell within this category. The equivalent figures for
the 5-8 kwacha range showed an opposite configuration. Sixty-one
percent of houses were within this group, but only 18 percent of families could afford to rent them. The great bulk of the remainder consisted of houses and families in the 8-12 kwacha range (10 percent
and ten percent) and the 12-17 kwacha range (7 percent and 3 percent,
respectively).[22]

The ultimate losers in this ill-starred marriage of labor and
housing in the Lusaka area were the employees rather than the employers. Labor was cheap because of its availability, and the price paid
for it as a commodity was low. Therefore, with rising accommodation
costs, the employer subordinated housing obligations to his desire for
overall profit. This consideration received priority over the employees'
living costs, and consequently wages were kept artificially low. The
employers might justify themselves by claiming that as housing and
service standards were constantly being raised, wage increases were
not necessary. Nonetheless, as many of them engaged labor at casual
rates for temporary periods, an African would face the loss of both
house and job. Unfortunately, this would not affect the amount of rent
for the house.

Employers in Lusaka seemed as oblivious to economic laws as
their government. Wages would not increase greatly during times of
prosperity. Instead, the effect in Lusaka was to induce more unskilled
labor to migrate to the town, thereby reinsuring the lopsided supply-
demand proportion in the employer's favor. This situation was partially
concealed by Lusaka's relatively low unemployment, which averaged
7.5 percent in the late 1950s and early 1960s.[23] It must be remembered that this was an overall percentage which obscured the fact
that there was an excess demand for certain types of semi-skilled

labor, such as artisans in the booming construction industry. Many of the labor migrants themselves preferred certain types of work and would often refuse work which they might consider beneath their dignity.[24] If the economic situation in the town became unfavorable, the worker—particularly if he was from a neighboring group—could always move out of Lusaka altogether. If he was not a member of a local group, he could move into one of the mushrooming unauthorized compounds located on the periphery of the city. There, rents averaged 1 kwacha to 2 kwacha per month.[25] Also the timing of rent collection was fairly flexible, and this enabled the rent payer to tide himself over during periods of sickness and unemployment. Eventually, when the labor situation in Lusaka brightened, he could return to the city.

The fairly reasonable rates of the unauthorized compounds also offered attractions to those Africans whose skills were in demand. In the 1960s, artisans in the construction trade constituted the largest single group of wage earners in these areas. It was also evident by then that those Africans who had the choice of being personally responsible for rent overwhelmingly opted for the squatter locations as opposed to Chilenje or Matero, the two largest African suburbs. The latter were generally the home of the higher wage groups and contained the largest proportion of nonpayers of rent.[26]

There were two possible solutions to the housing-cum-services problem, both of which required government action. One was the restriction of labor migration. As Lusaka's rural hinterland contained a sizable reserve of unskilled labor, the possibility would always exist of an oversupply of labor and a consequent depression of wages. In 1961 and 1962, at the annual conferences of the Municipal Association of Northern Rhodesia, the then mayor of Lusaka suggested that controls be instituted to restrict the influx of Africans to certain urban areas. The government turned down the suggestion on the grounds that it was beyond its physical power. Through the years, various laws controlling movements of Africans into urban areas had gradually lapsed or become inoperative. By 1958, even the pass, the forerunner of all segregative acts, had been repealed.[27]

The other possible solution would have revolved around the introduction of minimum wage legislation. A general minimum wage was never introduced during the colonial era. The nearest approach to it, however, was the Minimum Wages, Wage Councils, and Conditions of Employment Ordinance of 1961, which set up wage councils regulating the employment of Africans in the building industry, hotels, clubs, and restaurants, and shop workers. The effect of this ordinance on Lusaka was minimal as employees of the Northern Rhodesia government, any municipal council, the Rhodesia Railways, and domestic servants—the largest single group of wage earners in Lusaka—were specifically excluded. [28]

The net result of housing decisions was a vicious circle. Because labor was at a discount, wages were depressed and excessive labor was often employed. Housing therefore was in great demand, but due to its huge costs it had to be subsidized. This situation resulted in the employer's obligation to pay a set and rather high rent including services. As labor was tied to housing, he would compensate by keeping wages low. This fed on and was in turn fed by the excess of unskilled labor.

With the advantage of hindsight (the Lusaka of the 1970s still has its tied housing, its "disguised" housing subsidy, housing shortage, and gap between standard of accommodation and wages), one can attempt an evaluation of the short-term panaceas which were put forward in the late 1950s and early 1960s. It was suggested, for instance, that the government initiate a unit grant per house based on minimum standards and average spending power. It was argued that government had a "moral responsibility" to support the rents of housing of a standard which government thought desirable but which could not be afforded by the tenants. It was to be a stop-gap measure and was to be progressively lowered as average wages increased until the African wage earner was deemed capable of supporting himself the economic cost of the services with which he would be provided. The danger inherent in a proposal like this, which was intended to be temporary, was its likelihood of perpetuation in the manner of the housing subsidies. This was the case of a similar measure introduced in 1964. Its object was to encourage capital construction at a gradually decreasing unit grant of initially 12 kwacha per unit. The result has been the opposite of what was intended. Instead of withering away, the government has had to double its grant to 24 kwacha per unit. [29]

A second suggestion envisaged the transferring of the "native" tax of 1.50 kwacha, which all African males in the territory were obliged to pay, from the government of Northern Rhodesia to the municipality. It was argued that the native tax was originally a local tariff and it would be more appropriate that what little taxation urban Africans could afford to pay should be used to identify themselves with the affairs of their township and develop a participation in the provisions of local services. It was also argued that if the tax were levied on all Africans living in the municipal area, it would have the twofold advantage of providing a closer control of unauthorized compounds and perhaps inducing those who lived in them to move into the municipal housing areas. [30]

The proposal was not practical for two reasons. First, the amount to be collected was relatively minor in terms of the effort expended. It was estimated in 1960 that the total amount collected from the city would be about 40,000 kwacha.[31] Second, the source of income itself was already an anachronism, a relic of the time when an African was considered an interloper totally isolated from urban life. Events soon overtook this proposal. The personal levy ordinance of 1963 introduced the income tax to anyone, including Africans, who earned 500 kwacha.[32]

The third suggestion revolved around integrating African housing areas with the rest of the municipality financially making them ratable and including the expenditure of African housing area services in the General Rate Fund. But as Africans could not afford to pay the rates (computed at almost 21 kwacha a year),[33] the end result would have been to transfer liability from employers, based on the size of the labor force, to all ratepayers (based on property values).[34] Nevertheless, African housing areas did become ratable at independence. And as tied housing remained a feature in Lusaka, it was the employers who paid rates instead of rents.

As the colonial period ended, the problem centered on gradually transferring purchasing power from the non-African to the African sector. This process involved persuading employers to increase wages. It would probably entail a period of training and education, which would increase productivity to the point where an employer might feel justified in raising wages. In all, it seemed a long process before the umbilical cord between housing and labor would finally be severed.

POST-INDEPENDENCE

As the population increased over 250 percent in less than ten years, housing service problems have intensified in the first decade of independence. By the end of 1969, for example, the Lusaka City Council had a waiting list in housing of some 16,345 families and 3,636 single persons. In view of this situation, it is not surprising that by one estimate the number of unauthorized squatter settlements in the Lusaka area had reached 32 by 1970-71 and accounted for perhaps 40 percent of its inhabitants.[35]

Lusaka's position vis-a-vis other urban centers in Zambia continued to be unfavorable. It was calculated in 1971, for example, that out of a national squatter population of approximately 260,000, well over 100,000 lived in and around Lusaka.[36] Much of this differential continued to be caused by the nature of employment in Lusaka as opposed to that in the other cities, where the mines continued to be the major employers. The only major urban area even remotely comparable to Lusaka was Livingstone, which had a basically stagnant population. For the rest, employers in Lusaka as in other areas now had the option of paying a statutory housing allowance of 3.50 kwacha per month to their workers to satisfy their housing obligation. Most chose to exercise this option rather than provide housing. The majority of employer housing directly or indirectly was taken up by civil servants or employees of mines as opposed to the population at large. The mines accounted for one-fourth of permanent housing, and the Zambian government owned outright another 20 percent of houses. Indirectly, however, approximately one-fourth of the 30 percent of permanent housing owned by the local authorities had to be rented to civil servants. [37]

As a result of this situation, the favored approach to solving the urban services as revealed in the First National Development Plan and envisaged in the Second National Development Plan has been the "site and service" projects, whereby local authorities lay out the plots, provide roads, water, and sewage, supervise construction, draw up roofing plans, and charge inexpensive rents. [38] In Lusaka as elsewhere their purpose was not only to reduce the dependence of housing on employment but also to combat the spreading of squatter compounds. In the well-financed mining towns of the Copperbelt, local authorities were relatively successful in combatting the spread of squatter compounds through publicly-financed site and service schemes. [39] As has been seen, however, they have been notably ineffective in this last effect as far as Lusaka was concerned. However, until 1969 there was a notable obstacle to their success— continued non-African ownership of freehold land around Lusaka on which most of the squatter compounds were built. Under the terms of the constitution by which Zambia gained its independence, existing landowning rights were respected and could only be challenged by a referendum. This situation was changed by the plebiscite of August 1969, which did away with referenda and decreed that all matters affecting change of constitution, including land ownership, would henceforth be decided by the National Assembly. [40] In effect, land could now be taken over in the national interest.

Fifteen years after independence, the ultimate success or failure of site and service schemes remains in doubt. Their fate had become critical. It was estimated that in Zambia the urban squatter population was doubling every three to four years; so by 1972 one-third of the total urban population lived in illegal settlements. At that time, the problems of burgeoning unauthorized settlement and the possible solution afforded by site and service schemes were explicitly linked. The government decided to couple a site and service scheme with the renovation of salvageable squatter settlement. Therefore, in 1973, as part of its national program, the Zambian government secured financial aid from the World Bank to combine site and service arrangements with the improvement of squatter settlements. Due to the gravity of its particular housing situation within Zambia, Lusaka was selected for the pilot project. Ultimately, 30,000 households—approximately 40 percent of Lusaka's total—were affected. As part of this project, four squatter settlements were to be systematically upgraded. Initiated at the end of 1974, the project is still ongoing. Ultimately, it is hoped that the project will serve as a model for the rest of urban Zambia.[41]

There were two new features in the project. First, efforts were made to involve the affected community in the overall planning. Innovative to Lusaka, at least, was the provision for community facilities. Second, enabling legislation was passed. This law, the Zambian Improvement Areas Act, permitted the individual affected to acquire security of tenure through a thirty-year lease regardless of whether it would be in an upgraded squatter location or in a newly developed site and service residential area.[42]

In general, the method of application of site and service plans has varied from place to place. As applied to the Copperbelt, some programs sold building materials and made credit available for both technical and material help. In addition, community facilities with self-contained health, educational, and market units were furnished. As applied in Lusaka, an individual, in return for services—piped water, waterborne sanitation, access to graded roads, and refuse collection from the City Council (a basic unit as opposed to the normal unit did not provide sewage facilities)—and lots which average one-third to one-half acre, undertakes to build a structure on the site. Furthermore, in a minimum basic scheme, an individual commits himself to paying back a 72-kwacha loan over four years as well as a monthly rent of 2 kwachas. The government loan is in the form of materials. There are certain conditions attached; if the individual accepts the loan, the house must be built according to the prescribed standard set by the council and its inspectors. Tenure is based on a lease related to the standard of the building.[43]

The main criticism made against site and service schemes as they exist in present-day Lusaka is their extreme identification with a particular area at the expense of overall community development. In general, site and service schemes in Lusaka have tended to reflect the weaknesses inherent in all previous housing schemes—distance from the center, difficulties in economically sewering and providing water, and the usual problems of getting financial support.[44]

The last few years have brought about a somewhat reluctant acceptance of the role that "squatter" locations can play in urban areas. This acceptance has been caused by the pressures invoked by phenomenal population growth and financial considerations arising from budgetary limitation. Overall, the attitude toward unauthorized locations on the part of government has undergone three stages since the belated recognition of the permanence of African town dwelling over a quarter of a century ago. From the late 1940s to the late 1950s, the emphasis on "social engineering" resulted in the wholesale razing of illegal compounds which were either on Crown land or whose owners would accept government compensation for their property. This policy was successful in an urban area with a stationary or slow-growing population, such as Livingstone, where accommodation could be found for displaced people; it was not so successful in an urban area with an exploding population, such as Lusaka, where accommodation could not be found. This human suffering was even greater for those who had spent most of their urban lives in one area and had actually expended a considerable amount of capital as well as human investment on their homes. During the next decade, the emphasis was on site and service schemes which faced the twin obstacles of time and money in the wake of the country's rate of urbanization. As a result, the Zambian government has come to the realization that for the foreseeable future these unofficial living areas are here to stay. In token of this recognition, the Second National Development Plan, which covered the years 1972-76, continued to put the major stress on site and service schemes but has also earmarked five million kwacha for squatter area improvement.[45]

The attention beginning to be paid to unauthorized compounds should highlight the positive functions they have exercised during the colonial past and continue to perform in the present. From the standpoint of convenience, particularly in an urban area where even civil servants spent months and perhaps years on waiting lists for not very desirable accommodation (comparative statistics showed that in most respects the town with the squatter problem, Lusaka, ranked at the bottom or near bottom—for room space, permanent building materials, house size, electrification, water reticulation, waterborne sanitation—compared to other urban areas in Zambia at the end of the colonial period),[46] the available unauthorized locations must have appeared attractive. Although, with respect to quality, the distinction may have blurred between authorized and unauthorized locations, Africans not in "employment," whether unemployed or self-employed, appreciated the relative cheapness of the latter since the cost of tied housing was beyond their economic means. Moreover, as their residence was not tied to their employment, they enjoyed a greater security of tenure. When, as in the case of Lusaka, they worked in a decentralized urban center, which rendered municipal transportation unfeasible, they might actually be closer to their place of employment in an illegal compound than in a legal one. Aside from practical advantages, residence in an unauthorized location would have social and psychological benefits. Individuals would be able to construct their own lodgings from materials of their own choice and build to their own specifications. They were free to practice their own customs and traditions without undue interference from perhaps overzealous officials. In addition, squatter compounds were vital to the socialization process of the newly arrived rural migrant. They were the halfway houses between town and country, where a person could gradually acclimate himself to urban conditions.

From the perspective of today, the lack of available housing and of houses within the wherewithal of most people in the official municipal suburbs of Lusaka has not been disastrous to initial urban adjustment. It has contributed to the rise of de facto if not de jure living settlements where an individual can be free from Western or Westernized control to practice his own mixture of traditional and modern life styles. They have answered the needs of Africans defined as marginal through criteria originally imposed by the ruling non-African minority—the newly arrived, the self-employed, the unskilled and uneducated, and the traditional-minded. However, the rise of squatter settlements have not answered the needs of those Africans who may possess the means and/or desire to become totally committed to and integrated into the urban way of life. The prosperous merchant who may want a five-room house with existing conveniences— piped water, tarred roads, modern sewerage, electrification—still has many obstacles to face in the municipally administered suburbs and housing areas, which continue to be employee-oriented. Similarly, the civil servant with a standard six education who is far down on a municipal waiting list might not relish the prospect of residence in a nonofficial location miles away from schools for his children. For them, full urban adaptation has yet to come.

NOTES

1. Alan J. F. Simmance, Urbanization in Zambia, An International Urbanization Survey Report to the Ford Foundation (New York: Ford Foundation Press, 1972), pp. 18, 34.

2. Republic of Zambia, Lusaka: Existing Conditions (Doxiades Report) (Lusaka: Government Printer, 1965), pp. 60-90; Republic of Zambia, Greater Lusaka: A Guide to Residents (Lusaka: Government Printer, 1971), pp. 4-5; and Republic of Zambia, City of Lusaka— Facts (Lusaka Information Center, 1971), p. 7.

3. Richard Sampson, So This Was Lusaka (Lusaka: Northern Rhodesia Publicity Association, 1959), pp. 17-18.

4. See Republic of Zambia, Annual Reports of the District Commissioner 1914-1920, H.C. series (Lusaka: Zambian National Archives, 1920).

5. L. H. Gann, A History of Northern Rhodesia (London: Chatto and Windus, 1964), pp. 140-42.

6. "A History of Lusaka," Central African Post, July 10, 1952.

7. D. Hywel Davies, "Lusaka, Zambia: Some Town Planning Problems at Independence," Zambian Urban Studies 1 (1969): 4-5.

8. Ibid., pp. 7-9.

9. Ibid.

10. Republic of Zambia, Eccles Report: Report on the Administration and Finances of Native Locations in Urban Areas (Lusaka: Government Printer, 1953), pp. 3, 17-18; African Housing Ordinance no. 32, cap. 234 (Lusaka: Government Printer, 1948).

11. Republic of Zambia, Department of Local Government, Annual Report (Lusaka: Government Printer, 1952), pp. 2-3. See also Nightingale Report, Report on the Position of African and Eurafrican Housing in Lusaka (Lusaka: Government Printer, 1953).

12. Lusaka Chamber of Commerce, Minutes of meeting, n.p. March 17, 1958, Lusaka.

13. District Commissioner of Lusaka District, Annual Report (Lusaka: Government Printer, 1959), pp. 4-6.

14. George Kay, A Social Geography of Zambia (London: University of London Press, 1967), pp. 109-32.

15. Lusaka Chamber of Commerce, Minutes of meeting, August 2, 1957, Lusaka, p. 2.

16. Republic of Zambia, "Illegal Compounds," memo, June 16, 1955, file SA/II.

17. David Bettison, "Poverty in Central Africa," Rhodes Livingstone Institute (1959): 54-55.

18. Ibid.

19. Town Treasurer, Lusaka Review of Financial Policy (Lusaka: Government Printer, February 1960), p. 34.

20. Ibid., p. 17.

21. Ibid., p. 5.

22. Government of Zambia, Review of the Housing Accounts (Lusaka: Government Printer, September 1964), pp. 21-23.

23. Town Treasurer, Review, op. cit., p. 17.

24. David Boswell, "Personal Crises and the Mobilization of the Social Network," in Social Networks in an Urban Situation: Analyses of Personal Relationship in Central African Towns, ed. J. Clyde Mitchell (Manchester: Manchester University Press, 1969).

25. Town Treasurer, Review, op. cit., p. 21.

26. See Republic of Zambia, Social Survey of Nguluwe Compound (Lusaka: Department of Community Development, January 1961), p. 6; and also Republic of Zambia, Social Survey of Kalingalinga (Lusaka: Department of Community Development).

27. Interview with Richard Sampson, Mayor of Lusaka, 1961-63, January 28, 1970; and District Commissioner, Annual Report (Lusaka: Government Printer, 1958), p. 9.

28. Demographic Surveys on Northern Rhodesia (May-August 1960) (Salisbury: Central Statistical Office, 1961), p. 21.

29. Interview with L. M. Smale, Town Treasurer of Lusaka, 1952-68, February 19, 1970.

30. Sampson Interview, op. cit.

31. Town Treasurer, Review, op. cit., pp. 21-23.

32. Interview with Safeli Chileshe, Mayor of Lusaka, 1964-65, February 4, 1970.

33. Zambia, Review of the Housing Accounts, op. cit., p. 27.

34. Chileshe Interview, op. cit.

35. Simmance, Urbanization in Zambia, op. cit., pp. 28-29.

36. Ibid.

37. Ibid.

38. Ibid., p. 32.

39. See, for example, Franziska Hosken, "Urban Development and Housing in Africa," available at the libraries of Harvard University and the Massachusetts Institute of Technology, Cambridge, Massachusetts.

40. Chileshe Interview, op. cit.

41. C. E. Madavo, "Uncontrolled Settlements," Finance and Development 13-14 (1976-77): 18-19.

42. Ibid.

43. W. H. Dobkins, "A New Residential Pattern for Lusaka" (Architectural diss., School of Architecture, University of Edinburgh, 1966), pp. 40-50.

44. Simmance, Urbanization in Zambia, op. cit., pp. 55-64.

45. Ibid., pp. 32-33.

46. Demographic Surveys on Northern Rhodesia, op. cit., pp. 8-30.

Part Five

SOUTHERN AFRICA: DEVELOPMENT ISSUES

In view of their current political context, development issues
in the southern African nations are by necessity intertwined with
issues of political and economic domination of white minorities and
exploitation of the African majorities. Urbanization patterns and
planning approaches and policies have been, and still are, aimed at

preventing Africans from developing or acquiring a political or eco-
    nomic base or organization sufficient to tip the balance of power
    among the races;
protecting life and property of white minorities in the event of out-
    breaks of organized or spontaneous struggle or violence; and
maintaining a fragmented, ill-organized, and cheap African labor
    force.

Thus the essence of urbanization and planning approaches in southern
Africa is maintaining the marginality of the African populations. This
essence translates into policies of restricting their access to major
resources or centers of power, isolating them from white populations,
and limiting their ability to urbanize permanently or on a large scale.

The chapters in this section analyze these policies and the
resulting constraints and patterns of development both currently and
in their historical perspective.

The origins of urbanization in Namibia date back to the beginning
of the colonial period, and its development witnessed several restrictions on migration and unequal treatment of the African population.
The level of urbanization among the Africans is close to the average
of sub-Saharan Africa, and the towns have become more and more
dominated by non-Africans. Duality in the economy as well as in the
internal structure of towns persists. Whites lived apart from Africans,
who were relegated to marginal, peripheral locations. Recently they
have been pushed by municipal action and force to locations even
farther out. W. Pendelton describes this process of forced relocation
and other restrictions on the urban Africans' social interaction as a
result of the implementation of a South African model of apartheid.
If the towns are to play their normal role in the integration and development of the country, he concludes, the existing political and economic system would have to be radically altered.

Such radical restructuring of the society requires not only
political action but also major efforts in education and social development as well as investments in expanding the economy and creating
job opportunities for Africans in all sectors. Planning for such change
is likely to encounter many obstacles, as James Cobbe illustrates in
the case of Lesotho. Problems of data may be a feature in most
developing countries. However, when such lack concerns migrant
labor, the heart of planning issues in a dependent economy like

Lesotho's, it significantly affects the efficacy of planning exercises. Land tenure practices, administrative weakness, lack of expertise, vulnerability, and uncertainty are all features not unrelated to the historical dependent development process of Lesotho, and they constitute obstacles to comprehensive long-range planning.

Perhaps the origin of obstacles to self-development of the black population in Southern Africa can be best understood in South Africa itself. Here, according to Rogerson and Pirie, urbanization and regional development policies seek to foster the disjunction of a racially integrated economic space and a racially segregated social and political space. This separation guarantees the maintenance of the marginality of the black population and the preservation of a cheap labor system.

The southern African nations are still in the throes of establishing the basic rights of the majority of their populations to self-development, equality, and participation in the political process. Even when these rights are attained, they will still face the massive structural imbalances which have been institutionalized over decades of apartheid and white-dominated urbanization and economic systems.

16

URBANIZATION AND DEVELOPMENT IN NAMIBIA (South West Africa)

Wade C. Pendleton

Namibia is the name adopted by the United Nations for the territory of South West Africa. The territory is called South West Africa by South Africa, which administers the country under a mandate from the League of Nations. The United Nations abolished the mandate in 1966, but South Africa continues to administer the country. The International Court of Justice at the Hague has heard two cases about the territory, but their decisions have not altered the disputed international status of the territory. The United Nations continues its efforts to force South Africa to turn over the administration of the territory to them, and in 1975 South Africa supported the establishment of a Constitutional Conference with representatives from most racial and ethnic groups in the country with the notable exception of the South West African People's Organization (SWAPO). The conference, subsequently called the Democratic Turnhalle Alliance, has the task of drafting a constitution for the country and recommending a form of government for an independent Namibia. The outcome of the alliance, its acceptance or rejection by the people of Namibia, the United Nations, and liberation groups, the results of an independence election, and the influence of other outside forces, such as the United States, the Soviet Union, Cuba, Angola, and South Africa, could all be crucial factors in Namibia's future.

URBANIZATION

The history of urbanization in Namibia began with the colonial era. No precolonial urban areas existed in the country. The various Africans included hunters and gatherers (San and Damara), pastoralists

FIGURE 16.1

Geography of Namibia (South West Africa)

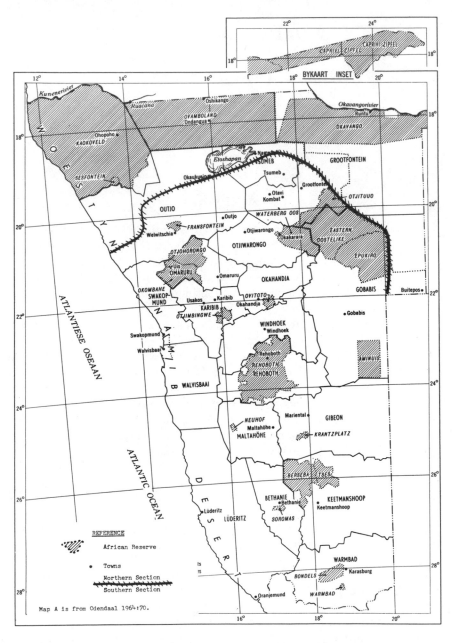

Source: Compiled by the author.

(Herero and Nama), and those pursuing an economy based on horti-
culture and pastoralism (Ovambo and Okavango groups). All these
people lived in small dispersed homesteads or camps which were
moved periodically.

The German colonial era (1889–1915) saw the beginning of
urbanization in the territory. By 1921, when South Africa was given
the country to administer as a class "C" mandate by the League of
Nations, a number of small towns had been established. These towns
were administrative and business centers. The most important of
these towns were Windhoek (the capital), Tsumeb, Grootfontein,
Otavi, Outjo, Okahandja, Omaruru, Karibib, Swakopmund, Walvis
Bay, Gobabis, Rehoboth, Bethanie, Berseba, Gibeon, Keetmanshoop,
Warmbad, and Lüderitz (see Figure 16.1).

The urban migration of Africans is closely tied to the history
of the German colonial era. Between 1889 and 1904, the African people
were subjected to increasingly difficult circumstances. The Germans
were not honoring their agreements and treaties with the various African people, Africans were receiving unequal and severe treatment in
German courts and under German law, and African land was continu-
ally being taken by treaty and purchase. Whites were establishing
farms on what was previously African land. Non–African traders were
also exploiting the African people. It was becoming increasingly difficult, especially for the Herero and the Nama, to continue their previous way of life.

The Herero revolted in 1904, and the Nama nine months later.
Both were decisively beaten by the German occupation army. According to H. Bley, 75 percent of the Herero population and 35–50 percent
of the Nama population may have died in these wars or later in
prisoner-of-war camps.[1] After these wars with the Africans, Germany
confiscated all Nama and Herero land and cattle. Racial discrimination
laws were passed, the Masters and Servants Act was passed, and
Africans were required to carry identity cards. Travel permits were
needed, and service contracts had to be carried. The cumulative effect
of all these factors was to force Africans to work for whites in order
to survive. Many Africans went to work on newly established white-
owned farms, and others migrated to the towns to seek work.

The people primarily affected by these events were the Damara,
Herero, and Nama. The Ovambo and other peoples in the northern
section of the country were not directly involved in these events. Beginning in 1911, the recruitment of Ovambo men as migrant laborers
began, and in that year 9,295 went to work in the mines and on railroad construction.[2] In later years, considerably larger numbers of
Ovambo men went to work as migrant workers in the towns, on farms,
and in the mines. W. G. Clarence-Smith and R. Moorson have shown
that the Ovambo became dependent on migrant labor through a series

of events beginning in the mid-nineteenth century.[3] Between 1845 and 1885, the Ovambo traded ivory with European traders until the elephant population was virtually extinct. They then traded cattle, which were often stolen from neighbors in southern Angola. Beginning in the early twentieth century, raiding became more difficult, and Ovambo kings and nobles demanded large numbers of cattle for taxation. Many Ovambo who had no cattle were forced to work as migrant laborers in the southern section to earn money. The Ovambo joined the Nama, Herero, and Damara, who were employed as unskilled laborers in the southern section of the territory.

The number of people living in urban areas between 1936 and 1970 increased 15.7 times. Windhoek had always dominated the urban areas, accounting for an average of 32 percent of the urban population. The percentage of whites in urban areas rose from 38 percent in 1936 to 75 percent in 1970, representing, in addition to natural increase, a movement to the towns and the fact that new white settlers have taken up residence in the towns. The percentage of "colored" people (people of mixed African and white ancestry) has increased to 63 percent in 1970, representing in part a townward migration of colored people who found jobs in the urban areas. The percentage of Africans in urban areas continued to increase from 6 percent in 1936 to 15 percent in 1970, in spite of government efforts to reduce African migration to towns. Government policy, implemented by urban area municipalities, attempted to reduce if not eliminate the number of Africans allowed to migrate and take up permanent residence in towns.

The percentage of Africans residing in urban areas (15 percent) is typical of the rest of Africa, where the continental average was about 17 percent for the period 1960-68.[4] Africans are being increasingly drawn to the towns, especially Windhoek, because of better paying jobs than on farms and greater employment opportunities. Structural factors and especially economic characteristics of the society are the primary influences in rural to urban migration, but some individual motivations may also be involved. For some it is a rite of passage proving their earning abilities,[5] and "city life" with its attractions and better facilities certainly brings some, i.e., the bright light theory.[6] Many Africans send their children to towns to stay with relatives in order to take advantage of the educational opportunities there, which are considered to be better than in rural areas. Education is seen as offering the possibility of a better job and life than the uneducated parents achieved. All of these factors play a role, but the greatest factor in migration must be the push of rural poverty with its limited wage-employment and the pull of the town or city where there are jobs.[7]

The movement of Africans to towns and the permanent establishment of many Africans in towns has created a sizable urban African population in the southern section of Namibia. Many Africans have been born in town, and many consider their permanent home to be in urban areas. The vast majority of urban Africans are poor, own little property, and have an insecure right to remain in town.

Africans and whites have lived apart since the establishment of the first towns in the territory. Africans lived in locations on the edge of the "white" town, building their own houses out of whatever materials were available. Beginning in the 1950s, new African locations were planned and built. They were farther out of town, and the houses were constructed by the municipality and rented on a monthly basis to tenants. There was much opposition to the forced relocation of Africans to these new locations. The new housing was in most cases superior to what the Africans had built for themselves, but the cost of living in the new houses was high. In the old Windhoek African location a housing site rented for R0.10 (U.S.$0.07) a month in 1968. In the new location, a four-room house rented for R4.10 (U.S.$5.74) a month—a substantial increase. In addition, the old houses were the Africans' most valuable property; they could be inherited, sold, and rooms rented for extra income. In Windhoek the new African township is so far out of town that many Africans have to ride buses, an extra expense. The name adopted for the Windhoek African township reflected the opposition and resentment of the forced move. The name the authorities chose was Katutura which in Herero means "place where we do not stay."[8]

The African population does stay in Katutura today, but the relocation did not take place without violence. On December 8, 1959, an effective boycott of the municipally operated facilities in the location was held, including the buses, beer hall, and cinema. On the night of December 10th, a protest meeting was held in the old location which developed into a confrontation with the police. The police shot and killed 11 Africans, and about 44 Africans required medical attention.[9] Immediately after the confrontation, 3,000 to 4,000 Africans fled the location and refused to return because they were afraid of further trouble. Many asked to be allowed to move to Katutura, and the authorities agreed to this, although Katutura was not yet completed. About 3,000 people subsequently took up residence in Katutura. In 1968, the old African location was closed, and the remaining people either moved to Katutura or left the area. Colored people, who previously lived in the old location, were moved to a new location exclusively for themselves. Animosity and increased social distance now exist between African and colored people in Windhoek, and their physical separation into two townships is in part to be blamed.

The urban African population of Namibia has little unemployment. Nearly all adult, and many juvenile Africans are employed by whites. Most employment is in unskilled work. They are messengers, make deliveries, do cleaning and janitorial work, and usually make the tea and coffee for their white employers. The average annual salary paid to African men in Windhoek in 1968 was R423, and about 78 percent made R50 or less per month.

African women have even fewer job opportunities. Most do part-time domestic servant work for which they earn about R9 per month from each employer; some women work for several employers in order to earn more money. Many women brew and sell beer and sometimes food to supplement their low incomes. Shebeens, as places where beer is sold are usually called, are popular places where men gather to visit and drink with friends. In 1967, a cost-of-living survey was conducted by a member of the Windhoek Non-European Affairs Department, and he calculated that an African family of five needed R52 per month to subsist.[10] The combined wages of an African man and woman are short of that figure for a majority of the population. It is fair to assume that a similar situation exists in other towns of the territory.

The stratification of the urban African population is not compli- cated. The vast majority are poor people who spend everything they make to get by from month to month. A small number of African ministers, teachers, clerks, and businessmen have a better than average income and life style. Those Africans who operate small general dealers shops in the African locations have the largest in- comes and are the wealthiest members of the African community.

The social organization of urban Africans in Namibia has no resemblance to traditional patterns. No lineage or clan organization exists, traditional homestead groupings are not found, and traditional marriage customs are not followed. The meaning of ethnic identity has been radically altered and is strongly influenced by numerous nontraditional factors that are part of the urban way of life.

Ethnic groups are no longer autonomous units pursuing unique patterns of culture. They have been transformed into ethnic groups with only modest differences. Ethnic groups are categories of people who share some normative patterns of behavior and are part of a larger population, consisting of other ethnic groups, which make up a social system.[11] The most obvious ethnic differences are in language, dress, and physical appearance. Beyond that, their life styles are basically the same. Ethnic group is a category of identification for sorting strangers and applying stereotypes to facilitate interaction. In this, Namibian urban ethnicity shares much in common with the rest of urban Africa. However, ethnicity has taken on much more significance in Namibia because political and administrative factors, which define much of the larger social system, have increased its importance. These administrative and political factors were imple- mentations of South African government policy, the purpose of which was to maintain the separation of racial and ethnic groups. In addition, by categorizing people as "tribesmen" it maintained the illusion that Africans were "primitive" and therefore could be exploited.

Africans live in townships physically separate from residential areas where white and colored people live. Within the townships people live in officially designated ethnic group sections. Official documents and passes require ethnic group identification, and township advisory boards are based on ethnic group representation. Separate schools are maintained for all African ethnic groups, and church congregations also cater to ethnic differences. The cumulative effect of the administrative, political, cultural, and racial boundaries around ethnic groups is to make people identify themselves to the world through their ethnic group and strengthen ethnic group membership. But an ethnic group is not a real group; it is only a social category. Most of the African ethnic groups have little real solidarity because they are unorganized and fragmented. The only group with an ethnic association are the Herero. In the African townships, very few of the associations or clubs exist that are so common in other parts of urban Africa. The only clubs found in most urban areas in Namibia are sports associations. Possibly the fear of being accused of political activism is what limits the numbers of voluntary associations.

One of the areas where urban African ethnicity manifests itself most strongly is in marriage. Urban African populations are ethnically heterogeneous, but most people choose marriage partners from their own ethnic groups. The ethnic endogamy rate for Katutura Africans in 1968 was 85 percent.[12] The most important type of conjugal union for urban Africans in Namibia is a church marriage. Its importance reflects both the influence of Christianity and the loss in importance of traditional unions. A church marriage is the only type of union that is a public ceremony, establishes new kinship obligations and responsibilities, and requires payment of bride price.

Mia Brandel and J. C. Mitchell have both discussed the function of urban bride price.[13] They suggest that in the urban situation, where lineage groups are absent, bride price is an acknowledgment of the bride's status. The higher her status the more bride price that must be paid. Urban Africans in all ethnic groups gave some evidence to corroborate this suggestion. They said bride price is a compensation paid to parents for having raised and trained their daughter. The more training and education she has the greater is their loss when she marries, and the more bride price must be paid.

Among urban Africans, the most frequent type of conjugal union is living together. It is also frequent among Africans living on farms and in reserves. Among Katutura Africans it accounted for 44 percent of all unions. Most Africans attach no stigma to living together. People cannot afford to get married; the minimum cost for a church marriage including bride price is about R120, and few Africans can afford that. To live together requires no permission from kinsmen, no bride price, no public ceremony, and the mother maintains rights over any children born. The large percentage of living together unions among Africans reflects the poverty of their socioeconomic condition. But the percentage of households that are not based on any conjugal union shows how serious the poverty and socioeconomic problems of the African people really are.

Among Katutura Africans, 55 percent of the households consisted of a single adult, usually a woman, and dependent children. Evidence indicates that similar high percentages of single-parent families exist in all towns in the territory. Women, who on the average in Katutura have more than two children in their household, support and make the smallest salaries of all urban Africans and have the heaviest burden. N. Gonzales suggests that such situations are the result of migrant labor and the presence of more women than men in the community.[14] Most important, they reflect the economic condition of the people. Where men are unable to make enough money to support a wife and family they will not establish permanent relationships with women and support the children they have fathered. The insecurity and uncertainty of living in an urban area in Namibia, where land cannot be owned by Africans and very few can afford to buy or build their home, only adds to the already serious conditions under which the people live.

DEVELOPMENT PLANNING

The vast majority of all recent development in Namibia was the result of implementations of the Report of the Commission of Enquiry into South West African Affairs 1962-1963, generally known as the Odendaal Commission Report. The development program that the Odendall Commission recommended and that was being implemented until about 1975 was based on the South African model of apartheid, or separate development. It perpetuated a dual economy—one African and one white—which put Africans in a very disadvantaged position. Most of the economic development in Namibia only helped the African population indirectly and did not alter the basic pattern of a racially stratified white-dominated society. Economic expansion of the important fishing, mining, and farming industries of the territory have only involved Africans as unskilled workers. The white population has by far received the greatest benefits.

The South African government has focused its African development programs on the rural areas, with the largest portion being concentrated in Ovamboland in the northern part of the country. The territory has experienced little industrialization, and the economy is based on cheap African labor which is used in the mines, farm work, fishing industry, and unskilled urban employment. This pattern must be altered and full occupational and career opportunities made available to African and colored people.

The role of urban areas in development could be considerable. People migrate to towns and cities for employment, the possibility of alternative life-styles, a better way of life, a higher standard of living, educational opportunities, attractions, and more and better facilities. But in Namibia few Africans are able to enjoy the opportunities that urban life makes possible for people in many other countries.

A development program should be implemented to alter the existing racial, economic, political, and social system in the country, but the problems of implementing such a program are considerable. Politically, it requires an end to job discrimination and lower pay scales for African and colored people. Many African and colored people will require vocational, occupational, primary, and/or secondary education. Additional educational and training facilities including a university must be built. Such training and education would qualify African and colored people for better qualified jobs. However, these jobs are now almost exclusively held by white people. The jobs must either be redistributed or more jobs created. It can also be expected that in an independent Namibia cheap African labor for farm work would be scarce. Many farm workers would come to the towns in search of better jobs and more opportunities. Without industrialization this would create high unemployment rates with accompanying social and economic problems.

Capital will be needed for industrialization and economic development, not only to help train Africans but to expand the economy so that Africans will have opportunities in every sector of the society. The urban areas will be the focus of this development. They must also be restructured. Separate residential areas for African, colored, and white people should be eliminated, and people must be free to live and own property wherever they want to. The towns and urban areas of Namibia can play a crucial role in the economic development of the country. They can also be the focus of other kinds of change. The towns of Namibia are the places where people of different racial and ethnic groups meet and interact. In the past this interaction was based on white domination of the society. In an independent Namibia let us hope the towns will function to integrate the country and break down the negative stereotypes that the colonial era created.

NOTES

1. H. Bley, South-West Africa Under German Rule 1894-1914 (London: Heinemann, 1971), pp. 150-51.

2. M. J. Olivier, Native Policy and Administration in the Mandated Territory of South West Africa (Ph.D. thesis, Stellenbosch University, 1964), chap. 6.

3. W. G. Clarence-Smith and R. Moorsom, "Underdevelopment and Class Formation in Ovamboland, 1845-1915," Journal of African History 16 (1975): 365-81.

4. William A. Hance, Population, Migration and Urbanization in Africa (New York: Columbia University Press, 1970), p. 228.

5. I. Schapera, Migrant Labor and Tribal Life (London: Oxford University Press, 1947), p. 114.

6. P. Gulliver, "Nyakyusa Labor Migration," Rhodes-Livingstone, Journal 21 (1956), pp. 40-51.

7. F. Wilson, Migrant Labour in South Africa (Johannesburg: Christian Institute and SPROCAS, 1972).

8. Wade C. Pendleton, Katutura: A Place Where We Do Not Stay (San Diego: San Diego State University Press, 1974).

9. I. Goldblatt, History of South West Africa (Cape Town: Juta, 1971), p. 262; and C. G. Hall, Report of the Commission of Enquiry into the Night of the 10th to the 11th December, 1959, and the Direct Causes Which Led to Those Occurrences, Report submitted to the Governor-General of the Union of South Africa (Pretoria: Government Printer, 1960), p. 3.

10. A. Venter, "Plasslike Nie-Blanke Werknemers," a memrandum prepared for the Windhoek City Council Steering Committee (Windhoek: City Council, September 18, 1967).

11. A. Cohen, Urban Ethnicity (London: Tavistock, 1974), pp. ix-x.

12. This and other statistics about Katutura and Windhoek are based on research conducted 1967-69, 1970, 1971-72, which included surveys and in-depth interviews. For details, see Pendleton, op. cit.

13. Mia Brandel, "Urban Lobolo Attitudes: A Preliminary Report," African Studies 17 (1958): 34-51; J. C. Mitchell, "The Anthropological Study of Urban Communities," African Studies 19 (1960): 169-72; and idem, "Theoretical Orientations in African Urban Studies," in The Social Anthropology of Complex Societies, ed. M. Banton (London: Tavistock, 1966), pp. 37-68.

14. N. Gonzales, Black Carib Household Structure (Seattle: University of Washington Press, 1969), p. 140.

17

PLANNING IN LESOTHO

James H. Cobbe

PLAN PURPOSES AND CONSTRAINTS ON PLANNING

Planning is a purposive attempt to attain a better outcome than would be possible without planning.[1] Development planning in Africa is intended to assist governments to achieve their development objectives, that is, to alter the pace and the structure, including the spatial structure, of development. Two conclusions follow immediately from this observation. First, development planning is popular in Africa and can be expected to continue to be found there because of the widespread dissatisfaction with the pace and structure of development experienced before independence and that expected to result from the unrestricted play of market forces. Second, planning is not just the production of plan documents; planning is a process, in fact, the whole process by which the government makes decisions affecting the pace and structure of development.[2] Much of this process does not even take place in planning offices.

However, in much of Africa, planning is thought of as something that happens in planning offices, and the most obvious activity in planning offices tends to be the periodic production of plan documents. Since these documents are frequently out of date by the time they are printed and appear to bear little relation to what actually happens in terms of development during the period they are supposed to cover, there has been much disillusion with "planning" as such.[3] Under the broad definition given above, planning in some form always takes place if there is a government that takes any interest in how the country it governs develops. The disillusionment, therefore, arises from the particular kind of planning that African countries

303

have attempted and the constraints on the process imposed by African conditions.

Generally, the view seems to have been that planning should be "comprehensive development planning." In other words, there should be a strategy of development, including specific objectives to be achieved; a centrally coordinated, internally consistent set of principles and policies, the optimal mix for the given strategy and objectives; coverage of the whole economy; use of models to insure optimality and consistency; and a set of projects, capital expenditures, physical plans, tax and expenditure policies, and so on, which will help achieve these aims.[4]

This view runs into two difficulties. The first is a fundamental criticism, namely that this technocratic view of planning starts from an implicit set of assumptions about government, government decision making, and administration, which is both naive and unrealistic.[5] If the model is adhered to at all rigidly, it results in pseudo-planning, the production of irrelevant plan documents, and the relegation of planners to positions of little influence within government. Fortunately, there are other reasons why comprehensive development planning cannot be attempted seriously in many African countries, which can lead to planners serving useful purposes.

This second set of reasons why comprehensive planning is bound to fail consists of practical aspects of the process. Comprehensive planning requires detailed and accurate information about the economy, an efficient and effective system of administration allowing government access to policy tools to influence all sectors of the economy, and the expertise, both technical and in terms of local conditions, to carry out the process. To a greater or lesser extent, all three tend to be lacking in Africa.[6] Hence, comprehensive planning and even, as in Lesotho, basic planning for urbanization and physical development in spatial terms may be simply impossible.

In what follows, these general observations will be illustrated by the example of Lesotho. The discussion will first set the scene with some information on Lesotho's economic and institutional background. Then, some particular development problems in Lesotho and specific constraints on planning will be discussed. In particular, the almost total lack of physical planning or planning for urbanization in Lesotho will be examined. Finally, some of the strengths and weaknesses of the planning process that does go on in Lesotho will be discussed.

THE ECONOMY AND ITS PROBLEMS[7]

Lesotho is perhaps the most anomalous of all the small African states to become independent since the 1950s as a result of the withdrawal of the imperial powers. However, Lesotho's peculiarities, some of which will soon become evident, are for the most part differences of degree compared to other former British territories. It is important to emphasize that the present economic and social structure of Lesotho is essentially the result of the same processes that were experienced elsewhere in Africa during the colonial period.

The differences are, nevertheless, striking. Lesotho is, territorially, a small enclave totally surrounded by the Republic of South Africa. Of a total area of some 11,716 square miles, about one-fourth is "lowland," i.e., between 5,000 and 6,000 feet above sea level, the rest being foothills and mountains rising to 11,000 feet. For a de facto population of about 1.2 million, there are only about 1 million acres of arable land—less than one acre per head. Moreover, most of this land has been cropped continuously for 100 years. Since animal dung is burnt as fuel because of the absence of trees, and stover is fed to livestock, little organic material is ever returned to the soil and soil erosion is widespread. Thus, it is not surprising that crop yields are low and probably have declined between 1950 and 1970.

The present structure of the Lesotho economy has its origins in the third quarter of the nineteenth century.[8] The Basotho (the people of Lesotho) had always kept livestock and grown grain to feed themselves. In the 1860s and 1870s, they developed a prosperous economy based on the export of agricultural products, mostly grain but also livestock products, to other parts of southern Africa. The plow was widely adopted, and the main administrative and trading centers of the country were established at this time. Very soon, though, a combination of political, economic, and natural events and changes undermined the Basothos' comparative advantage in southern African agricultural markets and set in motion a process of pauperization that was already evident early in this century and may not yet have been reversed.

Increasing population pressure on limited land, erosion and exhaustion of soils, discrimination in South Africa against Lesotho's exports, unequal and inadequate access to the southern African transport network, together with the inherent difficulties of dryland crop farming in uncertain weather conditions and of livestock farming under communal grazing patterns led to a situation in which increasingly the only method by which a man could hope to support himself and his family was by seeking wage employment in South Africa. This situation was compounded by a British administration which, until astonishly recently, assumed that eventually the territory would be incorporated into South Africa and thus its internal development could be neglected. Until the mid-1960s, there was only one mile of tarred road in the whole country; as early as 1935, it was clear that more than 50 percent of the adult males were normally absent from the country, [9] but until independence no real effort was made to change the situation.

Little firm statistical data exist for Lesotho, but the broad outlines of its economic and social problems have been clear for a long time. However, the perception of the problems has changed markedly—and continues to change. Nevertheless, in terms of operational suggestions and concerns, there has been a large measure of continuity in official statements concerning development policy over the last 40 years since the Pim Report. Although independence has seen a predictable shift of emphasis towards provision of domestic employment opportunities, away from dependence on South Africa, and towards nonagricultural activities, it will be argued below that some of the most important implications of recent changes in southern Africa for Lesotho's development have not yet been fully incorporated into official thinking.

DEVELOPMENT PLANNING AND STRATEGY

Development planning in Lesotho presents many of the inevitable problems of this exercise in any poor country, with little "redundancy" and facing extreme uncertainty, in exaggerated form. [10] Before independence, several fairly typical colonial development plans were produced, the earliest being in response to the 1946 offer of funds under the Colonial Development and Welfare Act. [11] These consisted of fairly short analyses of the economy, followed by a listing of government capital spending, with some justification for each project. Since independence, a Central Planning and Development Office has been established, and two plan documents produced. [12] Although both these documents are much fuller and more detailed than their colonial predecessors, it is still fair to say that they are basically government investment programs and not comprehensive development plans as normally understood. As suggested above, this is not in itself necessarily a bad thing. But in order to understand more fully why it should be and the tasks which the planning process can seek to achieve in Lesotho it is necessary to examine in detail three aspects of the local situation: the information and data situation, the economic, social and political structure, and the administrative framework.

It is a standard truism that statistics in African countries tend to be either unavailable, unreliable, or unuseful when collected according to an inappropriate conceptual framework. In Lesotho, the usual problems of inadequate and inappropriately trained manpower, inadequate resources, and neglect prior to independence are compounded by difficulties inherent in the nature and position of the country. In a mountainous country with few roads it is difficult and expensive to collect statistics nationally. In a country totally surrounded by another with which it is closely integrated economically, to the extent of using the same currency and belonging to one customs union, and where the border is mostly unguarded, it is almost impossible to compile accurate information on many variables of considerable interest from the point of view of national economic planning. As a result, there are many important aspects of Lesotho's economy for which little or no data has as yet been collected, since the limited resources of the Bureau of Statistics have been concentrated on collecting and improving the data with respect to a few areas officially judged to be of high priority—imports, cost-of-living data, employment and manpower, the population census, and so on. As a result, virtually all statistical data must be regarded as approximate, and for many important areas information is still almost totally lacking.

The extent of this information vacuum can be illustrated by considering the data available to the Central Planning Office for preparing the second plan document in 1975. The most recent national income accounts available were those for 1971-72. But these were considered to be of dubious reliability, the probable accuracy of most components being perhaps to within 20 percent and some even less accurate. A manpower survey was underway which had produced fairly accurate data for employment for regular cash wages within the country by sectors. However, there were as yet no data on the distribution of employees by skill classification, education and training, or earnings—although these data were also in the process of being collected. Trade data existed, but both imports and exports were universally believed to be underenumerated by a factor which had been declining in recent years. Population data were only available for 1966. Although it was believed that the population of some towns, notably Maseru and Teyateyaneng, had grown very rapidly (perhaps by 50 percent or more since 1966), no reliable recent data were available.[13] As to the most striking feature of Lesotho's economy, namely, labor migration to the Republic of South Africa, the situation was not one of lack of information, but an embarrassing set of conflicting estimates which were often not of the most helpful kind anyway.

LABOR MIGRATION

Since the reduction of dependence on employment in South Africa is the most stressed of Lesotho's development objectives, it is worthwhile to examine the information problem here in some detail. Historically, since the earliest European contact, some

Basotho have always migrated elsewhere for cash employment. Most
of this migration has been on a temporary basis; some, until comparatively quite recently, has been on a more permanent basis. From
the population censuses for various years it appears that the de facto
population increased at 2.3 percent per annum from 1904 to 1921,
0.8 percent from 1921 to 1936, and 0.7 percent from 1936 to 1956,
and the de jure population at 1.9 percent from 1956 to 1966 and 2.3
percent from 1966 to 1976. On the basis of demographic data collected in surveys in the late 1960s, the rate of population increase
was estimated at 2.2 percent per annum—unusually low for southern
Africa. (The South African rate is 2.6 percent.) Even allowing for
variations in coverage at the censuses and fluctuations in the absentee
population, it is clear that a substantial number of Basotho—perhaps
140,000 between 1936 and 1956[14]—have been permanently absorbed
into South Africa. Although controls over the movements of persons
in southern Africa have been tightened considerably since 1956, there
is reason to believe that there are still significant movements across
Lesotho's borders, in both directions, by persons who are not "temporary oscillatory migrants" in the normal statistical sense.

This may help to explain the confusion over the deployment of
Lesotho's labor force. Persons who regard themselves as Lesotho
citizens working in South Africa (some of whom may conceal this
view of their national status because of South African laws) can be
divided into five categories:

1. Workers on short-term contracts with gold mines;
2. Workers on short-term contracts with other mines;
3. Temporary migrants legally (under South African law) employed
   in agriculture and domestic service in South Africa;
4. Skilled or semiskilled workers, or workers with legal rights from
   long residence in South Africa, in contract or indefinite-duration
   legal employment in construction, manufacturing, and other
   sectors in South Africa; and
5. Persons working either temporarily or for indefinite periods in
   all sectors of the South African economy, in some respect
   illegally or irregularly under South African regulations, mostly
   unskilled but in some cases (e.g., construction) skilled.

Of these five groups, statistics on the first and second are good
because of organized recruitment procedures. On the third they are
not too bad; on the fourth dubious; and on the fifth basically not col-
lectable under present conditions. Persons in categories four and
five may, for example, be currently denying Lesotho citizenship in
order to remain in the republic, and, in the case of category five,
their existence may be totally unrecorded (e.g., illegally resident

domestic servants not even declared on census returns). It is also
clear that persons in categories four and five may have ties to Lesotho
as close as those of a contract mine worker (maintaining a family in
Lesotho, sending money home, and returning frequently) or as tenuous
as those of some illegal migrants in the United States with their countries of origin (a connection of birth with no economic significance).
Such vagueness of status perhaps explains why in 1970, for example,
a South African source put the number of migrants from Lesotho employed in South Africa at 209,000,[15] while a Lesotho source estimated
it at 150,000.[16] Estimates for 1975 varied from 138,000 to well over
200,000. In this case, however, the differences were caused by variations of definition; the low estimate included only categories one,
two, and three, and the contract portion of four, while the high estimate included them all. The government finally decided to use an
estimate of 140,000 "oscillating" migrants (i.e., workers with families and domiciles in Lesotho on fixed-term contracts) for planning
purposes. The existence of about 60,000 other workers with considerable family ties in Lesotho but not necessarily either having their
domicile there or working on fixed-term contracts, was also recognized. The 200,000 total is estimated to include 25,000 females.[17]

So much attention has been paid to the problem of measuring
migrant labor because it is at the heart of the planning problem in
Lesotho, first because it is generally accepted that the first priority
in Lesotho's planning should be to reduce migration. Second, without
knowledge of the numbers and qualifications of migrants, the government would not really know who it is planning for or what labor resources are available. Third, migrants' earnings and remittances
loom large in the economy of Lesotho; the earnings of mine workers
alone (some 100,000 workers earning, on the average, a cash wage
of about U.S. $125 per month in 1977) probably exceed Lesotho's GNP.
In fact, the rapid increase in black miners' cash wages in South
Africa over the past few years (the minimum rate increased fivefold
in money terms in four years)[18] may well have qualitatively changed
the development problem in Lesotho from a situation in which almost
all investment had to be financed externally to one in which the basic
problem is to channel and harness the earnings of migrants, above
basic consumption needs, to development purposes.

THE DOMESTIC ECONOMY

Turning to the economic, social, and political structure of the
country, one important point has already been made, namely, the
overwhelming dependence on South African demand for Basotho labor
as a source of income. Domestically, agriculture is the dominant

activity, probably still accounting for more than half of the GNP.
Although in practice the proportion of the landless population has
grown rapidly in recent decades (from about 7 percent of all households in 1950 to an estimated 15 percent in 1976), in theory all households are entitled to land under Lesotho law. Land is held in trust
for the nation by the king and allocated by the chiefs subject to the
regulation of government and appeal to the courts. Families only
receive rights to use it. It should be open to communal grazing after
cropping, and it can be reallocated if misused. Rights in land are
distributed in a relatively egalitarian manner, even allowing for the
landless, in comparison with many developing countries, on the basis
of rights to land. However, in practice, rights to use land are inherited, and attempts to reallocate land can easily result, as one Basotho
court put it, in "a matter of bloodshed."[19] The widespread practice
of sharecropping, by which a household allows another with better
access to draft power for plowing and working capital for seed and
fertilizer to cultivate its land in return for half the crop (or, in hard
bargains, half the net return), may have an unequalizing effect.
Once again, data are lacking; although some attempts have been made
to collect information on land use as opposed to rights, it is difficult
to get a true picture of the distribution of arable cultivation. Sharecropping arrangements may be quite complex and often involve an
employed individual who may himself be an urban resident, with
interests in fields scattered widely over many districts through as
many partners. Over 13 percent of households with land sharecropped
some of it in 1970, but the incidence tended to increase with the size
of the holding.

The largely unmodernized land law, together with some other
factors, goes a long way towards explaining the lack of physical planning in Lesotho. Land is a highly emotional and political issue.
Furthermore, the right to allocate land, both for agricultural purposes and for the construction of dwellings, rests in the first instance
with the chiefs and headmen. It is the main source of their power and,
on the outskirts of urban areas, also a source of income for some of
them through corrupt practices. An Administration of Lands Act was
passed in 1973, providing for the extension of urban areas and the
institution of transferable leasehold rights in land within them. Initially, this will probably apply only to parts of the capital, Maseru.
However, the implementation date for this legislation had still not
been decided in 1976. The chiefs have tended to support the government in Lesotho, and they have not tended to favor modernization of
land legislation.

The typical rural household does have two or three acres of
land, in two or three separate pieces, and some animals. Most land
(about two-thirds of the total cultivated) is used for subsistence crops;

maize and sorghum produced for home consumption. Relatively small quantities of peas, beans, wheat, and other crops are grown for sale. It has been estimated that fully 95 percent of farm households in 1970 earned less than U.S. $200 per year per adult from their agricultural activities (including livestock). In one district in the central lowlands it was found that, in 1974, the average farm household only derived 20 percent of its household income from agricultural activities. Thus, although wool and mohair are the country's principal exports and over 95 percent of the population lives in rural areas and holds or hopes to hold land, at present agriculture is for most people a secondary activity and source of income. Both land holdings and livestock are more important for security against disaster than the current income they provide.

In 1975, however, the rural areas contained about 340,000 economically active adults whose most obvious activity was agriculture. It was estimated that of the remaining 50,000 persons economically active within the country, 27,500 were in regular employment for cash wages and 22,500 had handicraft production and various "informal sector" activities as their main occupation (petty trade, beer brewing, repair and service activities, etc.). About half of the 27,500 employed were in the six main towns, one-third of them working directly for the government. Most of the remainder were engaged in service industries, notably education, and also in the new tourist industry, with only a couple of thousand each in construction and manufacturing.[20] Apart from government and the distributive trades, the modern sector is confined to tourism, construction, and a still tiny but fairly rapidly growing manufacturing sector. Tourism consists basically of two large hotels in Maseru catering to the desires of South Africans to indulge in minor "vices" (such as gambling) forbidden at home; and manufacturing consists of a dozen or so fairly small enterprises.

Lesotho's balance of trade is enormously lopsided—nearly U.S. $100 million of imports against little more than U.S. $10 million exports in 1974/75. But the trade deficit is probably more than covered by the remittances of migrant workers, tourist spending, and aid inflows. The estimate of government recurrent revenue for 1974–75 was a little over $40 million. Of this, almost $30 million was expected to consist of Lesotho's share of the common revenue pool for customs, excise, and sales duties with South Africa, Botswana, and Swaziland, and the compensatory payment to Lesotho for use of the rand currency.[21] Direct taxation contributed less than $6 million.

POLITICAL AND ADMINISTRATIVE STRUCTURE

Officially, Lesotho is a constitutional monarchy. However, the only elections since independence in 1966 were cancelled when it became clear that the ruling party, Prime Minister Chief Leabua Jonathan's Basutoland National Party (BNP), had lost to the opposition Basutoland Congress Party (BCP). This was in 1970, and it led to considerable bloodshed and a temporary suspension of British aid.[22] There were more disturbances in early 1974, albeit more localized, which drove most of the leaders of the opposition BCP out of the country. At present there is an appointed "Interim National Assembly," and the cabinet contains some non-BNP members, but it is generally agreed that the government is autocratic, and the country remains divided politically. The government has the support of most chiefs and of a significant proportion of the people, not necessarily a majority, and effective control of the country through the police, police reservists, paramilitary, and so on. But it is widely believed that a large proportion of the population, particularly among migrant workers and the more educated (in the churches, education, and the civil service) remain seriously disaffected, and this disaffection inevitably has detrimental effects on the implementation of policy, including development efforts.

The administrative structure for implementing government policy in Lesotho, though improving, remains weak. The country inherited an extremely weak civil service structure from the British. At the time of independence, Lesotho received budgetary grants-in-aid from the United Kingdom to balance its recurrent budget, amounting in the first financial year after independence to over half of current expenditure. In 1966-67, total current expenditure nevertheless amounted to barely U.S.$12 per capita. The Lesotho government made the elimination of dependence on British grants-in-aid for current expenditure a major objective which was given even more emphasis after the brief suspension of British aid in 1970. The last such grants were received in 1972-73. However, the objective was achieved at the cost of severely restraining current expenditure and thus the size of the civil service. Furthermore, secondary and higher education in Lesotho had been very little developed prior to the 1960s, and despite recent rapid expansion there is still a severe shortage of middle and high-level manpower. This shortage is exacerbated both by political problems (which result in some persons being unable or unwilling to work for government) and by the lure of higher salaries both in South Africa and further afield. As a result, there is heavy reliance on expatriate personnel in technical and specialized posts. Large numbers of established posts at graduate-entry and technical levels remain vacant, and continuity is compromised as the competent staff are moved rapidly from post to post as priorities change or as individuals move seeking promotion.

PLANNING STRATEGY

Given the realities of the situation, any attempt at full-blown comprehensive planning would be farcical. The plan documents themselves are to some extent cosmetic exercises. These documents serve as reference points, and their production as an occasion to take stock of progress, review policy, and identify public sector priorities and projects. This is reflected in the structure of the second plan document. It surveys the economy, assesses progress during the first plan period, and then gives the targets, programs, and projects for the second plan period. The impossibility of comprehensive planning is easily shown. It is clear that in recent years the two major binding constraints on development efforts have been personnel and construction; there is a severe shortage of all types of personnel at the technical, executive, and administrative levels, and the capacity of the domestic construction sector is very limited—in 1971-72 its value added was estimated to be only about U.S. $3 million. A further problem arises because the bulk of investment funds still comes from external sources. In the true public sector this is not too much of a problem since donors can be persuaded fairly easily to give at least the outlines of their intentions for the next few years— especially if given a reasonable picture of the broad outlines of development policy and an idea of the cost of projects that need finance. In fact, in 1975, during the preparations for the second plan, Lesotho took an unusual initiative by inviting all prospective donors to a "Donor Conference," at which policy and needs for the next five years were discussed in some detail. [23]

But with the private sector the situation is quite different. Lesotho puts considerable emphasis on the development of a manufacturing sector. The major vehicle for doing this is the Lesotho National Development Corporation (LNDC), a government-owned parastatal which assists prospective foreign investors, generally takes equity in new ventures, and has a number of wholly owned subsidiaries in sectors where foreign private capital could not be attracted or is not wanted. LNDC has had a somewhat checkered history but has recently been strengthened considerably and appears to be performing well. The problem is that Lesotho has no particular natural advantage as a site for foreign private investment of an obvious kind, no super-abundant raw materials, and a small and fragmented domestic market. Lesotho's advantages are basically man-made, "political" ones—free access to the South African and European Economic

Community (EEC) markets[24] for its manufactures and freedom from the racial restrictions on the use of labor that exist in South Africa, together with rather lower wage rates than in South Africa. Against these factors must be set transport problems and rather less advantageous investment incentives and tax concessions than exist in the "decentralization areas" in South Africa. The actual experience of any development corporation or similar agency involved in trying to attract investment, especially foreign investment, to a particular location is that there are far more inquiries than serious negotiations and more serious negotiations than actual new ventures. This may be as true in Appalachia or Northern Ireland as in southern Africa. Because of its small size, Lesotho is vulnerable to such uncertainties. One cannot foretell either which inquiries will actually lead to investment or how long it will take from first serious negotiation to the start of actual investment. If one is dealing with a fairly large region or country, so that inquiries are in the hundreds or thousands and actual new ventures agreed upon are several a month or a week, this would not be too important. In such a case one can rely on the laws of large numbers to give a reasonably steady flow which can be planned for without too frequent or too great a disruption. But in a situation like Lesotho's, it becomes impossible to program or plan private sector investment. The number of possible new investors is usually small; one cannot tell which negotiations will bear fruit when; and it is politically unacceptable to turn away any possible new venture that can be concluded on reasonable terms. This has certain implications for the planning process which in fact involve criticisms of the way that process now operates.

Since private sector investment activity cannot be predicted, even six months ahead let alone five years, it is perfectly acceptable not to try to plan comprehensively. This implies that the planning process should concentrate on three things: giving a clear outline of the government's development and economic policies; planning for those in which direct public decisions are all-important to development (social and physical infrastructure, agriculture); and facilitating development in the private sector. Lesotho's two post-independence plans have done well in the second area but score very poorly on the other two. The country's development strategy and its economic policy are not clear from the plan documents. There are a number of possible explanations for this. It could be that government itself is not clear, or that government is clear on its policies but considers it politically inexpedient to spell them out, or that the policy is internally inconsistent and that this is reflected in the plan. The most probable explanation is a mixture of all three, since there are both certain clear conclusions that can be drawn from government actions and statements and contradictions between them. At the same time, perhaps the most fundamental of these conclusions about actual policy is something which it would be difficult for government to state too explicitly. Thus, the stated policy of the government is that to reduce labor migration to South Africa as quickly as possible is of great priority, but actual planning proceeds on the assumption that labor migration will continue to grow. The overall development strategy seems to be to exploit the earnings opportunities and the safety valve of employment in South Africa to the full while strengthening the structure and cohesion of the domestic economy and making contingency arrangements against the possible emergency of a sudden mass return of unemployed migrants. This strategy is probably in the best long-term interest of the country, but government seems to feel that it is not one that can be stated too openly. One of the consequences of this feeling on the part of government seems to be a misplaced sense of urgency to be seen to be doing something. This results in a willingness to accept and encourage almost any halfway reasonable project with no concern for how it fits into the economy as a whole or into an overall strategy. This approach produces manpower shortages, construction delays, and other problems which in most other countries would be very serious; luckily, given the openness of the Lesotho economy, the lack of a foreign exchange constraint (a virtue of economic integration with South Africa), and a willingness to accept expatriate staff, in Lesotho it does not produce disasters. However, it does lead to a complete loss of any sense of overall direction to the economy and plays havoc with any attempt to establish priorities. Even when priorities are in theory established, they rapidly get lost because of the multiplicity of minor constraints not centrally controlled. To give one concrete example, there is a severe shortage of housing throughout Lesotho, especially the type of housing "suitable" for expatriates. But there is no overall attempt to relate the housing supply to the numbers of expatriates being hired. The result is that supposedly "high priority" projects may be held up because there is no housing available for essential expatriate staff, at the same time that less urgent projects are going ahead because they somehow obtained housing.

The example of housing brings us back to the spatial aspects of planning and the comparative failure of planning to facilitate private sector development. The two are related. Land tenure in Lesotho is rather complex, but basically there is no private ownership of land, only various forms of rights of use. A special law was passed to enable the predecessor of LNDC to give industrial and commercial firms long leases with security of tenure. As yet, physical planning has been almost totally neglected in Lesotho, another example of lack of paying attention to a constraint on development that could be binding while concentrating on ones much less likely to cause difficulty

(particularly finance for investment, which for Lesotho is very
unlikely to be a real problem, so long as the projects are viable).
When the first plan was written in 1970, there was no overall plan
for the development of any urban areas. By 1975, effectively this
was still true, although in the second plan reference is made to the
intention to produce plans for the main towns and to identify "growth
centers" in which provision of public services would be concentrated.
However, physical planning has clearly been given low priority—in
1975 there was not even a single Mosotho being trained as a physical
planner—and this lack of attention does create problems. Not only is
there a danger of a shortage of suitable serviced land for new industrial development, but also haphazard and relatively uncontrolled
urban and peri-urban growth creates a number of problems that must
be tackled in an ad hoc, and expensive, manner. Public health and
other considerations imply that some provision for sewerage and
water supply must be made. Unplanned development may also lead
to poor land use, which is of considerable importance in a country
where good arable land is so scarce.

Some of the problems arising from the lack of physical planning
and lack of personnel in that area were illustrated by events surrounding the 1976 "independence" of the Transkei. Lesotho, like all other
member nations of the United Nations except South Africa, does not
recognize the Transkei. However, Transkei borders on fairly large
portions of eastern Lesotho which have no reliable land transport
links with the rest of Lesotho, and which did have established transport and commercial links with urban centers in that part of South
Africa now known as the Transkei. Lesotho regarded the transfer of
the border posts in question from South Africa to the Transkei as a
technical closure of the border and appealed to the world community,
with the endorsement of a U.N. mission, for special aid funds for
the construction of road links to the affected areas.[25] But the lack
of physical planning meant that these roads, too, had to be developed
on an ad hoc, emergency basis.

Overall, then, Lesotho's planning efforts appear, at least on
the surface, to be rather poor according to normal criteria. Although
they show a praiseworthy concern with egalitarian and need-fulfilling
development rather than growth for its own sake,[26] the two plan documents that have appeared are basically government investment programs and statements of often conflicting policies and objectives.
There is no serious attempt to relate plans to constraints on resources
or to give a clear idea of the overall strategy and the relative priorities attached to different objectives. It is quite possible that this,
together with the ad hoc way in which projects get initiated and
approved, is a good adaptation to the realities of the situation—particularly the extreme uncertainties, the lack of a foreign exchange

constraint, and the extreme openness of the economy. Unfortunately, although this may be reasonable from the point of view of producing plan documents, it has certain very undesirable effects from the point of view of actual policy. These are of two types. First, overall policy and strategy is unclear, and therefore people feel a lack of purpose and direction and also, lacking clear guidelines, may make wrong or inconsistent decisions. The implicit overall strategy may also not be the best possible. Second, the ad hoc nature of actual decisions produces a permanent sense of crisis among officials dealing with planning; so emphasis is always being given to new planning for the future. As a result, great inefficiency may exist with respect to the actual current implementation of existing projects, which may receive nobody's attention until the inefficiency reaches "crisis" proportions—and then warrants an ad hoc solution. Plan implementation remains extremely weak in Lesotho; in spite of the emphasis given to the need to improve project reporting, monitoring, and implementation by former senior officials of the planning office, both expatriate and local, in practice very little attention is paid by the center to how projects are actually performing.[27]

Hence, much of the planning process suffers from the faults common in Africa and identified by critics such as Killick and Helleiner, namely, that too much attention is paid by planners to the plan document and to possible projects for the future, and not enough attention is given to the day-to-day efficiency of actual operation of government policy and development projects. But the lack of an explicit, clear, overall strategy and the danger that the implicit one is not the best possible is also serious. It can be illustrated with the question of agriculture.

Because in practice the plan is a public sector investment program and agriculture is far and away the largest domestic sector by any yardstick, agriculture naturally gets a great deal of attention in the plan documents—about a quarter of the whole in the first plan and a similar fraction in the second. It also receives a very large chunk of both public sector investment funds and recurrent government spending. Now, it is clear that on an average landholding of less than four acres rain-fed agriculture in Lesotho cannot provide income-generating opportunities for many households that are competitive with migration to South Africa or wage employment in Lesotho. There is some evidence that many Basotho households therefore regard their land and livestock mainly as a fallback, a form of security which also provides some income (but not, for most households, a substantial portion of total income). There are also some indications that at certain levels within government this is recognized and that the actual objectives of agricultural policy are to achieve self-sufficiency in food grains plus improvement in agricultural efficiency—both sensible objectives. But if this is the policy, it is not clearly articulated and not widely understood; nor is it consistently followed either at the very top or the operational bottom. What results is both a waste of resources (on projects that are not "high priority" in terms of the real policy) and disaffection, since policy is criticized because it is not understood. Government is criticized for wasting money on agriculture when Lesotho is "not an agricultural country," in the sense that it cannot support by agriculture alone the whole of the rural population at the consumption levels to which they are accustomed.[28] If government was to make clear what its objectives in agriculture were and to state clearly that it did not expect more than a small minority of the current rural population to have agriculture as their primary source of income then policy and projects might be more usefully assessed and efficiently implemented.

CONCLUSION

Planning in Lesotho faces peculiar difficulties. The result of planning thus far has been the production of plan documents, which are inaccurate public sector investment programs, together with a stock-taking of progress (a very useful exercise) and an unclear statement of policy. In practice, development planning proceeds in an ad hoc fashion from one project, one crisis, to the next. Except for the lack of an overall physical plan and a clearly stated economic strategy, this procedure probably represents a good adaptation to the situation. Unfortunately, the same attitude has been taken to the implementation and monitoring of projects, which is done on an ad hoc basis and given serious attention only when crises occur. This attitude is very detrimental to morale and has also probably resulted in inefficiency. The hope must be that in the future planning will pay more attention to real constraints, such as land use and physical planning, and more attention to its evaluative function, monitoring progress, and identifying what makes for success rather than failure.[29] One should add two final points. The first is to emphasize the strength of egalitarian sentiment in Lesotho and the real concern with social justice, which has resulted in an unwillingness to match South African wage and salary levels for skilled personnel and thus exacerbated manpower difficulties—less than 10 percent of the output of artisans from the government technical institute in 1974 and 1975 is employed in Lesotho.[30] Second, one must note a possible shift in planning strategy. Government appears to have concluded recently that the South African mining industry's demand for Basotho labor might fall sharply quite soon, and the minister of finance has called for the industry to plan jointly with the Lesotho government for a phased redeployment of Basotho miners, with the industry assisting to create income-earning opportunities in Lesotho for returning miners.[31]

However, in fact, Basotho employment in the gold mines in South Africa grew quite rapidly from 1974 to 1977, and the basic task has remained mobilizing the surplus earnings of migrants above their consumption needs for development purposes. As yet, the policy and institutional structure to achieve this basic task do not seem to have been devised.

NOTES

1. For definitions of planning, see A. Waterston, Development Planning: Lessons of Experience (London: Oxford University Press, 1966); or Tony Killick, "The Possibilities of Development Planning," Oxford Economic Papers, n.s., vol. 28, no. 2 (July 1976).

2. The process view is emphasized in N. Caiden and A. Wildavsky, Planning and Budgeting in Poor Countries (New York: Wiley, 1974).

3. See, e.g., G. K. Helleiner, "Beyond Growth Rates and Plan Volumes—Planning for Africa in the 1970's," Journal of Modern African Studies 10, no. 3 (October 1972); and Michael Faber and Dudley Seers, eds., The Crisis in Planning (London: Chatto & Windus, 1972).

4. This list owes much to Killick, op. cit. It reflects the concept that has been termed "narrow-planning." For an argument in favor of "broad-planning," involving much more of society than just the technocratic "planners," see Ray Bromley, "The Planning Process: Lessons of the Past and a Model for the Future," IDS Bulletin 9, no. 3 (February 1978).

5. The view is expounded in detail in Killick, op. cit. For an assessment of African experience that concludes that in the present unstable world, without the ability to implement by fiat, macro planning in Africa is bound to be inaccurate, see T. Y. Shen, "Macro Development Planning in Tropical Africa: Technocratic and Non-Technocratic Causes of Failure," Journal of Development Studies 13, no. 4 (July 1977).

6. See Helleiner, op. cit., especially on the expertise problem; and Wolfgang F. Stolper, Planning Without Facts (Cambridge, Mass.: Harvard University Press, 1966), on data problems.

7. On Lesotho's economy, see International Monetary Fund (IMF), Surveys of African Economies, vol. 5 (Washington, D.C.: IMF, 1973); World Bank, Lesotho: A Development Challenge (Baltimore: The Johns Hopkins University Press, 1975); Kingdom of Lesotho, Second Five Year Development Plan 1975/76–1979/80 (Maseru: Government Printer, 1976); and James H. Cobbe, "Growth

and Change in Lesotho," South African Journal of Economics 46, no. 2 (June 1978).

8. A satisfactory economic history of Lesotho has not been published. On political history, see David Ambrose, The Guide to Lesotho (Maseru and Johannesburg: Winchester Press, 1976), and references therein; also Paul Spray, "A Tentative Economic History of Lesotho from 1800," mimeographed, University of Sussex, United Kingdom, 1975.

9. Great Britain, Financial and Economic Position of Basutoland ("Pim Report"), cmd. 4907 (London: His Majesty's Stationary Office, 1935), p. 84.

10. Caiden and Wildavsky, op. cit.

11. Basutoland: Memorandum of Development Plans (Bloemfontein: Francis, 1946). There was also a Draft Development Plan 1955-60, a Five-Year Development Programme 1960-64, and a Development Plan 1963-66 (Maseru: Government Printer, various dates).

12. Kingdom of Lesotho, Lesotho First Five-Year Development Plan 1970/71-1974/75 (Maseru: Government Printer, 1970); and Lesotho Second Five-Year Development Plan 1975/76-1979/80 (Maseru: Government Printer, 1976).

13. The 1976 population census in fact showed that Maseru town had more than doubled its population since 1966. John Jilbert, "Notes on Population Change in Lesotho 1966-76," South African Journal of African Affairs 7, no. 1 (1977).

14. M. Ward, "Prospects for Full Local Employment with Special Reference to Changes in the Labor Force and the Pace of Industrialisation in Lesotho," Lesotho National Population Symposium 1974, mimeographed (Roma, Lesotho: University of Botswana, Lesotho, and Swaziland (UBLS), 1974), p. 15.

15. W. J. Breytenbach, Migratory Labor Arrangements in Southern Africa (Pretoria: Africa Institute, 1972), p. 41. It should be realized that the migrant labor system has many negative effects on social and economic life in Lesotho. For a discussion, see T. Eggenhuizen and D. Matsobane, eds., Another Blanket (Horison, South Africa: Agency for Industrial Mission, 1976).

16. L. S. Cooley, "The Deployment of the Labor Force in Lesotho (1970)," mimeographed (Maseru: CPDO, 1973), p. 3.

17. An indication that the 140,000 figure was about right for 1975 is given by an official South African figure of 160,634 workers from Lesotho in South Africa in February 1977, together with the fact that the number of Basotho in the gold mines alone increased by slightly over 20,000 between 1975 and 1977. Loraine Gordon et al.,

Survey of Race Relations in South Africa, 1977 (Johannesburg: South African Institute of Race Relations, 1978), pp. 223, 258.

18. The minimum underground weekly cash wage was R2.52 in June 1971, R3 in June 1972, but had reached R15 by June 1976; the rate of growth has slackened since 1975, reaching R15.9 in August 1977. Gordon, Survey of Race Relations in South Africa, 1977, op. cit., p. 260.

19. Moeno v. Moeno, J.C. 214/64, Rothe Local C.C. 4/64, quoted by I. Hamnett, "Land Shortage in Lesotho," African Affairs 72, no. 286 (January 1973): 44.

20. See Kingdom of Lesotho, Second Five-Year Development Plan, op. cit., chap. 5.

21. On the customs union agreement, see P. M. Landell-Mills, "The 1969 Southern African Customs Union Agreement," Journal of Modern African Studies 9, no. 2 (1971); and Paul Mosley, "The Southern African Customs Union: A Reappraisal," World Development 6, no. 1 (January 1978). Under the monetary agreement, Lesotho uses South African currency but receives a periodic compensatory payment from the Republic of South Africa equal to two-thirds of the interest rate on the most recent South African long-term internal debt issue, times the estimated currency circulation in Lesotho. For the text of the agreement, see Kingdom of Swaziland, Government Gazette 12, no. 678 (December 13, 1974).

22. See R. F. Weisfelder, "Lesotho," in Southern Africa in Perspective, ed. C. P. Potholm and R. Dale (New York: Collier-Macmillan, 1972).

23. See Kingdom of Lesotho, Report and Papers of the Donor Conference, April 1975 (Maseru: CPDO, 1975).

24. Under the customs union (note 21 above) and the Lomé Convention, respectively.

25. United Nations Mission to Lesotho, "Assistance to Lesotho," Objective: Justice 9, no. 2 (Summer 1977).

26. An International Labor Organization (ILO) survey praised Lesotho's first plan for its concern for the employment situation but noted the concern was "on the surface and the policies envisaged appear not consistent with the overall objective of maximisation of productive employment." S. B. L. Nigam, Employment and Income Distribution Approach in Development Plans of African Countries (Addis Ababa: Jobs and Skills Programme for Africa, ILO, 1975).

27. For an expatriate view, see P. Selwyn, "Report on Assignment to Lesotho," Institute of Development Studies (IDS) Discussion Paper no. 5, mimeographed, IDS, University of Sussex, 1971; for a local view, T. T. Thahane, "Planning for Development," in Accelerated Development in Southern Africa, ed. John Barratt et al.

(London: Macmillan, 1974). Lesotho is likely to introduce its own currency in the future.

28. The phrase quoted comes from a speech made by Mr. Joel Moitse, Minister of Commerce and Industry in the Lesotho Government 1974-75, after he had left office.

29. Many projects in Lesotho have been "failures." For a controversial hypothesis to explain this, see S. Wallman, "Conditions of Non-Development: The Case of Lesotho," Journal of Development Studies 8, no. 2 (January 1972).

30. For a fuller discussion of this problem, see James Cobbe, "Wage Policy Problems in the Small Peripheral Countries of Southern Africa, 1967-76," Journal of Southern African Affairs 2, no. 4 (October 1977).

31. Namely, remarks made by Minister of Finance E. R. Sakhonyana at the Matsieng Development Trust Conference, Maseru, March 10, 1976.

18

APARTHEID, URBANIZATION, AND REGIONAL PLANNING IN SOUTH AFRICA

Christian Myles Rogerson
Gordon Harvey Pirie

INTRODUCTION

Policies falling under the rubric of "urbanization and regional planning" in the Republic of South Africa are inextricably linked to the evolution of the national economy, society, and polity. Racial ideology in South Africa and the political practice in which it is reflected has always stood in a complex reciprocal relationship with changing social and economic conditions. Consequently, an understanding of the emerging apartheid* complex must be rooted in an

---

*In this paper apartheid is applied as a generic term to the policies, practices, and ideology of the National Party since its accession to power in 1948. While the terms separate development and multinationalism are also in current usage, apartheid remains the term most widely used to designate the present system in South Africa.

This essay was originally prepared in November 1975. A full revision of the paper to consider apartheid in the aftermath of the Soweto rebellions and subsequent events in South Africa has not been possible because of the continental separation of the two authors. Grateful thanks are due to Miss J. G. Rouse, University of Witwatersrand, Johannesburg, for the preparation of diagrams accompanying this chapter.

initial appreciation of this symbiosis of the economy, society, and political ideology.

In the past the South African economic system encompassed two diverse modes of production, the white-focused capitalist mode and the black-focused redistributive mode.[1] The South African economy, anchored on the growing domination of the capitalist mode, was based at first on mineral exploitation, a phase succeeded by burgeoning industrialization and expansion of the tertiary sector.[2] Together these events accounted for South Africa's economic advance from a pre-industrial stage of national economic development to Rostowian "drive to maturity" in less than 60 years. However, there occurred another side to capitalist development in the country. As Colin Bundy proffers,

> the crucial post-mineral period was one in which non-market forces predominated; in which discriminatory and coercive means were utilized by the wielders of economic and political power to disadvantage the African peasantry; and that an economy was created whose structure was such as to render "market forces" highly favourable to the White capitalist sector. The decline in productivity and profitability of African agriculture—and the corollary of greater dependence of Africans on wage labor—is in an important sense the outcome of the nature of capitalist development in South Africa.[3]

The salient feature of black wage labor was its migratory and temporary nature, with migrants returning to the Reserves* between periods of employment in "white areas." The migrant retained a means of subsistence in the redistributive economies of the black areas, thus creating a geographical separation of the two processes of labor-force maintenance and renewal. The costs of welfare facilities, education, and social security were accordingly transferred to the communal context of the precapitalist economy. Capital in South Africa was thus able to pay its black workers less than might otherwise have been the case as the burden of labor renewal fell upon the subsistence economy.[4]

---

*The term "Reserves" refers to the black areas, or black race space, in South Africa. In recent years the term has been superseded by the designation "Homelands." Recent consolidation of the black areas has resulted in the creation of nine Homelands, with the possible future establishment of a tenth.

The roots of this exploitative labor system began to be undermined with the progressive dissolution of the traditional reserve economies. These areas' rural economy decayed as soil erosion and overpopulation made the extraction of a viable existence there increasingly arduous. It is in this setting that there occurred in 1948 a shift in the application of policies of segregation to those of apartheid. Although it is a widely held conception that apartheid is essentially little more than a continuation under a new guise of pre-1948 policies, Harold Wolpe argues the existence of fundamental differences.[5] Most important is that apartheid serves to insure, in the period of South Africa's industrialization, the availability of a cheap and controlled labor force in the face of the disintegration of the precapitalist systems of production in the black areas.

These changes from an economy based on capitalist and precapitalist modes of production to one founded essentially upon capitalism wrought a considerable restructuring of southern African space.[6] In the period of post-mineral discoveries, the Witwatersrand emerged as the economic locus of the subcontinent, and, more generally, all economic progress was geographically concentrated on the white metropolitan or core areas. By contrast, the black reserves, experiencing rural deterioration, economic decay, and pauperization, emerged as the outer peripheries of national economic space. To borrow from the language of André Gunder Frank, the black reserves of South Africa proceeded from a condition of undevelopment to one of underdevelopment.[7]

The expansion of capitalism in South Africa resulted in the institutionalization of a massive structural imbalance in the relationship between the geographical location of job opportunities and the settlement pattern of the black population.[8] Thus, a situation was created whereby a rapid increase in the migration of blacks to the white ecumene on either a temporary or permanent basis was inevitable. The advantages to capital and white fears of a permanently established black proletariat in the towns settled the issue in favor of migrant labor. The decision to work as a migrant is not in the hands of the black worker himself; rather the decision must be viewed as a byproduct of policies over which he had no input. The migrant labor system of South Africa is part and parcel of the political economy of capitalism.[9]

Predicated upon the belief that racial contact inevitably occasions racial conflict, the National Party began implementation of its apartheid programs. Faced with the dilemma of controlling a de facto multiracial society consisting of a white-dominated capitalist economy wedded to black labor, apartheid planners set about moulding two distinctive geographical spaces, namely, a racially-integrated economic space and a racially segregated social and political space.[10]

FIGURE 18.1

The Spatial Fabric of Black and White Race Space in South Africa

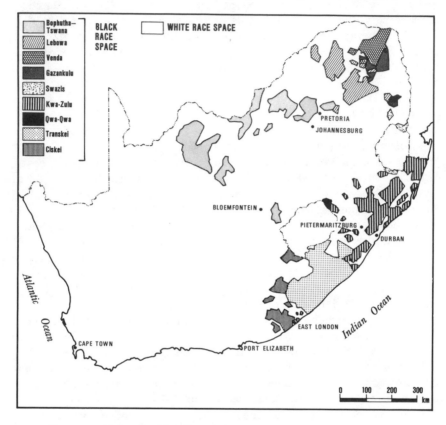

<u>Source</u>: Compiled by the authors.

(See Figure 18.1.) The separation of these two geographical spaces
is a reflection of the state's efforts to reorder the relations between
capital and labor in South Africa. The sustaining of a system of
cheap labor makes control over the geography of black employment
and settlement imperative. These controls comprise a suite of policies that may be subsumed under the broad designation of "urbanization and regional planning." Among the most notable of these policies
are constraints upon permanent black urbanization, resettlement
programs, economic decentralization, and associated strategies for
the "development" of black areas.

MIGRANT LABOR

Migratory labor as an oscillating movement between a home in some rural area and place of work is a long-established feature of the South African scene.[11] Labor migrancy, rather than mass black proletarianization, has been and remains the linchpin of economic progress in South Africa. The reasons for this are enumerated by Bundy:

> The embedding of migrant labour in the economic struc-
> ture conferred benefits upon all major interests which
> possessed a political voice in the State. For urban em-
> ployers it meant that labour was kept cheap, unorganized
> and rightless, that overhead costs were kept to a mini-
> mum, and the formation of an urban proletariat was
> restricted. For White workers it provided the security
> of membership of a labour elite. For White farmers it
> meant that low wages and the impermanence of com-
> pound life kept the labour force close at hand.[12]

In light of these advantages, it is not surprising that steeling the migrant labor system is the keystone of apartheid. The forces under-pinning oscillatory migratory labor patterns have been modeled by Francis Wilson.[13] As shown in Figure 18.2, the urban pull force,

FIGURE 18.2

Rural-Urban-Rural Population Flow Model

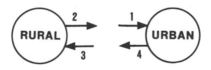

Source: Francis Wilson, Migrant Labour in South Africa (Johannesburg: South African Council of Churches and Spro-Cas, 1972), p. 153.

(1) representing the economic and sociological attractions of town life, has operated in tandem with those push forces (2) impelling blacks to leave rural areas. Over time, force 1 in South Africa as

in other countries, has become progressively stronger. However, it has been force 2, the rural push, that has strengthened most during the period of national economic development. The rising importance of the rural push is the consequence of extensive agricultural mechanization in white farming locations and of the continual erosion of the economic base of the black areas.

In Wilson's model, forces 3 and 4 function to return workers from urban to rural environs. Of particular historical significance in South Africa has been the attachment, for ethnic or personal security reasons, of black migrants to the land (force 3). Increasing poverty in the densely settle reserves and a growing inability of these areas to fulfill their traditional role of providing social security have, however, steadily weakened the pull back to rural areas. Emasculation of force 4, the urban push, has also occurred; economic progress has been accompanied by increasing demands for black labor in ever more skilled employment which, for urban employers, has meant the increased attractiveness of a permanent rather than a migratory labor force.

The historic role of economic growth in extending the compass of forces 1 and 2 while, at the same time, weakening forces 3 and 4, creates a situation in which temporary migration yields to a condition of permanent urbanization. In view of the benefits that would be foregone by white South Africa if the migrant worker were to be replaced, official policy aims at 'migratizing' the entire black work force; the single male contract laborer, shuttling back and forth between place of work in the white cities and residence in a black area, is now viewed as the ideal "labor unit." In support of this policy, blacks seeking work in white cities are required to register at labor bureaus in the Homelands. The control so exercised serves also to boost the ever weakening urban push force (4), for migrants are compelled to return to the reserves after completion of an eleven-month labor contract in white areas.

The extent and current significance of migrant labor within the South African complex is the subject of extensive documentation. An investigation by Jill Nattrass places the total number of migrants in the modern sector of the economy at approximately 1,750,000.[14] Indeed, 60 percent of the modern sector work force in South Africa are oscillating migrants, and eight out of ten black modern sector workers are normally resident outside the sector. In its effect on the migration source areas, the system of migratory labor has had a devastating impact: the ratio of migrants to economically active males in the Homelands is as high as 7:3, and on average is 6:5. Two-thirds of a typical Homeland family's income derives from migrant remittances; and at least one-third of the economically active males in the Ciskei and Transkei are working as migrant laborers at any particular time.[15] These statistics belie the notion that the migrant labor system in South Africa could ever be swiftly "ended."[*] Far from a general reallocation of population in response to changing geographical demand patterns for labor, continuing capitalist development in the republic has meant swelling the stream of temporary migrants.

CONSTRAINED URBANIZATION

Efforts to nourish migratory labor have been supplemented by and, in turn, complement, a set of policies that seek to retard the shift from temporary to permanent migration and from that to a permanently urbanized black proletariat.

Restrictions upon permanent black urbanization take several forms, the most important stemming from the massive influx of blacks into the cities of post-1945 South Africa. Between 1946 and 1960, there occurred a near doubling in the urban black presence; by 1970, blacks accounted for slightly under half of the republic's urban population groups (Table 18.1). Only one-third of blacks were urbanized by 1970, compared to 86, 74, and 83 percent, respectively, for Asians, coloreds, and whites.

The migrant flood and emergence of shanty towns[16] that distinguished the immediate postwar years of surging industrial expansion provided economic and social rationales for policies to constrain black urbanization. Mass movement of blacks into white race space, however, poses a potential threat to the authority of the dominant white elite. In terms of what John Friedmann designates urbanization, "the geographic concentration of population and non-agricultural activities in urban environments of varying size and form,"[17] that is, the cityward movement of blacks, heightens the potential for crystallization of black class formations which subsequently may confront white rule. Strenuous efforts are made by the South African state to counter the process of urbanization. So forcefully have a set of legislative weapons been applied that it has been suggested that there is now no more coveted right, including the vote, anywhere in the world

---

[*]While it is possible that the bargaining position of migratory laborers may improve with the onset of Homelands independence (implemented for the Transkei in October 1976 and Bophuthatswana in December 1977), it is inconceivable that sufficient work opportunities will ever be provided in the Homelands so as to halt migrancy.

TABLE 18.1
Urban Population, by Race, 1946-2000
(in thousands)

	Blacks	Coloreds	Asians	Whites
1946				
Total	1,902	580	208	1,793
% urban population	42.4	12.9	4.6	40.0
% urbanized	24.3	62.5	72.8	75.6
1960				
Total	3,471	1,031	397	2,582
% urban population	46.4	13.8	5.3	34.5
% urbanized	31.8	68.3	83.2	83.6
1970				
Total	4,989	1,494	539	3,258
% urban population	48.5	14.5	5.2	31.7
% urbanized	33.1	74.0	86.8	83.6
2000				
Total	20,661	3,967	1,205	5,642
% urban population	65.6	12.6	3.8	17.9
% urbanized	75.0	87.0	92.0	93.0

Source: G. M. E. Leistner, Economic and Social Forces
Affecting the Urbanization of the Bantu Population of South Africa,
Occasional Paper no. 32 (Pretoria: Africa Institute, 1972).

than the qualification of a black to (a degree of) permanent residence
in the republic's white cities.[18]
    South Africa has, in its history, an impressive record of
attempts to control the concentrated settlement of blacks in white
race space.[19] Nonetheless, machinery for systematic restraint over
black migration was not instituted until the promulgation of the Native
Laws Amendment Act of 1937. A subsequently introduced measure,
the Native (Urban Areas) Act of 1945, is more chiefly employed at
present to combat the movement of blacks from rural to urban set-
tings and is colloquially termed "influx control." As regards still
newer regulation, little that can be described as innovative has been
introduced since 1948. The apartheid ideology, however, provides
the government with a terminology and an implicit justification for
the most recent and systematic phase of labor coercion.[20] Blacks

are deemed temporary "sojourners" in white cities, having neither claims, rights, nor privileges comparable with urban whites. Such privileges are only granted blacks in their own race space, and even those blacks born in white cities are now to regain links with the "lost Homelands." Under the details of the 1945 Act, certain blacks (and their dependents) with comparatively long employment and residence records in the white areas were granted a degree of permanence, being allowed to rent but not own family houses. Further to this range of directives, there exist practically no legal limits under which economically inactive blacks can be legislated out of urban areas. The catalogue of controls upon urbanization means that all blacks are but de jure temporary residents in white urban areas.

The measures tailored to constraining urbanization discussed here go far beyond an attempt to arrest only the flow of population to the cities. As Thomas J. D. Fair and Charles F. Schmidt argue, "implicitly and explicitly they are also aimed at reducing the perception of permanence of Africans in urban areas and at inhibiting urbanization as a modernizing process among them."[21] Retardation of this modernization process, designated urbanization by Friedmann,[22] forms a second aspect of apartheid controls in the urban realm. Comprehension of this urbanization process in South Africa is assisted by using Lawrence Schlemmer's three-phase model of the incorporation of workers from the periphery into a developing industrial system: disposability, mobilization, and integration.[23] At each successive stage, curbs on black advancement obtain. In particular, progress towards the critical final phase of integration is vitiated through a galaxy of what may be termed counter-urbanization measures. These seek to exclude blacks from the process of modernization in an indirect fashion through slowing acculturation and detribalization. By way of example, blacks and whites are denied contact in schools and universities and are not permitted to share many civic and cultural facilities. Active black participation in urban affairs is considerably discouraged. Furthermore, black trade unions are not condoned, and the activities of black traders, professionals, and entrepreneurs are severely circumscribed. Nonetheless, as Schmidt maintains,

> The Blacks cannot be expected to reside in the main towns
> and cities, to function in a modern economic system and
> to conform to the moral and social values of the dominant
> White elites without undergoing cultural changes which
> make them increasingly aware of their lack of functional
> and spatial mobility as well as their subdominant position
> throughout the entire South African society.[24]

For blacks, permanent repatriation or voluntary migration to a Homeland provides the only alternative to continued subjugation under
urbanization strategies.

RESETTLEMENT

Associated with government attempts to stem cityward flow of
migrants are counterpoising programs to settle blacks away from
white areas. The excision of blacks from white race space assumes
an important role in the total effort to relocate blacks en masse and
may be viewed as the reverse flow of migratory labor. Workers who,
with their families, may leave towns for a variety of reasons are
allowed to return to the white areas on a contract basis but may not
take their families with them. Under Section 10 of the Native (Urban
Areas) Act of 1945, the aged, young, infirm, and dependent are
classed as "unproductive" and may be forcibly relocated from the
cities to resettlement townships in the Homelands. Justification for
such removals from white urban areas is reflected in the official
pronouncement that "the White areas should not be regarded as the
dumping grounds for the surplus labor which comes from the Bantu
Homelands."[25]
Removal of population from urban areas is, however, only one
component in the total program for black resettlement. The abolition
of labor tenancies and elimination of squatting on white farms, as
well as the eradication of black spots has occasioned the removal of
more than 1 million blacks.[26] Resiting black townships, establishing
dormitory towns, and programs for Homeland consolidation involve
additional mass removal of blacks.[27] One estimate of the projected
scale of black population shifts places the total at 4 million.[28] However, there are presently some 8 million blacks (more than half the
total black population in the republic) domiciled in white areas and
eligible for resettlement in terms of prevailing government policy.
Resettlement camps are appearing as distinctive features in
nearly all the black Homelands, with the notable exception of the
Transkei. Such locations have been variously styled "rural ghettos,"[29]
"ghost villages,"[30] and "dumping grounds."[31] These terms capture
the nature of life in centers of enigmatic urbanization[32] where there
exists no economic base and where, as a consequence, poverty is
endemic. As Wilson perceptively remarks, "There is as yet no word
in English to define accurately places such as Itsoseng, Witsieshoek,
or Dimbaza where people live in close proximity to each other in a
community which is neither agricultural nor near jobs in any urban
area."[33] Graphic descriptions of camp conditions are available,[34]
and these contrast markedly with the government-sponsored picture

of slumbering rural retreats. In the present context, suffice it to say
the poverty and lack of work opportunity in these settlements neces-
sitate migrancy among eligible males and, thus, cheap labor.

REGIONAL PLANNING—INDUSTRIAL DECENTRALIZATION

Attention has so far been directed towards urbanization policies
and cheap labor power as they serve the seemingly contradictory
goals of economic integration and social and political separation in
South Africa. Regional planning represents one further tool in the
present government's efforts to "modernize racial domination."[35]
In fact, Wolpe goes so far as to suggest that the policy of industrial
decentralization and associated strategies for Homelands development
can only be understood when seen as alternatives to migration as
mechanisms for maintaining a cheap labor supply.[36] Given that blacks
were not to be accorded social and residential rights in white areas,
it followed that economic activities should move to locations of concentrated black labor. Here the energies of a recently impoverished
peasantry could be tapped without incurring the additional costs
attendant upon permanent urbanization. Moreover, here also a lesser
degree of black worker organization and other factors enable industry
to pay lower wages than in white core areas.[37]
The policies for manufacturing decentralization within South
Africa have enjoyed a checkered history.[38] During the mid-1950s,
the Report of the Tomlinson Commission,[39] which is generally con-
ceded as laying the blueprint for the evolution of apartheid in South
Africa, commended the encouragement and establishment of white-
owned factories inside the black areas. Rejecting this proposal, the
Verwoerd government introduced in 1960 the program for industrial
movement to select white towns bordering upon Homelands. In the
first generation of border area towns, locations appending the existing
metropolitan areas provided the focus of attention. Examples are
Hammarsdale, Pietermaritzburg, and Rosslyn. Progress in border
area development in its early years was, however, glacial, and in
an attempt to catalyze the program (and also to contain the influx of
blacks into metropolitan areas more effectively), the government
strengthened its legislative armory. The passing of the Physical
Planning and Utilization of Resources Act in 1967 imposed restrictions upon the development of new industrial land in certain of the
metropolitan areas, most notably within the country's prime economic
core, the Witwatersrand. In addition, the act introduced a ceiling on
the black labor complement of factories located in these controlled
areas. In terms of the 1971 Government White Paper on Decentralization,[40] manufacturers in these proscribed areas are only legally

FIGURE 18.3

The Geography of Industrial Decentralization in South Africa

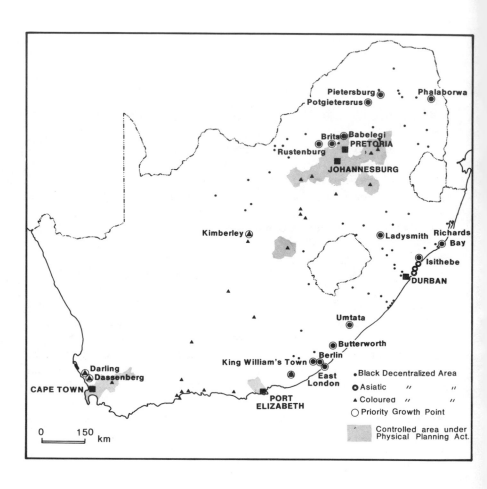

Source: Compiled by the author.

permitted to expand their black work force provided that a 1:2 ratio of white to black employees is not exceeded. The existence of such controls disposes "once and for all of claims that location policy in South Africa is governed by a need to increase the productive capacity of the economy or to improve the distribution of income."[41]

Enactment of such constraints upon industrial expansion in the leading metropolitan areas parallels a contemporaneous shift in the spatial direction of policy. A second generation of border area towns, now termed growth points, was declared to comprise centers such as Ladysmith, Phalaborwa, and Pietersburg, at some distance from the major existing national centers of production and consumption (Figure 18.3). It has been towards these and like locations in the inter-metropolitan periphery of the national space-economy that the government has directed efforts to deflect black labor-intensive manufacturing activity.*

To date, the impact of government decentralization efforts has been limited. Eighty percent of work opportunities in the manufacturing sector remain focused in the four metropolitan areas (Table 18.2). If decentralization is defined in terms of the total spatial system as a relative diminution in the importance of the center, then, at least at the macro scale, it is clear that polarization tendencies in the industrial space economy have not been arrested.[42] Fair concurs:

> While the space economy is long past the transitional
> stage dominated by a single national center and backward
> periphery, its present multi-nuclear structure of core
> and strong peripheral subcenters . . . has still not pro-
> vided a vehicle for the diffusion of economic activity
> such that dispersion from the core, either nationally or
> regionally, has set in.[43]

Assuming that even in the absence of official policy the decentralized locations would have maintained their percentage share of the national manufacturing work force, Trevor Bell attributes to the

---

*The decentralization program was extended in 1965 to encompass South Africa's Asian and colored peoples and centers designated for the receipt of appropriate government financial assistance. The geography of such centers is indicated in Figure 18.3. All these centers are designed wherever possible to reduce the number of coloreds and Asians in the metropolitan areas, especially Cape Town in the former case and Durban in the latter.

TABLE 18.2

Employment in Manufacturing, by Area

Area	1959–60		1961–62		1967–68		1969–70	
	Number	Percent	Number	Percent	Number	Percent	Number	Percent
Major industrial complexes	494,150	79.8	540,083	79.0	793,644	80.3	866,023	79.2
Pretoria–Witwatersrand–Vereeniging	283,929	45.9	302,733	44.3	448,626	45.4	484,729	44.3
Western Cape	104,121	16.8	112,530	16.5	155,451	15.7	168,382	15.4
Durban–Pinetown–Inanda	76,907	12.4	84,765	12.4	130,914	13.2	149,821	13.7
Port Elizabeth–Uitenhage	29,193	4.7	40,055	5.9	58,653	5.9	63,091	5.8
Remainder of South Africa	124,961	20.2	143,432	21.0	195,302	19.7	228,121	20.8
Total South Africa	619,111	100.0	683,515	100.0	988,946	100.0	1,094,144	100.0

Source: Trevor Bell, "Some Aspects of Industrial Decentralisation in South Africa," *South African Journal of Economics* 41, no. 4 (December 1973).

government the creation of only an additional 11,579 job opportunities in decentralized locations during the decade 1960-70.[44] But, included in this definition of decentralized areas are the two most successful border areas of Rosslyn and Hammarsdale, which represent the thinly veiled spread of the existing metropolitan areas. Excluding the employment figures for these two centers, government-sponsored locations experienced a net decline in their relative share of national industrial employment during the years 1960-70. Underscoring the lack of success of policy measures is Anne E. Ratcliffe's contention that the absolute amount of employment created in the decentralized locations has certainly been exceeded by the amount of potential black employment refused in the controlled areas in terms of the Physical Planning Act.[45]

One reason for the limited success of South Africa's decentralization program is the misapprehension of the nature of processes shaping the industrial landscape.[46] That apartheid planners have grossly overestimated the spatial mobility of the nation's manufacturing sector was shown by Christian M. Rogerson who, in extensive study, demonstrates that South Africa's industrial employment geography is broadly etched by the two factors of distance (accessibility) to the major metropolitan areas and hierarchical status of urban place.[47] High order centers and those locations with good access to major centers of production and consumption constitute the major poles of economic expansion. The most successful decentralized growth points have therefore been those enjoying good access to the existing centers of production and/or those which are high order centers themselves. Accordingly, locations in the outer periphery of national economic space and those of low hierarchical status have evidenced little sign of industrial advancement. This situation is not at all surprising given that any such "development" as does occur within black areas must be seen in the broader context of these areas' function within the political economy of apartheid in South Africa, that of renewing a cheap labor supply for the core areas.

BLACK HOMELAND "DEVELOPMENT"

In terms of the "development" of the black Homelands, the border area program may be described as a "red herring," as it served only decentralization within white race space. Indeed, Gavin M. Maasdorp has declared that the period 1955-70 may be appositely termed the "locust years" of industrial planning in South Africa.[48] Failure of the border area industries to galvanize substantial economic progress within the black areas encouraged a volte-face on earlier thinking and introduction of the first incentives to activate manufacturing development at selected growth nodes within the black Homelands. Commencement of this phase of industrial planning in 1968 represents a significant new step in regional policy in South Africa. Regional planning is being harnessed more closely to the attainment of what is frequently referred to within the country as "grand apartheid." If apartheid planners are to succeed in their objectives of Balkanizing the existing South African ecumene and establishing political units of reserve or Homeland areas, which comprise the underdeveloped parts of the national economy, considerable efforts are required to provide these nascent states with some degree of economic viability. Towards this end, the state perceives secondary industry as the prime vehicle whereby this objective may be realized. [49]

A series of industrial growth points for the black Homelands has been established. [50] White entrepreneurs are now being bribed, cajoled, and hectored into considering the location of black labor-intensive manufacturing operations inside a Homeland. Additionally, much effort is being expended to entice foreign firms to operate at these locations. In particular, the government is assiduously promoting the advantages of industrial location at the four priority growth points (Figure 18.3) of Babelegi (in Bophuthatswana), Isithebe (in KwaZulu), Butterworth, and Umtata (in the Transkei). Except for the highly core-oriented growth point of Babelegi (40 kilometers north of Pretoria), the remaining Homelands growth foci occupy locations in the extreme outer periphery of the national space economy. All, excluding Umtata, are places which were either too insignificant to merit inclusion in Ronald J. Davies and Gillian P. Cooks' research on the South African urban hierarchy or did not exist until a short time ago. [51] In view of their location within the space economy and their hierarchical status, it is to be expected that efforts to attract manufacturing enterprise to these areas have fared little better than those for the border area locations. Most successful of the Homelands growth points is the Bophuthatswana growth node of Babelegi, [52] which has appropriated almost half of all industrial employment opportunities in black areas. Significantly, the overwhelming problems encountered in attempting to generate manufacturing activity at locations far distant from the country's major growth poles have been covertly acknowledged in the realignment of development efforts in the northern Homelands away from industry and in favor of agriculture. [53]

The extent of the employment requirements of the black Homelands is staggering. Most recent estimates place the average job requirements of all these areas as 105,000 per annum. While recognizing that some Homelands possess an unexploited agricultural potential, official writings defer that "the fast growing labor force of the various homelands will have to be absorbed chiefly by the industrial sector and to a lesser extent by the service industries."[54] Given the fact that one black industrial job at a growth point spawns only one other in the tertiary or service sector,[55] fully 52,500 industrial jobs must annually be provided in the Homelands to stave off rising unemployment. Yet, from the inception of the program for Homelands industrialization to 1975, only some 13,000 job opportunities in manufacturing, or less than 3,000 jobs per annum, had been initiated. On average the cost of activating one black industrial job is estimated at R8,400;[56] therefore, to satisfy the annual employment needs of the Homelands would demand an annual expenditure of R441,000,000.[*] This potentially massive cost to white South Africa of apartheid and the imperative of generating viable work centers within the Homelands led to proposals, derived from the experience of Puerto Rico, for the establishment in the Homelands of industrial parks which it was envisaged would reduce the cost of job creation by almost four-fifths.[57]

CONCLUSION

The distinguishing feature of urbanization and regional planning strategies in the Republic of South Africa is their accordance with the political economy of apartheid. More specifically, urbanization and regional policies seek to foster the disjunction of a racially integrated economic space and a racially segregated social and political space. Separation of these twin geographical spaces in South Africa undergirds the maintenance of a cheap labor system.

The fundamental challenge facing apartheid in the future was succinctly expressed in a statement by Prime Minister Vorster that "the greatest danger confronting South Africa is not so much the threat from outside the borders, serious though that may be, but mass unemployment and disturbed race relations."[58] Just as the structures of apartheid perpetuate the comparative cheapness of black labor, so do they insure that the problems of unemployment are displaced sociologically onto blacks and geographically onto the Homelands.[59] Yet, it is apparent that at present rates of Homelands

---

[*]On current exchange rates (floating) in November 1975. R100 equals U.S.$155, or British £56. The figure of R441,000,000 should be seen in the light of a total expenditure on industrial development in the Homelands in 1974 cumulated from the program's inception of approximately R60,000,000.

"development," achievement of the necessary employment creation
in these areas is an objective that is unrealistic and even chimeric.
Even if, as Alan S. Mabin and Sally E. Biesheuvel argue, the decentralization efforts of the past two decades are only now coming to
fruition,[60] the fundamental forces guiding the geography of development and underdevelopment in South Africa militate against immediate
advances in these outermost segments of national economic space.

The unemployment exigencies of the Homelands notwithstanding,
it was in the black townships girdling the core areas of South Africa
that resistance to the policies associated with apartheid was forcefully expressed in the events of June 1976 and thereafter. In Soweto,
a black city appending Johannesburg, schoolchildren and the young
unemployed led the rebellion.[61] The time has not yet come to make
a final judgment about the protests in Soweto and the other black
townships; however, from the tide of current events in southern
Africa as a whole, it seems clear that the era of exclusively white-
initiated "solutions" to the problems of capitalist development in
South Africa is approaching an end. Increasingly, blacks are going
to participate, either through cooptation or confrontation, in shaping
the urban and regional fabric of this southernmost part of Africa.

NOTES

1. Harold Wolpe, "Capitalism and Cheap Labour-Power in
South Africa: From Segregation to Apartheid," Economy and Society
1, no. 4 (November 1972): 431-33.

2. See D. Hobart Houghton, The South African Economy (Cape
Town: Oxford University Press, 1973).

3. Colin Bundy, "The Emergence and Decline of a South African
Peasantry," African Affairs 71, no. 4 (October 1972): 371.

4. See Bernard Magubane, "The 'Native Reserves' (Bantustans)
and the Role of the Migrant Labor System in the Political Economy of
South Africa," in Migration and Development, ed. Helen I. Safa and
Brian M. Du Toit (The Hague: Mouton, 1975), pp. 225-67.

5. Wolpe, "Capitalism and Cheap Labour-Power in South
Africa," op. cit., pp. 432-33. See also Martin Legassick, "South
Africa: Capital Accumulation and Violence," Economy and Society
3, no. 3 (August 1974): 269-81.

6. For details of the structure of the South African spatial
system, see Christopher Board, Ronald J. Davies, and Thomas J. D.
Fair, "The Structure of the South African Space Economy," Regional
Studies 4, no. 3 (1970): 367-92; John G. Browett and Thomas J. D.
Fair, "South Africa 1870-1970: A View of the Spatial System," South
African Geographical Journal 56, no. 2 (September 1974): 111-20.

7. André Gunder Frank, Capitalism and Underdevelopment in Latin America (New York: Monthly Review Press, 1967).

8. Jill Nattrass, "The Migrant Labour System and South African Economic Development," South African Journal of Economics 44, no. 1 (March 1976): 78.

9. Magubane, op. cit., pp. 259-60.

10. David M. Smith, "Race-Space Inequality in South Africa: A Study in Welfare Geography," Antipode 6, no. 2 (July 1974): 42.

11. Francis Wilson, Migrant Labour in South Africa (Johannesburg: South African Council of Churches and Spro-Cas, 1972).

12. Bundy, op. cit., p. 372.

13. Wilson, op. cit., pp. 144-68.

14. Nattrass, op. cit.

15. Johan Maree and Pieter J. de Vos, Underemployment, Poverty and Migrant Labour (Johannesburg: South African Institute of Race Relations, 1976), p. 13.

16. An excellent discussion of shantytowns in the metropolitan Durban region is provided in Gavin G. Maasdorp and A. S. B. Humphreys, From Shantytown to Township (Cape Town: Juta, 1975).

17. John R. P. Friedmann, Urbanization, Planning and National Development (Beverly Hills, Calif.: Sage, 1973), p. 65.

18. Muriel Horrell et al., A Survey of Race Relations in South Africa, 1972 (Johannesburg: South African Institute of Race Relations, 1973), p. 162.

19. For details, see Rodney Davenport, "African Townsmen? South African Native (Urban Areas) Legislation Through the Years," African Affairs 68, no. 2 (April 1969): 95-109.

20. Stanley Trapido, "South Africa in a Comparative Study of Industrialization," Journal of Development Studies 7, no. 3 (April 1971): 318.

21. Thomas J. D. Fair and Charles F. Schmidt, "Contained Urbanisation: A Case Study," South African Geographical Journal 56, no. 2 (September 1974): 159.

22. Friedmann, op. cit., p. 65.

23. Lawrence Schlemmer, "Human Resources Utilisation in Southern Africa—Policy Alternatives?" (Paper prepared for the Conference on Resources of Southern Africa, Today and Tomorrow, Associated Scientific and Technical Societies of South Africa, September 22-26, 1975, Institute for Social Research, University of Natal, Durban). "Disposability" involves "the erosion and selective rejection of elements of traditional culture in response to the need to adapt to the demands and constraints of industrial work." "Mobilization" occurs "when workers begin to aspire actively towards mobility and progress in the modern world of work." In the stage of "integration," workers "have fully acquired urban-industrial life-

styles, a substantial degree of incorporation into public life via
political participation and who, as a consequence of an appreciable
power-base, are more or less coherently organised to engage in
economic conflict, which is typically along institutional lines in most
modern economies."

24. Charles F. Schmidt, "A Spatial Model of Authority-Dependency Relations in South Africa," Journal of Modern African Studies 13, no. 3 (September 1975): 489.

25. T. N. H. Janson, in Republic of South Africa, House of Assembly Debates, May 17, 1973.

26. Alan Baldwin, "Mass Removals and Separate Development," Journal of Southern African Studies 1, no. 2 (April 1975): 215-27; also, idem, Uprooting a Nation: The Study of 3 Million Evictions in South Africa (London: Africa Publications Trust, 1974).

27. See Alan C. G. Best and Bruce S. Young, "Homeland Consolidation: The Case of Kwazulu," South African Geographer 4, no. 1 (September 1972): 63-74.

28. Baldwin, op. cit., p. 217.

29. Francis Wilson, "Unresolved Issues in the South African Economy: Labour," South African Journal of Economics 43, no. 4 (December 1975).

30. Wilson, op. cit., p. 106.

31. The name derives from a television film made after the publication of Cosmas Desmond, The Discarded People (Johannesburg: The Christian Institute, 1971).

32. Christian M. Rogerson, "New Towns in the Bantu Homelands," Geographical Review 64, no. 4 (October 1974): 58.

33. Wilson, op. cit., p. 106.

34. See Desmond, op. cit.; and Liz Clarke and Jane Ngobese, Women Without Men (Durban: Institute for Black Research, 1975).

35. The phrase derives from Heribert Adam, Modernising Racial Domination: The Dynamics of South African Politics (Berkeley: University of California Press, 1971).

36. Wolpe, op. cit., p. 452.

37. Martin Legassick and David Hemson, Foreign Investment and the Reproduction of Racial Capitalism in South Africa (London: Anti-Apartheid Movement, 1976), pp. 7-8.

38. For details, see Trevor Bell, Industrial Decentralisation in South Africa (Cape Town: Oxford University Press, 1973).

39. South Africa, Socio-Economic Development of the Bantu Areas Within the Union of South Africa, Summary of the Report of the Commission (Tomlinson) U.G. 61/1955 (Pretoria: Government Printer, 1955).

40. Republic of South Africa, White Paper on the Report by the Inter-Departmental Committee on the Decentralisation of Industries (Pretoria: Department of Industries, 1971).

41. Trevor Bell, "Some Aspects of Industrial Decentralisation in South Africa," South African Journal of Economics 41, no. 4 (December 1973): 427.

42. Christian M. Rogerson, "Government and the South African Industrial Space Economy," Environmental Studies 14, Occasional paper, Department of Geography and Environmental Studies, University of Witwatersrand, Johannesburg, 1975.

43. Thomas J. D. Fair, "Polarisation, Dispersion, and Decentralisation in the South African Space Economy," Urban and Regional Research Unit, University of Witwatersrand, Occasional paper no. 7, 1975, p. 12.

44. Bell, "Some Aspects of Industrial Decentralisation in South Africa," op. cit., pp. 402-05.

45. Anne E. Ratcliffe, "Industrial Decentralization in South Africa" (review article), South African Journal of Economics 42 (January 1975): 160.

46. Christian M. Rogerson, "Industrial Decentralization in South Africa: The Planning Uncertainties," Standard Bank Review (October 1974): 19-25.

47. Christian M. Rogerson, "Industrial Movement in an Industrializing Economy," South African Geographical Journal 57, no. 2 (September 1975): 88-103.

48. Gavin G. Maasdorp, Economic Development for the Homelands (Johannesburg: South African Institute for Race Relations, 1974), p. 30.

49. Alan S. Mabin and Sally E. Biesheuvel, "Spatial Implications of Apartheid: The Role of Growth Centres in South Africa," Pan-African Journal 9, no. 1 (1976): 1-16; and Johannes A. Lombard, "Problems of Regional Economic Programming in the Development of the Bantu Homelands," South African Journal of Economics 39, no. 4 (December 1971): 388-401.

50. For details, see Christian M. Rogerson, "Industrialization of the Bantu Homelands," Geography 59, no. 3 (July 1974): 260-64; and South Africa, Homelands: The Role of the Corporations in the Republic of South Africa (Johannesburg: Chris van Rensburg Publications, 1975), pp. 97-138.

51. Ronald J. Davies and Gillian P. Cook, "Reappraisal of the South African Urban Hierarchy," South African Geographical Journal 50 (1968): 116-32.

52. Christian M. Rogerson, "Growth Point Problems—The Case of Babelegi, Bophuthatswana," Journal of Modern African Studies 12, no. 1 (May 1974): 126-30.

53. The Star (Johannesburg), April 29, 1974.

54. South Africa, Homelands: The Role of the Corporations, op. cit., p. 23.

55. Management (Johannesburg) (August 1975): 29.

56. South Africa, Homelands: The Role of the Corporations, op. cit., p. 103.

57. Natal Mercury (Durban), August 9, 1975. The program, however, has not been operationalized.

58. Republic of South Africa, House of Assembly Debates, September 14, 1970.

59. Martin Legassick, "Legislation, Ideology and Economy in Post-1948 South Africa," Journal of Southern African Studies 1, no. 1 (October 1974): 28.

60. Mabin and Biesheuvel, op. cit.

61. Alex Callinicos and John Rogers, Southern Africa After Soweto (London: Pluto Press, 1977), pp. 157-73.

BIBLIOGRAPHY

AARDES (Association algérienne pour la recherche demographique, économique et sociale). Enquête sur les budgets familiaux auprès des ménages algériens. 7 vols. Algiers: AARDES, 1970.

Abdi, N. "Reforme agraire en Algerie." Maghreb-Machrek (1975): 34-35

Abeggien, James C. "The Japanese Factory: Aspects of its Social Organization." In Urbanism in World Perspective: A Reader, edited by Sylvia F. Fara.

Abercrombie, Patrick. The Master Plan for Addis Ababa. Addis Ababa: The Addis Ababa Municipality, 1956.

Abraham, Willie. The Mind of Africa. Chicago: University of Chicago Press, 1962.

Abu-Lughod, Janet. "Developments in North African Urbanism: The Process of Decolonization." In Patterns of Urbanization and and Counter-Urbanization, edited by Brian Berry, pp. 202-05. Beverly Hills, Calif.: Sage, 1976.

___. "Moroccan Cities: Apartheid and the Serendipity of Conservation." In African Themes: Essays in Honor of Gwendolen Carter, edited by Ibrahim Abu-Lughod, pp. 77-111. Evanston, Ill.: Northwestern University Program of African Studies, 1975.

___. "Urban Structure under Decolonization: The Factorial Ecology of Rabat-Salé, Morocco." New York, June 1976. United Nations.

Adam, Herbert. Modernizing Racial Domination: The Dynamics of South African Politics. Berkeley: University of California Press, 1973.

Adams, Robert. The Evaluation of Urban Society: Early Mesopotamia and Prehistoric Mexico. Chicago: Aldine Press, 1966.

Addis Ababa Municipality. Draft Report on Housing in Addis Ababa: Results from the Census of September 1976. Addis Ababa: The Municipality of Addis Ababa, March 1972.

345

Adedeji, A. and L. Rowland, eds. Management Problems of Rapid Urbanization in Nigeria. Ile-Ife: University of Ife Press, 1973.

Adeniyi, E. O. "The Institutional Framework for Planning and Managing Urban Settlements in the Developing Countries of Africa." Planning and Administration 2 (Spring 1975): 71-74.

Advisory Committee for Reconstruction. Terms of Reference for Planning Sadat City. Cairo: Ministry of Housing, 1975.

Agency for Industrial Mission. South Africa: A Good Host Country for Migrant Workers? Horison, South Africa: Agency for Industrial Mission, 1976.

"A History of Husaka." Central African Post, July 10, 1952.

Akalou, Wolde Michael. "Some Thoughts on the Process of Urbanization in Pre-Twentieth Century Ethiopia." Ethiopian Geographical Journal 5 (December 1967): 35-38.

Akesson, Towald, and Ikakem Belletétch. "Survey of Housing Conditions in Tekle Haimonot and Lidetta Districts of Addis Ababa, Ethiopia, 1962." Addis Ababa: Ethio-Swedish Institute of Building Technology, Research Department, Housing Section, 1962.

Almond, Gabriel, and G. Bingham Powell, Jr. Comparative Politics: A Development Approach. Boston: Little Brown, 1966.

Ambrose, David. The Guide to Lesotho. Maseru: Winchester Press, 1976.

Amicale des Algériens en Europe. Nouvelle perspectives pour l'émigration algérienne. Assemblée Générale des Cadras, Nancy, February 12-13, 1977.

Amin, S. L'Économie du Maghreb 1965-1966. Paris: Éditions du Minuit, 1966.

_____. The Maghreb in the Modern World. Harmondsworth, England: Penguin Books, 1970.

Amos, J. C. "A Development Plan for Addis Ababa." Ethiopia Observer 6, no.1 (1962): 5-15.

Ampene, E. "Obuasi and Its Miners." Ghana Journal of Sociology 3, no.2 (1973): 73-80.

Anderson, Perry. Passages From Antiquity to Feudalism. London: New Left Books, 1974.

Apter, David E. The Political Kingdom of Uganda: A Study in Bureaucratic Nationalism. Princeton: Princeton University Press, 1961.

____. The Politics of Modernization. Chicago: University of Chicago Press, 1965.

Armor, Murray. Unauthorized Compounds in Lusaka Urban District. Lusaka: privately printed, 1957.

Ashton, A. H. "Liquor Laws in Central Africa." Paper given at the 9th annual conference of non-European administrators, 1960, Livingstone.

Asmarom, Legesse. "The Genesis of Ethiopian Urbanism. Sociological Development and Ethnographic Context of Addis Ababa." Paper presented at the Third International Congress of Africanists, December 1973, Addis Ababa.

Assefa, Mehretu. "Diffusion of Banking in Ethiopia; An Appraisal of the Process of Spatial Integration." Ethiopian Journal of Development Research 1 (April 1976): 31-70.

Baldet, Henri. "Urban Study of Dire Dawa." B.A. thesis, Department of Geography, Haile Sellassie I University, 1970.

Baldwin, Robert F. Economic Development And Export Growth. A Study of Northern Rhodesia 1920-1960. Berkeley: University of California Press, 1966.

Barber, William J. The Economy of British Central Africa: A Case Study of Economic Development in a Dualistic Society. Stanford: Stanford University Press, 1961.

Barbour, K. M., ed. Planning for Nigeria. Ibadan: Ibadan University Press, 1972.

Bardhan, Paul. "External Economies, Economic Development, and the Theory of Protection." Oxford Economic Papers 16, no 1 (March 1964): 40-54.

Bardinet, C. "Problèmes demographiques de l'urbanisation en Algérie dans la période 1962-72." Bulletin de la société languedocienne de géographie 6, no. 1 (January-March 1972): 11-33.

_____. "La répartition géographique de la population." In La démographie algérienne, Dossiers Documentaires 19-20. Algiers: Ministry of Information and Culture, 1972.

Barratt, John, et al., eds. Accelerated Development in Southern Africa. London: Macmillan, 1973.

Bascom, W. R. "The Urban African and His World." Cahier d'Études Africaines 4 (1963).

Bax, Mart. "The Political Machine and Its Importance in the Irish Republic." Political Anthropology 1 no. 1 (March 1975): 6-20.

Bekele, Haile. "Typical Urban Conditions in Developing Countries; Brief Focus Through Ethiopia's Experience." Unpublished Paper. Addis Ababa, August 1971.

Beleky, Louis. "The Development of Liberia." The Journal of Modern African Studies 2, no. 1 (1973): 43-60.

Bell, Trevor. Industrial Decentralisation in South Africa. Cape Town: Oxford University Press, 1973.

_____. "Some Aspects of Industrial Decentralisation in South Africa." South African Journal of Economics 41 (1973): 401-37.

Berg, F. J. "The Coast from the Portuguese Invasion." In Zamani: A Survey of East African History, edited by B. A. Ogot, pp. 115-34. Dar es Salaam: Longman Tanzania, Ltd., 1973.

Bernard, F. E. "East of Mount Kenya: Merv Agriculture in Transition." Ph. D. dissertation, University of Wisconsin, 1968.

Berry, Brian J. L., and A. Pred. Central Place Studies; A bibliography of Theory and Application with Supplement. Philadelphia: Regional Science Institute, 1965.

Best, Alan C. G., and Bruce S. Young. "Homeland Consolidation: The Case of Kwazulu." South African Geographer 4 (1972): 63-74.

Bettisson, Davidson. "Poverty in Central Africa." Rhodes Livingstone Institute (1959): 54-55.

Blacker, J. G. C. "Population Growth and Urbanization in Kenya." In United Nations Mission to Kenyan Housing, pp. 59-63. Nairobi: Government Printer, 1964.

Blake, G. H. Misurata: A Market Town in Tripolitania. Durham: University of Durham Research Paper in Geography, no. 9. 1968.

____. "Oil production in Libya." Geography 4 no. 2 (1969): 221-23.

Blamo, J. Bernard. "Nation-Building in Liberia: The Use of Symbols in National Integration." Liberian Studies Journal 4, no. 1 (1971-72): 21-30.

Bley, H. South-West Africa Under German Rule 1894-1914. London: Heinemann, 1971.

Board, Christopher; Ronald J. Davies; and Thomas J. D. Fair. "The Structure of the South African Space Economy." Regional Studies 4 (1970): 367-92.

Bolton, Hennessey, and Partners. Report on the Development Plan. Addis Ababa: Municipality of Addis Ababa, May 1961.

Bondestam, Lars. "A Draft Report on Urbanization of Addis Ababa." Mimeographed. Addis Ababa: Central Statistical Office, 1971.

____. "Prostitution in Addis Ababa." Mimeographed. Addis Ababa: Government Printer, 1972.

Bookchin, Murray. The Limits of the City. New York: Harper & Row, 1974.

Boserup, Ester. Woman's Role In Economic Development. London: George Allen and Unwin Press, 1970.

Boswell, David. "Personal Crises and the Mobilization of the Social Networks." In Social Networks in an Urban Situation: Analyses of Personal Relationship in Central African Towns, edited by J. Clyde Mitchell. Manchester: Manchester University Press, 1969.

Boudeville, J. R. Problems in Regional Economic Planning. Edinburgh: Edinburgh University Press, 1966.

Brenon, L. A., and Melvin Albdum. "On Rural Settlement in Israel and Model Strategy." In Models of Spatial Variation, edited by H. McConnell and D. W. Yesseen. De Kalb: Moners Northern Illinois University Press, 1971.

Brethen, Henry L. Power and Politics in Africa. Chicago: Aldine, 1973.

Breytheback, W. J. Migratory Labor Arrangements in Southern Africa. Pretoria: Africa Institute, 1972.

British South Africa Company. Report of the Acting Administrator for Mashonaland, Mr. W. H. Milton, for the Eighteen Months Ending the 30th September, 1898, the British South Africa Company Reports on the Administration of Rhodesia 1897-1898. London: British South African Company, 1899.

Bromley, Ray. "The Planning Process: Lessons of the Past and a Model for the Future." Institute of Development Studies Bulletin 9, no. 3 (February 1978).

Browett, John G., and Thomas J. D. Fair. "South Africa 1870-1970: A View of the Spatial System." South African Geographical Journal 56 (1974): 111-20.

Bundy, Colin. "The Emergence and Decline of a South African Peasantry." African Affairs 71 (1972): 369-88.

Caiden, Naomi, and A. Wildavsky, Planning and Budgeting in Poor Countries. New York: Wiley, 1974.

Callinicos, Alex, and John Rogers. Southern Africa After Soweto. London: Pluto Press, 1977.

Carter, Gwendolen M. The Politics of Inequality. London: Thames and Hudson, 1954.

Carvalho, Mario E. F. C. "Regional Physical Planning in Kenya: A Case Study." Ekistics 27, no. 161 (1969): 232-37.

Casetti, E., et al. "On the Dentification of Growth Poles in Spatial-Temporal Context." Proceedings of Canadian Geographers (1971): 35-54.

Casson, W. T. "Architectural Notes on Dar es Salaam." Tanzania Notes and Records 71 (1970): 181-83.

Central Agency for Public Mobilization and Statistics (Campas). Population and Development. Cairo: Campas, 1973.

Central Bank of Libya. "The Post-Revolution Industrial Situation in the Libyan Arab Republic." Economic Report 14, no. 7-12 (1974): 31-32.

Chadwick, G. A. A Systems View of Planning: Towards a Theory of the Urban and Regional Planning Process. Oxford: Pergamon Press, 1971.

Chittick, N. "The Coast Before the Arrival of the Portuguese." In Zamani: A Survey of East African History, edited by B. A. Ogot, pp. 98-115. Dar es Salaam: Longman Tanzania, 1973.

Clarence-Smith, W. G., and R. Moorsom. "Underdevelopment and Class Formation in Ovamboland, 1845-1915." Journal of African History 16 (1975): 365-81.

Clark, D. "The Formal and Functional Structure of Wales." Annals of the Association of American Geographic 63 (March 1973): 71-84.

Clark, Paul G. Development Planning in East Africa. Nairobi: East African Publishers House, 1965.

Clarke, J. I. "The Growth of Capital Cities in Africa." Afrika Spectrum 2 (1971): 33-40.

____. "Oil in Libya: Some Implications." Economic Geography 39 (1963): 40-59.

Clarke, Liz, and Jane Ngobese. Women Without Men. Durban: Institute for Black Research, 1975.

Clower, Robert, et al. Growth Without Development: An Economic Survey of Liberia. Evanston: Northwestern University Press, 1966.

Cobbe, James. "Wage Policy Problems in the Small Peripheral Countries of Southern Africa, 1967-76." Journal of Southern African Affairs 2, no. 4 (1977).

Cohen, A. Urban Ethnicity. London: Tavistock, 1974.

Cohen, Abner C. Custom and Politics in Urban Africa: A Study of Hausa Migrants in Yoruba Towns. Berkeley: University of California Press, 1969.

Coleman Report: Report of the United African Services Committee
    Appointed to Review the Financing of Services and Amenities
    Provided for Africans in Urban Areas. Lusaka: Government
    Printer, 1960.

Comité Permanent d'Études, de Développement, d'Organisation et
    d'Aménagement de l'agglomeration d'Alger (Comedor). Equipe
    bidonvilles—Rapport no. 1 Exploitation de l'enquête bidonvilles—
    enquête realisée par la wilaya d'Alger 1972, 1973.

____. Algiers, Étude pour la renovation de la Casbah d'Alger, vol. 4.
    Les transformations de tissu de la Casbah pendant la période
    coloniale, 1970.

Comhaire, Jean. "Urbanization in Ethiopia." Dialogue (Addis Ababa)
    1 (October 1967): 26-33.

Conroy, Michael E. "Rejection of Growth Center Strategy in Latin
    American Regional Development Planning." Land Economics
    49, no. 4 (November 1973): 371-80.

Cooley, L. S. The Deployment of the Labor Force in Lesotho (1970)
    Maseru: Central Planning and Development Office, Mimeo, 1973.

Cornaton, M. Les regroupements de la décolonisation en Algerie.
    Paris: Les Éditions ouvrières, 1967.

Darkoh, Michael B. K. "Toward A Planned Industrial Reallocation
    Pattern in Ghana." Urbanization, National Development and
    Regional Planning in Africa (ed.) Salah El-Shakhs and R. A.
    Obudho New York: Praeger, 1974: 110-129.

Darwent, D. F. "Growth Poles and Growth Centers in Residual
    Planning: A review." Environmental Planning 1 (1954): 5-32.

Davenport, Rodney. "African Townsmen? South African Native
    (Urban Areas) Legislation through the years." African Affairs
    68 (1969): 95-109.

Davidson, Basil. Africa in History. New York: Macmillan, 1968.

Davies, D. Hywel. "Lusaka, Zambia—Some Town Planning Problems
    at Independence." Zambian Urban Studies 1 (1969): 4-5.

Davies, Ronald J., and Gillian P. Cook. "Reappraisal of the South African Urban Hierarchy." South African Geographical Journal 50 (1968): 116-132.

De Blij, Harm. Dar es Salaam: A Study in Urban Geography. Evanston: Northwestern University Press, 1963.

De La Casiniere, H. Les municipalités marocaines: leur developpement, leur législation. Casablanca: Imprimerie de la Vigie Marocaine: 1924.

de Tocqueville, Alexis. Oeuvres Complètes. Paris: Gallimard, 1962.

____. The Old Regime and French Revolution. Garden City, N.Y.: Doubleday and Co., 1954.

Descloitres, R.; J. Cl. Reverdy; and Cl. Descloitres. L'Algérie des bidonvilles. Le Tiers Monde dans la cité. Paris: Mouton, 1961.

Desmond, Cosmas. The Discarded People. Johannesburg: The Christian Institute, 1971.

Despois, J. L'Afrique du Nord. Paris: Presses Universitaires de France, 1964.

Deutsch, Karl. Nerves of Government: Models of Political Communications and Control. New York: Free Press, 1963.

Diamant, Alfred. "The Nature of Political Development." In Political Development and Social Change, edited by Jason L. Findle and Richard W. Gasve. New York: Wiley, 1966.

Dobkins, W. H. "A New Residential Pattern for Lusaka." Architectural dissertation, School of Architecture, University of Edinburgh, 1966.

Doxiades Report: Report on the Greater Lusaka Area. Lusaka: Government Printer, 1969.

East Africa High Commision, East Africa Statistical Department. African Population of Kenya Colony and Protectorate: Geographical and Tribal Studies. Nairobi: Government Printer, 1950.

Easton, David. A Systems Analysis of Political Life. New York: Wiley, 1965.

Eaton-Tomer, G. W. A Short History: Ashanti Goldfield Corporation Ltd. 1897-1947. Ashanti, Ghana: Ashanti Goldfields Corp. Ltd., 1947.

Eccles Report: Report on the administration and finance of Native Locations in urban areas. Lusaka: Government Printer, 1944.

Economic Commission for Africa, (ECA). Cooperative Housing Pilot Project. (Kijitonyama) Dar-Es-Salaam: (UNESCO, 1972).

Eggenhuizen, Toine, and Dan Matsobane, eds. Another Blanket. Horison: African Inland Mission, 1976.

Egypt, Ministry of Housing and Reconstruction. The Planning of Sadat City: Status Report No. 1. Cairo: Ministry of Housing Reconstruction, 1974.

Ehret, C. "Cushites and the Highland and Plains Nilotes to A.D. 1800." In Zamani: A Survey of East African History, edited by B. A. Ogot, pp. 150-69. Dar Es Salaam: Longman Tanzania, Ltd., 1973.

Eisenstadt, S. N. The Political Systems of Empires. New York: Praeger, 1963.

Elkan, Walter. Migrants and Proletarians. Oxford University Press, 1960.

El-Sadat, President Anwar. October Working Paper. Cairo: Government Press, 1974.

El-Shakhs, Salah. "National Factors in the Development of Cairo." Town Planning Review 42, no. 3 (July 1972).

____. "New Cities in the Desert: Pattern of Forced Urbanization and Modernization in Egypt." Paper delivered at the Middle East Studies Association's Annual Conference, 1974, New York City.

El-Shakhs, Salah S., and R. A. Obudho. Urbanization, National Development and Regional Planning in Africa. New York: Praeger, 1974.

Engels, Frederick. Anti-Duhring. New York: International, 1939.

Epstein, A. L. "The Network and Urban Social Organization." In Social Networks in Urban Situations: Analyses of Personal

Relationships in Central African Towns, edited by J. Clyde
Mitchell, pp. 77-116. Manchester: Manchester University Press,
1969.

____. Politics in an Urban African Community. Manchester:
Manchester University Press, 1958.

Escallier, R. "La croissance urbain au Maroc." Annuaire de
l'Afrique du Nord. 11 (1973) 145-73.

Etherington, D. M. "Projected Changes in Urban and Rural Population in Kenya and its Implication for Development Policy."
East African Economic Review 1, no. 2 (1965): 1-19.

Ethiopia, Central Statistical Office. Population and Housing Charac-
teristics of Asmara; Results of the 1968 Population and Housing
Censuses. Statistical Bulletin, no. 2. Addis Ababa: Government
Printer, December 1974.

____. Population of Addis Ababa. Statistical Bulletin, no. 8. Addis
Ababa: Crown Stationery Office, 1972.

____. Survey of Major Towns in Ethiopia. Statistical Bulletin, no. 1.
Addis Ababa: Crown Stationery Office, December 1968.

____. Urbanization in Ethiopia. Statistical Bulletin, no. 9. Addis
Ababa: Crown Stationery Office, August 1972.

Ethiopia, Ministry of Interior. General Analysis and the Report on
the Master Plan for Harar. Addis Ababa: Ministry of Interior,
Municipalities Department, 1966.

____. "Municipalities Department Work Report and Development
Plan." Translated by Seleski Sisaye. Addis Ababa: Municipalities
Department, 1971.

Ethiopia, Planning Commission. Ethiopia's Third Five-Year Development Plan (1968-1973). Addis Ababa: Planning Commission, 1968.

____. "A Summary Assessment of Past Performance." Addis Ababa:
Planning Commission, 1971.

Evers, Hans-Dieter. "Urban Expansion and Landownership in Underdeveloped Societies." Urban Affairs Quarterly 11 (September
1975): 117-29.

Faber, Michael, and Dudley Seers, eds. The Crisis in Planning. London: Chatto & Windus, 1972.

Fadiman, J. A. "Early History of the Men of Mt. Kenya." Journal of African History 14, no. 1 (1973): 9-27.

Fair, T. J. D. "Growth Centre Strategy in South Africa." In, Proceedings of the Urban and Regional Development Seminar, edited by Keith S. O. Beavon, and T. J. D. Fair, pp. 152-60. Johannesburg: South African Geographical Society, 1973.

____. "Polarisation, Dispersion and Decentralisation in the South African Space Economy." Urban and Regional Research Unit Occasional Paper, no. 7. Witwatersrand: University of the Witwatersrand, 1975.

____. "A Regional Approach to Economic Development in Kenya." South Africa Geographical Journal 45 (1963): 55-77.

____. "Some Spatial Aspects of Black Homelands Development in South Africa." Urban and Regional Research Unit Occasional Paper, no. 6. Witwatersrand: University of the Witwatersrand, 1975.

____, and Charles F. Schmidt. "Contained Urbanisation: A Case Study." South African Geographical Journal 56 (1974): 155-66.

Famoriyo, S. "Land Transactions and Agricultural Development in Nigeria." Eastern African Journal of Rural Development 7, nos. 1-2 (1974): 179-88.

Fanon, Frantz. The Wretched of the Earth. New York: Coneve Press, 1963.

Fearn, Hugh. An African Economic Study of the Economic Development of Nyanza Province of Kenya 1903-1953. London: Oxford University Press, 1961.

Fikru, Dessalegne. "Financial Administration in the Municipality of Addis Ababa." B.A. thesis, Haile Sellassi I University, Department of Public Administration, 1973.

Franchet, J. "La formulation de l'espace algérien." In Villes et sociétés au Maghreb—études sur l'urbanisation, pp. 39-53. Paris: Centre Nationale de la Recherche Scientifique, 1974.

Frank, F. E., and M. L. McNulty. "A Strategy for Co-ordination of Human and Technical Reserves in Planning: The Lagos-Ibadan Corridor." In Urbanization, National Development and Regional Planning in Africa, edited by Salah El-Shakhs and R. A. Obudho, pp. 177-99. New York: Praeger, 1974.

French Mission for Town Planning. The City of Addis Ababa: Master Plan Surveys. Secretariat des Missions d'Urbanisme et d'Habitat, 1967.

Friedman, John. "The Concepts of a Regional Plan, The Evolution of the Idea in the United States." In Regional Development and Planning, edited by John Friedman and William Alonso, pp. 497-518. Cambridge, Mass.: Massachusetts Institute of Technology Press, 1964.

____. "A General Theory of Polarized Development." In Growth Centers in Regional Economic Development, edited by N. Hansen, pp. 82-107. New York: Free Press, 1972.

____. "The Role of Cities in National Development." In Latin American Urban Policies and Social Sciences, edited by John Miller and Ralph A. Gakenheimer, pp. 167-208. Beverly Hills, Calif.: Sage, 1973.

____. "The Strategy of Deliberate Urbanization." Journal of the Institute of American Planners 24, no. 6 (November 1968): 364-73.

____. Urbanization, Planning, and National Development. Beverly Hills, Calif.: Sage, 1973.

____, and W. Stohr. "The Uses of Regional Sciences, Policy Planning in Chile." Papers and Proceedings of Regional Science Association 18 (1967): 207-22.

____, and Flora Sullivan. "The Absorption of Labor in the Urban Economy: The Case of Developing Countries." Economic Development and Cultural Change 22, no. 3 (April 1974): 385-413.

Ganiage, J. Les affaires d'Afrique du Nord de 1930 à 1958. Paris: Centre de Documentation Universitaire, 1972.

Gann, L. H. A History of Northern Rhodesia. London: Chatto and Windus, 1964.

Gans, Herbert. The Urban Villagers; Group and Class in the Life of Hatian Americans. Glencoe, Ill.: Free Press of Glencoe, 1962.

Garretson, Peter P. A History of Addis Ababa from its Foundation in 1886 to 1910. Ph. D. dissertation, University of London, 1974.

General Organization for Physical Planning (G.O.P.P.). Suez Canal Plan. Cairo: G.O.P.P., 1974.

Georgulas, N. Settlement Patterns and Rural Development in Tanganyika. Program of East African Studies, Maxwell School of Citizenship and Public Affairs, Occasional Paper, no. 29, Syracuse: Syracuse University, 1967.

Ghana, Republic of. Report of the Commission of Enquiry into Obuasi; Disturbances 1969. Accra: Government Printer, 1970.

____, Census Office. 1970 Population Census of Ghana. Volume II: Statistics of Localities and Enumeration Areas. Accra: Government Printer, 1972.

Gibb, Sir Alexander, and Partners. A Plan for Dar-Es-Salaam. London: Government Printer, 1949.

Glass, Y. "Industrialization and Urbanization in South Africa." In Problems of Transition, edited by J. F. Holleman, et al., pp. 52-80. Durban: Institute for Social Research, University of Natal, 1964.

Gold, J. M. "African Urbanization in Kenya." Journal of African Administration 13, no. 1 (January 1961): 24-28.

Goldblatt, I. History of South West Africa. Cape Town: Juta, 1971.

Gonzales, N. Black Carib Household Structure. Seattle: University of Washington Press, 1969.

Gordon, Loraine et al. Survey of Race Relations in South Africa 1977. Johannesburg: South African Institute of Race Relations, 1978.

Gould, W. T. S. "Problems of Secondary School Provision in African Cities: The Example of Addis Ababa, Ethiopia." Department of Geography, Working Paper, no. 5. Liverpool: University of Liverpool, 1973.

BIBLIOGRAPHY / 359

Goulet, Denis. The Cruel Choice. New York: Atheneum, 1971.

Gouvernement Cherifien. Annuaire statistique de la zone française du Maroc, 1952. Rabat: Service Central des Statistiques, 1952.

Gray, R. The Two Nations: Aspects of the Development of Race Relations in the Rhodesias and Nyasaland. London: Oxford University Press, 1960.

Great Britain. Financial and Economic Position of Basutoland. (Pim Report), cmd. 4907 (London: Her Majesty's Stationary Office, 1935).

____, Colonial Office. Report of the East Africa Commission. London: Her Majesty's Stationery Office, 1956.

Greater Cairo Planning Commission (G.C.P.C.). General Plan for Greater Cairo. Cairo: G.C.P.C., 1970.

Green, L. Nigeria: Population Models for National and Regional Planning 1952-67. Ibadan: National Institute of Social and Economic Research, 1969.

____, and V. Milone. Urbanization in Nigeria—A Planning Commentary. New York: Ford Foundation, 1973.

Griffin, Keith B., and John L. Enos. Planning Development. Reading, Mass.: Addison Wesley, 1970.

Grillo, Ralph D. "African Railwaymen." African Studies Series no. 10. London: Cambridge University Press, 1973.

Gutkind, Peter C., ed. The Passing of Tribal Man in Africa. Leiden: E. J. Brill, 1970.

Hamnett, I. "Land Shortage in Lesotho." African Affairs. (January 1973): 72-86.

Hance, William A. Population, Migration, and Urbanization in Africa. New York: Columbia University Press, 1970.

Hanna, William, and Judith Hanna. Urban Dynamics in Black Africa: An Interdisciplinary Approach. Chicago: Aldine, 1977.

Hansen, L. M. et al. The Economic Development Prospects of Tanzania, Vol. I: The Main Report. Washington, D.C.: International Bank for Reconstruction and Development, 1972.

Harris, John, Henry Rempel, and Michael Todaro. "Rural-Urban Labor Migration: A Tabulation of the Responses to the Questionnaire in the Migration Survey." Institute for Development Studies, Discussion Paper, no. 92. Nairobi: Nairobi University, March 1970.

Harroy, Jean-Paul. "The Politican, Economic, and Social Role as Urban Agglomeration in Countries of the Third World." Civilizations 17 (1967): 167-70.

Harsch, Ernest. "Cities in Decay." International Society Review 34, no. 6 (1973): 137.

Hartley, R. G. "Libya: Economic Development and Demographic Responses." In The Populations of the Middle East and North Africa, edited by J. I. Clarke and W. B. Fisher. London: University of London Press, 1972.

Harvey, David. Social Justice and the City. Baltimore: The Johns Hopkins University Press, 1973.

Hasselman, Karl-Heinz. "Migrancy and its Effect on the Economy in Liberia." The Liberian Economic and Management Review 11, no. 1 (1973-74): 3-34.

Hauser, P. M., and L. F. Schnore. The Study of Urbanization. New York: Wiley, 1965.

____. "Urbanization: An Overview." In The Study of Urbanization, edited by Phillip Hauser and L. Schnore. New York: Wiley, 1967.

Helleiner, G. K. "Beyond Growth Rates and Plan Volumes-Planning for Africa in the 1970's." Journal of Modern African Studies 10, no. 3 (October 1972).

Henissart, P. Wolves in the City—the Death of French Algeria. London: Rupert Hart-Davis, 1970.

Hill, Polly. "A Plea for Indigenous Economics: The West African Example." Economic Development and Cultural Change. (1966).

Hirschmann, Albert O. The Strategy of Economic Development. New Haven: Yale University Press, 1958.

Horton, Frank E., and Michael L. McNulty. Problems in the Application of Planning Methodologies in Developing Countries. Institute of Urban and Regional Research Technical Report, no. 22. Iowa City: University of Iowa, 1973.

Horrell, Muriel, et al. A Survey of Race Relations in South Africa, 1972. Johannesburg; Institute of Race Relations, 1973.

Horsch, Ernest. "Cities in Decay." International Society Review 34, no.6 (1973).

Horvath, Ronald J. "Towns in Ethiopia." Erdkunde 22 (1968): 41-52.

____. "The Wandering Capitals of Ethiopia." Journal of African History 10, no.2 (1969): 205-19.

Hosken, Franziska. "Urban Development and Housing in Africa." Harvard University Library, Cambridge, Mass.

Hunter, Guy. Modernizing Peasant Societies: A Comparative Study of Asia and Africa. London: Oxford University Press, 1969.

Iichman, Warren F., and Norman T. Uphoff. The Political Economy of Change. Berkeley: University of California Press, 1971.

Imoagene, O. "The Impact of Industrialization and Urbanization on the People of Nigeria." Presence Africaine 96 (1975).

Internation Union of Local Authorities. Urbanization in Developing Countries. The Hague: Martinus Nijhoff, 1968.

International African Institute. Social Implications of Industralization and Urbanization in Africa South of Sahara. Paris: UNESCO, 1956.

International Bank for Reconstruction and Development (IBRD). "Appraisal of the Addis Ababa Water Supply and Sewerage Project." IBRD report. Addis Ababa, IBRD, March 1972.

Isard, Walter, and R. E. Kumene. "The Impact of Steel Upon the Greater New York-Philadelphia Industrial Region." Review of Economics and Statistics (November 1953): 389-401.

Jilbert, John. "Notes on Population Change in Lesotho 1966-76." South African Journal of African Affairs 7, no. 1 (1977).

Johnson, E. A. J. The Organization of Space in Developing Countries. Cambridge: Harvard University Press, 1970.

Johnson, G. E., and W. E. Whitelaw. "Urban-Rural Income Transfers in Kenya: An Estimated-Remittances Function." Economic Development and Cultural Change 22, no. 3 (April 1974): 477-78.

Jones, D. Caradog. The Social Survey of Merseyside. London: Oxford University Press, 1934.

Jordan, Robert S., and John P. Renninger. "The New Environment of Nation Building." Journal of Modern African Studies 13 (June 1975): 187-207.

Kay, George. A Social Geography of Zambia. London: University of London Press, 1967.

Kenya, Republic of. Kenya Colony and Protectorate, Geological Survey. Mining Pamphlet, no. 1. Nairobi: Government Printer, 1953.

Kenya, Republic of, Ministry of Finance, Economic Planning and Development, Statistics Division. Development Plan, 1970-1974. Nairobi: Government Printer, 1970.

____. Population Census 1962, Advance Report of Volumes I and II. Nairobi: Government Printer, 1964.

____. Ministry of Finance and Economic Planning, Directorate of Economic Planning. Kenya Population Census 1962, Vol. I: Population of Census Areas by Sex and Age Group. Nairobi: Government Printer, 1964.

____. Kenya Population Census 1962, Vol. II: Populations of Location and Country Council Wards by Race, Tribe and Sex. Nairobi: Government Printer, 1963.

____. Kenya Population Census 1962, Vol. III: African Population. Nairobi: Government Printer, 1966.

____. Kenya Population Census 1969. Vol. I. Nairobi: Government Printer, November 1970.

Kenya, Republic of, Ministry of Lands and Settlement. "The Future Growth of Kenya's Population and Its Consequences." Kenya Statistical Digest 9, no. 2 (June 1971): 3-4.

____. "Population Growth and Urbanization in Kenya." Kenya Statistical Digest 2, no. 2 (September 1964): 3-4.

____. "Population Growth in Kenya, 1948-1962." Kenya Statistical Digest, 1, no. 1 (September 1953): 3-4.

____. A Study of the Possible Distribution of Urban Growth in Kenya as a Framework for Physical Planning. Nairobi: Town Planning Department, 1969.

Kenya, Republic of, Ministry of Lands and Settlement, Statistics Division. Kenya Population Census 1969, Vol. II: Data on Urban Population. Nairobi: Government Printer, 1971.

____. Kenya Population Census 1969, Vol. III: Data on Education, Relationship to Head of Household, Birthplace and Marital Status. Nairobi: Government Printer, 1971.

Killick, Tony. "The Possibilities of Development Planning." Oxford Economic Papers 28, no. 2, (July 1976).

Kimani, S. M., and D. R. F. Taylor. Growth Centers and Rural Development. Thika, Kenya: Maxim Printer, 1973.

Knupfer, Genevieve. "Portrait of the Underdog." Public Opinion Quarterly (Spring 1947): 103-14.

Koehn, Peter. "The Municipality of Addis Ababa, Ethiopia: Performance, Mobilization, Integration, and Change." Ph. D. dissertation, University of Colorado, 1973.

____, and John M. Cohen. "Local Government in Ethiopia: Independence and Variability in a Deconcentrated System." Quarterly Journal of Administration 9 (July 1975): 369-86.

Koenigsberger Report: Report on the Infrastructure Problems of the Cities of Developing Countries. New York: Foundation Press, 1971.

Komarovsky, Mirra. "The Voluntary Associations of Urban Dwellers." American Sociological Review 11 (December 1946): 689-98.

Konjit, Meshesha. "Empty Spaces in Addis Ababa." B.A. thesis, Department of Geography, Haile Sellassie I University, May 1967.

Kuklinski, Antoni R. "Education for Regional Planning." In Issues in Regional Planning, edited by David Dunham and Joseph Hilborst. The Hague: Mouton, 1971.

_____. Growth Poles and Growth Centers in Regional Planning. Paris: Mouton, 1972.

Kuznets, S. "Industrialization, Urbanization and Consumption." In Industrialization and Society, edited by B. Hoselitz and W. Moore. Paris: UNESCO, 1963.

"La circulation routière à Ouagadougou." Le développement voltaique 25 (1975): 9-10.

Lampard, E. C. "The Histories of Cities in the Economically Advanced Areas." Economic Development of Cultural Change 3 (January 1955): 81-137.

Landell-Mills, P. M. "The 1969 Southern African Customs Union Agreement." Journal of Modern African Studies 9, no. 2 (August 1971).

Lapham, R. J. "Population Policies in the Maghreb." Middle East Journal 26, no. 1 (Winter 1972): 1-10.

Lawless, R. I. "Centrality and the Evolution of a Central Place Hierarchy in Western Algeria." Paper presented at the Developing Areas Study Group meeting on Marketing and Central Place Systems in Less Developed Countries, Annual Conference, Institute of British Geographers, January 1975, Oxford.

_____, and G. H. Blake. Tlemcen: Continuity and Change in an Algerian Islamic Town (Epping, Essex: Gower Press, 1976).

Le Coz, J. "De l'urbanisation sauvage a l'urbanisation integrée." Bulletin de la Société Languedocienne de Géographie 6, no. 1 (January-March 1972): 5-9.

Ledda, Romana. "Social Classes and Political Struggle." International Socialist Journal 2 (August 1967).

Legassick, Martin. "Legislation, Ideology and Economy in Post-1948 South Africa." Journal of Southern African Studies 1 (1974): 3-35.

_____. "South Africa: Capital Accumulation and Violence." Economy and Society 3, no. 3 (1974): 253-91.

_____, and David Hemson. Foreign Investment and the Reproduction of Racial Capitalism in South Africa. London: Anti-Apartheid Movement, 1976.

Lerner, Daniel. "Comparative Analysis of Process of Modern-ization." In The City in Africa, edited by Horace Miner, pp. 21-38. New York: Praeger, 1967.

Leslie, J. A. K. A Survey of Dar es Salaam. London: Oxford University Press, 1963.

Lesotho, Kingdom of. Lesotho First Five-Year Development Plan 1970/71-1974/75. Maseru: Government Printer, 1970.

_____. Report and Papers of the Donor Conference, April 1975. Maseru: Central Planning and Development Office, 1975.

_____. Second Five Year Development Plan 1976/76-1979/80. Maseru: Government Printer, 1976.

Libyan Arab Republic. Housing and Establishment Census Preliminary Results. Tripoli: Ministry of Planning, Census and Statistical Department, 1973.

_____. Population Census, Preliminary Results. Tripoli: Ministry of Planning, Census and Statistical Department, 1973.

Liebenow, Gus J. Agriculture, Education and Rural Transformation. Bloomington, Ind. Carnegie Seminar on Political and Administrative Development, 1969.

_____. The Evolution of Privilege. Ithaca, N.Y.: Cornell University Press, 1969.

Little, Kenneth L. West African Urbanization: A Study of Voluntary Associations in Social Change. Cambridge: Cambridge University Press, 1965.

Lloyd, Peter C. Africa in Social Change: Changing Traditional Societies in Modern World. Baltimore: Penguin Books, 1969.

Logan, M. I. "Key Elements and Linkages in the National System: A Focus for Regional Planning in Nigeria." In Planning for Nigeria, edited by K. M. Barbour, pp.16-39. Ibadan: University of Ibadan, 1972.

Lombard, Johannes A. "Problems of Regional Economic Program-ming in the Development of the Bantu Homelands." South African Journal of Economics 39 (1971): 388-401.

Lublin McGaughy (Libya) Ltd. Planning Report for the New Town of El Marj. Benghazi: Barce Reconstruction Organisation, 1964.

Lusaka, City Council of. Greater Lusaka: A Guide to City Residents. Lusaka: Government Printer, 1970.

Lusaka, City of, Information Centre. Facts on Lusaka. Lusaka: Information Centre, 1970.

Lwabuti, J. V. "Urban Housing Cooperatives." Mimeographed circular, Dar es Salaam: Registrar of Cooperatives, 1973.

Maasdorp, Gavin G. Economic Development for the Homelands. Johannesburg: South African Institute of Race Relations, 1974.

_____, and A. S. B. Humphreys. From Shantytown to Township. Cape Town: Juta, 1975.

Maaza, Bekele, and Lars Bondestam. "Ethiopia: A Case of the Interrelations of Population with Economic and Social Development." Paper presented to the African Population Conference, December 9-18, 1971, Accra Ghana.

Mabogunje, Akin L. "Regional Planning and the Development Process: Prospects in the 1970-74 Plan." In Planning for Nigeria, edited by K. M. Barbour. Ibadan: University of Ibadan Press, 1972.

_____. "Towards an Urban Policy in Nigeria." Nigerian Journal of Economic and Social Studies 16, no. 1 (March 1974): 85-97.

_____. Urbanization in Nigeria. New York: Africana Publishing Company, 1968.

_____. "Urbanization Problems in Africa." In Urbanization, National Development and Regional Development, edited by Salah El-Shakhs and R. A. Obudho, pp. 13-25. New York: Praeger, 1974.

Mabin, Alan S., and Sally Biesheuvel. "Spatial Implications of Apartheid: The Role of Growth Centres in South Africa." Pan-African Journal 9, no. 1 (1976): 1-16.

McCallum, J. S. "Planning Theory in Planning Education." The Planner Journal of the Royal Town Planning Institute 60, no. 6 (1974): 738-41.

McClintock, Hugh. "The Planning of Kisumu's Peri-Urban Areas." The Planner 7, no. 59 (July-August 1973): 328-29.

McGaughy, K., et al. Master Plan for the City of Misratah 1988. Tripoli: Ministry of Planning and Development, Kingdom of Libya, 1967.

MacKay, J. R. "The interactance Hypothesis and Boundaries in Canada: A Preliminary Study." The Canadian Geographer 2 (1958): 1-8.

McKee, S. Ian D. "Towards a National Physical Planning for Kenya." In Report of the Proceedings of the Town and Country Planning Summer School, pp. 65-69. University of Swansea, 1970. (London).

McNulty, M. L. "African Urban Systems, Transportation Networks and Regional Inequalities." African Urban Notes 6, no. 3 (1972).

Madavo, C. E. "Uncontrolled Settlements." Finance and Development 13-14 (1976-77): 18-19.

Magubane, Bernard. "The Native Reserves (Bantustans) and the Role of the Migrant Labor Systems in the Political Economy of South Africa. In Migration and Development, edited by Helen I. Safa and Brian M. Du Toit, pp. 225-67. The Hague: Manhen, 1975.

_____, and A. Moriotti. "Urban Ethnology in Africa—Some Theoretical Issues." A paper presented at the IXth International Congress of Anthropological and Ethnological Sciences, August-September, 1973.

Manchotte, Marie-Therese. Les Quartiers Spontanes de Ouagadougou. Ouagadougou: Ministry of Public Works, Transportation, and Urbanism, March 1973.

Mandel, Ernest. Marxist Economic Theory Vol. II translated Brian Pearce New York: Monthly Review Press, 1968.

Maree, Johan and Pieter J. de Vos. Underemployment, Poverty and Migrant Labour. Johannesburg: South African Institute of Race Relations, 1975.

Markakis, John. Ethiopia: Anatomy of a Traditional Polity. London: Oxford University Press, 1974.

Maroc, Royaume du, Division du Plan et des Statistiques. La situation économique du Maroc en 1964. Rabat: Service Central des Statistique, May 1965.

Maroc, Royaume du, Direction des Statistiques. Population légale du Maroc d'après le recensement général de la population et de l'habitat, 1971. Rabat: Direction des Statistiques, December 1971.

Maroc, Royaume du, Service Central des Statistiques. Recensement démographique, Juin 1960: Population légale du Maroc. Rabat: Service Central des Statistiques, June 1961.

____. Résultats du recensement de 1960, I: Nationalité, Sexe, Age. Rabat: Service Central des Statistique, 1965.

Martelot, R. "Les bidonvilles encasernés: Contribution a l'étude du surpeuplement à Alger." In Les influences occidentales dans les billes Maghrebines a l'epoque contemporaine. Études Méditerranéenes 2, 74: 123-33.

Marx, Karl Genesis of Capital Moscow: Progress Publishers, 1969.

____, and Frederick Engels. On Britain. Moscow: Foreign Language Publishing House, 1962.

Mason, P. The Birth of a Dilemma. London: Oxford University Press, 1958.

Mayer, Phillip. Townsmen or Tribesmen. Capetown: Oxford University Press, 1961.

Mehmel, Ozay. "Administrative Machinery for Development Planning in Liberia." Journal of Modern Africa Studies 13, no. 3 (September 1975): 310-11.

Meillasoux, Claude. Urbanization of an African Community: Voluntary Associations in Bamako. Seattle: University of Washington Press, 1968.

Mesfin, Wolde Marian. "Problems of Urbanization." In Proceedings of the Third International Conference of Ethiopian Studies; Addis Ababa, 1966, vol. 3, pp. 20-38. Addis Ababa: Haile Sellassie I University, Institute of Ethiopian Studies, 1970.

____. "The Rural-Urban Split in Ethiopia." Dialogue (Addis Ababa) 2 (December 1968): 7-16.

Mintz, Sidney. "Men, Women and Trade." Comparative Studies in Society and History 13, no. 3 (July 1971): 247-69.

Mitchell, J. C., ed. Social Networks in an Urban Situation. Manchester: University of Manchester Press, 1969.

_____. Tribalism and the Plural Society: An Inaugural Lecture. London: Oxford University Press, 1960.

Mlia, N. Justice. "National Urban Development Policy: The Issues and the Options." In Urbanization, National Development and Regional Planning in Africa, edited by Salah El-Shakhs and R. A. Obudho, pp. 75-87. New York: Praeger, 1974.

Montagne, Robert. Naissance du prolétariat marocaine: Enquête collective executée de 1948 à 1950. Paris: Peyronner et Cie., 1950.

Moore, C. H. "Old and New Elites in North Africa: The French Colonial Impact in Comparative Perspective." In Les influences occidentales dans les villes maghrebines à l'époque contemporaine, pp. 17-37. 1974.

Morgan, W. T. W. "Urbanization in Kenya: Origins and Trends." Proceedings and Transactions of Institute of British Geographers 46 (March 1969): 167-78.

Moriaty, Denis. "Kenya Houses Its Africans." Town and Country Planning 23 (August 1955): 369-74.

Morrison, G., et al. Black Africa: A Comparative Handbook. New York: Free Press, 1972.

Mosley, Paul. "The Southern African Customs Union: A Reappraisal." World Development 6, no. 1 (January 1978).

Mumford, Lewis. The City in History. New York: Harcourt, Brace & World Inc., 1961.

Murdock, G. P. Africa: Its People and Their Cultural History. New York: McGraw-Hill, 1958.

Murphy, E. J. History of African Civilization. New York: Delta, 1972.

Murray, Roger, and I. Wengraf. "The Algerian Revolution." New Left Review 22 (1963): 14-65.

Myrdal, Gunnar. Rich Lands and Poor. New York: Harper & Brothers, 1957.

Naipaul, V. S. In A Free State. Harmondsworth: Penguin Books, 1973.

Nattrass, Jill. "The Migrant Labour System in South Africa's Economic Development." South African Journal of Economics 44, no. 1 (1976): 65-83.

Neal, D. F. "Liberia's Trade Pattern 1940-1968." Liberian Studies Journal 4, no. 1 (1971-72): 1-17.

Nigam, S. B. L. Employment and Income Distribution Approach in Development Plans of African Countries. Addis Ababa: International Labor Organization, ILO Jobs and Skills Programme for Africa, 1975.

Nigeria, Federal Government of Ministry of Economic Development. The Third National Development Plan 1975-1980. Lagos: Government Printer, 1976.

Nigeria, Federal Ministry of Information. The Report of Committee on the Location of the Federal Capital of Nigeria. Lagos: Government Printer, 1976.

Norris, M. N. "Ethiopian Municipal Administration and the Approach to Local Government Reform." Planning and Administration (Winter 1974): 47-74.

Nwosu, S. "Obstacles to Economic Development," Africa 22 (June 1973): 48.

Nyerere, Julius. Ujamaa: Essays on Socialism. London: Osgood University Press, 1968.

Nystuen, J. D., and M. F. Dacey. "A Graph Theory Interpretation of Modal Regions." Papers and Proceedings of the Regional Science Association 7 (1961): 29-42.

Obudho, R. A. "The Central Places in Nyanza Province, Kenya." African Urban Notes 5, no. 4 (Winter 1970): 71-88.

____. "The Hierarchy of Urban Centers in Kenya." Town Planning Institute Journal 56, no. 8 (September-October 1970).

____. "The Urban Geography of Kisumu, Kenya: Materials and Research." A Current Bibliography on African Affairs 16 (November 1971): 391-96.

____. "Urbanization and Regional Planning in Western Kenya." In Urbanization, National Development and Regional Planning in Africa, edited by Salah El-Shakhs and R. A. Obudho, pp. 161-76. New York: Praeger, 1974.

____. "A Note on Urbanization and Development Planning in Africa." Pan African Journal 8, no. 3 (1975): 243-45.

____. "A Strategy in Periodic Market, Urbanization and Regional Development Planning in Africa." Pan African Journal 8, no. 3 (1975): 319-45.

____. "Urbanization and Development in Kenya: An Historical Appreciation." African Urban Notes 1, no. 3 (Fall 1975): 1-56.

____, and Constance E. Obudho. Urbanization, City and Regional Planning of Metropolitan Kisumu: A Bibliography Survey of an East African City. Council of Planning Librarian Exchange Bibliography, no. 278. Monticello, Ill.: CPLE, April 1972.

____, and Peter P. Waller. "City, Urbanization and Regional Planning in Africa: An Intranational and International Problem." Pan Africa Journal 9, no. 2 (1976): 89-91.

____. Periodic Markets Urbanization and Regional Planning. Westport, Conn.: Greenwood Press, 1976.

____. "Spatial Dimension and Demographic Dynamics of Kenya's Urban Subsystems." Pan African Journal 9, no. 2 (1976): 103-34.

____. "Social Indicators for Housing and Urban Development in Africa: Towards a New Development Model." Social Indicators Research Journal 3, no. 314 (December 1976): 431-50.

O'Connor, A. M. "New Railway Construction and the Pattern of Economic Development in East Africa." Transaction Institute of British Geographers 36 (June 1965): 21-30.

Odingo, R. S. The Kenya Highlands Land Use and Agricultural Development. Nairobi: East Africa, 1972.

O'Donnell, G. A. Modernization and Bureaucratic-Authoritarianism: Studies in South American Politics. Berkeley: California Institute of International Studies, 1973.

Ogendo, R. B. Industrial Geography of Kenya with Special Emphasis on the Agricultural Processing and Fabricating Industries. Nairobi: East African, 1972.

_____. "Location and Structure of Kenya's Industries." In Studies in East Africa Geography and Development, edited by S. H. Ominde, pp. 230-38. Berkeley: University of California Press, 1971.

_____. "Manufacturing Industries." In Nairobi City and Region, edited by W. T. W. Morgan, pp. 121-290. Nairobi: Oxford University Press, 1967.

_____. "Some Aspects of Geography of Electricity in Kenya." In Proceedings of East Africa Academy, pp. 835-90. Nairobi: Longmans, 1965.

_____. "The Significance of Industrial Zoning to Rural Industrial Development in Kenya A Study of the Facts and Methodology." Cahiers d'études africaines 7 (1967): 444-84.

Ogot, B. A. Peoples of East Africa: History of the Southern Luo, Vol. I: Migration and Settlement 1500-1900. Nairobi: East African, 1967.

_____, ed. Hadith 1. Nairobi: East African, 1968.

_____. Hadith 2. Nairobi: East African, 1970.

_____, and J. A. Kieran. Zamani: A Survey of East African History. Nairobi: East African, 1968.

Ojany, F. F., and Ogendo, R. B. Kenya: A Study of Physical and Human Geography. New York: Longmans, 1974.

Olivier, M. J. Native Policy and Administration in the Mandated Territory of South West Africa. Ph.D. dissertation, Stellenbosch University, 1964, chap. 6.

Oloo, Dick, ed. Urbanization, Its Social Problems and Consequences. Nairobi: East Africa, 1969.

Ominde, S. H. Land and Population Movements in Kenya. Evanston, Ill.: Northwestern University Press, 1968.

____. "Migration and Child-Bearing in Kenya." In Economic Growth and Economic Development in Africa, edited by S. H. Ominde and C. N. Enjiogu, pp. 193-97. London: Heinemann, 1972.

____. "Migration of the 15-44 Year Age Group in Kenya." In Proceedings of the Social Science Council Conference 1968/1969 Geography Papers, pp. 43-62. Kampala: Consolidated Printers, Ltd. , 1969.

____. "Population Movements to the Urban Areas of Kenya." Cahiers d'études africaines 5, no. 20 (1965): 593-617.

____. "Problems of Land and Population in Lake Districts of Western Kenya." In Proceedings of the East African Academy, pp. 23-36. Nairobi: Oxford University Press, 1964.

____. "Rural Economy in West Kenya." In Studies in East African Geography and Development, edited by S. H. Ominde, pp. 207-29. Berkeley: University of California Press, 1971.

____. "Rural Population Patterns and Problems of the Kikuyu, Embu and Meru Districts of Kenya." In Proceedings of the East Africa Academy, Vol. II, 1964, pp. 36-45. Nairobi: Longmans, 1966.

____. "The Semi-Arid and Arid Lands in Kenya." In Studies in East African Geography and Development, edited by S. H. Ominde, pp. 145-61. Berkeley: University of California Press, 1971.

____. Studies in East African Geography and Development. Berkeley: University of California Press, 1971.

____, and Charles N. Ejiogu. Population Growth and Economic Development in Africa. London: Heinemann, 1972.

Orde-Brown, G. St. The African Labourer. London: Frank Cass, 1967.

Owusu, Maxwell. Uses and Abuses of Political Power. Chicago: University of Chicago Press, 1970.

Paden, John. Religion and Political Culture in Kano. Berkeley: University of California Press, 1973.

Pal, Dilip K. "Urban Development Potential in Libya; a Speculation in Form and Structure." Paper presented at the Faculty of Arts International Geographical Conference, University of Benghasi, Libya, March 1975.

Palen, John J. "Housing in a Developing Nation: The Case of Addis Ababa." Land Economics (November 1974): 428-34.

Pankhurst, Rich. "Notes on the Demographic History of Ethiopian Towns and Villages." Ethiopia Observer 9, no. 1 (1965): 60-83.

_____. State and Land in Ethiopia. Monographs in Ethiopian Land Tenure, no. 3. Addis Ababa. Institute of Ethiopian Studies and Faculty of Law, Haile Selassie I University, 1966.

Parker, Mary. "Municipal Government and the Growth of African Political Institutions in Urban Areas." Zaire 3 (June 1949): 649-62.

_____. "Social and Political Development in Kenya Urban Society." Problèmes de l'Afrique Centrale 1, no. 15 (1962): 12-19.

Pauwels, I. J. "The Importance of Planned Urbanization and of the Development of the Construction Industry in Developing Countries." Planning and Administration 2 (September 1975).

Pechoux, P. Y., et al. "La part des quartiers d'habitat précaire dans la croissance récente de Mostaganem." Bulletin de la société languedocienne de géographie 6, no. 1 (January-March 1972).

Pendleton, Wade C. Katutura: A Place Where We Do Not Stay. San Diego, Calif.: San Diego State University Press, 1978.

Perkin, David J. Neighbors and National in an African City Ward. Berkeley: University of California Press, 1969.

_____. "Types of African Marriage in Kampala." Africa 36 (1966): 269-85.

Perloff, Harvey. "Education for Regional Planning in Less Developed Countries." In Issues in Regional Planning, edited by David Dunham and Jos. Hilhorst. The Hague: Mouton, 1971.

Perroux, François. "The Domination Effect and Modern Economic Theory." Social Research (1959): 188-205.

_____. "Economic Space: Theory and Applications." In Regional Planning and Development: A Reader, pp. 21-34. Cambridge, Mass.: M.I.T. Press, 1964.

_____. "Economic Space: Theory and Applications." Quarterly Journal of Economics (February 1950).

____. L'Économie du xxieme siècle. Paris: Presses Universitaires de France, 1962.

____. "Note on the Concept of Growth Poles." In Regional Planning: Theory and Practice, edited by D. L. McKee; R. D. Dean; and W. H. Leahy, pp. 93-104. New York: Free Press, 1970.

____. "Note sur la notion de pôle de croissance." Économie Appliqué (January-June 1955): 307-30.

Plotnicov, Leonard. Strangers to the City. Pittsburgh: University of Pittsburgh Press, 1967.

Pons, Valdo. Stanleyville: An African Urban Community under Belgian Administration. London: Oxford University Press, 1969.

Portes, Aleiandro. "Comparative Urbanization and National Development." Paper presented at 71st Annual Meeting of the American Sociological Association, New York: 1968.

Potholm, C. P., and R. Dale, eds. Southern Africa in Perspective. New York: Collier-Macmillan, 1972.

Powdermaker, Hortense. Copper Town: Changing Africa; the Human Situation of the Rhodesian Copperbelt. New York: Harper & Row, 1962.

Programme of Eastern African Studies. The Role of Railway Transportation in the Economic Development of East Africa by David Macharia. Syracuse, New York: Program of Eastern Studies, 1966.

____. A Select, Preliminary Bibliography on Urbanism in Eastern Africa by Barbara A. Skapa. Syracuse, New York: Program of East African Studies, 1967.

Project Planning Associates. National Capital Master Plan Report, Dar es Salaam. Toronto: Project Planning Associates, 1968.

Public Administration Service. Establishment of the Addis Ababa Water and Sewage Authority. Chicago: Public Administration Service, 1970.

Pusic, Eugen, and Annmarie H. Walsh. Urban Government for Zagreb, Yugoslavia. New York: Praeger, 1968.

Pye, Lucian. Politics, Personality and Nation Building. New Haven: Yale University Press, 1962.

Ratcliffe, Anne E. "Industrial Decentralization in South Africa." South African Journal of Economics 42 (1974): 157-76.

Rempel, Henry, and M. P. Todaro. "Rural to Urban Labor Migration in Kenya." In Population Growth and Economic Development in Africa, edited by S. H. Ominde and C. M. Ejiogu, pp. 214-34. London: Heinemann, 1972.

Resources for the Future, Inc. Design for a Worldwide Study of Regional Development: A Report to the United Nations on a Proposed Research-Training Program. Washington, D.C.: Resources for the Future, Inc., 1966.

Richardson, Boyce. "Saskatoon: The City as Landowner." Canadian Forum (May 1972): 42-43.

Ridley Report: Report to Consider the Provisions of the Liquor Licensing Ordinance. Lusaka: Government Printer, 1956.

Riggs, Fred W. Administration in Developing Countries: The Theory of the Prismatre Society. Boston: Houghton Mifflin, 1964.

Rodney, Walter. How Europe Underdeveloped Africa. Dar es Salaam: Tanzania Publishing House, 1972.

Rodwin, Lloyd. "Choosing a Region for Development." In Regional Development and Planning, edited by Friedman and Alonso, pp. 37-58. Cambridge, Mass.: M.I.T. Press, 1964.

_____. "Metropolitan Policy for Developing Countries." In Regional Economic Planning Techniques and Analysis for Less Developed Areas, edited by Walter Isard and John H. Cumberland, pp. 221-31. Paris: European Productivity Agency of the Organization for European Economic Cooperation, 1961.

Rogerson, Christian M. Environmental Studies. Department of Geography and Environmental Studies, Occasional paper no. 14. Johannesburg: University of Witwatersrand, 1975.

_____. "Growth Point Problems—The Case of Babelegi, Boputatswana." Journal of Modern African Studies 12 (1974): 126-31.

_____. "Industrial Decentralization in South Africa: The Planning Uncertainties." Standard Bank Review (October 1974): 19-25.

_____. "Industrial Movement and South Africa's Decentralization Programme." Journal of Southern African Studies (1976).

_____. "Industrial Movement in an Industrializing Economy." South African Geographical Journal 57 (1975): 88-103.

_____. "Industrialization of the Bantu Homelands." Geography 59 (1974): 260-64.

_____. "New Towns in the Bantu Homelands." Geographical Review 64 (1974): 579-83.

Ross, Lynette E. "The Spatial Organization of the South African Population 1904-1970." South African Geographical Journal 57 (1975): 73-87.

Ross, M. H. The Political Integration of Urban Squatters. Evanston, Ill.: Northwestern University Press, 1973.

Sada, P. O. "Urban Growth and Development in Nigeria." Journal of Tropical Geography 13 (June 1974): 45-53.

Safier, Michael, ed. The Role of Urban and Regional Planning in National Development of East Africa. Kampala: Milton Obote Foundation, 1970.

Sampson, Richard. So This is Lusaka. Lusaka: Northern Rhodesia Publicity Association, 1959.

Sanson, R. P. H. "La symbolique rurale et la symbolique urbaine du néocitadin algérien." In Les influences occidentales dans les villes maghrébines à l'époque contemporaine. Études méditerranéennes, no. 2, 1974, pp. 135-41.

_____. "Prise de la ville, prise du pouvoir." In Villes et sociétés au Maghreb—études sur l'urbanisation, pp. 21-28. Paris: Centre National de la Recherche Scientifique, 1974.

Sari, D. "La restructuration des centres urbains en Algérie." In Villes et sociétés au Maghreb—études sur l'urbanisation, pp. 55-75. Paris: Centre National de la Recherche Scientifique, 1974.

_____. Les villes précoloniales de l'Algérie occidentale—Nedroma, Mazouna, Kalaa. Algiers: Société Nationale d'Édition et de Diffusion, 1970.

Schapera, I. Migrant Labor and Tribal Life. London: Oxford University Press, 1947.

Schatz, L. Industrialization in Nigeria—A Spatial Analysis. Munich: Weltforum Verlag, 1973.

Schlemmer, Lawrence. "Human Resources Utilisation in Southern Africa—Policy Alternatives." Paper prepared for the Conference on Resources of Southern Africa, Today and Tomorrow, Associated Scientific and Technical Societies of South Africa, Institute for Social Research, University of Natal, Durban, September 22–26, 1975.

Schmidt, Charles F. "A Spatial Model of Authority-Dependency Relations in South Africa." Journal of Modern African Studies 13 (1975): 483–90.

Schultz, Willi. "Liberia." In Africa South of the Sahara 1977–78. London: Europa, 1977.

Segal, Edwin S. Peri-Urban Settlement Patterns: Policy Implications. Research report prepared for the Ministry of Lands, Housing, and Urban Development. Dar es Salaam: Government Printer, 1974.

Selwyn, Percy. Industries in the Southern African Periphery. London: Croom Helm, 1975.

_____. "Report on Assignment to Lesotho." Brighton: Institute of Development Studies (IDS) Discussion Paper No. 5 (University of Sussex, mimeographed, 1971).

Shelton, Austin. Igbo-Igala Borderland: Religion and Social Control in Indigenous African Colonialism. Albany: State University of New York Press, 1971.

Shen, T. Y. "Macro Development Planning in Tropical Africa: Technocratic and Non-Technocratic Causes of Failure." Journal of Development Studies 13, no. 4 (July 1977).

Shevky, Eshref, and Wendell Bell. Social Area Analysis: Theory, Illustrative Application and Computational Procedures. Stanford, Calif.: Stanford University Press, 1955.

Shibli, Khalid. "Metropolitan Planning in Karachi: A Case Study."
In Metropolitan Growth: Public Policy for South and Southeast
Asia, edited by Leo Jakobson and Ved Prakash, pp. 109-36.
New York: Halsted, 1974.

Simmance, Alan J. F. "An International Urbanization Survey Report
to the Ford Foundation." In Urbanization in Zambia. New York:
Ford Foundation Press, 1972.

Simms-Hamilton, Ruth. Urbanization in West Africa: A Review of
Current Literature. Evanston, Ill.: Northwestern University
Press, 1965.

"Sir Patrick Abercrombie's Town Plan." Ethiopia Observer 1
(March 1957): 35-44.

Sjoberg, G. "Rural-Urban Balance and Models of Economic Development." In Social Structure and Mobility in Economic Development,
edited by N. J. Smelser and S. Lipset. Chicago: Aldine, 1966.

"Skikda: les retombées du boom industriel." El Moudjahid, August 6,
1974.

Skinner, Elliott P. African Urban Life: The Transformation of
Ouagadougou. Princeton, N.J.: Princeton University Press, 1975.

Sklar, Richard. Nigerian Political Parties: Power in an Emergent
African Nation. Princeton, N.J.: Princeton University Press,
1963.

Smailes, P. J. "Some Aspects of South Australian Urban Systems."
The Australian Geographer 11, no. 1 (1969): 29-51.

Smith, David M. "Race-Space Inequality in South Africa: A Study in
Welfare Geography." Antipod 6 (1974): 42-69.

Smith, H. L. London Life Laboin. London, n.p., 1930-33.

Smock, Audrey. Ibo Politics: The Role of Ethnic Unions in Eastern
Nigeria. Cambridge, Mass.: Harvard University Press, 1971.

Société Africaine d'Études et de Développement (S.A.E.D.). A Qui
Appartiendra Ouagadougou? Ouagadougou: S.A.E.D., 1976.

Soja, E. W. "Communications and Transaction Flow Analysis."
East Lakes Geographer 4 (1968): 39-57.

____. The Geography of Modernization in Kenya: A Spatial Analysis of Social, Economic & Political Change. Syracuse, N.Y.: Syracuse University Press, 1968.

Sommer, John W. "Several Aspects of Urbanization and Political Integration in Sudan." In Urbanization, National Development & Regional Planning in Africa, edited by Salah El-Shakhs and R. A. Obudho. New York: Praeger, 1974.

South Africa, Republic of. Homelands: The Role of the Corporations. Johannesburg: Chris van Rensburg, 1975.

____. (Stallard Commission) Report of the Local Government Commission. Pretoria: Government Printer, 1972.

____. Socio-Economic Development of the Bantu Areas within the Union of South Africa, Summary of the Report of the Commission. Pretoria: Government Printer, 1955.

____. White Paper on the Report by the Inter-Departmental Committee on the Decentralisation of Industries. Pretoria: Department of Industries, 1971.

Southall, A. W. "Kampala-Mengo." In The City in Modern Africa, edited by Horace Miner, pp. 297-332. London: Praeger, 1967.

____, and Peter C. W. Gutkind. Townsmen in the Making: Kampala and its Suburbs. Kampala: East African Institute of Social Research, 1957.

Spengler, J. J. "Bureaucracy and Political Development." In Bureaucracy and Political Development, edited by Joseph La Palombar, pp. 199-232. Princeton, N.J.: Princeton University Press, 1963.

Spray, Paul. A Tentative Economic History of Lesotho from 1800. Mimeographed. University of Sussex, U.K., 1975.

Stohr, Walter. "Development Planning for Depressed Areas: A Methodological Approach." Journal of American Institute of Planners 30, no. 2 (May 1964): 123-31.

Stravenhagen, Rodolfo. Social Classes in Agrarian Societies. Garden City, N.Y.: Doubleday, 1975.

Stren, Richard. "The Evolution of Housing Policy in Kenya." In Urban Challenge in East Africa, edited by John Hutton, pp. 57-96. Nairobi: East Africa Publishing House, 1972.

____. Housing the Poor in Africa: Policy Politics and Bureaucracy in Momlasa. Berkeley: University of California, Institute of International Studies, 1978.

____. "Urban Policy and Performance in Kenya and Tanzania." Journal of Modern African Studies 13 (June 1975): 267-94.

____. "Urban Policy in Africa: A Political Analysis." African Studies Review 15, no. 3 (December 1972).

Stryker, Richard. "Political and Administrative Linkage in Ivory Coast." In Ghana and Ivory Coast, edited by P. Fuste and Aristide Zolberg. Chicago: University of Chicago Press, 1971.

Sudarkasa, Niara. Where Women Work: A Study of Yoruba Women in the Market Place and in the Home. Ann Arbor: University of Michigan Press, 1973.

Sutton, J. E. G. "Dar es Salaam: A Sketch of a Hundred Years." Tanzania Notes and Records 71 (1970): 1-20.

Swaziland, Kingdom of. Government Gazette 12, no. 678 (December 13, 1973).

Taaffe, E. J.; R. L. Morrill; and P. R. Gould. "Transport Expansion in Underdeveloped Countries: A Comparative Analysis." Geographical Review 53 (October 1963): 503-29.

Taylor, D. R. F. "The Internal Trade of Fort Hall, Kenya District Kenya." Canadian Journal of African Studies 1, no. 2 (November 1967): 111-22.

____. "New Central Places in East Africa." African Urban Notes 3, no. 4 (December 1968): 15-29.

____. "The Role of the Smaller Urban Place in Development: The Case of Kenya." In Urbanization, National Development and Regional Planning in Africa, edited by Salah El-Shakhs and R. A. Obudho, pp. 143-58. New York: Praeger, 1974.

____, and R. A. Obudho, eds. The Computer and Africa: Applications, Problems and Potential. New York: Praeger, 1977.

Thomlinson, Ralph. "Les relations entre les rangs des villes et leurs populations au Maroc: 1936-1971." As-Soukan 1, no. 2 (June 1973): 9-24.

_____. "The Primate City in Morocco: Casablanca or Rabat or None?" Population Review: Demography of Developing Countries 19, nos. 1, 2 (January-December 1975): 24-33.

Thompson, J. W. An Economic and Social History of the Middle Ages (300-1300). New York: The Century Company, 1928.

Tindall, P. E. N. A History of Central Africa. New York: Praeger, 1958.

Tisdale, Hope. "The Process of Urbanization." Social Forces 20 (1942): 311-16.

Toynbee, Arnold. Cities on the Move. New York: Oxford University Press, 1970.

"Town Planning Revolves Around the People: A Record of Ten Years." Tanzania Notes and Records 76 (1975): 179-84.

Trapido, Stanley. "South Africa in a Comparative Study of Industrialization." Journal of Development Studies 7 (1971): 309-20.

Uchendu, Victor. "The Passing of Tribal Man: A West African Experience." In The Passing of Tribal Man in West Africa, edited by Peter C. Gutkind, pp. 64-70. Leiden: E. J. Brill, 1970.

United Nations, Centre for Housing, Building, and Planning, Economics Commission for Africa. Missi Report: Upper Volta. New York: United Nations, June 8, 1971.

United Nations, Department of Economic and Social Affairs. Local Government Reform: Analysis of Experience in Selected Countries. New York: United Nations, ST/ESA/SER.E, 1975.

_____. Popular Participation in Decision Making for Development. New York: United Nations, ST/ESA/31, 1975.

_____. Urban Land Policies and Land-Use Control Measures, I: Africa. New York: United Nations, ST/ECA 1167, 1973.

_____. "Urbanization: Development Policies and Planning." International Social Development Review 1 (1968).

_____, Mission to Lesotho. "Assistance to Lesotho." Objective: Justice 9, no. 2 (Summer 1977).

United Nations, Development Program (UNDP). Le Financement de l'Habitat. Ouagadougou: UNDP, June 1974.

_____. Liste d'attributaires—Cissin pilote. Ouagadougou: UNDP, 1974.

"Upper Volta." In Africa South of the Sahara, 1974. London: Europa, 1975.

Venter, A. Plasslike Nie-Blanke Werknemers. Memorandum prepared for the Windhoek City Council Steering Committee. Windhoek: City Council, September 18, 1967.

Vincent, Joan. "The Dar es Salaam Townsman: Social and Political Aspects of City Life." Tanzania Notes and Records 71 (1970): 149-56.

Wagner, Gunter. The Bantu of North Kavirondo, vol. 1. London: Oxford University Press, 1949.

_____. The Bantu of North Kavirondo, vol. 2. London: Oxford University Press, 1956.

Waller, P. P. "The Delineation of a Planning Region: A Case Study from West Kenya." East Africa Geographical Review 8 (April 1970): 55-60.

_____, and Rolf Ofmeier. "Methoden zur Bestimmung der Tragfähigkeit ländlicher Gebiete in Entwicklungslanden dargestellt am Beispiel West Kenias." Die Erde 4 (1968): 340-48.

Wallerstein, Immanuel, ed. Social Change: The Colonial Situation. New York: Wiley, 1966.

Wallman, Sandra. "Conditions of Non-Development: The Case of Lesotho." Journal of Development Studies 8, no. 2 (January 1972).

Walsh, Annmarie H. The Urban Challenge to Government: An International Comparison of Thirteen Cities. New York: Praeger, 1969.

Ward, M. "Prospects for Full Local Employment with Special Reference to Changes in the Labor Force and the Pace of Industrialisation in Lesotho." In Lesotho National Population Symposium 1974. Roma: University of Botswana, Lesotho, and Swaziland, 1974.

Warner, William Lloyd, and Paul S. Lunt. The Social Life of a Modern Community. New Haven: Yale University Press, 1941.

Warren, Dennis M. "Voluntary Associations in a Market-Agricultural Secondary City: The Case of Techiman, Ghana." Paper presented at the African Studies Association, Syracuse, New York, November 2, 1972.

Waterburg, John. Egypt: Burdens of the Past, Options for the Future. Hanover, N.H.: The American University Field Staff, 1973.

Waterston, Albert. Development Planning: Lessons of Experience. Baltimore: The Johns Hopkins University Press, 1965.

Watkins, R. J. The Growth of Metropolitan Cairo and Alexandria. Cairo: Ministry of Housing and Reconstruction, 1976.

Weber, Max. The City. New York: Free Press, 1958.

Welin, Herbert H. Governing an African City; a Study of Nairobi. New York: Africana, 1974.

Whitaker, C. S. "A Dysrhythmic Process of Political Change." World Politics 20, no. 2 (January 1967): 190-207.

_____. The Politics of Tradition: Continuity and Change in Northern Nigeria, 1946-1966. Princeton, N.J.: Princeton University Press, 1970.

Whiting Associates International. Benghasi Master Plan Final Report: The Social Structure of the Italian Slum. Benghasi: Municipality of Benghasi, Libya.

_____. Master Plan for the City of Sebha, Southern Region Preliminary Report, vol. 2. Tripoli: Ministry of Planning and Development, Kingdom of Libya, 1967.

_____. Tripoli Master Plan Final Report. Tripoli: Ministry of the Interior, Libyan Arab Republic, 1969.

Whyte, William Foote. Street Corner Society. Chicago: University of Chicago Press, 1955.

Williams, Eric. Capitalism and Slavery. London: Andre Deutsch, 1964.

Williams, Raymond. The Country and the City. New York: Oxford University Press, 1973.

Williamson, J. B. "Regional Inequality and Process of National Development: A Description of the Patterns." Economic Development and Cultural Change 13, no. 4 (July 1964).

Wilsher, Peter. "Everyone, Everywhere is Moving to the Cities." The New York Times, June 22, 1975.

Wilson, F. Labour in the South Africa Gold Mines 1911-1969. Cambridge: Cambridge University Press, 1972.

_____. Migrant Labour in South Africa. Johannesburg: South African Council of Churches and Spro-Cas, 1972.

_____. "Unresolved Issues in the South African Economy and Labour." South African Journal of Economics 43, no. 4 (1975): 516-46.

Wina, Arthur. "Pluralism and Conflict Situation in Africa: A New Look." African Social Research 7 (June 1969): 1-5.

Wincott, N. E. "Aspects of the Growth and Development of African Urban Society." B. Litt. dissertation, Department of Social Anthropology, Oxford University, 1966.

Wingo, L. "Issues in a National Urban Development Strategy for the U.S." Urban Studies 9, no. 1 (1972): 15-20.

Wirth, Lewis. "Urbanism as a Way of Life." In Urbanism in World Perspective: A Reader, edited by F. Fava. New York: T. Y. Crowell, 1968.

_____. "Urbanism as a Way of Life." American Journal of Sociology 44 (July 1938): 3-24.

Wolpe, Harold. "Capitalism and Cheap Labour-Power in South Africa: From Segregation to Apartheid." Economy and Society 1 (1972): 425-56.

_____. Urban Politics in Nigeria. Berkeley: University of California Press, 1974.

Wood, Anthony S. John. Northern Rhodesia: The Human Background. London: Pall Mall Press, 1961.

World Bank. Lesotho: A Development Challenge. Baltimore: The Johns Hopkins University Press, 1975.

Wunsch, James D. "Voluntary Associations: Determinants of Associational Structure and Activity in Two Ghanaian Secondary Cities." Ph.D. dissertation, Indiana University, 1974.

Young, Michael, and Peter Willmott. Family and Kinship in East London. Harmondsworth: Penguin, 1962.

Yudelman, Montague. Africans on the Land: Economic Problems of African Agricultural Development in Southern, Central, and East Africa, with Special Reference to Southern Rhodesia. Cambridge, Mass.: Harvard University Press, 1964.

Zambia, Republic of. Lusaka: Existing Conditions (Doxiades Report). Lusaka: Government Printer, 1971.

_____. Report on the Administration and Finance of Native Locations in Urban Areas. Lusaka: Government Printer, 1953.

_____. Report on the Position of African and European Housing in Lusaka. Lusaka: Government Printer, 1953.

Zolberg, Aristide. Creating Political Order: The Party States of West Africa. Chicago: Rand McNally, 1966.

INDEX

Bricker, Gary, 177-93
British: in Kenya, 245, 246; in Lesotho, 305-06, 312; in Nigeria, 197-98; in Tanzania, 262-63
Bundy, Colin, 324, 327
Burgess, Ernest, 21
bush, 40, 47

Cairo (town—Egypt), 62, 116, 118, 119, 123-27, 129
Cambodia, 91
capital: accumulation of, 36, 37, 41, 43-44, 50, 51; export of, 50; investment of, 32, 37
capital-intensive, 51
capitalism, 32, 33, 34, 36, 37-44, 48, 53
Capitalism and Slavery (Eric Williams), 44
capitalist mode of production, 36, 41, 43-44, 46, 51
Casablanca (town—Morocco), 63, 65, 67, 68, 69, 74, 75, 76, 84
Casbah (section—Algiers), 80, 84, 93, 94
cash-crop farming, 38, 49; see also agriculture
census taking, 6
Ceuta (town—Morocco), 65
Chad, 109
Chicago school, 44
Christopher, Garland, 157-76
Cissin Habitat Project (Upper Volta), 189-92. See also Ouagadougou (town—Upper Volta)
cities, 31-54
civil strife, 10
civilized, 45
Clarence-Smith, W. G., 295
class(es), 34, 36, 41, 46-47
class structure, 39, 41-42, 45, 50, 51

classical world, 34-35
clustering, 26
Cobbe, James, 291, 303-18
Cohen, Abner, 26
colonial: administration(s), 8, 42; dependency, 37-40; domination, 2; era, 49; experience(s), 7, 11, 59, 60; governments, 46; pattern of development, 12; relationships, 9; societies, 49; towns, 37-38
colonialism, 13, 19, 37, 38
colonies, 37, 41
communication, 21, 50
Communist Manifesto (Marx and Engels), 33
community atomization, 23
comparative studies, 32
Condition of the Working Class in England 1844, The (Friedrich Engels), 43
Congo, 53
conspicuous consumption, 50
Constantine (town—Algeria), 79, 83, 87, 91, 92
"consumatory" values, 22
contemporary metropolitanism, 48
Cook, Gillian P., 338
Copper Town (Hortense Powder-maker), 21
core units, 5
credit association, 24
crosscultural comparisons, 32
Cuba, 293
cultural change, 45
cultural relativity, 26
Cyrenaica (province—Libya), 104, 105, 107, 112

Dakar (town—Senegal), 39
Damara (tribe—Namibia), 293, 295-96
Dar es Salaam (region—Tanzania), 39, 213, 258-69. See also Tanzania

distribution and growth of urban settlements in, 218-23; expropriation of property in, 227-28; French Mission Plan, 224; future of urban development planning in, 233-34; ghebi (palace compound) in, 215; history of urbanization in, 215-23; material conditions of urban life in, 223; Ministry of Public Works and Housing, 233, 234; Ministry of Urban Development and Housing (MUDH), 229, 230, 233; Provisional Military Administrative Council (PMAC), 229-34; rural-urban migration in, 220-21, 223; urban planning under Emperor Haile Selassie I in, 224-28; urban planning under the provisional military government in, 228-33

ethnic consciousness, 25-26
ethnic groups, 25-26
Euro-American, 23, 25
Europe, 36, 44-45, 49, 51, 52, 53, 243
European: experience, 44, 51; technology, 24; towns, 38
European Economic Community (EEC), 313-14
Europeans: in Algeria, 80, 81, 83-87, 88, 93, 94; in Morocco, 28, 59, 61, 68-70, 75, 76
Evian accords (Algeria), 89
exploitation, 2, 32, 36-39, 42, 46, 49
export-oriented, 9
export trade, 49
extended family, 10, 27
extended kin ties, 46
external governments, 9

Fair, Thomas J. D., 251, 331

family structure, 45
Fanon, Frantz, 38-39, 41
farming associations, 24
Fava, Sylvia, 44
favelas (slums), 42. See also shanty towns; slums
Fer Kessdougou (town—Ivory Coast), 174
feudal society, 35
Fez (town—Morocco), 62, 63, 65, 67, 68, 74, 107
Florence (town—Italy), 36
"foreign aid," 78; capital, 48, 49, 50; corporations, 9; "experts" (or advisors), 7, 11, 49; governments, 9; investment, 52
Fort Hall (town—Kenya), 246
Fort Ternan (town—Kenya), 246
Frank, André Gunder, 325
French: in Algeria, 79, 80, 81, 85, 96; in Morocco, 61, 63, 67, 68, 69, 70, 74-77; in Upper Volta, 177-78
French West Africa, 140, 143, 178
Friedmann, John, 4, 329, 331
"functional complementarities," 5
functionalism, 22

Gans, Herbert, 26
Gbadamosi, Rasheed, 42
Gemu Goffa (province—Ethiopia), 219
German East Africa Company, 261
Germans, in Tanzania, 261, 262
Ghana, 9, 24, 135, 138-54, 189; "Aliens Compliance Act," 141, 143, 145; Ashanti Goldfields Corporation (AGC), 143, 145; conflict resolution in, 149-50, 152-53; development strategy in, 153-54; local councils in, 141, 142, 147, 148, 149, 151;

mining in, 143, 144, 145;
Muslims in, 140, 141, 145;
northern, 139, 140, 143, 145;
political development of, 148-
53; traditional councils in,
139, 141-42, 147, 148-51,
153; urban councils in, 147-
48; Zongo councils in, 142,
147, 148, 151, 153
ghebi (palace compound—Ethi-
opia), 215
Gibb, Sir Alexander (Dar es
Salaam), 262, 263
Goans, 247
Godfrey, E. M., 164
Gonzales, N., 300
Graeco-Roman antiquity, 34-35
Grand-Bassam (town—Ivory
Coast), 159
Great Britain, 7, 41, 47, 61;
see also England
Green, L., 199
greetings (ritual), 24-25
"growth pole theory," 4-5
Guelma (town—Algeria), 91
Guinea, 158, 177
Gulf of Sirte (Libya), 105, 113
Gumel (town—Nigeria), 197
Gutkind, Peter C. W., 23, 24

Habitat Project (Upper Volta),
189-92
Hadjar Soud (town—Algeria), 91
Hammarsdale (town—South
Africa), 333, 337
Hanna, Judith, 25
Hanna, William, 25
Harar (town—Ethiopia), 217,
219, 226
Harris, J. R., 164
Harris-Todaro model, 164
Harsch, Ernest, 35
Harvey, David, 32, 43, 48
Hausa (tribe), 26-27, 28, 142,
143, 197

Hauser, Phillip, 44
Helleiner, G. K., 319
Herero (tribe—Namibia), 295-96,
297, 299
highways. See roads
hinterland(s), 36, 43, 44, 48, 53;
in Egypt, 128, 129, 130; in
Kenya, 243, 254, 255, 256
Hirschman, Albert O., 4, 11
Horton, Frank E., 1-13
housing, in Lesotho, 315. See
also shanty towns; slums

Ibadan (town—Nigeria), 26-27,
28, 197, 200
ideology, 4, 50
Igbo (tribe), 25
Igbo-Igala borderland, 20
Ilorin (town—Nigeria), 197, 200
Imoagene, O., 207
Imperial British East Africa Company (IBEAC), 243, 245
imperialism, 34, 36, 38, 44, 49,
52, 61
import substitution, 49
Indians, in Kenya, 245, 246
indigenization, 9
indigenous, "economics," 6;
norms, 20, 23, 27; urban
theory, 6
indigenously generated change, 23
industrial development, 27, 51,
52
industrialism, 31
industrialization, 37, 49, 50, 51
infrastructural development, 9,
11, 12
infrastructural linkages, 4
innovation, 23
instrumental values, 22
integration (of planning), 3, 13
inter-African cooperation, 13
internal market, 59
international organizations (or
agencies), 4, 9

International Court of Justice, 293
inter-regional integration, 13
intra-ethnic interaction, 26-27
intransigents, 22
invasion of privacy, 6
Islam, 62. See also Muslims
Islamic invasions, 35
Isusu Union (Nigeria), 24
Ivory Coast, 135, 139, 157-76, 179, 189; cash crops in, 159, 162, 173; conventional eco nomic theory applied in, 165-66; creation of regional growth poles in, 166, 169-74; iron ore in, 171; northern savannah zone of, 159, 164, 174; process of urbanization in, 159-66; projects of a grand scale in, 169-74; regional development in the savannah zone of, 174; regional economic plans of, 166-74; revolving national independence festivals in, 167-68; rural-urban income inequality in, 161-65; rural-urban migration in, 157-58, 159-60, 163-66, 174-76; southern forest zone of, 159, 160, 164, 174; southwestern region of, 169, 171-73; timber industry in, 171, 173, 175; unemployment in, 157-58, 164, 175

Japan, 27
Jews: in Algeria, 80, 81, 85; in Morocco, 65, 68, 70, 75
Johnson, G. E., 8
Jonathan, Prime Minister Chief Leabua (Lesotho), 312
Jos (town—Nigeria), 199
Jukawa (town—Nigeria), 197

Kaduna (town—Nigeria), 199, 200, 202

Kamm, Henry, 39, 41
Kano (town—Nigeria), 25, 28, 197, 198, 199, 200
Kariakoo (section—Dar es Salaam), 262, 267
Katanga region (Congo), 53
Katatura (town—Namibia), 297, 299, 300
Katsina (town—Nigeria), 198
kebele (local cooperative—Ethiopia), 230-33
Kenitra (town—Morocco), 63, 65, 74, 75, 76
Kenya, 8, 242-56, 260; Arabs in, 245, 246, 247; Asians in, 246, 247; bomas (towns) in, 243, 245, 247; British in, 245, 246; caravan towns in, 243, 245; Central Highlands region in, 246; central places in, 242-43, 245, 246, 248, 253-54, 255; coastal strip in, 243, 245; colonial urbanization in, 245-48; elites in, 247; export enclaves in, 254, 255, 256; hinterland(s) in, 243, 254, 255, 256; Indians in, 245, 246; non-Africans in, 243, 245-47, 248, 249, 255; periodic markets in, 242, 245, 247-48, 254-55, 256; postcolonial urbanization in, 248-49; precolonial urbanization in, 243-45; rural development in, 253, 254; rural to urban migration in, 248, 249, 254; Swahili traders in, 245; toward a regional planning strategy in, 250-55; trading centers in, 247-48; Western Kenya Region in, 252
Kenya Highlands, 246
Khouribda (town—Morocco), 63
kinship patterns, 48
Kisumu (town—Kenya), 242, 246, 250
Kitale (town—Kenya), 243

393

Koehn, Eftychia, 213, 215-34
Koehn, Peter, 213, 215-34
kolanut presentation (ritual), 25
Koolfu (town—Nigeria), 197
Korhogo (town—Ivory Coast), 174
Kossou, Dam of (Ivory Coast),
   173-74
Koudougou (town—Upper Volta),
   179
Kumasi (town—Ghana), 139, 140,
   143, 144

labor force (or power), 42, 46,
   49, 51, 52, 53; in Zambia,
   275-81; See also migrant labor
labor-intensive, 52
labor-saving, 52
Lagos (town—Nigeria), 23, 25,
   39, 42, 198, 199, 200, 206
Lake Nasser (Egypt), 127
Lake Victoria (Kenya), 246
land: rights, 45-46; use patterns,
   39
landowners, 34, 37
Larache (town—Morocco), 65, 75
Latin America, 38, 53
Laurenti, Luigi, 251
Lawless, Richard, 59, 79-96
League of Nations, 293, 295
leisure activities, 21-22
Lerner, Daniel, 51
Leslie, J. A. K., 263
Lesotho, 291-292, 303-18; Ad-
   ministration of Lands Act, 310;
   agriculture in, 305, 309-11,
   317-18; Basutoland Congress
   Party (BCP), 312; Basutoland
   National Party (BNP), 306;
   British in, 305, 312; Bureau
   of Statistics, 307; Central
   Planning and Development
   Office, 306, 307; Colonial
   Development and Welfare Act,
   306; development planning and
   strategy in, 306-07; economy

of, 304-06, 309-11; first plan,
   313, 314, 316, 317; housing in,
   315; labor migration in, 305,
   307-09, 315; mine workers in,
   308-09, 318; National Development Corporation (LNDC), 313;
   Pim Report, 306; planning
   strategy in, 313-18; political
   and administrative structure,
   312-13; population of, 305, 307-
   08, 309; private sector investment in, 313-14; relationship
   with South Africa, 305-06, 307-
   10, 311, 312, 313-14, 315, 316,
   317, 318-19; rights in land in,
   309-11, 315; second plan, 307,
   313, 314, 316, 317; sharecropping in, 310
Libya, 59, 99-113; Barce Reconstruction Organisation, 107;
   First Five Year Plan, 109;
   manufacturing industry in, 108-
   12; master-plans for, 106-07,
   109; medina(s) in, 107-08;
   migration in, 99, 106; national
   urban development strategy in,
   103-05; 1976-1980 Plan of Economic and Social Transformation, 109; oil in, 104-05, 106,
   107; town planning in, 105-08;
   urban growth in, 99-104
linear progression, 19, 23, 26,
   27, 28
Little, Kenneth, 23
Liverpool (town—England), 44
Livingstone (town—Zambia), 281,
   284
Lloyd, Peter C., 24
London (England), 23, 48, 53
long-range planning, 9, 11
Losch, August, 48
Lourenço-Marques (town—Mozambique), 39, 40
Luanda (town—Angola), 39, 40
Lusaka (town—Zambia), 213, 272-

394

109; bidonvilles in, 68, 77;
capital city rotation in, 62;
coastal regions in, 62; colonial
transformations in the urban
system in, 63-69; decolonization in, 69-77; Europeans in,
28, 59, 61, 68-70, 75, 76;
French in, 61, 63, 65-67, 68,
70, 75-77; French zone of, 62,
63, 68, 69; Jews in, 65, 68,
70, 75; medinas in, 68, 75,
76, 80; Muslims in, 26, 65,
68, 69, 75, 76; "native quarters" in, 68, 70, 75; precolonial roots of urbanism in, 61-
63; protectorate period in, 63,
65, 68; segregation in, 59, 68,
76; Spanish in, 61-62, 70;
Spanish zone of, 62, 63, 65,
69
mosques, 80, 83, 140, 217
Mossi (tribe—Upper Volta), 177-
78
Mossi Plateau (Upper Volta), 177,
178
Mozambique, 39
M'sila (town—Algeria), 92
Murdock, G. P., 259
Murphy, E. J., 259
Murray, Roger, 52
Muslims: in Algeria, 80, 81-87,
93; in Ghana, 140, 141, 145;
in Morocco, 26, 65, 68-69,
75-76
Myrdal, Gunnar, 4, 5

Naipaul, V. S., 47
Nairobi (town—Kenya), 8, 23, 39,
249, 250, 252-53, 259
Nakuru (town—Kenya), 250
Nama (tribe—Namibia), 295-96
Namibia (South West Africa), 291,
293-301; bride price in, 299;
Coloured people in, 296, 297,
301; Democratic Turnhalle

Alliance, 293; development
planning in, 300-01; education
in, 296, 301; ethnic groups in,
293-96, 298-99, 301; German
colonial era in, 295; marriage
in, 298, 299-300; migrant
labor in, 295, 296, 300; northern section of, 295, 301;
Odendaal Commission Report,
300; racial discrimination in,
295-98, 299, 300; Report of the
Commission of Enquiry into
South West African Affairs, 300;
rural to urban migration in,
295-97, 301; southern section
of, 296, 297; unskilled laborers
in, 296, 297, 300; urbanization
in, 293-300; women in, 298,
299-300
national planning (or plans), 3, 4,
13
native quarters (Morocco), 68,
69, 70, 75
Nattrass, Jill, 328
Nazreth (town—Ethiopia), 215, 219
neocolonial, 9, 13, 49, 53
New Valley (region—Egypt), 127
New York (U.S.A.), 23, 53
Ngoni (tribe—Tanzania), 259, 260,
261
Niger, 177, 178
Nigeria, 9, 26, 116, 135, 140,
196-214; associations in, 24;
British in, 197-98; emerging
national urban hierarchy in,
199-200; evolution of the urban
system in, 197-98; federal military government, 199; growth
pole methodology in, 4; national
strategy of urbanization for,
203-07; new federal capital in,
12, 135; railroads in, 198;
rituals in, 23, 24-25; rural to
urban migration in, 204-06;
Second National Development

396

production, capitalist mode of, 36, 40-41, 43-44, 46, 51
proletariat, 36, 37, 50
proto-modern norms, 28
"public good," 2
public sector, 11
Puerto Rico, 339

Qattara Depression (region—Egypt), 127

Rabat (town—Morocco), 62-63, 65-67, 68-69, 74, 75-77, 84
racial discrimination, in Namibia, 295-98, 299, 300. See also apartheid; segregation
radio, 21-22
railways, 48; in Nigeria, 198; Abidjan-Niger, 178, 179; Addis Ababa-Djibuti, 215
Ras Lanuf (town—Libya), 105
Ratcliffe, Anne E., 337
raw materials, 46, 48, 50-52, 54
regional: development, 4, 12; growth center, 5; planning, 3, 12, 13
Reissman, Leonard, 44
reserve army of labor. See labor force
resilience, 22, 28
resource(s), 2, 3, 43, 50
Rhodesia, 273. See also Zambia
Rif Mountains (Morocco), 69, 75
rituals, 23-25
roads, 48; Accra-Tema motorway (Ghana), 9; Unity Highway (Morocco), 75
Rodney, Walter, 37
Rogerson, Christian Myles, 292, 323-40
Roman, 79, 116; Empire, 35, 116; Republic, 34
Rosslyn (town—South Africa), 333, 337
rotating credit association, 24

Rothman, Norman C., 272-85
rural, 23, 37, 42, 43, 45, 47, 52, 53; development planning, 3
ruralization, 59
rural to urban migration: in Algeria, 85, 87-89, 91, 95; in Ethiopia, 220-22, 223; in Ivory Coast, 157-58, 159-60, 164-66, 174-76; in Kenya, 248, 249, 254; in Namibia, 295-97, 300-01; in Nigeria, 204-06
Russia. See Soviet Union (USSR)

Sabhah (town—Libya), 107
Sabo (town—Nigeria), 26
Sadat, Anwar el- (president of Egypt), 127
Safi (town—Morocco), 63, 67
Safier, Michael, 250-51
Sahara (desert), 177, 197
Sahelian drought, 175
Salau, Ademola T., 196-214
Salé (town—Morocco), 63, 65, 67, 74, 76
Salisbury (town—Rhodesia), 273
San Pedro, Port of (town—Ivory Coast), 169-73, 174, 175
Sanson, R. P. H., 85
Savannah Zone (Ivory Coast), 159, 164-65, 174, 175
Schatzl, L. L., 202
Schlemmer, Lawrence, 331
Schmidt, Charles F., 331
secondary production, 50
Seers, Dudley, 3
Sefrou (town—Morocco), 67
Segal, Edwin, 214, 258-69
segregation: in Algeria, 85, 94; in Morocco, 59, 68, 76. See also apartheid; racial discrimination, in Namibia
Selassie, Emperor Haile, I (Ethiopia), 224, 229, 234
Senegal, 177
Senufos (tribe—Ivory Coast), 174

Sequela (Ivory Coast), 168
Sétif (town—Algeria), 80, 91
settlers' town, 38
shanty towns, 37, 40, 42, 53, 84.
  See also bidonvilles; slums
Shelton, Austin, 20, 22
Shevky, Eshref, 20
Shoa (province—Ethiopia), 219
Sidi bel Abbès (town—Algeria), 80
Sijilmasa (town—Morocco), 63
Skikda (town—Algeria), 80, 91,
  93
slums, 37-38, 41, 42, 48, 50.
  See also bidonvilles; shanty
  towns
social: change, 20, 23, 27, 28;
  integration, 13; justice, 13
socialism, 34
Society for International Development (SID), 10
sociocultural change(s), 19, 21,
  27
Sokoto (town—Nigeria), 197, 198
Souk Ahras (town—Algeria), 91
souks (markets—Algeria), 80
South Africa (region), 46, 53,
  272, 273, 291-340
South Africa (Republic of), 323-
  40; apartheid in, 291-92, 323-
  26, 330-33, 337; black wage
  labor in, 324-29; black Reserves in, 325, 328, 337-38;
  border areas in, 335, 337,
  338; constrained urbanization
  in, 329-31; growth points (or
  nodes) in, 335, 337, 338;
  homelands, 328, 331, 332,
  333, 337-40; industrial decentralization in, 333-37; migrant
  labor in, 324-29, 332-33;
  National Party in, 325; Native
  Laws Amendment Act of 1937,
  330; Native (Urban Areas) Act
  of 1945, 330, 332; Physical
  Planning and Utilization of

Resources Act, 333, 337;
  regional planning in, 323, 333-
  37, 338, 339-40; relationship
  with Lesotho, 304-06, 307-09,
  311, 312, 313-14, 315, 316,
  317, 318; resettlement of blacks
  in, 331-33; Stallard Commission, 46; Tomlinson Commission, 333; white paper on
  decentralization, 333-35
Southall, A. W., 22
South West Africa, 293. See also
  Namibia
South West African People's
  Organization (SWAPO), 293
Soviet Union (USSR), 13, 293
Soweto (town—South Africa), 340
space, 21, 41
Spanish, in Morocco, 61, 70
spatial: patterns of development,
  12; planning, 3-4; system, 4,
  39
spread effects, 5
squatter neighborhoods, in Upper
  Volta, 183-87, 189-94. See
  also shanty towns; slums
stabilization, 45
structural model of urbanization,
  20
Suez Canal, 117-19, 127
"sunk capital," 12
Swahili (language), 259, 263
Swaziland, 311
synchronic method, 28

Tagiura (town—Libya), 104
Tamale (town—Ghana), 139
Tangiers (town—Morocco), 63,
  69, 75, 76
Tanzania, 213, 258-69; Arabs in,
  259, 260, 261; Arusha Decla-
  ration, 263; Asians in, 262;
  British in, 262-63; Dar es
  Salaam Master Plan, 263;
  First Five Year Plan, 263;

ABOUT THE EDITORS AND CONTRIBUTORS

R. A. OBUDHO is Planning Analyst, Johnson & Johnson Worldwide, and formerly was Instructor of Geography, Rutgers University. He is currently a member of the board of editors, Social Indicators Research Journal and African Studies Review Journal. He is also a member of the International Geographical Union Working Group on Market Distribution Systems.

Dr. Obudho's principal research includes the urbanization process and regional planning in the developing countries, with particular emphasis on Africa. His publications include several articles and bibliographies on the spatial and quantitative aspects, geography, and statistical techniques of urbanization, development planning, and demography. He has been contributor to and editor of The Computer and Africa: Problems, Prospects, and Potentiality; co-author of Urbanization, City and Regional Planning in Metropolitan Kisumu, Kenya: Bibliographical Survey of an East African City; editor of and contributor to Urbanization, National Development and Regional Planning in Africa; co-author of Periodic Markets, Urbanization and Regional Planning—A Case Study from Western Kenya; author of The Nature of Kenya Urban Hierarchy: Implication for Regional Planning Strategy; and editor of and contributor to Urbanization and Development Planning in Kenya.

Dr. Obudho holds an A.A.Sc. from the State University of New York College at Cobleskill, a B.Sc. from the State University of New York at Albany, a Diploma in Education from the University of Nairobi, and an M.A. and Ph.D. from Rutgers University, New Brunswick, New Jersey.

SALAH EL-SHAKHS is Professor of Urban Planning and Policy Development, New Brunswick Chairman of Urban Studies, and Director of the Program on Middle Eastern Studies at Rutgers University. He is a member of the advisory board of the Institute of Middle Eastern and North African Affairs and Associate Editor of the Journal of the American Institute of Planners. His research and professional interests center on comparative urbanization and planning in developing nations, settlement patterns, and regional development. He has been a consultant to a number of international agencies and planning firms, with particular experience in Egypt, Nigeria, and Libya.

Dr. El-Shakhs has published extensively on urbanization and development planning and systems of cities. He has recently been contributor to and editor of <u>Urbanization, National Develop-</u><u>ment and Regional Planning in Africa</u> (Praeger, 1974); "Contemporary Alexandria," <u>International Encyclopedia of Architecture, Engineering</u><u>and Urban Planning</u>, ed. A. Tzonis and D. Schodek; and "Cairo," <u>The Great Spectrum Encyclopedia</u>. His other publications have appeared in <u>Town Planning Review</u>, <u>Pan African Journal</u>, <u>Northeastern</u><u>Regional Science Review</u>, <u>Journal of Developing Areas</u>, <u>American</u><u>Behavioral Scientist</u>, <u>The Pyramids Economist</u>, and <u>Ekistics</u>.

Dr. El-Shakhs received his B.Sc. from Cairo University in Egypt, and his M.C.P. and Ph.D. from Harvard University.

JANET L. ABU-LUGHOD is Professor of Sociology and Urban Affairs at Northwestern University.

GERALD H. BLAKE is Senior Lecturer in Geography and Director of the M.A. course in the Geography of the Mediterranean and Middle East at the University of Durham, England, where he is closely associated with the work of the Centre for Middle Eastern and Islamic Studies.

GARY BRICKER is continuing his work with A.I.D. in Tunis, where he is assigned to the Regional Housing and Urban Development Office and is specializing in shelter-related programs in developing countries.

GARLAND CHRISTOPHER is currently Assistant Research Scientist at the Center for Research on Economic Development, University of Michigan. He has previously taught at California State University, Rohner Park, and the Université de Paris, Nanterre. From 1975 to 1977 he was Research Associate at the Université Nationale de la Côte d'Ivoire.

JAMES COBBE is currently Assistant Professor of Economics, Florida State University, Tallahassee. Formerly he has lectured in economics at the London School of Economics (1973-76) and at the University at Roma, Lesotho (1976-78).

AZUKA A. DIKE is a Senior Lecturer at the University of Nigeria, Nsukka. Formerly he was a lecturer at the New School for Social Research (N.Y.), Marymount College (N.Y.), Montclair State College (N.J.), and Ramapo State College (N.J.).

FRANK E. HORTON is Vice President for Academic Affairs and Research and Professor of Geography at Southern Illinois

University at Carbondale. He was formerly Dean for Advanced Studies and Professor of Geography at the University of Iowa.

EFTYCHIA F. KOEHN is presently conducting research in gerontology at the University of Montana. From 1973 to 1975 she was a part-time instructor in the Department of Sociology, and from 1970 to 1972 she lectured in the Department of Sociology at Haile Selassie I University in Addis Ababa, Ethiopia.

PETER KOEHN is Associate Professor of Political Science at the University of Montana. In 1978-79, he will be principal research fellow in the Department of Research and Consultancy, Institute of Administration, at Ahmadu Bello University in Zaria, Nigeria. From 1970 to 1972, Dr. Koehn lectured in public administration at Haile Selassie I University in Addis Ababa.

RICHARD I. LAWLESS is currently Research Officer at the Centre for Middle Eastern and Islamic Studies, University of Durham, England.

BERNARD MAGUBANE is Associate Professor of Anthropology at the University of Connecticut, Storrs. He also has taught at the University of Zambia, U.C.L.A., and the State University of New York at Binghamton.

MICHAEL L. McNULTY is Professor of Geography and Director of the Center for Development Studies, University of Iowa. Formerly he was Visiting Lecturer at the University of Ibadan (1970-71) in Nigeria. During 1976-77, Dr. McNulty served as Urban and Regional Department Advisor with the Office of Urban Development, U.S. Agency for International Development, under the auspices of the Intergovernmental Personnel Act.

WADE C. PENDLETON is Professor of Anthropology at San Diego State University. He has also taught Social Anthropology at the University of Cape Town and Witwatersrand University in Johannesburg. During 1978-80 he will be Professor of Sociology at Ahmadu Bello University in Zaria, Nigeria.

GORDON HARVEY PIRIE is Assistant Lecturer in the Department of Geography and Environmental Studies at the University of Witwatersrand, Johannesburg.

CHRISTIAN MYLES ROGERSON is a Ph.D. candidate in geography at Queen's University, Kingston, Canada. During 1972-74 he was Junior Lecturer in Geography at the University of Witwatersrand, Johannesburg, and in 1975, Lecturer in Geography at the University of Natal, Durban.

NORMAN C. ROTHMAN is currently chairperson of the Departments of History, Political Science, and Geography, and the Division of Social Sciences, Morris Brown College, Atlanta University Center.

ADEMOLA T. SALAU, a former town planning officer for the old northwestern state of Nigeria, is now writing a Ph.D. dissertation in urban planning at Rutgers University.

EDWIN S. SEGAL is Associate Professor of Anthropology at the University of Louisville.

SOUMANA TRAORÉ is Founder and Executive Director of the Société Africaine d'Études et de Développement (S.A.E.D.), a private research and development firm in Ouagadougou.

JAMES WUNSCH is Associate Professor of Political Science at Creighton University.